The Nazis, Capitalism, and the Working Class

The Nazis, Capitalism, and the Working Class

Donny Gluckstein

Haymarket Books
Chicago, IL

This edition published in 2012 by
Haymarket Books
PO Box 180165
Chicago, IL 60618
773-583-7884
info@haymarketbooks.org
www.haymarketbooks.org

ISBN: 978-1-60846-137-0

Distributed to the trade in the US through Consortium Book Sales and
Distribution (www.cbsd.com) and internationally through Ingram Publisher
Services International (www.ingramcontent.com).

This book was published with the generous support of Lannan Foundation and
Wallace Action Fund.

Special discounts are available for bulk purchases by organizations and
institutions. Please call 773-583-7884 or email info@haymarketbooks.org for
more information.

Cover design by Josh On. Cover images of Nazi stormtroopers gathered at Luit-
pold Arena to listen to a speech by Adolf Hitler on "Brown Shirt Day" at the
1937 convention of the Nazi Party in Nuremberg, Germany. © Associated Press
photo.

Printed in the United States.

Entered into digital printing July 2020.

Library of Congress cataloging-in-publication data is available.

10 9 8 7 6 5 4 3 2

Contents

Acknowledgements

Several people have assisted with research and advice in preparing this book. Special thanks are due to Chris Bambery, John Charlton, Tony Cliff, Neil Davidson, Henry Maitles, Dave Renton and Ian Slattery.

Glossary and list of abbreviations

ADGB—Allgemeiner Deutscher Gewerkschaftsbund. General Confederation of German Trade Unions, also known as Free Trade Unions. Linked to SPD.

AfA-Bund—Allgemeiner freier Angestelltenbund. General Confederation of salaried employees. White collar union affiliated to ADGB.

Antifas—Anti-fascist committees in 1945.

Betriebsrate—Factory councils.

BVP—Bayerische Volkspartei. Bavarian People's Party (Catholic).

Communist International—Comintern. The Third International. After Stalinisation became an instrument of rule from Moscow.

DAF—Deutsche Arbeitsfront. German Labour Front; the Nazi 'trade union'.

DAP—Deutsche Arbeiterpartei. German Workers' Party; precursor of the Nazi Party.

DDP—Deutsche Demokratische Partei. Left of centre middle class party.

DHV—Deutschenationaler Handlungsgehilfenverband. German National League of Commercial Employees. Far right wing white collar association.

DNVP—Deutschenationale Volkspartei. German National People's Party, right wing middle class party (Conservatives).

DVP—Deutsche Volkspartei. German People's Party, centre right middle class party.

Einsatzgruppen—SS task forces responsible for shooting large numbers (especially Jews) in Nazi occupied territories.

Freikorps—Free Corps. Armed units used to repression revolution, 1918-19.

Gau—Nazi geographical unit headed by a Gauleiter or local party boss.

Gestapo—Geheime Staatspolizei. State secret police.

Gleichschaltung—'coordination' or Nazification process.

Grossraumwirtschaft—macro-economic community, planned for post-war Nazi Europe.

HJ—Hitler Jugend. Hitler Youth.

ISK—Internationale Sozialistische Kampfbund. League of International Socialist Struggle.

KdF—Kraft durch Freude. 'Strength through Joy' movement, linked to DAF.

KPD—Kommunistische Partei Deutschlands. German Communist Party.

KPO—Kommunistische Partei Opposition. Left Opposition (Communist), a breakaway from the KPD.

Kristallnacht—Night of Broken Glass, 9-10 November 1938. Anti-Jewish pogrom.

Lebensraum—Living space. Expansionist policy.

NSBO—Nationalsozialistische Betriebszellen-Organisation. National Socialist Factory Cell Organisation.

NSDAP—Nationalsozialistische Deutsche Arbeiterpartei. German National Socialist Workers Party, the Nazis.

RDI—Reichsverband der Deutschen Industrie. National Federation of German Industry.

Reichswehr—German army under the Weimar Republic.

RGO—Revolutionäre Gewerkschafts Opposition. Revolutionary Trade Union Opposition. The KPD's trade union organisation.

SA—Sturmabteilung. Stormtroopers, or 'Brownshirts'.

SAP—Sozialistische Arbeiter Partei. Socialist Workers' Party; a split from the SPD.

SOPADE—Monthly reports of the Social Democratic Party of Germany in exile.

SPD—Sozialdemokratische Partei Deutschlands. German Social Democratic Party.

SS—Schutzstaffeln. Literally 'Protection Squads'. Elite Nazi paramilitary force which later ran the camps and armed units. 'Blackshirts'.

USPD—Unabhängige Sozialdemokratische Partei Deutschlands. Independent Socialists. A split from the SPD.

Volksgemeinschaft—'National', 'Folk' or 'People's' Community. Supposed non-class solidaristic society established under Third Reich.

Wehrmacht—German army under Third Reich.

ZAG—Zentralarbeitsgemeinschaft. Central Working Community. A body established after November Revolution with equal employer/union representation.

Introduction

The Nazi regime of 1933 to 1945 brought horror into the world on a scale almost impossible to comprehend. After just six years in power it detonated the largest single military conflict in history that consumed some 55 million lives. Six million Jews were coldly butchered in a deliberate campaign of extermination.[1] By 1945, of five million Soviet prisoners of war, only one million survived. The German population, with some six and a half million dead or wounded, faced a devastated country in which one fifth of its housing was uninhabitable.[2]

The deeds of Nazism were such that the commandant of Auschwitz concluded they were 'so terrible that no one in the world will believe it to be possible'.[3] Human history continues to witness terrible experiences of inhumanity. What made Nazism unique until that time was the scale and deliberate calculation involved. Target groups were selected for extermination—mental and physical 'defectives', gays, Sinti and Roma ('Gypsies'), political opponents and, of course, the Jews—old, young, women, men, most of whom could not possibly be a threat—all annihilated using 'state of the art' capitalist methods. One of these was the concentration camp: 'the modern facility for isolating and destroying the "dispensable".'[4]

For many who witnessed the liberation of the camps in 1945, their awful lesson was so self evident that simply recounting what had happened seemed sufficient to immunise future generations from a repetition. Thus the British editor of Hitler's book *Mein Kampf* wrote in 1969, 'The plague has run its course. It is now for the scientists to isolate and examine the bacillus'.[5] Tragically this is not true. The brown plague has returned and, although fascism first came to power in Italy in 1922, Nazi Germany is the model that inspires the new followers. The danger is visible in the movements of Le Pen in France, Haider in Austria, Zhirinovsky in Russia, and fascists who were recently in the Italian government. Though in public these movements wear smart suits, the graffiti betrays their true character. Their symbol is the swastika; their message is murder.

An analysis of Nazism cannot be a matter of antiquarian interest; it must be a means of combating its resurgence today. Studies emphasising

Hitler's role or the 'German national character' cannot explain contemporary Nazism or its international spread. Warning of the dangers, or appealing to humanitarian anti-racist feelings, while essential, are not enough. Such warnings and appeals were deployed by anti-Nazis in the early 1930s, to tragically little effect.

This book will argue that the most effective explanation (and therefore the most effective guide to counter-measures) is social; Nazism was based on class forces operating within a capitalist context. But this concept has come under sustained criticism from every corner of the academic world. We are told, 'National Socialism overcame boundaries of class';[6] it 'does not conform to any class pattern';[7] or was 'a classless popular party'. The Nazi state 'cannot be explained in terms of class'.[8] This approach reaches its logical conclusion in an article which says:

> The chain of causality implied by even a modified social interpretation has been severed. Realms of historical events, politics and culture, that in the older conception were driven from underlying economic and social factors, have been granted an autonomy... Ritual drama, rhetoric and symbolism have become causal forces in their own right.[9]

The contrary viewpoint, an understanding of Nazism from a class point of view, suggests that, in Trotsky's words, Nazism was a 'movement of counter-revolutionary despair'.[10] It also points towards a force which has both the social weight and interest in preventing the victory of such a movement—the working class.

Note
To give an accurate picture of the Nazis and their views in this work it has been necessary to quote passages which are deeply objectionable and offensive. Unfortunately, it is not possible to investigate the contents of a cesspool without looking at excrement. While apologising in advance for having to do this, no one should misconstrue the intention of this book, which is to assist the struggle to banish Nazism forever.

Chapter 1

Backward or modern? The course of German history

Conventional interpretations of fascism often portray it as the product of a 'special path' of national development in Germany and Italy that predates the First World War.[1] Nazism, it is argued, arose because 'the Germans have believed with a desperate conviction...that they have a divine mission'.[2] A key role here is given to the 'ideology of power and community' justified through 'a unique Germanic-Pagan pre-history'.[3] This explanation would be plausible if the Nazi movement had been isolated or lain dead and buried after 1945. However, it was part of a Europe-wide phenomenon stretching in time from the inter-war period through to today.[4] Clearly, while Nazism owes something to German history, it must have also shared many characteristics with other countries.

A more subtle approach has been to bracket Germany with countries which together shared a system of 'totalitarianism':

> National Socialism represents the right wing variant of modern totalitarianism, the ideological counterpart of Communism, or left wing totalitarianism... The major reason why Germany and several other countries turned to totalitarianism resides in their failure to integrate traditional institutions with the requirements of modern industrial civilisation.

In other words they had not achieved liberal market capitalism and the 'end of history'. Thus Nazism was generated because of 'capitalism maturing in a late feudal setting'.[5]

There were indeed long term features of German history that played a part in the triumph of Nazism, such as an influential and reactionary army. However, these institutions were not contradictory to capitalism; indeed, they mirrored its very development.

Unification and industrialisation

Nineteenth century Germany was dominated by two processes—the creation of the unified national state and industrialisation. The key moments in unification were the failed liberal nationalist revolution of 1848 and a series of wars between 1864 and 1870. During the latter period Germany amalgamated its separate states. Unification in turn became the springboard for large scale industrialisation.

After 1815 the territory consisted of a confederation of 38 states run mostly by autocratic princes or kings, each of whom jealously guarded their sovereign independence. The Revolution of 1848 aimed to merge these states into one national unit organised on a democratic basis. Leadership of the movement fell to an elected assembly in Frankfurt. The deputies there included 49 university professors, 157 magistrates, 118 higher civil servants, but not a single worker and just one peasant.[6] Mindful of the way the French Revolution had turned to Jacobinism, this thoroughly middle class crowd, while wanting national unity and democracy, were afraid to rouse the sort of mass action that might uproot the old ruling groups who resisted unification. Engels explained the dilemma of the 1848 parliamentarians:

> It is a peculiarity of the bourgeoisie, in contrast to all former ruling classes, that there is a turning point in its development after which every further expansion of its agencies of power, hence primarily of its capital, only tends to make it more and more unfit for political rule. 'Behind the big bourgeois stand the proletarians.' As the bourgeoisie develops its industry, commerce and means of communication it produces the proletariat...[and] begins to notice that its proletarian double is outgrowing it. From that moment on, it loses the strength required for exclusive political rule; it looks around for allies with whom to share its rule, or to whom to cede the whole of its rule, as circumstances may require... These allies are all reactionary by nature.[7]

The Frankfurt parliamentarians feared that if 'the mob' was stirred up to dispose of kings and princes it might turn on lesser property owners afterwards. Rather than go down this road they offered the king of Prussia the crown of a united Germany, hoping he would provide the physical force to complete their project. The offer was contemptuously refused. Soon after the Frankfurt parliament was easily dispersed and with it went the possibility of national unification on a bourgeois democratic basis.

Still, Germany was unified. The means used were 'blood and iron', in the words of its architect, the Prussian chancellor Bismarck. In wars against Denmark (1864), Austria (1866) and France (1870), a single state was forged under the hegemony of the Prussian king (now the 'Kaiser'). Thus was achieved the bourgeois goal of national unity without any real bourgeois democracy. The new political system did not allow the parliament (Reichstag) to choose the government or chancellor. It could only advise. Power, apparently, remained with feudal institutions—the monarchy and Junkers (aristocratic landowners from eastern Prussia, the most economically backward area of the country).

Proponents of a special German history, or of totalitarian theory, conclude that failure to develop bourgeois democracy proves that Germany had been halted on the 'normal path' of development towards capitalism. But capitalism and parliamentary democracy are not always paired. Capitalism can function with a variety of state forms. Parliamentary democracy was linked with the rise of capitalism in cases where the mass of the population was drawn in to smashing old state structures so the new society could be born. England in 1640, the US in 1776 and France in 1789 fitted this pattern of mass involvement. But parliamentary democracy is not a necessary component of capitalist advance and even where it is present it may be limited. For example in Britain the vast majority of the population (all women, and one third of men) lacked the vote until 1918.

In Germany the capitalists preferred an alternative to physical confrontation with the traditional state, opting for cooperation and transformation from within. For its part, the Prussian state played along with the bourgeoisie and indeed encouraged it. Bismarck knew that industrial capitalism was vital if an army was to be built that was strong enough to forge a central European state under the noses of its jealous neighbours (Austria and France), and in the teeth of local particularism from German royal houses. For him the key issue was the common interest of exploiters: 'For the security and advancement of the state, it is more useful to have a majority of those who represent property'.[8]

Even if it retained an archaic political appearance, the German state championed the creation of capitalist society. In Engels' words, the new Reich had 'outgrown the old Prussian Junker-feudalism. In this way the very victories of the Prussian army shifted the entire basis of the Prussian state structure'.[9] The German capitalists may not have remade the state, but it fitted their needs. A German state inimical to capitalist interests would have been an obstacle to development, but:

> ...industrial development went ahead at a tumultuous pace... German steel production, roughly equivalent to that of France in 1880, exceeded its closest rival by almost four to one by 1910. Germany's coal output increased seven times over between 1870 and 1913, a period in which British coal production increased less than two and a half times.[10]

Between 1860 and 1910 Germany's industrial output per head out-stripped that of Britain, France and the US.[11] In just 12 years (to 1907) machine production increased by 160 percent, mining by 69 percent and metallurgy by 59 percent.[12] Whereas 63 percent of the population lived in the countryside when Germany was unified, on the eve of the First World War 60 percent lived in towns.[13]

This was not achieved in spite of the state, but with its assistance through measures such as:

> Freedom of movement for goods, capital and labour; freedom of enter-prise from guild regulation; the 'emancipation of credit'; favourable legal conditions for company formation; the metric system of weights and measures, a single currency and unified laws of exchange; a federal consular service and standardised postal and telegraphic communica-tions; patent laws and the general codification of the commercial law.[14]

These were rendered possible by the unification achieved by force of Prussian arms under Junker leadership.

Unlike the scenario painted by totalitarian theory, this was not a frustrated rising capitalism facing a 'neutral force above the competing particular interests of party and class',[15] but a partnership in which there was a division of labour. Bismarck admitted as much, describing the new system as an alliance of baronial landowners and industrialists—'the marriage of iron and rye'.[16] There were tensions. Bismarck resented attempts by the party of business (the National Liberals) to directly in-fluence the state, a domain he reserved exclusively for his circle, drawn from the Junker landowning class. In the end the bourgeoisie accepted a subordinate role in the political sphere in return for economic dom-inance and physical protection.

In this the state was no impartial arbiter between the various classes of German society. The commitment of the army to the preservation of capitalism from the threat of the working class and its Social De-mocratic Party was summed up by General von Einem, minister of war: 'I have hated the Social Democrats all of my life [and] waged the struggle against them with the purest conscience and from innermost conviction'.[17] Thus, as one historian writes, 'The very modernity of the institutional framework created out of the unification settlement made "democratisation" (or further liberalisation) unnecessary'.[18] The po-sition of the big business sector was put superbly by the industrial magnate Fritz Thyssen, who became an ardent supporter of Hitler:

> An industrialist is always inclined to consider politics a kind of second string to his bow—the preparation for his own particular activity. In a

well ordered country, where the administration is sound, where taxes are reasonable, and the police well organised, he can afford to abstain from politics and devote himself entirely to business.[19]

Therefore, the roots of Nazism and the crisis that brought it to power did not reside in a hybrid half-feudal society, but in a thoroughly capitalist one. As Trotsky put it, 'German capitalism is going through the severest convulsions just because it is the most modern, most advanced and most dynamic capitalism on the continent of Europe'.[20] This does not mean German society was identical to other capitalist societies. Each has its own characteristics.

Organised capital

One early development in Germany was the close collaboration of state and capital. In Britain, the world's first industrial power, the traditionally dominant landowners had initially seen commerce and industry as a useful source of revenue. This led to a policy of 'mercantilism' where the state funded its operations by levying customs duties on foreign imports. Early British industry was hamstrung by the high cost of foreign raw materials and customs barriers. Therefore the battle cry of the rising industrial bourgeoisie was *laissez-faire* and free trade—there should be minimal government intervention in economic affairs. The pursuance of 'Manchesterism' from the 1840s onwards was highly successful and made Britain 'the workshop of the world'. Leaving nothing to chance the state bolstered its position by conquest of vast colonies (closely followed by France).

By the time German capitalism arrived to compete on the international scene Britain had international economic hegemony. Far from resenting protectionism, many German industrial capitalists (along with the Junkers who were fast becoming agricultural capitalists in their own right) rejected *laissez-faire* because they needed state support against competitors in the shape of tariff barriers. Not all sectors viewed protection in the same light. Successful export industries would come to reject the imposition of tariffs because other countries retaliated by introducing their own on German goods. This was not the predominant view, however, and the demand for protection was given added urgency by the Great Depression—a dip in world prices that lasted from 1873 to 1896. Thus in 1879 the German government introduced a series of protective tariffs so that 'from now on economic, domestic and foreign policy were completely dominated by the unity of interest between agriculture, industry and the leaders of the state'.[21]

Although the degree of collaboration between capital and the state may be disputed,[22] the close integration of the two was one contributory factor in the triumph of Nazism in 1933 and continued to shape the regime's policies right through to 1945.

Another consequence of German industrialisation following Britain's was that its capital tended to be far more concentrated. British industry had begun in the 1760s with small production units and numerous entrepreneurs. Only gradually did competition whittle down numbers and increase the size of factories. Industrialising a century later, Germany began with larger units leading to an 'organisation of individual capitals and the "organisation of capitalism" [which] was the most developed of any country by 1914'.[23] The electrical industry, which was virtually non-existent at the time of the 1882 census, had 107,000 workers in 1907 and was controlled by just two firms—AEG and Siemens-Halske.[24] The town of Hamborn was dominated by three pits, employing 6,000, 11,000 and 14,000 miners respectively.[25] In the financial sector Germany's nine giant banks wielded immense power by 1914, their involvement with industry linking many separate units together.[26]

Hilferding described large scale German industry, with its high level of integration through cartels, banks and the state, as a new and high stage of development called 'finance capital'. He concluded his path-breaking book of 1910 on that subject with this prediction of war and revolution:

> Finance capital, in its maturity, is the highest stage of the concentration of economic and political power in the hands of the capitalist oligarchy. It is the climax of the dictatorship of the magnates of capital. At the same time it makes the dictatorship of the capitalist lords of one country increasingly incompatible with the capitalist interests of other countries, and the internal domination of capital increasingly irreconcilable with the interests of the masses of the people exploited by finance capital but also summoned into battle against it.[27]

Although the trend was strongest in Germany, Hilferding saw finance capital as an international phenomenon.

While the concentration of capital was characteristic of some sectors of the German economy, it is important to realise how uneven the situation was. For example, in 1907 the average number of workers per company was 164 in mining and 142 in metallurgy. At the opposite end the figures for transport, woodworking and clothing were five, four and two respectively.[28] This meant that in some sectors the middle class had been transformed into full capitalists. However, a substantial middle class (or petty bourgeoisie) remained. This also had an impact on the working class. There continued to be a mass of artisans, craftsmen and others still working in close proximity to their employers. The concentration of modern capitalism at the top of German society generated a fierce class antagonism, but the continuing existence of a broad middle class milieu should not be ignored.

By the 20th century, German workers had achieved a scale of organisation unknown anywhere else. Founded in 1875, in its early days the Social Democratic Party was committed to revolutionary Marxism. By 1912 the party had won 35 percent of the vote, making it by far the most popular party. It had at this time over one million members,[29] with 11,000 of them on local councils and an estimated 100,000 working in its various offshoots or affiliated bodies (insurance institutions and so on).[30] Workers' organisation was not limited to the political sphere, for direct conflict between capital and labour took place in the factories and mines. The Free Trade Unions (ADGB) grew in membership even more dramatically than the German Social Democratic Party (SPD). Established by the SPD, the ADGB's numbers rose from 237,000 in 1892 to 2.6 million in 1912.[31] What lay behind this stormy development of the labour movement?

Firstly, 'Compared to Great Britain and France, German industrialisation was the most rapid, giving workers the least time to adapt to the conditions and labour demands of the industrial system'.[32] The very success and scale of capitalist growth had created a political reaction among those the new industrialists sought to exploit. Secondly, much of the working class was politicised by its experience of an authoritarian state in a capitalist society. The sham of democracy was brought out sharply by the imposition of the Anti-Socialist Laws which operated between 1878 and 1890. It was no accident that their introduction virtually coincided with the protectionist moves of 1879. Both reflected the coming together of state and capital. Under the Anti-Socialist Laws 1,500 prison sentences were handed down[33] and even after repeal repression did not stop. Members of the SPD were sentenced to a total of 1,244 years in prison between 1890 and 1912.[34] Such moves were welcomed by industrialists such as Alfred Krupp who told his employees, 'Higher politics requires more time and a greater insight into conditions than are given to the workers... You will do nothing but damage if you try to interfere with the helm of the legal order'.[35] Whereas in France in 1789 the democratic bourgeoisie mobilised the common people in its fight against the aristocracy, in Germany the situation was different:

> [The] labour movement had to concentrate all its energies on the attainment of democracy in a bitter struggle against the combined forces of the emperor, the landed aristocracy (with its offspring, the Prussian army) and…capitalist interests.[36]

So German Marxism was closely identified with the struggle for parliamentary democracy. On the other side was a ruling class committed to opposing such democracy. This identification of the working class movement with democratic rights, and of capitalism with denial of such rights, would play a part in the rise of Nazism.

Class antagonisms had an impact on the German petty bourgeoisie or middle class. Historically this class has had the potential to play a variety of political roles, from far left to far right. In the English and French revolutions it formed the most radical wings in Cromwell's New Model Army and the Jacobin clubs. In 1930s Germany it would tend to support Nazism. Such volatility arises from its position between the two key social classes. The middle class can identify with the workers, because it too lacks the wealth and privilege of the capitalists, falls into debt with banks, or is a victim of big capital in the unequal competition to survive. However, there can be another influence. As Engels put it, 'The petty bourgeois, artisans and shopkeepers hope to climb, to swindle their way into the big bourgeoisie; they are afraid of being thrown down into the proletariat, hovering between fear and hope'.[37] The middle class can also identify with the capitalist class because both own property (even if the disparity in size of property is great) and it sees itself as superior to the working class in wealth and education.

In much of late 19th century Europe the middle class often found itself roughly equidistant from both capitalists and workers, forming the backbone of liberalism—the middle road. In Germany such an option barely existed. The intensity of class struggle and the structure of the state forced a choice between the two hostile armies. The right wing Conservative Party won over large numbers of middle class supporters from the ailing liberal parties over the question of protection in 1879. It skilfully diverted attention from the clash between big capital and the middle class by using anti-Semitic rhetoric. The eventual result was an almost complete collapse of the 'middle road' in politics. Unlike in Britain, in Germany:

> Manchester liberalism, which expressed the free competition of independent entrepreneurs, became an ideological anachronism in the age of high imperialist cartelisation, concentration and monopolisation… The rise of working class organisation eventually meant that…an increasing

proportion of the industrial employers and the trading middle class regarded parliamentary government as a threat to their interests.[38]

Thus far it is clear that the background to Nazism was not the failure of capitalism to develop but, on the contrary, its turbulent progress, which had consequences for other classes in society.

Anti-Semitism and war

A class approach is relevant for two other aspects that are often portrayed as especially German traits and independent factors in their own right—anti-Semitism and the drive to war. The roots of both lay in capitalism. A society where a tiny number enjoy vast wealth and exploit the majority cannot long exist without an ideology which obscures the real social relationship by suggesting a common interest between exploiter and exploited (nationalism). This can easily lead to blaming the ills of society on 'non-national' scapegoats. In 19th century Britain, for example, racism was focused against the Irish; more recently it has been against black people. These groups have become convenient targets because of the imperial connection with Ireland and Africa.

Though the basic determinants were the same, the target of German racism was primarily the Jews. Anti-Semitism is sometimes portrayed as a non-class or middle class phenomenon. In fact it had its roots in the development of German capitalist society. During the 1789 Revolution the bitter struggle of the French middle class against feudalism meant that it drew a wide coalition of forces into the battle. This was fought under the general banner of freedom which included emancipation of the Jews. In Germany the timid and compromising character of the 1848 revolution and the later settlement with the establishment meant no such general freedoms were obtained. Richard Wagner, for example, could be involved in the 1848 events and yet be a vicious anti-Semite.

Anti-Semitism was prevalent at the very summit of German society. In 1901, for example, Kaiser Wilhelm II waxed lyrical about the 'massive primeval Aryan-Germanic feeling which lay slumbering within me'.[39] He thought 'our aim must certainly be firmly to exclude Jewish influence',[40] and was 'completely under the spell' of Houston Chamberlain.[41] As a leading anti-Semite the latter wrote to Hitler in 1923, 'With one blow you have transformed the state of my soul. That Germany, in the hour of her greatest need, brings forth a Hitler—that is proof of her vitality'.[42] However, anti-Semitism was also a useful tool for controlling those beneath the elite.

Significantly, organised mass anti-Semitism began in 1878, the very same year as the passing of the Anti-Socialist law, with the formation of Stöcker's Christian Social Party. A year later it was joined by the League of Anti-Semites and in 1880 by the Social Reich Party and German Reform Party. All made anti-Semitism their key policy.[43] However, anti-Semitism was not the exclusive property of one-issue groups. The much bigger Conservative Party used it to build up influence amongst the middle class. At a time when German industrialists and Junkers were pushing for state curtailment of competition through protectionist measures, it suited them to attack Jewish businessmen who were portrayed as representatives of free market capitalism. Towards the end of the century the crises of decaying feudalism and capitalist growth in Eastern Europe led to pogroms and immigration towards the West. This was used by anti-Semites in Germany and especially in Austria where Hitler was growing up.

The class origins of anti-Semitism are denied by Daniel Goldhagen, who writes that 'no non-anti-Semitic alternative image of the Jews found institutional support (the SPD partially excepted)'.[44] He conveniently fails to mention that the SPD was by far the biggest political party by the end of the 19th century. Its chief thinker, Kautsky, wrote that 'there is nothing more inimical to social democracy than anti-Semitism, [its] most dangerous opponent'.[45] The SPD was founded by the joining together of political currents led by Marx and Lassalle, both Jews, while among its most prominent leaders were Jews such as Rosa Luxemburg, Eduard Bernstein and Kurt Eisner. The contrast between the attitude of the SPD and pro-bourgeois parties towards Jews was sharp because anti-Semitism and the class structure of German society were so clearly linked.

The idea that the drive to war was some exceptional German trait is also false. It should not be forgotten that in the 19th century Germany's future foes, with political systems ranging from British liberal democracy to French republicanism and Russian autocracy, had been conquering whole continents by force of arms. Thus Trotsky wrote that Germany 'squeezed into the heart of Europe, was faced—at a time when the whole world had already been divided up—with the necessity of conquering foreign markets and redividing colonies which had already been divided'.[46] Germany's position—a population of 65 million, 16 percent of world industrial output, but only 12 million people in its colonies—contrasts with that of the British capitalism. With a domestic population of 45 million it had 14 percent of world industry and an empire of 394 million.[47]

Internal social factors also played a part in the German state's calculations. In its fight against the rise of Social Democracy the government wanted to 'consolidate the position of the ruling classes with a successful imperialist foreign policy, [since] war would resolve growing social tensions'.[48] Even this was not peculiarly German. The same social imperialist current existed in Britain around Lord Milner.

The First World War cost 13 million lives and left another 36 million wounded. For Germany this meant 1.7 million dead and 4.2 million wounded.[49] The nature of the 'patriotic' employers was also put to the test: 'Only when the army was willing to grant high profits and suppress labour did it receive the full support of the industrialists'.[50] As a result of this blackmail corporate earnings soared from a pre-war annual sum of 1.6 billion to 2.2 billion marks in 1917-18. In metal industries (which served the war effort directly), earnings rose from 34 million marks to 111 million in the same period.[51]

War also caused a split in the SPD. Reformists joined in the carnage to defend 'their' capitalist state against other capitalist states. However, the pretence that the war was anything other than imperialist was exposed by the vicious Treaty of Brest-Litovsk which the German military imposed on the newly formed Russian Soviet state in early 1918. This cost the Bolshevik government 26 percent of its population, one third of its townspeople, 28 percent of industry and 75 percent of coal and iron reserves.[52] Only a small minority of revolutionaries, led by Luxemburg and Liebknecht, remained internationalist and condemned the war from the beginning.

In spite of SPD support for the war effort the state eventually cracked apart. Imminent defeat and a mutiny by Kiel sailors initiated a revolution. The imperialist war also produced an imperialist peace—the Treaty of Versailles—in which the victors carved up the country, taking 13 percent of its territory and 10 percent of its population.[53]

Writing a year after its outbreak, Luxemburg warned prophetically that the war was an imperialist conflict that confronted humanity with 'a dilemma; either a transition to socialism or a return to barbarism'.[54] These choices were to be played out in the years that followed.

Chapter 2

The origins of Nazism: revolution and counter-revolution, 1918 to 1923

Though there is a continuity within German history, it is undeniable that the ferocity of Nazism marked it out from anything that had come before. The prison sentences handed out under the Anti-Socialist law cannot be compared to the torture and murder of millions in concentration camps. This has led German conservatives to argue that 'it is a very great mistake to believe that [Nazism] is in any way the heritage and continuation of the old, monarchic power of the princes. Neither Frederick the Great, Bismarck nor Wilhelm II were the historical precursors of Adolf Hitler', and because the Nazi leader was an Austrian (who only acquired German nationality in 1932), 'The historical origins of Hitlerism are to be found outside the Reich'.[1] This is wrong. The difference between Nazism and previous forms of capitalist rule is between the birth and development of the system and the agonies of its increasing old age. A key stage in this process was the experience of revolution and the reaction against it by the German ruling class.

The November Revolution

Many historians write off the possibility of socialist revolution in the period from 1918 to 1923. In doing so they minimise the importance of counter-revolutionary currents. Both these approaches were belied by opinion at the time. On 10 January 1919 Stinnes, the richest man in Germany, led 50 industrialists from the most illustrious firms in establishing a fund which financed the 'General Secretariat for the Struggle against Bolshevism', the 'Anti-Bolshevist League', the 'Union for the Struggle against Bolshevism', the 'Freikorps Publicity Bureau' and various other bodies.[2] The upper classes, who had lorded it over the masses for generations were suddenly terrified for their property. Prince von Bülow wrote, 'In Berlin on November 9, I witnessed the beginnings of revolution... I have seldom witnessed anything so nauseating, so maddeningly revolting and base, as the spectacle of half grown louts, tricked out with the red armlets of social democracy'.[3] The industrialist Thyssen wrote that 'during an entire year, 1918-1919, I felt that Germany was going to sink into anarchy. Strikes follow one another... It was impossible to reorganise industrial production'.[4] Thyssen had reason to fear the revolution. At one stage he was arrested by his workers and shipped to Berlin for trial by a revolutionary tribunal. Another industrialist complained that 'all authority had collapsed; monarchy, state, army and bureaucracy'.[5]

The immediate impact of the November Revolution was to overthrow the Kaiser (on 9 November) and to stop the war. However, its potential did not end there. War weariness and revolution shattered the hold of the army officers. As early as June 1918, for example, the 41st Infantry Division quit the trenches in a mass desertion.[6] Later attempts to use conscripted front line soldiers to repress the left at home failed as the hoped for troop units simply dissolved away. All over Germany revolutionary soldiers' councils linked up with workers' councils in a pattern similar to the Russian soviets. The head of the army, General Groener, reported:

> The influence of the workers' and soldiers' councils prevails among whole sections of the army... All authority on the part of officers and junior officers is being undermined by the propaganda of the Independents and Spartakists. The High Command is powerless and no help can be expected from the government.[7]

As the repressive powers of the old state disintegrated, the outline of a socialist alternative emerged in the workers' and soldiers' council movement. The changes that workers wanted went far beyond the establishment of the parliamentary democracy denied them under the Kaiser. The atmosphere in Berlin's factories in late November was captured by the right wing *Deutsche Tageszeitung*:

> The employers are as powerless as the managerial staff. All power is in the hands of the workers' committees. On all questions ranging from the reconversion of the factory to peacetime production, the supply of labour, the employment of demobbed soldiers, the implementation of agreements, work methods and sharing out of work—on all these the workers' committees have the last word.[8]

The November Revolution showed the potential for a revolutionary democracy in which the mass of producers collectively controlled the wealth that they created. It was this spectre which terrified the once secure ruling groups.

In the face of a powerful opponent the ruling class had two options. One was to seek compromise and ride out the storm. The other was head-on confrontation. Both carrot and stick were employed, although the balance between them varied according to circumstances and the tactical judgements of those giving the orders. With the army in tatters, direct military collision with workers on a broad scale was not an immediate option. The relation of forces was clearly in labour's favour so a compromise strategy predominated. Its progress was smoothed by the influence of reformism in the working class. No doubt the mass of German workers wanted a better standard of living, plus freedom from exploitation and war; however, only a small minority regarded revolution as the necessary means to achieve it. This minority was to be found mainly in the new Communist Party of Germany (KPD), formerly the Spartakist League. The vast majority of workers supported the reformist SPD or the Independents (USPD) who vacillated between the alternatives of reform and revolution.

So, for the old rulers of Germany the main path to salvation was through compromise, and in the SPD and the unions they found willing partners. At first sight this might seem strange. It was not so long ago that socialists and trade unionists had been jailed by these very people. However, a remarkable transformation had occurred within the upper circles of the SPD and unions. The logic of their reformist politics had always been to work within the capitalist system to win changes. Now revolution not only threatened that system, it had catapulted them into powerful positions. Later on Tarnow, an SPD leader, asked, 'Are we now to stand at the sick bed of capitalism merely as the diagnostician, or also as the doctor who seeks to cure? We are condemned to act as the doctor who earnestly seeks the cure'.[9] Thus the SPD set its face against the revolution.

The army had its own pressing reasons for working with the SPD. General Groener wrote, 'At first, of course, we had to make concessions... The task was to contain and render harmless the revolutionary movement.' So he telephoned the SPD leader, Ebert, to tell him that in return for putting the army at the government's disposal:

> The officer corps expected the support of the government in the maintenance of order and discipline in the army. The officer corps expected the government to fight against Bolshevism and was ready for the struggle. Ebert accepted my offer of an alliance. From then on we discussed the measures which were necessary every evening on a secret telephone line between the Reich Chancellery and the High Command.[10]

Parallel to the Ebert-Groener alliance were the negotiations between unions and employers. The chair of the iron and steel employers was 'happy that the unions are still prepared to negotiate as they have; for only by negotiations can we avoid anarchy, Bolshevism, Spartakist rule and chaos—call it what you will'.[11] In return for limited concessions, the union leaderships would prevent workers taking over the factories and mines. The result was most satisfactory to the employers:

> It is no exaggeration to say that this cooperation...saved Germany in the early years from chaos and from Bolshevik revolution... What happened in all other revolutions, that the workers turned against the employers, did not happen here because the unions cooperated with the employers in the preservation of order.[12]

Nevertheless, the social crisis which had led to revolution could not be wished away by the army or SPD. The lack of real change spurred the most militant workers into action. During the so called 'Spartakus Week' of January 1919 the revolutionary left in Berlin responded to a government provocation by launching a movement which turned into an insurrection. Now the compromise with the SPD and unions paid off. One tangible result had been the formation of the Freikorps. This was a new right wing volunteer force assembled out of what remained of the disintegrated Imperial Army. Over 400,000 strong, it was composed of mercenaries, ex-officers and soldiers torn out of society by the degrading experience of war. Financed by big business and led by Noske, the Social Democrat and 'bloodhound of the revolution', it was deployed to smash opposition wherever it could be found. In Berlin, Freikorps troops took control through fierce house to house fighting. Some 200 people were killed, 90 percent coming from the revolutionary side and including the leaders of the KPD, Rosa Luxemburg and Karl Liebknecht.[13]

Although the KPD had acted prematurely in early 1919 and so lacked the support needed to succeed, disappointment with the meagre results of reformism in government continued and grew deeper. One barometer of this was elections to the Reichstag. In the first election under the republic (January 1919) the socialist parties attracted 13.8 million votes, of which 11.5 million went to the SPD and 2.3 million to the more left wing USPD. By the next election in June 1920 the SPD vote had more than halved—reaching just 5.6 million, while the USPD's had more than doubled, at 4.9 million. To this should be added the KPD's vote of 0.4 million.[14] The leftward trend showed itself in other ways. Within the USPD itself there was a vote to merge with the KPD. The new body, the 'United KPD', grew from 50,000 to 450,000 by December 1920. More important than the elections was the continuous stream of radical activities, including a rising strike wave (5,000 strikes in 1919 to 8,800 in 1920)[15] and periodic uprisings.

Therefore the final outcome of the revolution was not decided by the crushing of the Berlin left in the Spartakus Week. In the months that followed, Freikorps units, with the blessing of the SPD government and the finances of industrialists and bankers,[16] sought to eradicate revolution all over Germany. The power of the workers' and soldiers' councils, which represented the rudiments of an alternative system to capitalism, was systematically destroyed. Lacking an effective leadership, the centres of the revolutionary left were picked off one at a time. The small but ruthless roving force of right wing soldiers swept down from Bremen in the north, via central Germany to the Ruhr and Bavaria in the south.

Bavaria would be of particular importance, because it was here that Nazism first developed. Although this part of Germany was amongst the least industrialised, the workers of the regional capital, Munich, were highly radical, the Independents gaining a third of the popular vote in local elections in the summer of 1919.[17] Between February and April 1919 Bavaria also saw Germany's poorly organised but most ambitious seizure of power. The Bavarian Soviet Republic was led at first by disparate elements of the far left, but in the end Leviné of the KPD felt obliged to step in and give some coherence to it even though he knew it was likely to fail. The hope was that outside assistance would save the day. This was not forthcoming and very soon Hoffmann, the SPD representative, was installed by brutal Freikorps tactics. Chris Harman writes that 'the outcome was a disastrous defeat for the whole working class. From that point on the Freikorps and the extreme right had a free reign in Bavaria'.[18]

'Swastika or Soviet star'—the origins of Nazi ideology[19]

The various social forces opposing the revolution were not all agreed on the tactics to adopt. On one side there were those like Groener or Stinnes who judged that it was initially best to compromise and to collaborate with the SPD in efforts to stabilise the situation. While this did not preclude bloody civil war against radical workers, it did mean combining forces (if only temporarily) with Ebert and supporters of the new republic.

However, there was another current which believed that the best form of defence against revolution was direct counter-revolutionary attack. This group included the Freikorps whose lives and livelihoods were committed to the cause. As one of them put it:

> Completely disconcerted, a bourgeois generation faced the new world of 1918... Fighting had become our life purpose and goal; any battle, any sacrifice for the might and glory of our country [in] the battle against the Reds.[20]

Many such Freikorps troops became Nazis such as Ritter von Epp (whose activities including crushing the Bavarian Soviet Republic), and Captain Röhm, later the leader of the Nazi Stormtroopers (SA). The history of the early Nazi Party is inextricably bound up with such active counter-revolution.

Hitler's biography makes this clear. Son of a minor government official in Austria, he had drifted from doss house to doss house in Austria and Bavaria, painting postcards to earn a living. Initially evading conscription, war service for Germany gave his existence a structure and purpose. During the war Hitler rose to the rank of corporal and earned the Iron Cross for bravery. Many of those who formed the cadre of Italian and German fascism in the 1920s and 1930s shared a similar experience. In November 1918 Hitler was dismayed by the way that the revolution not only signalled the end of his way of life, but also Germany's military defeat and a challenge to society. He later claimed that it was at this point that he determined to enter politics. Branding the republican forces 'November criminals', he echoed Field Marshal Hindenberg's contention that 'the German army was stabbed in the back' by revolution at home.[21]

Hitler was in Munich when, in 1919, counter-revolution triumphed over the Bavarian Soviet Republic. His superior officer instructed him to help link up the reactionary army with right wing civilian politics. He was to make contact with the German Workers' Party (Deutsche Arbeiterpartei or DAP) which was, despite its name, a fanatical nationalist grouping. In March 1920 Hitler was demobilised because the clauses of the Versailles Treaty limited the Reichswehr to 100,000. Five months later his rhetoric had won him the DAP's leadership and it was renamed the National Socialist German Workers' Party (NSDAP).

What was the ideology of Nazism? This is a surprisingly difficult question to answer because it was an incoherent mass of prejudices, hatred and plain untruths. Policies were designed to win converts rather than reflect the real thinking of the leadership. Nevertheless at the core of Nazi concerns we see an extreme caricature of the prevailing capitalist ideas.

One element was social Darwinism, which Hitler expressed in this way:

> In the end, only the urge for self preservation can conquer. Beneath it so called humanity, the expression of a mixture of stupidity, cowardice and know it all conceit, will melt like snow in the March sun. Mankind has grown great in eternal struggle, and only in eternal peace does it perish.[22]

The idea of survival of the fittest matches the character of market capitalism with its ruthless competitive drive. Thus, 'Men dispossess one another, and one perceives that, at the end of it all, it is always the stronger who triumphs. Is that not the most reasonable order of things?'[23]

In Hitler's version the struggle is transposed into a struggle of nation against nation or race against race. Hitler was obsessed by the idea of imperialist expansion and *Lebensraum* (living space): 'The purpose of domestic policy is to secure for the race the power needed for its external policy claims'.[24] Many historians take the Nazis' extreme nationalism and denial of class at face value and see the ideology as therefore being above class. Certainly Hitler wanted it that way, declaring in a debate on whether the immense wealth of the German princes should be confiscated, that, 'For us there are today no princes, only Germans'.[25] However, the concept of 'nation', which does indeed deny the importance of class, is thoroughly rooted in capitalist (class based) society. Luxemburg accurately described the bourgeois nature of nationalism:

> In a class society, 'the nation' as a homogeneous socio-political entity does not exist. Rather, there exist within each nation classes with antagonistic interests and 'rights'. There literally is not one social area, from the coarsest material relationships to the most subtle moral ones, in which the possessing class and the class conscious proletariat hold the same attitude, and in which they appear as a consolidated 'national' entity. In the sphere of economic relations, the bourgeois class represents the interests of exploitation; the proletariat the interests of work. In the sphere of legal relations, the cornerstone of bourgeois society is private property; the interest of the proletariat demands the emancipation of the propertyless man from the domination of property.[26]

There was therefore nothing original about the Nazis' expansionist aims. The goal of *Lebensraum*, of 'Middle Europe under German leadership', had been set out by the German chancellor, Bethmann Hollweg, as early as September 1914. His plan almost exactly matched Hitler's conquests a quarter of a century later because it encompassed France, Belgium, Holland, Denmark, Austria, the Austrian Empire (Poland, Czechoslovakia, Hungary, etc) and eventually Italy and Norway.[27]

Hitler's attitude to nations and races infected his views on every other aspect of society right down to the individual:

> [This outlook] by no means believes in an equality of the races, but along with their difference it recognises their higher or lesser value and feels itself obligated, through this knowledge, to promote the victory of the better and stronger, and demand the subordination of the inferior and weaker in accordance with the eternal will that dominates this universe. Thus, in principle, it serves the basic aristocratic idea of nature and believes in the validity of this law down to the last individual. It sees not only the different value of the races, but also the different value of individuals.[28]

What a justification of the capitalist system! It derives from the 'eternal will' and laws of 'nature'. He concluded, 'The capitalists have a right to lead due to their abilities; for they have worked their way to the top, and on the grounds of this selection, proved their higher race'.[29]

Elitism in politics followed. Hitler divided society into three groups: 'the great mass of the people and consequently...the simplest minded part of the nation', a smaller middle group and finally 'the smallest; it consists of the minds with real mental subtlety, whom natural gifts and education have taught to think independently...splendid people'.[30] Democracy is therefore wrong because, 'today, when the ballot of the masses decides, the chief weight lies with the most numerous group, and this is the first: the mob of the simple or credulous'.[31]

Hitler's approach to politics was only one variety of bourgeois thinking and a minority one at this stage. Under capitalism the controllers of the means of production rule those who lack these by a number of methods, both indirect (ideological) and direct (economic and political). As long as workers 'know their place' and the system of exploitation is secure, a degree of rotation of top political jobs through parliamentary democracy is an attractive strategy. It allows flexibility in the executive of the state which 'is but a committee for managing the common affairs of the whole bourgeoisie'.[32] In this way it reflects the changing needs of capital and gives the appearance of popular control, thus helping maintain popular cooperation.

Hitler's counter-revolutionary strategy would only become popular in crisis conditions where even rudimentary compromise of the parliamentary kind was anathema for important sections of capitalism.

This set it apart from the usual tenor of ruling class ideology and its extremism took it on to another plane. Thus while the Kaiser had detested democracy, his chancellor, Bismarck, had gone through the motions of consulting the people by introducing universal male suffrage in 1871, which predated Britain by 47 years.

Anti-Semitic ideology

Many historians emphasise the anti-Semitic character of the movement. There can be no doubt that this was a key feature. Hitler's first political statement of 16 September 1919 dripped with anti-Semitism. It blamed Jews for 'the racial tuberculosis of the nation', the solution for which 'must be the total removal of all Jews from our midst'.[33] Anti-Semitism was a cancer running throughout Hitler's life. In 1928 he wrote, 'The higher the racial merit of a people, the higher is their general right to life'.[34] Hitler's very last statement, dictated just before his suicide in the Berlin bunker on 29 April 1945, ends with this curse: 'Uphold the race laws to the limit and resist mercilessly the poisoner of all nations, international Jewry'.[35] Nazi anti-Semitic beliefs went far beyond anything envisaged by the Kaiser's governments.

This has led historians to explain Nazism by referring to its racism: 'In regard to Hitler's ideology, the critique of the republic, democracy, parliamentarism, Marxism, socialism and so forth should be viewed as entirely subordinate to his anti-Semitism'.[36] Such a conclusion is understandable. However, the deranged actions of a deluded individual and the account that person gives for their actions do not reveal the real causes. Irrational ideas and actions have rational explanations and causes which lie beneath the surface. If this is true for the individual, it is also valid for a movement.

One causal factor that can be excluded from the start is Jewry itself. Jews were not the cause of anti-Semitism. Forming just 0.76 percent of the German population, the obsessive and fanatical anti-Semitism of Nazism cannot be explained by anything Jews did.[37] The delusion must therefore be explained by other conditions.

Abram Leon argues the origins of anti-Semitism were rooted in the development of European capitalist society. In pre-capitalist times the conventional society was based on landed production and Jews were assigned a special role in commerce and banking which it could not supply. In this sense the Jews were both an ethnic group and had 'a specific social function'—they formed a 'people-class'.[38]

To fulfil their role they could not assimilate into the rest of society as happened to countless other ethnic groupings over the centuries.

When feudalism went into decline, the Jews, to whom nobles might be in debt, became the object of ruling class hatred. Since the aristocracy possessed political and ideological power, officially sponsored anti-Semitism was encouraged and pogroms organised. The simultaneous rise of capitalism brought no respite as Jews were now seen as rivals and competitors to 'native' capitalists. The pattern of feudal decline and rising capitalism occurred first in western Europe, spreading successively to central and then eastern Europe.

In Britain, therefore, the period of most intense anti-Jewish riots was in the 12th century, culminating in massacres in London, Lincoln, Stafford and York (1189-90). By the 20th century British capitalism had been firmly entrenched for centuries and so the social force of anti-Semitism was a pale shadow of its former self. However, where feudalism was replaced more recently by capitalism, such as Russia, Poland, and, crucially for Nazism, Hitler's Austria, the ideological power of anti-Semitism tended to be greater. Thus when Hitler arrived in Vienna in 1907 the mayor, Lüger, was a leading anti-Semite as was his chief political rival, von Schönerer. In addition the semi-feudal Austrian Empire was in the last stages of decay. It would not survive the war, being replaced in 1918 by new independent states such as Czechoslovakia and Poland. Hitler ascribed the weakness of the Austrian state to the presence of different national groupings and the Jews in particular.

According to Abram Leon's analysis, while anti-Semitism existed throughout pre-war Europe it was not likely to be most virulent in Germany. As one writer put it recently:

> Surveying European society in 1914, it would have taken a great leap of imagination to nominate Germany as the future perpetrator of genocide against the Jews. Tsarist Russia, with its government-encouraged pogroms, the Hapsburg lands [Austrian Empire]…may have seemed likelier candidates.[39]

So how can the extreme position of the NSDAP be explained? Some authors blame it entirely on Hitler and his individual psychology. This is a weak argument for a mass movement and even in the case of Hitler it does not stand up. Focusing on events like the unsuccessful treatment of Hitler's dying mother by a Jewish doctor,[40] the fact that four members of the committee that rejected his application to art school were Jewish[41] or that Hitler read anti-Semitic literature in Austria are not convincing. Although probably a racist from early on, racism did not become a crusade for him until 1919. Only then was there a real compulsion behind his all embracing and politically motivating hatred—defeat and revolution.

This was what turned Hitler and his immediate followers to polit-ical action based on anti-Semitism. Already imbued with a ruling class ideology of nationalism and authority, they were confronted with the impact of the Russian and German revolutions, surrender, virtual civil war between revolutionaries and establishment, and finally de-mobilisation. The military's ambitions had brought untold suffering, but in Hitler's view, 'What the German people owe to the army can be briefly summed up in a single word, to wit: everything'.[42]

It was primarily this hatred of revolution and working class organ-isation that powered his anti-Semitic political activity. Significantly, his first political statement, quoted above, also includes the phrase that 'the driving force of the revolution [are] the Jews'.[43] A list of Hitler's 22 early speeches shows that only two mentioned Jews in the title while 11 alluded to the consequences of war and revolution.[44] References to the centrality of counter-revolution abound in Hitler's later speeches and writings.

Hitler's *Mein Kampf*, written in 1924, fulminates against Marxism, 'a doctrine that must lead to the destruction of all humanity'.[45] The anti-war movement was made up of 'treacherous murderers of the nation', whose leaders 'should at once have been put behind bars, brought to trial, and thus taken off the nation's neck. All the imple-ments of military power should have been ruthlessly used for the ex-termination of this pestilence.' He considered, 'The scum of our people then made the revolution... It was not the German people as such that committed this act of Cain, but its deserters, pimps, and other rabble that shun the light'.[46] Hitler's autobiography described his first activ-ities as 'The Struggle against the Red Front'.[47]

His criticism of the establishment was that the tactics employed against the left were too weak and ineffective: 'The revolution had been possible thanks only to the disastrous bourgeois leadership of our people.' In arguing this Hitler showed the contradictory character of Nazi ideas. Like most leading Nazis he was personally an outsider to the ruling class yet he was filled with its ideas in an extreme form. He therefore had contempt for their collective failure to protect their so-ciety. Later he talked of 'that riff-raff of a bourgeoisie', whose behav-iour was such that 'I don't blame the small man for turning Communist'.[48] By contrast to the old establishment his group had 'the fists to protect the German people... And how these lads did fight!'[49] The aim was spelled out:

> If we are victorious Marxism will be destroyed, and completely de-stroyed. We shall not rest until the last newspaper has been destroyed,

the last organisation liquidated, the last centre of education wiped out and the last Marxist converted or exterminated.[50]

If Hitler's public utterances are not to be believed (as he was a self confessed inveterate liar), his private comments are more reliable. In a letter written in 1932 Hitler claimed, 'It was solely to save Germany from the oppression of Marxism that I founded and organised a movement'.[51] During the approach to Operation Barbarossa, the invasion of Russia in 1941, Goebbels, Hitler's propaganda chief, said, 'We shall now destroy what we have fought against for our entire lives. I say so to the Führer and he completely agrees with me... This plague will be driven out of Europe'.[52]

It would be wrong to counterpose Nazism's counter-revolutionary character with its anti-Semitism, or to suggest one outweighs the other. The two were inextricably linked in the Nazi leadership's fevered imaginations. If there was any genuine connection between anti-Marxism and anti-Semitism it was the prominent part played by internationalist Jews in socialist and revolutionary movements—from Marx in Germany, to Luxemburg, a Pole, to Trotsky, a Russian, and so on. In other words counter-revolution was the real basis of the Nazis' deluded belief system. *Mein Kampf* brings this out:

> Only a knowledge of the Jews provides the key with which to comprehend the inner, and consequently real, aims of Social Democracy. The erroneous conceptions of the aim and meaning of this party fall from our eyes like veils, once we come to know this people, and from the fog and mist of social phrases rises the leering grimace of Marxism.[53]

Himmler, arch-racist, elitist and leader of the SS (the fanatical Nazi Blackshirts), was equally convinced of the link between Jewry and workers' revolution:

> Time and again the Jews have stirred up the various systems of government by means of wars and revolutions, not only political but economic and intellectual revolutions... As the proletariat cannot lead a state, leadership comes into the hands of the Jews.[54]

Nazi anti-Semitism also derived from another source which reflected the class composition of the party. According to Kater, in the NSDAP 'the relative proportion of elite elements was higher among the leadership than in the party at large or in the Reich population. [It] tended to increase with rank [and] was particularly influential.' Overall, however, in the leadership the middle class 'were in the absolute majority'.[55] As already mentioned, the right wing petty bourgeoisie has a peculiar relationship to capitalism, both aspiring to become big capitalists and suffering from the development of capitalism in which large capitals squeeze out small ones; commerce and banking challenge the security and survival of individual enterprises, and so on. As a typical representative of the petty bourgeoisie, Hitler came to associate what he saw as the regrettable side effects of capitalism with Jews: 'Business was depersonalised, ie Judaised... It became the object of speculation. Employer and worker were torn asunder'.[56] Thus in Germany 'a 60 million strong people sees its destiny to lie at the will of a few dozen Jewish bankers'.[57] The Jews served the Nazis' purpose well by being the scapegoat both for a hatred of the labour movement and anger at the inevitable workings of the capitalist system: 'How wonderfully the stock exchange Jew and the leader of the workers...cooperate. Moses Kohn on the one side encourages his association to refuse the workers' demands, while his brother Isaac in the factory incites the masses'.[58]

This is nonsense, but it does show, in a distorted way, the sequence of causality—from the real pressure of the external world through to the fantasy of anti-Semitism. As a result we can reject the notion that Hitler and his circle derived anti-Semitism from some form of mental derangement, or that all Germans subscribed to such ideas. The history of ideology is suffused with irrational belief systems, but the explanation lies outside the individual mind and is to be found in social conditions. Nazis were not racist to the exclusion of class, but because of class.

National Socialism?

It would be a mistake to portray Nazism as a typical ruling class current of thought, however. There were important differences that went beyond a readiness to take extreme measures and use brutal violence. Hitler believed that capitalism as then constituted was incapable of successfully combating revolution: 'The struggle of the bourgeois world against the Marxist International must fail completely. It has long since sacrificed the foundation which would have been indispensably necessary for the support of its own ideological world'.[59] The problem was that 'it had not from the outset laid its chief stress on winning supporters from the circles of the great masses'.[60]

These statements confirm a characteristic of capitalism that Trotsky highlighted: 'The economically powerful big bourgeoisie, in itself, constitutes an infinitesimal minority of the nation. To enforce its domination it must ensure a definite mutual relationship with the petty bourgeoisie'.[61] This does not mean the relationship between the petty bourgeoisie and capitalism is a comfortable one: 'In its mass, the petty bourgeoisie is an exploited and oppressed class. It regards the bourgeoisie with envy and often with hatred'.[62]

Hitler's approach was to try to re-establish this 'definite mutual relationship' between the ruling class and the masses that had been disrupted by revolution. In doing so he exhibited resentment at capitalism, but at the same time insisted that his movement alone could save it by providing the necessary links with the population. This aspect was given special emphasis when the attempt to seize power by direct military means in 1923 failed completely. In 1924 he wrote in *Mein Kampf* that the masses were to be won back by propaganda which he said 'must be popular and its intellectual level must be adjusted to the most limited intelligence among those it is addressed to'.[63] Genuine argument is no part of this because, 'The people in their overwhelming majority are so feminine by nature and attitude that sober reasoning determines their thoughts and actions far less than emotion and feeling'.[64]

It is in this light that we should approach the official 25 point programme of 1920 which aimed to provide the 'foundation' for the support of the bourgeois 'ideological world' that capitalists failed to create. This was to be done by binding the mass of the population to the interests of capital through nationalism and racism flavoured with 'Germanic socialism'. Points 1 to 3 of the programme included a rejection of the Versailles Treaty and a demand for territorial expansion. Points 4 to 10 involved racism against Jews and foreigners.

Points 11 to 14 dealt with the so called 'socialism' of the Nazis. Clause 11 demanded 'abolition of income unearned by labour or effort; breaking the bondage of interest'. Point 12 asked for 'complete confiscation of all war profits', point 13 for the 'nationalisation of all incorporated companies', point 14 for 'profit sharing'. (The later points, 15 to 25, dealt with a variety of subsidiary issues such as small businesses, education, farming, health, law and religion).[65]

Do points 11 to 14 invalidate the assertion that Nazism was a ruling class current? Not at all. The driving force and philosophy of the movement was clearly counter-revolutionary, but an appeal to the masses through lying propaganda had to be included if the deficiencies of previous bourgeois movements were to be overcome. Whenever Hitler was compelled to define 'socialism' the contradictions emerged.

Unbelievably, the Kaiser's system was regarded as close to socialism: 'The old Reich had at least made an honourable attempt to be socially minded (*sozial*)... That the old Reich was in this sense 'social', that it did not allow itself to regard its people merely as numbers—this it was which constituted its greatest danger to the supporters of the world stock exchange'.[66] Nazism's phoney socialism was nothing new. As long ago as 1848 Marx had summed up its characteristics in *The Communist Manifesto*: 'This form of socialism aspires...to cramping the modern means of production and of exchange within the framework of the old property relations that have been, and were bound to be, exploded by those means. In either case it is both reactionary and utopian'.[67] Some 80 years after these lines were written the idea of returning to the former structures of capitalism was completely impractical and so only the reactionary aspect was left.

When in 1922 property owners expressed worries about NSDAP 'socialism' they were calmed:

> You are thinking of the false Jewish socialism (Marxism) of the *Sozis* [socialists] and Communists. National Socialism expressly recognises private property but demands that every producer subordinates his private interests to the interests of the German folk community.[68]

In 1933 Hitler told the Reichstag that one of the three aims of his party was 'to maintain the idea of property as the basis of our culture'.[69] In private he would later add, 'My plan is that we should take profits on whatever comes our way'.[70] Asked what would happen to people like Krupps under National Socialist rule, Hitler maintained, 'But of course things would remain as they were'.[71]

Expressions of concern for the working class were in reality designed to leave it economically exploited but to end its opposition to capitalism by incorporating it ideologically within the existing structure of state and society:

> The new movement categorically rejects any class or status division...and is for the formation of a unified national body through the immediate incorporation of the so called fourth estate in a people's community... It wants the millions strong masses to be led away from their current internationalist and most un-German seducers and leaders and their full incorporation into the framework of the nation and the state.[72]

Thus, Hitler's definition of socialism was:

> He who is prepared so completely to adopt the cause of his people that he really knows no higher ideal than the prosperity of this—his own—people, he who has so taken to heart the meaning of our great song 'Deutschland, Deutschland, Über Alles', that nothing in this world stands for him higher than this Germany, people and land, land and people, he is a socialist.[73]

Shortly afterwards he declared 'the highest socialist organisation is the German army'.[74]

All the capitalist elements mentioned so far—social Darwinism, imperialism, elitism, anti-democracy, anti-Semitism, counter-revolution, rejection of the Versailles Treaty and territorial expansion—were fully acted upon when Hitler attained power. None of the so called 'socialist' points 11 to 14, such as nationalisation, profit sharing or abolition of interest, were put into effect.

A third way?

Is it possible that instead of identifying Hitler with ruling class counter-revolutionary thinking he should be linked with ideas developing in the middle class at that time? It is clear that Hitler eventually got massive support from the middle class, but this was only in the 1930s and reflected middle class acceptance of capitalist ideas rather than its own autonomous position. But what of Nazi ideology at the moment it was taking shape? The fact is that in the formative period the middle class was moving to the left and away from the ideology being formulated for the NSDAP. There were a number of indicators for this. One was the changing electoral pattern.

Pre-war German politics was characterised by a working class that mostly voted socialist, and a middle class that generally voted Liberal or Conservative. The minority Catholic Centre Party cut across these divisions by combining a section of middle and working class voters. In 1919 the political landscape had been transformed. The Liberal vote had split, with four fifths of it moving left to form the German Democratic Party (DDP); the traditional Liberals, Stresemann's German People's Party (DVP), were now a rump. Conservativism continued in the shape of the German National People's Party (DNVP). The Catholic vote (now shared by the Centre Party and a Bavarian off-shoot, the BVP) remained little changed. Though the socialist vote had split into two groups, its overall share had risen dramatically.

A comparison of the percentages of the vote won in the 1912 and 1919 elections brings out these shifts:[75]

	Conservatives	Liberals	Catholic	Socialist
1912	12.2	26.0	16.4	34.8
1919	10.3	23.0[1]	19.7	45.5[2]

[1] Left Liberal DDP: 18.6, Old Liberal DVP: 4.4 / [2] SPD: 37.9, USPD: 7.6.

There must clearly have been a swing of large numbers of middle class votes from the right towards the left in the shape of the DDP and even the socialist parties.

Even more striking than electoral statistics was mass unionisation of white collar workers, who traditionally regarded themselves as middle class. Before the war only 80,000 white collar employees belonged to the socialist affiliated union, the AfA-Bund. By contrast, 600,000 were in the professional association dominated by the far right DHV.[76] The impact of the revolution was demonstrated very quickly. The ZdA, an even more left wing organisation than the AfA-Bund, grew from 66,000 to 138,000 in the first quarter of 1919.[77] By 1920 the AfA-Bund itself had multiplied over eight times to 690,000 members.[78] Meanwhile the DHV's share had fallen to 463,000.[79] The very fact of mass unionisation suggested to contemporaries that 'the middle class associations of white collar workers decided to acknowledge that their members were indeed members of the labour force—something they had not only previously denied, but sometimes denied in a doctrinaire manner.' And striking 'lost its stigma for the first time'.[80] Salaried employees could now be regarded as 'standard bearers of the revolution'.[81]

Why was the middle class now surging to the left? When, through revolution, the workers' movement offered the hope of a better society, it could win large numbers of the middle class. Without that alternative the middle class could, and did, get dragged along by ruling class influence. For the left to consolidate middle class support it needed to be clear of its own objective. As Trotsky explained:

> The petty bourgeoisie, even when completely thrown off the conservative road by circumstances, can turn to social revolution only when the sympathies of the majority of the working class are for a social revolution.[82]

Political evolution after 1919 meant that the middle class would later become a bulwark of Nazism, but this in no way invalidates the point that the development of Nazi ideology did not reflect the trend of middle class opinion. It went against it.

It could still be argued that even if Nazi ideology did not mirror the middle class, it does not follow that it reflected the ruling class. Could it have been outside class? Certainly there were enough cranks, eccentrics and pathetic social misfits in the party's minuscule ranks to make a case for the NSDAP being a simple aberration. Hitler may well have had 'multiple personality disorders including borderline personality...schizotypal, histrionic, narcissistic and anti-social personality'.[83] It is true the chief Nazi 'philosopher', Alfred Rosenberg, seriously insisted on 'the existence of a Nordic pre-historic culture centre' located in Atlantis,[84] that Jesus was 'non-Jewish'[85] and that the Roman Empire was brought down by '400 years of race destroying democracy'.[86] However, such raving should not make us overlook the real social content of Nazi ideology and its links with sections of the ruling class, both military and civilian. The Nazi belief in open counter-revolution went well beyond its ranks. This was clear from the Kapp Putsch.

From the Kapp Putsch to the Beer Hall Putsch

In March 1920 the Erhardt Brigade, wearing swastikas and supported by the prominent Reichswehr Generals Lüttwitz and Ludendorff, chased the SPD led government from Berlin. The putsch installed a retired civil servant, Kapp, as the new chancellor. (Three years later Ludendorff would jointly lead the 'Beer Hall Putsch' with Hitler.) Kapp like Hitler, warned of the threat of 'destruction and violation by war-like Bolshevism'. He too pretended to be above both capitalist and worker claiming his government would 'not be a one sided capitalist one. It will rather save German work from the hard fate of slavery to international big business… In the best German tradition the state must stand above the conflict of classes and parties, [although] striking is treason to the nation, the fatherland and the future.' The seriousness of this ruling class effort was underlined by the refusal of von Seekt, chief of the army High Command, to lift a finger against Kapp. The army had supported the republican government against the revolutionary left and the militant workers, but now that the Freikorps had accomplished its gruesome task, might it perhaps be safe to dispose of the SPD too? Seekt was unsure of the answer and decided to bide his time to see if Kapp could succeed. The same attitude prevailed in industry where 'the leading men of big business proclaimed their "neutrality", which amounted to according the new government parity with the old. Only when the failure of the venture became evident did they distance themselves from the putschists'.[87]

The putsch was defeated when the ADGB unions launched a massive general strike. Not only was Kapp's government forced to resign, soon the workers' offensive, which had been subdued by a year of Freikorps bloodletting, resumed. In the Ruhr a broad front of 'Red armies' arose. However, once again the Social Democrat leaders were able to disarm this workers' movement, avoid a thorough purging of the army and resurrect the Ebert-Groener compromise. Kapp's tactics had failed, but this did not rule out future attempts under other leaders.

In Bavaria, however, the outcome was different. Only here did the putsch succeed. During Kapp's brief rule the local SPD failed to promote the general strike. Hoffman's Social Democratic government was 'persuaded' to resign and a right winger called Kahr took over. When the putschists were finally swept away in Berlin and elsewhere, Kahr remained in office. From this point on Bavaria was even better disposed towards extreme right wing groups, among them the NSDAP.

The benefits to Nazism of this arrangement became evident in June 1922 after right wing fanatics murdered Rathenau, the foreign minister, who was also Jewish. There was fury across Germany and the NSDAP was banned in almost every state. Yet in Bavaria, where the Party's activities continued unabated,[88] Hitler enjoyed the 'patronage'[89] of Munich's police chief and of Frick, head of its political department. Links with the ruling class also went beyond this. Turner, who seeks to minimise Nazism's connections with capitalism, tells us that as early as 1919 Hitler had been invited to Berlin's 'National Club' of army officers, senior civil servants and businessmen. Meetings with the League of Bavarian Industrialists, the Herrenklub and Merchants' Guild followed.[90] By 1922 Hitler had the backing of one of the most venerable firms of heavy industry—Borsig. The Bechsteins (piano makers) and Bruckmann (the publisher) were also converts, along with Thyssen,[91] giving Hitler a 'respectability' in polite society that 'played an invaluable role'.[92]

Hitler's ambiguous position as the leader of an extreme faction of ruling class politics was illustrated by events surrounding May Day 1923. The NSDAP was planning to attack trade union demonstrations in Munich. In order to do so Captain Röhm 'borrowed' a supply of arms from a barracks. This was going too far for the military commander. While Hitler waited for the arms to arrive, Röhm 'was standing to attention before an angry General von Lossow and being reminded of his duty as a soldier'.[93] The fact that Hitler almost acquired arms in this way shows that he was far from an outsider to the ruling class. However, the withholding of those arms when they threatened to create an unpredictable civil war situation showed his strategy was not yet shared by everyone in the ruling circles.

As 1923 wore on Germany was hit by the 'Great Inflation'. It had many causes—the way the war effort had been financed, reparations, invasion of the Ruhr by French and Belgian troops to enforce payment, and finally the pressure of the great industrialists to withdraw concessions made to labour. The impact on the economy was astonishing. In January 1913 the exchange rate was one mark to the dollar, but in 1923:

The mark plunged down, not from month to month, or from week to week, but from day to day—indeed, hour to hour. On 13 November 1923 the dollar was quoted officially at 840 milliards [billion], the day after at 1,260 milliards, after another 24 hours at 2,520 milliards, and, on 20 November, when the rate reached its maximum, at 4,200 milliards [or 4,200,000,000,000 marks].[94]

The crisis swelled the fortunes of individuals like Stinnes to obscene proportions. He bought up failed businesses on borrowed money which instantly lost its value. For the rest of the population life became far more difficult. Workers struggled to keep up with price increases; a kilo of rye bread retailed at 0.29 marks in 1913 but cost 428,000,000,000 marks in November 1923.[95] The average wage did not provide half the subsistence needed for a family of four.[96] Many middle class people on pensions or with savings saw these wiped out in value. While ruin was not universal, it is calculated that by 1925 the total income of small investors was just 3-4 percent of its pre-war sum.[97]

What would be the outcome of this immense crisis? In the previous four years the reformist workers' parties had ensured that the Kaiser's state largely remained intact while the workers' movement was reined in. Denied a radical solution to Germany's problems, the middle class had swung back to the right. However, in the midst of a capitalist system apparently bent on self destruction, the left was also growing. The KPD had become a mass party.[98] Even after the revolutionary wave had passed, it still attracted four votes to every six of the SPD in the 1924 election.[99] Around Germany armed organisations called 'Proletarian Hundreds' were springing up and huge strikes swept the country.

In late 1923 revolution was clearly on the cards, a fact recognised on all sides of the political spectrum. Accordingly the KPD planned meticulously for an uprising. The spark was supposed to come from a defence of the KPD-backed governments in Saxony and Thuringia. The tense atmosphere was described by one Communist:

A silent, almost inconceivable drama. A million revolutionaries, ready, awaiting the signal to attack: behind them the millions of the unemployed, the hungry, the desperate, a people in pain, murmuring, 'Us as well, us as well.' The muscles of this crowd were ready, the first already clasping the Mausers that...were going to oppose...the armoured cars of the Reichswehr.[100]

Demands by the army to dissolve the Saxon and Thuringian governments were supposed to have been the prelude to a general strike and revolt. However, on 21 October 1923 the KPD backed off from issuing this call. Only Hamburg, which did not receive the order to retreat, rose up.

There is no space here to discuss the reasons for this turnaround, nor to speculate on the chances of success for a workers' revolution in autumn 1923. But the perception on the right is relevant. Hitler had witnessed the developing crisis and revolutionary mood with growing anticipation. In 1922 Mussolini had been invited into power after the march on Rome. This encouraged Hitler to attempt the same thing in Germany, although conditions were rather different. In the south, economic development had been less thorough, which meant that both the Italian capitalist class and the working class movement were weaker. Compared to the Nazis, Italian fascism did not have to take such a 'pure' form; its machine would not have to be as powerful, nor its ideology so racist (as a means of steeling its cadre). Hitler trusted that the threat of proletarian revolution in 1923 would bring him more determined ruling class support than had been available to Kapp in 1920. Bavaria was selected as the launching pad for a march through central Germany to wipe out the Saxon and Thuringian governments. It would then continue on to Berlin to take power.

In October the prospects for such an enterprise were good. At this time there was an 'unholy alliance between the Reichswehr and the paramilitary', for 'over 50 percent of all stockpiles and ammunition in Germany were owned or seized by these groups'.[101] The Bavarian government had already come into conflict with the central government in Berlin in September when the latter agreed to fulfil reparations demands in order to win French and Belgian withdrawal. Denouncing this as a betrayal of the national cause, a state of emergency was decreed in Bavaria and State Commissioner Kahr dared Berlin to do its worst. When Berlin tried to remove Lossow, the head of the Bavarian Reichswehr, Kahr stepped in to block this move. Together with Seisser, the state police chief, the three men formed a dictatorship.

This did not necessarily mean the way was open for Hitler. Firstly, differences existed between Kahr's government and the Nazis. The former wanted either monarchical restoration or independence for Bavaria and were not convinced that Bavaria could launch a successful armed counter-revolution on a national scale. Such an attempt might unleash a workers' movement even stronger than the one that had toppled Kapp in 1920. Secondly, in Berlin von Seekt was still more cautious. A right wing coup would, he said, 'unleash civil war' which the workers might win.[102]

Seekt's stance was based purely on a tactical estimate of the balance of class forces rather than any belief in democracy or hatred of Nazism.

In 1923 Seekt himself was working on plans for a military coup in which Stinnes would play a leading role.[103] The latter wanted a dictatorship which would demand two hours unpaid labour per day and ban strikes.[104] Later on, in 1930, Seekt was asked if the Nazis should be in government and replied, 'Yes indeed and I would go further—it is a necessity'.[105]

Hitler's strategy depended on the backing of significant sections of the ruling class, especially in Bavaria. To attract this he needed revolution as an immediate threat. He believed that Communist 'civil war' would crystallise support for a direct counter-attack: 'And there will be only two possibilities: either Berlin marches and ends up in Munich, or Munich marches and ends up in Berlin! A Bolshevist North Germany and a Nationalist Bavaria cannot exist side by side'.[106] Hitler's scenario seemed to be unfolding in October, when he was busy hatching his plans.

But the scrapping of the KPD-planned revolt threw Hitler's calculations off course and drove him to desperate measures. On the evening of 8 November a meeting with Kahr in the Munich Beer Hall was surrounded by Hitler's troops. The 'Führer' leapt on to a chair to announce the formation of a new government. This would be no overthrow of the establishment. The government was to be headed by the Kaiser's old war leader, Ludendorff. Kahr was to rule Bavaria; Lossow would be army minister and Seisser Reich police minister.[107] By this time, however, Kahr, Lossow and Seisser had got cold feet and so it was only under duress that they promised to play their allotted roles. As soon as they were out of Hitler's clutches they rescinded their pledge, one influence being the telegram from Seekt demanding an end to the putsch. The Nazis could not turn back now and on 9 November marched through Munich. As they reached the centre a police cordon blocked their passage. In the shooting that followed 16 Nazis were killed. This was the end of the 'National Revolution'. It failed so pathetically because, as Hitler himself admitted, 'We never thought to carry through a revolt against the army: it was with it that we believed we should succeed'.[108]

Conclusion

Once again we are confronted with the fact that the Nazi leadership was not some third force distinct from capitalist institutions, but an extreme counter-revolutionary wing of the ruling class. If there was any doubt of this it was dispelled by Hitler's treason trial that followed the putsch. Unbelievably, these were the words of the state *prosecutor* about the accused:

As a brave soldier [in the First World War] he showed a German spirit, and afterward, beginning from scratch and working hard, he created a great party, the National Socialist German Workers' Party, which is pledged to fighting international Marxism and Jewry, to settling accounts with the November criminals, and to disseminating the national idea among all layers of the population, in particular the workers. I am not called to pass judgement on his party programme, but his honest endeavour to reawaken the belief in the German cause among an oppressed and disarmed people is most certainly to his credit. Here, helped by his unique oratorical gift, he has made a significant contribution.[109]

Not surprisingly Hitler received the minimum sentence of five years, a promise of early probation,[110] and a prison 'cell' that looked 'like a delicatessen store. You could have opened up a flower and fruit and wine shop with all the stuff stacked there'.[111] Beloved of Munich salons and patronised by police chiefs and industrialists, the future Führer spent just over eight months in jail. Five days after his release this convicted criminal had a personal interview with the Bavarian prime minister who kindly agreed to lift the ban on his newspaper, the *Völkischer Beobachter*.[112]

Although the immediate prospect of revolution receded after 1923, Hitler had established his credentials as leader of a movement that took organised counter-revolution seriously. This book will continue to use the term 'counter-revolutionary' as shorthand for Nazi ideology even though there was a change in its practical meaning. After 1923 the Nazi programme was one of destroying the potential of revolution, ie smashing the working class and its organisations.[113] In the mid-1920s there was little call for the NSDAP's services, as the situation had apparently stabilised. The appearance of calm was misleading.

Chapter 3

The crisis of Weimar: Hitler becomes chancellor

If Nazism is understood in a class context, although individuals and groups of activists remain important, what they are able to do depends very much on the social framework. This is strikingly demonstrated by the history of the NSDAP. Nazi ideology with its obsessive hatreds, contempt for human beings, elitism and irrationality underwent little change from its inception in 1920. In the years that followed the Nazis spouted their racist filth and the Stormtroopers stomped around Germany, fists flying, but with negligible results. Until 1930 the NSDAP remained an eccentric collection of counter-revolutionary misfits on the outer margins of politics. Yet in 1933 Hitler was made chancellor of Germany. How could this happen?

One widespread view is that Germans were intrinsically inclined towards Nazi views such as anti-Semitism. Goldhagen states: 'Whatever else Germans thought about Hitler and the Nazi movement, however much they might have detested aspects of Nazism, the vast majority of them subscribed to the underlying Nazi model of Jews'.[1] This simply cannot explain why the most overtly anti-Semitic party, the NSDAP, could attract only 2.6 percent of the popular vote in 1928 and never won a popular mandate to rule.

Another approach suggests that social considerations played little part in the creation of the Third Reich: 'In the decision making process of 1930-33 the primacy of politics must be placed in the foreground'.[2] This is because, as another author puts it, Nazism involved 'the decoupling of political goals from any rational and recognisable socio-economic foundations'.[3] The trouble with this is that events at the state/political level cannot be divorced from those taking place in society and the economy generally—they are dialectically interrelated.

The decision to appoint Hitler, it is generally agreed, was arrived at by the German 'elite'. This included big business and the army. As we saw in Chapter 1, though these forces may function in discreet areas and be far from homogeneous within themselves, they were separate parts of a single social class—the capitalist ruling class. In Germany the relationship between the two was closer than in many other states. So accounts which rightly stress the role of the military in giving Hitler the chancellorship must ask what role was the army trying to fulfil, how it was financed, and what was its ideology?

The army was closely bound to capitalist industry at a number of levels. It was directly concerned with the arms industries like heavy engineering and chemicals. There was also a 'mental alliance' between the army and industry in terms of a defence of the stability of the state and its social underpinnings. Finally there was a surprisingly high degree of individual interconnections and crossover of personnel.[4] All of these take us back to society in general and capitalism in particular.

Pointing out the class context of the Nazi rise to power does not mean that there was a cunning capitalist conspiracy to install Hitler. Guerin oversimplifies when he writes, 'At a given moment the capitalist magnates no longer use the Blackshirts or Brownshirts merely as anti-labour militia, but launch fascism for the conquest of the state'.[5] The Beer Hall Putsch had demonstrated a number of key points in this regard. Hitler had attempted to seize power believing that support would be forthcoming from the establishment. However, the fact that the putsch failed so pathetically demonstrated how wary key sectors of the ruling class were of Hitler's high risk strategy. Only in an extreme crisis would capitalism dare to resort to the extreme measures proposed by Hitler. Thus, Nazism was a semi-autonomous force. Trotsky described the interrelationship of capitalism and fascism in these terms:

> The bourgeoisie does not like the 'plebeian' means of solving its problems…for the shocks and disturbances, although in the interests of bourgeois society, involve dangers for it as well. This is the source of the antagonism between fascism and the traditional parties of the bourgeoisie… The big bourgeoisie dislikes this method, much as a man with a swollen jaw dislikes having his teeth pulled.[6]

The problems of German capitalism

The appointment of Hitler was connected with the crisis of capitalism. Some basic features of German development have already been explored—its dynamism combined with intense class conflict and location in a recently unified country. This led to a high level of business concentration, close cooperation with the state, and frustration with both the constraints of internal class struggle and well established competitors. Between 1914 and 1918 this led to the explosive attempt to break through the barriers by means of imperialist war which failed, bringing defeat and revolution.

One consequence was the Treaty of Versailles, a settlement by imperialist victors imposed on their rival. This involved the loss of all colonies, 73 percent of iron and 26 percent of coal supplies.[7] The reparations bill was set at £6.6 billion, which equalled 1.5 times the total gross national product of Germany in 1929.[8] While the Nazis made much of these facts, the treaty merely added to the losses accumulated earlier. Even before the discussions at Versailles, war had reduced industrial output to just 37 percent of the pre-war level.[9] This decline was greater than that of its competitors. Germany's share of world industrial production had tumbled from 16 percent to 8 percent by 1923.[10]

In the mid-1920s the prospects for capitalism improved. The 1923 hyper-inflation, while catastrophic for some, actually benefited big capital which was able to wipe out its debts and buy out rivals for a song. In late 1923 the number of business insolvencies declined dramatically,[11] while capital became still more concentrated.[12] After 1923 the economy was stabilised on the basis of a new currency, the Rentenmark. Recovery was rapid with production returning to pre-war levels by 1928. This was Germany's roaring twenties. In just one year (summer 1926 to autumn 1927) overall industrial production leapt by 50 percent and capital goods output by 70 percent.[13]

However, beneath the surface problems remained. Growth and reparations repayments were assisted by foreign loans. Between 1924 and 1931 foreign credits amounted to 14 billion Rentenmarks of which 11 billion went on reparations.[14] To service these debts there was an emphasis on external trade,[15] which left Germany dangerously dependent on outside factors. Even in the 'golden years' Germany carried a heavy balance of payments deficit.[16]

Some sectors of industry found life easier than others. By 1927 consumer industries exceeded their pre-war output by 16 percent. During the war heavy industry had supplied a war machine of 13 million soldiers. Afterwards its military market was cut by the Treaty of Versailles to 100,000 troops. In 1927 heavy industrial output was still 2 percent below pre-war figures.[17] In this sector economic turmoil produced concentration, extensive rationalisation and automation. Second only in productive potential to the US,[18] the outcome was a modernised 'leaner, fitter' industry which soon bumped up against limits of demand. For example, in 1925 steel works were producing at just 60 percent of capacity, and by 1930 the figure had fallen to 55 percent.[19]

The German economic pattern exhibited the same basic trend as its neighbours, but it was manic depressive in its mood swings. So the roaring twenties were followed by a massive slump after October 1929. Signs of weakness in the German economy predated the 1929 Wall Street Crash, with industrial shares falling 25 percent in the summer of that year.[20] The very success of Germany's roaring twenties had been built upon 'an astonishing intensification of the productive process in important key industries. In no other country, apart from the US, were technical improvements as far reaching as in Germany.' In this very process of raising productivity by an average 20 percent, one million jobs also disappeared.[21] So the Depression and mass unemployment were not just externally generated disasters, although the situation was obviously exacerbated by world events and the withdrawal of US loans. While global industrial production fell 29 percent between 1929 and 1932, Germany fared still worse. Three years after 1929 national income had fallen by 43 percent, industrial production was half its pre-crash level, while heavy industry once again suffered most, falling to one third of the 1928 level.[22] Overall investment in 1932 was just one sixth of the level in 1928.[23] The starkest evidence of the crisis was unemployment, which even in the difficult years of 1919-23 had usually remained low. Unemployment statistics are notoriously dependent on methods of calculation. One estimate puts the real (as opposed to official) figure at ten million by the end of 1932.[24] The government reported the figure of 5.6 million, or 30 percent of the workforce at this time.[25] Trade union figures tell the same story. Unemployment in the metal workers' union averaged 4 percent between 1907 and 1928. In December 1932 the figure was 43 percent and rising.[26]

Despite its severity, the crash was part of the 'normal' process of capitalist crisis. Whatever its specific difficulties, it should be remembered that the basic trends of German economic development in the war years and 1920s broadly followed that of world capitalism as a whole. During the First World War the overall output of belligerents had fallen by one third.[27] World trade, which grew by almost half in the decade before the war, managed only an 8.5 percent increase in the decade after the war.[28] Even hyper-inflation was not a peculiarly German phenomenon. Austria saw prices rise to 14,000 times the pre-war level, Hungary 23,000 and Poland 2,500,000.[29] The 1929 crash was near universal, with falls in industrial output for the US and Poland outpacing even Germany's drop.[30] If the precise contours of the crisis that hit the Weimar Republic were 'without precedent in the history of industrial capitalism',[31] Germany was, nonetheless, very much part of that common process.

The ransom paid to class struggle

Economic crisis alone is not sufficient to explain the victory of Nazism, since other capitalist states suffered without following the same path. One factor was the particular character of German class relations. The period from 1918 to 1923 had seen a workers' revolution which had gone only half way, leaving the capitalist class intact but in a fragile position. Long before, the French Jacobins had warned about the dangers of such a situation: 'Those who half make a revolution dig their own graves'.[12] This is a major reason why politics in Germany did not take the British form of a 'National Government' (incorporating a spectrum of politicians from Tory to renegade Labour), or the US pattern of Roosevelt's 'New Deal'. For German capital any solution to the economic problems could not be separated from a decisive alteration of the political class balance.

The revolutionary events after November 1918 did not overthrow capitalist society, but it was only saved by a series of concessions. A substantial ransom had had to be paid. This included the establishment of the ZAG (Central Working Community) in which unions and employers had parity. Its task was to oversee the regulation of working conditions. Though shortlived, the ZAG led the way to the introduction of an eight hour day (without loss of pay), short-time payments, full collective bargaining over working hours, sick pay, employment of war invalids, and job protection. Perhaps most important of all were two laws. One legally established the *Betriebsrat* or works committee. In 1919 these had been the centre of the revolutionary effort to seize control of the factories, but they were now reduced to the functions of a shop stewards' committee. The second law brought state arbitration to bear on industry wide disputes.[13] Though all this fell far short of a social transformation it did create a bridgehead of workers' organisation into a system where the employer had, till then, regarded himself as *Herr im Hause* (lord in his own house). As a result the Free Trade Unions' membership rose from 2.9 million in 1918 to 8.5 million in 1920.

The compromise of 1918-19 was regarded by the employers as temporary. They intended to withdraw it when the balance of forces moved in the right direction. The bosses could achieve a certain amount within the framework of the republic. The buffeting suffered by workers' organisations in the early 1920s saw many of the immediate post-war gains taken back. In 1923, for example, inflation was used as the excuse to abrogate the eight hour day.[14] However, the power of workers' organisation was not destroyed and by 1928 the majority of workers had clawed back shorter hours.[35] Union membership may have fallen, but in 1930 it still stood at 62 percent of its post-war peak.[36] Under the impact of mass unemployment wages may have declined, but in 1932 they were still ahead of their pre-war level,[37] and taking 62 percent of national income as compared with 46 percent before the war.[38]

The ransom needed to head off revolution did not stop there. A broad system of social welfare was built up. This provided benefits for sickness and accidents, and improved unemployment provision. Compared to 1913, at the end of the Weimar Republic spending in real terms on social insurance had doubled, health and welfare quadrupled, and public housing expenditure rocketed 25 times. In contrast defence and the economy (roads, industrial subsidies) fell to a quarter of the 1913 level.[39] Despite savings in these departments, overall government spending was running at twice the pre-war level at the very moment the economy crashed.[40]

The balance of classes within the state

The Weimar system included a political compromise. On the one hand, workers' political representatives were allowed to play their allotted role in the Reichstag. Under the constitution providing one deputy to every 60,000 voters, elections were held and the SPD was even allowed to rule for three out of the 14 years that the Weimar Republic existed.[41] For the first time the government was formally accountable to the reichstag and 15 successive coalition administrations were formed.[42] In a country where the majority of the population were workers, and many of them radical, this represented a considerable concession from the old political groupings.

However, the public political process and the state are not one and the same. If, as Marx argued, the state's primary role is the maintenance of the ruling class and its key element is 'bodies of armed men' (such as the army, police, courts and prisons), then parliament was not the most important institution. The core of the Kaiser's state had been preserved, and transferred wholesale into the republic. Symbols are often evidence of deeper processes. The new political system 'retained the name Deutsches Reich (German Empire), with its imperial and authoritarian undertones'.[43] Its other title, the Weimar Republic, betrays the fact that it was deliberately concocted in a quiet non-industrial town far away from 'Red Berlin'. Still more important, tucked away in the constitution was a clause (Article 48) which said, 'In the event that public order and security are seriously disturbed or endangered, the Reich president may take the measures necessary for their restoration, intervening, if necessary, with the aid of the armed forces'.[44] In context this meant that if democracy should ever threaten capitalist 'order and security' the president could establish a dictatorship to defend it.

Thus the political compromise was no less strained by class conflict than was the socio-economic compromise in the 1920s. One SPD leader sensed the danger when he said, 'Essentially we have governed according to the old forms of our state life... I believe that the verdict of history...will be severe and bitter'.[45] Doubts about the democratic credentials of the state machine arose not only from the army but also the courts system. We have seen how Hitler was treated for his treasonous behaviour. Writing in 1922, this is how one observer described Weimar 'justice':

> Virtually all of the relatively small number of assassinations of reactionaries have been atoned for through severe penalties; of the very numerous assassinations of men of the left, on the other hand, not one has been atoned... The judge, who himself belongs to the former upper classes, has an age old familiarity with the thought that this economic order must be defended. His own position, after all, rests upon it.[46]

A comparison between those arrested after the fall of the Bavarian Soviet Republic in 1919 and the Kapp Putsch is instructive. In the former case 2,209 were murdered on the spot and those who escaped were given prison sentences amounting to 4,092 years. In the latter 705 charges of high treason were laid but no one was punished. Between 1919 and 1922 the right were responsible for 354 political murders, the left only 22, yet the former almost always escaped punishment.[47]

Liberal historians like Bracher tend to blame the problems of the Weimar Republic on a lack of faith in the 'middle road' of politics. From this viewpoint the left is as much to blame as the right: 'The trouble is not the lack of a "complete" revolution...but rather the reluctance to have a fully parliamentary regime...the original flaw of the Weimar Republic'.[48] This ignores the character of the state in capitalist society, which is to preserve the existence of that society. In circumstances of crisis and worker resistance it was impossible to achieve a smooth running system of exploitation based on consent. Therefore a stable parliamentary democracy could not be created. At the time supporters of such a system realised that it represented no more than a defeat of the initial revolutionary upsurge accompanied by concessions to a still powerful workers' movement:

> Even he who supports the republican state will have to recognise the fact without ado that the German republic was not the result of a great

republican movement and of republican aspirations of broad circles of our people, but that it arose as *the only possible form for the new state* after the collapse at the end of the world war.[49]

To fully grasp the relationship between the social context of postwar Germany and political events such as the Nazi assumption of power, it is useful to consider Marx's statement, 'The mode of production of material life conditions the general process of social, political and intellectual life'.[50] The mode of production in Germany was capitalism of the most advanced kind. Marx also affirmed:

The need to distinguish between the economic conditions of production …and the legal, political, religious, artistic or philosophic—in short, ideological forms… Just as one does not judge an individual by what he thinks about himself, so one cannot judge a period of transformation by its consciousness, but, on the contrary, this consciousness must be explained from the contradictions of material life.[51]

This dialectical approach to the relationship between capitalist society and politics is invaluable in the context of the rise of Nazism. Some historians claim that unless one can find individual capitalists who not only financed Hitler, but personally placed him in the seat of power, there is no connection between capitalism and Nazism. Stalinist historians countered by an equally undialectical response that Nazism equals capitalism. Connections existed between capitalism and the NSDAP; but this does not mean the Nazis were either robots programmed by the bosses, or free agents making up their own minds and acting as they pleased.

From the end of parliamentary democracy to the cabinet of barons

In 1930 the last democratically accountable government was removed from office, unravelling a sequence of events which would bring the Nazis to power three years later. It is often argued that the Depression, like some climatic phenomenon outside of human control, made this happen. This is wrong for a number of reasons. Firstly, the Depression was very much man made, since capitalism is a human institution. Secondly, the intensifying class struggle and assault on the post-war political and economic settlement began before the crash of 1929.

On the one hand there was a marked swing to the left in the years 1926-28. At the 1928 Reichstag election KPD and SPD votes increased by 17 percent and 14 percent respectively.[52] In this period

strike days rose from 1.3 million to 20.3 million and led to a significant increase in workers' victories. At the same time the employers
were continually resorting to lockouts which multiplied 11 times over
in the same period.[53] These battles reached a peak in the Ruhr and,
significantly, involved the state. The background to the Ruhr strike
was a wage dispute which was, as the law envisaged, taken to compulsory state arbitration. The government's partial pay award infuri-
ated the employers who declared war 'on the principles of pay
arbitration'.[54] In direct defiance of the government they locked out
250,000 workers. The result was a lower settlement for the workers,
but it was still enough to leave the industrialists feeling 'deprived of
a decisive victory over the "trade union state" by what they saw as the
subservience of politicians to the masses'.[55] So even in the years of
economic boom capitalists resented the price they paid for limited
democracy.

The arrival of the Depression dampened the conflict on the shopfloor
but focused the class struggle even more sharply on the state. An 'en-
lightened' businessman remarked, 'Personally, I do not believe that
the hard times we are in at present are to be explained solely or to a
large extent by the world crisis... We have not only lost a war, but we
have had a fundamentally new government, which has been concerned
for ten or 12 years to distribute charity to all sides'.[56] In 1930 a 'Grand
Coalition' headed by Hermann Müller of the SPD was in government.
With the onset of mass unemployment it attempted to reduce rising dole
costs,[57] but could not prevent a growing deficit, expenditure rising from
1.2 billion marks in 1928 to 2.7 billion in 1930.[58] The attitude of industrialists in December 1929, at this key moment of crisis, was expressed by the German Society for Industry or RDI (the German
equivalent of the CBI in Britain):

> Expenditures for welfare state purposes must be cut; the bureaucracy must
> be pared down; state interference in labour management disputes must
> be limited...direct taxes...must be reduced; indirect taxes on mass con-
> sumption items must be increased... The time had come, the RDI pro-
> claimed, for an end to compromising with socialism.[59]

Carl Duisberg of IG Farben, the chemicals giant, who was seen as progressive and pro-republican, said, 'Capital is being destroyed through the
unproductive use of public funds... Only an immediate and radical reversal in state policies can help'.[60] On 12 December 1929 a special RDI
meeting was told that political parties 'inevitably strive for compromise, which at best can only produce half measures. For us half measures
will no longer do... In Germany there will only be economic peace

when the 100,000 party functionaries are out of the country. (Cries of "Bravo!" and "Mussolini!")'.[61]

The German president was Paul von Hindenburg. Formerly one of the Kaiser's field marshals, he was an ageing reactionary who replaced Ebert in 1925. In 1930 he stepped up plans to overthrow the Müller coalition. In the words of his state secretary, Meissner, the president was concerned 'that the opportunity of forming an anti-parliamentary and anti-Marxist' government might again be lost. In that case the president would find it impossible ever to 'get away from governing with the Social Democrats'.[62]

In March the opportunity to end parliamentary democracy presented itself. The Grand Coalition fell apart when the SPD failed to win approval from its bourgeois partners for raising employers' contributions to unemployment funds. Hindenburg now used Article 48 of the constitution to install a new chancellor over the head of the Reichstag. Henceforth, the affairs of government were run by emergency decree and often without parliamentary approval. The three years that followed saw a succession of Hindenburg-nominated chancellors beginning with a right wing politician of the Catholic Centre Party, Brüning, followed by von Papen, von Schleicher and eventually Hitler.

What lay behind the collapse of parliamentary democracy? Turner insists:

> The assault on the democratic institutions of the republic that began in the spring of 1930 came not from big business but rather from another, but much more politically potent, remnant of the imperial era, the military. As Germany's capitalists looked on passively, and unconsulted, the generals stepped in and set in motion a reshaping of the political institutions of the country.[63]

There is a problem with this approach. It does not explain why the generals' programme consisted of bolstering up capitalism, nor why the supposedly 'politically potent' Reichswehr staggered from one crisis to another between 1930 and 1933. In fact the Reichswehr's disdain for democracy was cheered on by sections of business. Since the forced compromise with the unions, top capitalists like Stinnes longed for the day 'big business and all those who rule over industry will some day recover their influence and power'. Thyssen said, 'Democracy with us represents nothing,' and von Siemens stated that German people 'were not ready for democracy'.[64] On the eve of the Grand Coalition's fall the *Deutsche Zeitung* wrote, 'Industry must take advantage of the position of power it still retains to wipe out Social Democracy. It can only accomplish that if it eliminates parliamentarism'.[65]

Trotsky had a better explanation of what was going on after 1930:

> As a matter of fact, the government is…a sort of political commission of the Reichswehr. But for all its preponderance over the government, the Reichswehr nevertheless cannot lay claim to any independent political role. A hundred thousand soldiers, no matter how cohesive and steeled they may be…are incapable of commanding a nation of 65 million torn by the most profound social antagonisms. The Reichswehr represents only one element in the interplay of forces, and not the decisive one.[66]

The German government was, in his view, a manifestation of 'Bonapartism':

> As soon as the struggle of two social strata—the haves and the have nots, the exploiters and the exploited—reaches its highest tension, the conditions are established for the domination of bureaucracy, police, soldiery. The government becomes 'independent' of society. Let us once more recall: if two forks are stuck symmetrically into a cork, the latter can stand even on the head of a pin. That is precisely the schema of Bonapartism. To be sure, such a government does not cease being the clerk of the property owners. Yet the clerk sits on the back of the boss, rubs his neck raw and does not hesitate at times to dig his boots into his face.[67]

Trotsky derived this picture of Bonapartism from Marx's work on the failure of the workers' revolt in France in 1848 and the subsequent rise of Louis Napoleon. The analogy with Germany is a valuable one and many of the points raised by Marx explain quite clearly the problems the continued existence of the Weimar constitution posed for the ruling class. But how can one talk of a capitalist state in Hindenburg's Germany if the capitalists were not in charge? Marx explained such Bonapartism with these words:

> [To] establish peace and quiet in the country its bourgeois parliament must first of all be laid to rest; that its political power must be broken in order to preserve its social power intact; that the individual bourgeois can only continue to exploit the other classes and remain in undisturbed enjoyment of property, family, religion and order on conditions that his class is condemned to political insignificance along with the other classes.[68]

The severe crisis of German capitalism after 1929 generated forms of Bonapartism. Many of the features described here (in terms of the need to deny democracy or even direct bourgeois rule) would also be valid for the Nazi state. However, as we shall see, Nazism itself displayed certain features that mean that the analogy with Bonapartism should not be taken too far.

If there was any doubt about whose side Brüning was on, it was soon dispelled by a vicious austerity programme designed to balance the budget and restore capitalist stability. To do this he hit the millions already suffering misery. The emergency decrees worsened the social position of the working class as a whole, halving real wages between 1929 and 1932.[69] This does not mean, as the KPD argued at that time, that Brüning and his successors were fascist. He was a Bonapartist, balancing the contending forces in the interests of capital. Despite weakening the influence of the Reichstag, the Bonapartist balancing act meant successive governments sought to reconstruct a popular consensus by means of elections and appeals to reformist labour. Indeed, these chancellors very much depended on the acquiescence of the SPD to survive politically. Schleicher's brief ministry in 1933 even involved an attempt to construct a governing alliance in which the trade unions were to play a key role. This did not mean that Hindenburg's clique cared about parliamentary arithmetic, but class relations determined that, though the Reichstag had lost much prestige, those in charge feared the risks entailed in open counter-revolution.

Splits among the capitalists

One reason for the resort to Bonapartism was division amongst the capitalists themselves. There was no common agreement about how the immense crisis could be solved. This showed up in the various bourgeois political factions within the Reichstag, the German National People's Party (DNVP), standing mainly for landed and heavy industrial interests, with other bourgeois parties such as the German People's Party (DVP) representing the rest. This was one reason why a viable governing coalition could not be constructed.

At all times there are differences within the ruling class about how their interests will be best served. Capitalists form a band of 'hostile brothers' who share a common interest as a class but are also in competition with each other, company by company and sector by sector. These disagreements become even sharper after 1929.

The fault lines within the capitalist class have been described in these terms: 'Despite the intersection of numerous points of organisational and political points of interest, heavy industry and light industry were antagonistic currents in the Weimar Republic'.[70] Another historian distinguishes between dynamic industries interested in exports and concentrated in the chemicals and electrical sector, and backward industries relying on products like coal and steel.[71] The roots of such differences were numerous. Those industries that came into the category of light industry produced modern goods for which there was high demand both nationally and internationally. In the period in question consumer goods were more profitable than those of heavy industry and not only did the employers have some room for compromise, they did not want the incomes of their customers reduced too savagely. They also had no interest in an aggressive foreign policy which might cut off markets or lead to high taxation for armaments. By contrast heavy industry suffered a crisis of profitability even before the 1929 crash and, as was the case in the Ruhr, tended towards open confrontation with the unions. Producing goods which depended mainly on domestic markets, heavy industry did not fear alienating foreign customers and it looked forward to lucrative contracts from a government favouring rearmament.

One measurable contrast between the two sectors was relative labour costs. In mining these formed over 50 percent of all costs, while in chemicals the figure was 15 percent.[72] In a slump, when investment plummeted, heavy industry suffered much more than light industry which relied on a base of consumption needs. A concerted attack on organised labour was more attractive to bosses in heavy industry than in light industry. Other capitalist sectors were also predisposed towards extreme right wing politics. Influential farming interests, like heavy industry, were in crisis and, like that group, looked to nationalist policies of protectionism. German banks, as we have seen, were closely connected with industrial operations and so these too were drawn into the various political debates.

The divisions between the economic factions of capitalism were paralleled by divisions within the political sphere. The battle was not between democracy and dictatorship, however. As one writer puts it:

> In its internal debates, the ruling class was now only concerned with the form the authoritarian state should take and with the extent to which repression against the left was necessary. The majority, particularly firms in the chemical and electrical sectors, were in favour of an authoritarian presidential system like the one which was in power from 1930 to January 1933. This regime based itself primarily on the state power apparatus and the emergency powers of the president and was relatively independent of elections, parties, and parliamentary majorities. However, it left parliamentary forms and procedures intact insofar as all parties and unions could voice their opinions and had opportunities for

mobilisation. On the other hand, strong forces located in heavy industry and among large landowners pushed for a radical change in the form of government, for an open dictatorship and for a complete suppression of the democratic and socialist forces.[73]

In Chapter 2 we saw how the Nazis developed a potential strategy for crisis-ridden capitalism—that of direct counter-revolution. In 1923 the ruling elite had rejected this strategy and the Nazis were checked as a result. To understand why Nazism became the favoured solution for the ruling class in 1933 we must look at some of the changes that had taken place in the party since the Beer Hall Putsch.

Nazism's respectable veneer

Hitler had learnt from the failure in 1923: armed uprising was not a viable tactic, at least for the time being. Therefore, while still in Landsberg prison he decided to:

> ...pursue a new line of action... Instead of working to achieve power by armed conspiracy, we shall have to hold our noses and enter the Reichstag against the Catholic and Marxist deputies. If outvoting them takes longer than outshooting them, at least the results will be guaranteed by their own constitution.[74]

This did not mean he had altered his hatred for democracy which 'must be defeated with the weapons of democracy'.[75] Goering put it equally crudely: 'We are fighting against this state and the present system because we wish to destroy it utterly, but in a legal manner... we said we hated this state, [now] we say we love it—and still everyone knows what we mean'.[76] This tactic has been well learnt by present day Nazi groups. Their public face can be respectable but their policies are still as dangerous, and those who believe that Nazis should be allowed free use of democratic rights to destroy them have not learnt from the past.

The Nazis' legalistic policy even applied to the Stormtroopers who had originally been formed to spearhead a military assault on the state. Now Hitler told the press that the Stormtrooper units 'were set up exclusively for the purpose of protecting the party in its propaganda, not to fight against the state... I did everything I could to prevent the SA from assuming any kind of military character'.[77] Such tactics were forced upon the Nazis by circumstances of comparative economic prosperity and an easing of social tension. But there was more to it than that. The Munich fiasco proved to Hitler that he needed more than rabid anti-Semitism, military plots and the odd war hero like Ludendorff to earn ruling class backing. If influential circles were to regard him as a serious contender for power with the ability to deliver counter-revolution he would need leverage in the form of popular backing. This did not mean relinquishing his contempt for the 'masses'. His directive to the SA was that:

> The struggle against the present state will be raised above the atmosphere of petty acts of revenge and conspiracy to the greatness of an ideological war of extermination against Marxism... What we need is not 100 to 200 daring conspirators, but 100,000 and hundreds of thousands more fanatical fighters for our *Weltanschauung* (ideology). We must not work in secret conventicles but in huge mass marches.[78]

The new approach combined electoral campaigns and street marches in a delicate balancing act between electoralism and force. The SA was forbidden to bear weapons, but kept ticking over through the organisation of street demonstrations and low key thuggery. It had to be ready for the exercise of counter-revolutionary violence after the taking of power.

The same calculated ambiguity applied to propaganda. On the one hand to gain mass support the Nazis had to echo some of the discontent engendered by capitalist social crisis. At the same time, the party dared not appear too anti-capitalist because this would have alienated the very sections that were to give Hitler power. Its title—the National Socialist German Workers' Party—contained both sides of the single tactic. In so far as it was national(ist) and German it presented its credentials as a pro-ruling class faction. The terms socialist and workers pointed the opposite way. The two sides were in flat contradiction. It was impossible to serve both masters simultaneously yet the nature of the middle class is to be angry with both big business and workers, both of whom pose a threat. The title National Socialist, while objectively irrational, cleverly encompassed these middle class resentments.

What, then, was the real essence of Nazi politics, and what was there simply for show? Enough has already been said about the early years to suggest that Hitler's motivation was clearly counter-revolutionary. But Hitler was not the Nazi Party. Were there, perhaps, other important Nazis who took the left side of the equation more seriously?

It has been argued that there was a Nazi 'left'. If there were a case for this it would be strongest for the period following Hitler's incarceration when he lost direct control of the movement. As the NSDAP grew beyond its Bavarian origins, it won members in industrial areas of the north. Here leaders like the Strasser brothers, Gregor and Otto, and Joseph Goebbels regarded themselves as the party's left conscience. In 1925 Goebbels, for example, posed the following question in his diary: 'National and socialist! What goes first and what comes later? First the socialist redemption, then the national liberation'.[79] In 1928 his newspaper made the bizarre claim that it opposed 'the bourgeois parties and Marxism alike because both are sworn enemies of the approaching workers' state'.[80] He published a letter entitled 'National Socialism or Bolshevism' to 'My dear friend from the left', declaring, 'We agreed about the causes. No honest thinking person today would want to deny the justification of the workers' movements'.[81]

To judge whether or not such left wing utterances were anything more than a front requires a consideration of the NSDAP's internal workings. It was divided into areas called Gaus, headed by Gauleiters. Describing the evolution of these local sections in the 1920s the Hamburg Gauleiter Krebs said, 'The general discussion developed into a sort of order receiving session. There was always the chance to ask questions and express opinions, but decisions were not reached by a vote any more—they were simply handed down from above. The system of free and secret election also atrophied'.[82] The result was 'the triumph of the fascist/totalitarian tendency within what was originally at least a halfway democratic popular movement'.[83] Krebs saw this as the natural consequence of a deeply elitist movement led by a 'Führer clothed with the glory of political infallibility'.[84]

Even if the Nazi left had been genuine, which it was not, it lacked even the ghost of a chance of influencing the NSDAP. In 1926 Hitler demolished any lingering left illusions at a special meeting in Bamberg, Bavaria. Goebbels' diary tells the tale:

> Hitler speaks for two hours. I am virtually wiped out. What sort of Hitler is this? A reactionary?... He says our task is the destruction of Bolshevism. Bolshevism is a Jewish thing... Compensate the aristocrats... Don't disturb private property. Horrendous!... We are socialists. We don't want to have been so in vain![85]

But it was in vain. The encounter obliterated any naive ideas that Goebbels had that the NSDAP was remotely socialist and his capitulation was total. Later diary entries concerning Hitler contained phrases like this: 'He is such a great man. One can only feel reverence in the face of his greatness'.[86] The farce seen at Bamberg would recur. The party needed to claim vague left wing credentials to win a mass base and was bound to fool some Nazis into believing the words were meant seriously. Later on Hitler would cure such misconceptions with an execution squad.

Towards the abyss

In July 1930 Brüning's austerity programme was thrown out by the Reichstag.[87] Hindenburg then used emergency powers both to implement the policies and dissolve the parliament. An election followed. By installing Brüning as chancellor and abrogating the powers of the Reichstag, the intention of Hindenburg and his chief adviser, General von Schleicher, had been to create a government above party which could stabilise Germany. To counter the organised working class such a government would only be viable in the long term if it had at least some right wing popular support. The 1930 election was called in the hope that the parties ready to back Brüning would gain ground. The opposite happened. The Nazis, who were hostile to Brüning, gained 6.4 million votes and at 18 percent of the total vote stood second only to the SPD. The KPD came third.[88] This was clear evidence of political polarisation and the failure of the government strategy.

The actions of Hindenberg and his clique had opened a new path to power for the Nazis:

> If Hitler could persuade these men to take him into partnership and make him chancellor with the right to use the President's emergency powers— a presidential, as opposed to a parliamentary government—then he could dispense with the clear electoral majority which still eluded him and with the risky experiment of a putsch.[89]

How was Hitler to prove his suitability for the chancellor's position? It was now that the tactic of Nazi 'legality' plus controlled street violence could come into play. Mass electoral support, while never enough to form a government, could supply what the army clique desperately lacked, a social base for right wing anti-democratic policies. However, this in itself was not enough. After all, the army clique cared very little for formal political influence that rested on the counting of votes. Hitler's chief policy, and key selling point for the ruling class, was his determination and growing ability to wage a counter-revolutionary assault on the working class.

For a country run by military dictatorship, elections abounded in the years 1930-33 and each was an opportunity for the NSDAP to shine. In May 1931, for example, elections to the Oldenburg Landtag registered a 37.2 percent Nazi vote. In the spring of 1932 came a new presidential election. Hitler stood against Hindenburg, winning 30.1 percent in the first round and 36.8 percent in the run-off.[90] A fresh turning point came in July 1932 when the Nazis received 37.3 percent of the vote, the highest they would ever receive in a 'free' election. This was still less than the SPD's 37.9 percent vote in 1919 (the more left wing USPD also taking 7.6 percent at the same time). Thus Goldhagen's assertion that the Nazis gained power 'through electoral means' is simply wrong.[91]

So how was it done? The endgame of the Weimar Republic was, at one level, a convoluted series of manoeuvres and intrigues involving the military clique. At another level it was a lot simpler. Hitler convinced the ruling class that he should be given power. It did not depend entirely on the NSDAP gaining votes. Even before its spectacular successes sections of big business were beginning to rethink their attitude to Nazism. In the approach to the 1930 election the influential mouthpiece of Ruhr industrialists, bankers and shipping firms, the *Deutsche Allgemeine Zeitung*, advocated voting either Nazi (despite the Nazis winning only 2.6 percent of the votes in the previous election) or DNVP because 'every vote won for the right means a weakening of social democracy'.[92] After the election the *Berlin Stock Exchange Journal* lamented that in spite of Nazi growth, 'The National Socialists have not managed…to tear the German working class from internationalism and draw the German socialist workers to nationalism'.[93]

Following the election, direct contacts with big business and the government increased rapidly. Von Stauss, a director of one of the largest German banks, was an early convert to the idea the Nazis should be in government.[94] Even more prestigious was Schacht, former long standing president of the Reichsbank.[95] Heavy industry was represented by Thyssen, now chair of the massive United Steel Works.[96] Thyssen's memoirs are entitled *I Paid Hitler*. He details how he was introduced to Hess, Hitler's deputy leader, through Kirdorf, the director general of the Rhenish-Westphalian Coal Syndicate.[97] Thyssen was kind enough to arrange a foreign loan which enabled the Nazis to retain their headquarters, the Brown House, in Munich,[98] and modestly admits, 'I have personally given altogether one million marks to the National Socialist Party'.[99] Other friends of Nazism willing to help out included Grauert, managing director of the employers' association of the Ruhr iron and steel industry, and Poensgen, its chair. Then there was Brandi, chair of the coal operators' association, Tengelmann, chair of a major independent coal mining firm, the Essener Steinkolhenbergwerke, Springorum of the Hoesch company and Vögler, general director of United Steel.[100]

One source of business support was the 'circle of friends' organised by Keppler. He recounts that in May 1932 Hitler presented this group with his programme:

Abolition of trade unions and abolition of all parties other than the NSDAP. No one raised any objection. On the contrary, these policies of the Führer's met with the fullest approval of the members of the circle of friends. They only expressed their apprehension that he would not be able to carry out these excellent ideas.[101]

Not all such sympathisers were enthusiastic, mainly because they could not see that the radical language the Nazis needed to construct their mass base was merely rhetoric. Schacht of the Reichsbank wrote to Hitler that while a 'row of gentlemen' were ready to finance the NSDAP, some were put off by 'the mere mention of socialism' in the party's name, an attitude that he found 'plain silly'.[102]

When, in 1931, Hitler wanted to raise cash to arm the SA in the event of a civil war, Funk, his Berlin contact, installed him in the large and fashionable Kaiserhof Hotel across the street from the Reich Chancellery, and that afternoon:

> Funk brought two prominent executives of one of Germany's largest insurance firms, the Allianz... The two callers had pledged five million marks to the SA in the event of a civil war... Hitler's astonishment at the magnitude of this sum left him briefly speechless—a truly extraordinary condition for the Nazi leader. And Funk had only begun. During the following days Funk paraded a succession of prominent Berlin businessmen through Hitler's hotel suite... When the procession ended, the total amount pledged came...to 25 million marks.[103]

Turner suggests that these businessmen were rarely out and out Nazis, often retaining their affiliations with other right wing parties, and were simply 'adding additional coverage to the political insurance policies many had carried'.[104] The structure of one such insurance policy, however, is revealing. The big industrialist, Otto Wolff, disbursed his funds as follows: in 1931 he gave 7,500 marks to the DVP and 16,900 to the NSDAP; in 1932 the figures were 1,000 marks to the DVP, 15,000 to the DNVP and 160,800 to the Nazis![105] Much funding did come from ordinary NSDAP members. But this by no means invalidates the argument that capitalist backing was essential. While Nazism represented merely one ruling class strategy, as one writer puts it, 'Even if only a minority of the employers were actively for the NSDAP, the plan put forward by the leading bodies of the economy was still one of disciplining the ranks of the working class, restricting the rights of the unions and elimination of the parliamentary system'.[106]

Although the move to install Hitler as chancellor was not instigated by the industrial wing of the ruling class, as one historian suggests, 'It was a move they were prepared to tolerate. This, it seems, and not who actually financed the Nazis and how much they gave, is the crucial point about the industrial elite in the Weimar Republic'.[107] Indeed, support for Nazism often went beyond toleration. During Hitler's attempt to oust Hindenburg as president in the spring of 1932, 'The Reichsland Association, which was by far the greatest industrialist association, recommended, with all due respect to Hindenburg, the election of Hitler'.[108] The essence of the relationship between business and the NSDAP is given in the following exchange between Schacht and Reusch in March 1932. The latter led the Ruhrlade, a secret organisation of 12 top industrialists with control over 'the largest political fund of big business, and probably of any special interest group, in Germany'.[109]

Schacht said, 'The Nazis are not to be circumvented; more than that, they are the positive force. We should contribute to them and their efforts and assist them in altering some of the utopian aspects of their economic policies.'

Reusch said, 'After a productive two hour talk with Hitler yesterday, I fully and completely agree with your suggestions... I find myself in complete sympathy with the National Socialists, though they are a bit tactless'.[110]

Such attitudes had been carefully cultivated. Hitler learned in 1923 that support from the ruling class could not be taken for granted. His new approach balanced on a knife edge between gaining the necessary mass support to make him a serious player in the game of power politics and alienating the ruling class because of connections with the vulgar masses. Equally the policy of legality and respectability had to be tempered with SA thuggery which both proved the NSDAP to be an awesome force to be reckoned with, and one capable of smashing the left.

The level of violence could sometimes be great. At one notorious incident in Potempa, five SA members kicked a KPD member to death in front of his mother. Hitler had to hold his movement together as well as win respectable friends and so he sent a telegram protesting against their prosecution.[111] In Prussia alone 82 people were killed and 400 badly wounded in political incidents between 1 June and 20 July 1932. For public consumption Hitler would later portray this as a heroic period during which the SA began the 'Nazi revolution's' seizure of power. The truth was very different. The state was never the target. Fully 83 percent of those killed were either Nazis (38) or Communists (30). These details show that the real purpose of the SA was far from revolutionary; it was deliberately counter-revolutionary:

For all their violent rhetoric, the Stormtroopers did not engage in frontal attacks against the power of the state; these Nazi activists may have been fanatics, as Hitler was so fond of boasting, but they were not so fanatical as to attack police stations and army barracks...and the concern which was felt within the SA not to be caught with firearms betrayed a considerable respect for the forces of law and order.[112]

The Nazi approach to big business was nowhere better illustrated than in Hitler's address to the influential Düsseldorf Industry Club on 27 January 1932. It was staggering in its crude daring, but also in its fawning. Hitler began by reminding his audience that the main reason for their difficulties lay in the 'internal division' of society. He then described the crisis of overproduction gripping German capitalism which left their factories idle. He warned that 'if Bolshevism as a world idea tears the Asiatic continent out of the human economic community, then the conditions for the employment of these industries which have developed on so gigantic a scale will be no longer even approximately realised'.[113] This already contained the idea of Operation Barbarossa—the conquest of Russia to enhance German capitalism's prospects.

Harking back to the early experience of capitalism under Bismarck he argued that 'it was not German business which conquered the world and led to the development of German power, but in our case, too, it was the power-state which created for the business world the general conditions for its subsequent prosperity.' So he offered the Nazi state as guarantor of future profitability. Then, turning to the failure of official bourgeois parties and pointing to the SA, he asked, 'Where is the organisation which can boast, as ours can, that at need it can summon 400,000 men into the street, men who are schooled to blind obedience and are ready to execute any order—provided that it does not violate the law?'[114] Hitler admitted that SA tactics might be noisy and unpleasant: 'In the evening a tumult and commotion arises, then the bourgeois draws back the window curtain, looks out, and says, "Once more my night's rest disturbed: no more sleep for me." Gentlemen, if everyone thought like that...then the bourgeois today could not venture into the street'.[115]

Now the keystone was fitted into the arch: 'Today we stand at the turning point of Germany's destiny. If the present development continues, Germany will one day of necessity land in Bolshevik chaos.' His alternative was that 'our people must be taken into a school of iron discipline'.[116] Such speeches were effective and by November 1932 letters were sent by leading bankers, industrialists and large landowners to Hindenburg begging him to make Hitler chancellor, arguing that 'whatever the circumstances, almost the whole of industry wants the appointment of Hitler'.[117]

Support from industry was an important element in the elevation of Hitler to chancellor. Hitler was also assisted by other right wing political forces. The pro-nationalist *Deutsche Allgemeine Zeitung* was arguing for the inclusion of the Nazis in a coalition government.[118] Since the Nazis were a rival force, support was not unqualified:

> A right wing government, but not sole rule by the National Socialist folk. We are of the firm conviction that the pursuit of the open dictatorship of a single party, even when it possesses the powerful national merits of the National Socialists, would end in tragedy. The participation of Hitler in government has been our demand for years.[119]

On 11 October 1931 the Nazis were invited to join the 'Harzburg Front', consisting of an impressive collection of right wing forces, from Hugenberg's DNVP (nationalists) to the Stahlhelm paramilitaries, the Junkers' Land League and industrialists. Though the front would fall apart because Hitler was not prepared to be a junior partner in this arrangement, it was invaluable in giving added respectability to Nazism, as well as cultivating useful connections with Hugenberg's media empire.

However, in the Bonapartist system then operating, manoeuvres by traditional political parties were less important than before. The direct steps that would lead to a Nazi regime were taken by the military clique around Hindenburg. What motivated them? The Weimar army's outlook had grown even closer to mainstream capitalism than in prewar days. In breaking from its Junker ways of thinking (if not its Junker social origins) it was 'once again well in advance of its British or French counterparts':

> A close analysis of this ideology...would show that it resembles the technocratic ideals of state management more than traditional aristocratic values and that it bears a closer relationship to contemporary conditions than to the traditions of the past.[120]

Like the industrial capitalists, the army elite would need convincing of the NSDAP's merits. Hitler was given every opportunity to do this. He was received by Chancellor Brüning in October 1930. A year later the contacts multiplied, partly driven by Schleicher, the 'grey eminence' behind Hindenburg. It was he who arranged meetings with the chancellor and president in October 1931. Schleicher met Hitler on several occasions and concluded, 'Faced with the forces he controls, there is only one policy to adopt—to use him and win him over'.[121]

At this point the Nazis suffered a setback. At the end of 1931 papers arising from secret Nazi discussions in the Hesse area came to light. These showed what local Nazis thought would happen if they got into power: executions of opponents, abolition of private property and compulsory work service.[122] The 'Boxheim papers' were repudiated by Hitler, and for good reason. They not only showed how shallow the claims to legality were, but the local group suggested a left wing radicalism that was out of step with the party's efforts to win the ruling class. The damage could not be undone, however. With SPD-dominated Prussia leading the campaign, Brüning banned the SA and the black shirted SS on 14 April 1932.

An army leadership truly 'above' class politics would have welcomed this blow against paramilitaries who disrupted its monopoly of force and of 'law and order'. In fact, amidst deepening social division, subduing the Nazi right could only assist the Communist left. The Reichswehr's aloofness proved a hollow sham. Schleicher began intriguing to topple Brüning and exploited the social conflict between left and right to bring him down. The complaints against Brüning included his unpopular austerity programme which earned him the title 'hunger chancellor' and showed no sign of resolving the crisis. Industrialists felt that he was not hard enough on labour. Brüning had also threatened to expose the gigantic swindle of the 'eastern aid' programme which siphoned public funds into the pockets of East Prussian Junkers, amongst whom Hindenburg was now counted. The president demanded Brüning's resignation and received it on 30 May 1932. He was replaced by a more right wing figure—von Papen.

The new chancellor called a Reichstag election and, following Schleicher's advice, lifted the ban on the SA. As a result, within one month 99 people were dead and 125 gravely wounded.[123] It is important to note that the SA did not fight their way back to legality; it was granted by the government. This is not to say that the military clique wanted to aid Hitler directly. When Hindenburg was asked if Hitler would be made chancellor, he exclaimed, 'This Bohemian corporal wants to become Reich chancellor? Never! At most he could be my postmaster general. Then he can lick me on the stamps from behind'.[124] This was not just an expression of aristocratic contempt; the basis of Bonapartist rule was to stand 'above' the forces of a crisis ridden society. To accomplish this the left and right political forces had to balance out. While the strongholds of working class organisation—the mass parties, trade unions and SPD state governments, such as Prussia—remained fundamentally intact, the boot boys of the right could not be too much encouraged or too severely curbed.

As the crisis wore on increasing sections of the ruling class were won to the idea of a counter-revolutionary regime. Only this could decisively redress the balance of international capitalist competition abroad and class forces at home. They wanted all this for free, without risk and without having to pay the price demanded by a Hitlerian protection racket. However, almost every step the von Papen government took, from unbanning the SA onwards, narrowed its room for manoeuvre and made a Nazi government more likely.

Nowhere was this better illustrated than with the overthrow of the state government in Prussia. Von Papen and his cronies believed this would be their master stroke, giving them real power over the situation. The result was the opposite to that intended. The state of Prussia was a stronghold of the left. It had large KPD concentrations in the crucial area of Berlin and a SPD state government under Braun, with its own powerful police force. A Nazi invasion of the working class district of Altona in Hamburg, and the ensuing street warfare (which cost 17 lives, including some police) gave von Papen the excuse to stage a legal coup against Braun's Prussian government on 20 July 1932. No resistance was offered. If von Papen and the Reichswehr had been a genuinely potent and independent force, this should have massively enhanced its control, establishing a stronger dictatorship over 38 million Germans. But in a situation of Bonapartism, the unstable balance of class forces was tilted to the right; the cork wobbled on its pinhead and would soon fall off:

> No other decision of the [von] Papen government had promoted the later Nazi seizure of power more effectively than the coup against Prussia... The bulwark of the republic was razed to the ground well before the Nazis took over in early February 1933.[125]

The humiliation of the SPD in Prussia helped the Nazis to their greatest success in a free Reichstag election 11 days later. During the campaign the *Deutsche Allgemeine Zeitung* hoped that 'two or three National Socialists will enter the von Papen government'[126] and warned that:

> If, against all expectations, it is not [von] Papen but Braun who wins the Reichstag election, then the German state would be thrown back to 1919. There would be a situation with no way out and unthinkable consequences in all areas of politics and the economy.[127]

On 31 July the NSDAP scored a 37.3 percent vote by capturing a mass of mainly middle class votes to become the largest single party in the Reichstag. Hitler once more pressed his claims for the chancellorship, arguing that 'the Reich cabinet belongs to men who have the trust of the people'.[128] There was something tragi-comical in this man, who despised democracy, demanding his electoral rewards from Hindenburg, who despised it too.

How the decision was made

Histories which deny the relevance of class cannot adequately explain the twists and turns of the situation in the ensuing months which gave Hitler power at the very moment his influence began to wane. If a liberal democratic perspective is adopted, then voting arithmetic really expresses power in capitalist society. The best chance for Hitler should have come in July 1932. By the same token, his prospects should have worsened when, in November 1932, new elections brought a dramatic loss of two million votes for the NSDAP. The same problem applies if we adopt the 'power politics' approach and conceive of the military dominated state in isolation from its class basis. Hitler was manifestly less of a threat to the army in November than in July, yet power was still handed over.

What happened must be explained on the basis of changes in the balance of class forces. In July the very strength of Nazism meant it served as a useful counter-balance to the working class. Schleicher was explicit on this point: 'In the form of the Nazis there exists a counter-weight.' He added that 'although the Nazis are not very honourable brethren either, and have to be treated with the utmost caution, if they did not exist, one really would have to invent them'.[129]

As yet there was no need or desire to pay Hitler's price—the post of chancellor. After November the risk that the Nazi Party would disintegrate meant that it had to be saved (so that in turn it could save capitalism). The threat of its dissolution worried business circles intensely.[130] Trotsky described the thinking of the ruling class:

> It was not with a light heart that the high and mighty clique made a deal with the malodorous fascists. There are too many, all too many fists behind the unbridled upstarts; and therein lies the dangerous side of the brown shirted allies; but in that very same thing is also their fundamental, more exactly, their only, advantage. And this is the advantage that decides, for such are the times now that there is no guaranteeing property except with fists. There is no way of dispensing with the Nazis.[131]

If the background motive forces were capitalism and class, in the foreground the key moves were determined by the machinations of individual members of the German ruling class. The first reaction by von Papen and Co to the July election result was to offer Hitler the vice-chancellorship. He turned this down flat; only the top job would do. In insisting on an all or nothing approach Hitler was playing a dangerous game. To press the NSDAP's claims for attention he exploited the dire economic crisis, middle class fears and radical rhetoric to assemble a mighty voting machine plus an SA hundreds of thousands strong. An economic improvement might sap mass support; a long delay would explode the unstable combination of ruling class ideology and radical rhetoric. Hitler did not have much time, and he knew it. Nevertheless, in addition to personal ambition, there was a political logic to his demand for the chancellorship. To carry out his counter-revolutionary strategy required an untrammelled concentration of power. Anything less, such as a vice-chancellorship under von Papen, would blunt that offensive and tie him to a doomed Bonapartist regime.

Von Papen had his own difficulties when the Nazis refused to cooperate. His government might for the moment have the power of the army to back it up, but its popular basis was non-existent. This was soon revealed when the Reichstag met and passed a motion of no confidence in the government by 513 votes to 32. Another election followed on 5 November 1932. This saw the Nazi vote shrink by 4 percent and its seats in the Reichstag fell from 230 to 196 (out of 608).[132]

Goebbels, leader of the Berlin Gau, described the 'lapse into depression. Everywhere we are plunged into anger, strife and dissension'.[133] Financially the situation was 'quite hopeless. Only outgoings, debts and obligations, together with the complete impossibility of obtaining any reasonable sum of money after this defeat'.[134] The year 1932 had been an 'eternal misfortune. Everything is smashed... The past was hard, and the future looks dark and gloomy; all prospects and hopes have quite disappeared'.[135]

The reaction of the bourgeois press at the turn of the year 1932-33 is interesting, because it shows a debate within the ranks of the ruling class over what should follow. The *Berliner Tageblatt*, allied to the DVP, feared a Nazi takeover and interpreted the November election as ending such a prospect. On 2 January 1932 it wrote of 'new hope': 'Hitler is no dark threat any more. He is a political factor to be reckoned with who certainly should be taken seriously because of his supporters, but nothing more'.[136] A few days later it added:

> The new year holds out no great promise for the National Socialists, but great perplexity... Their papers and speakers no longer call out: 'The new year will bring us to power'; 'Hitler will be Reichspresident!' no longer 'Hitler will be Reichschancellor'.[137]

The liberal *Frankfurter Zeitung*, like the *Berliner Tageblatt*, also had grave doubts about the Nazis, but it was impatient for a solution. Its front page article was entitled 'Either/Or':

> In broad circles of the economy hopes have begun the year 1933. It may be possible, by energetic and planned efforts, to take advantage of the quite considerable signs of a change in the economic situation. For this to happen nothing is more urgent than a stable political basis... For more than a year efforts have been spent on drawing the National Socialists into government. Either do it, or leave it be.[138]

The *Deutsche Allgemeine Zeitung*, the most right wing of the three newspapers and closely allied with heavy industrial interests and the DNVP, saw the Nazis' very weakness as a reason for bringing Hitler into government. How was this odd conclusion reached? Power must be given, and without delay, since another election might bring further Nazi losses:

> [A] new electoral campaign for the National Socialist movement would be an extraordinarily difficult burden for it to undergo, probably the most difficult since the establishment of the party. It would be a missed opportunity if the elements of the right in parliament did not find a common agreement with the government at the eleventh hour. Otherwise, sooner or later, the left would again triumph, for they are already gloating over the constant signs of crisis in the NSDAP.[139]

This fear of missing a golden opportunity to uproot the gains of the working class was sharpened by a realisation that the economic cycle had indeed turned. By the end of 1932 production was already 15 percent higher than at the depth of the Depression.[140]

So from the point of view of Bonapartism and the military clique, the November election had solved nothing. Hindenburg's chancellors were still faced with problems which they could do nothing to resolve. They lacked the power to crush the workers, and lacked the support of the middle class which was mostly in Nazi hands. Balancing on the head of a pin became impossible in conditions of turbulence. Von Papen's failure to find a means of producing a stable government while respecting the last vestiges of democratic procedures led him to formulate a plan which 'would involve a breach of the present constitution by the president'.[141] This would have been received as a declaration of open counter-revolution. Yet without a deal with the Nazis the capitalist interest would be represented by an isolated and despised military regime. This would have been very dangerous, and Schleicher feared it would produce a civil war with the army fighting against the working class on the left while confronting Nazi hostility on the right.

At the same time, in letters to Hindenburg, Hitler pressed his case hard for a counter-revolutionary government with himself in charge:

> Now, after governing for six months, the von Papen cabinet has—as I anticipated—become hopelessly isolated... The Bolshevisation of the broad masses is proceeding apace. If a new government is to assume this terrible political, economic and financial heritage, then its efforts can only be crowned with success if it combines great authority with strong popular support.[142]

During the rest of November meeting followed meeting, letter followed letter, but doubts about the risk of relinquishing control to an unbridled counter-revolutionary movement persisted. A deal with Hitler could not be made, but neither could a continuing von Papen government be tolerated. Eventually the latter was toppled when Schleicher 'played his trump card'. He withdrew army support from von Papen because of the 'risk of civil war'.[143]

With support narrowing to vanishing point, the last hopes of the Bonapartist regime now rested on Schleicher, the army leader, who emerged out of the shadows, where he had been kingmaker to Brüning and von Papen. Made chancellor on 2 December 1932, he had to operate in the open. His Bonapartist solution was to try and break out of isolation by winning a mass base from trade unions on the left and from a wing of the Nazis on the right. Schleicher accordingly wooed Leipart, leader of the Free Trade Unions, Gregor Strasser, the Nazi organisation chief, and business representatives.[144] These efforts exasperated those sections of the ruling class who, like the *Deutsche Allgemeine Zeitung*, did not want to lose the chance of rolling back the Weimar compromise and solving German capitalism's problems by breaking the working class once and for all.

They reasoned that if Brüning, von Papen and Schleicher could not solve the problems of capitalism, then there was only one alternative, distasteful though it might be. Hitler must be put into power, and since he would accept nothing less, it would have to be largely on his terms. The manoeuvres that made Hitler chancellor reveal with full clarity the class character of the process. They began on 4 January 1933 with a meeting between Hitler and von Papen at the home of a banker—Schröder. The background to this meeting was:

> ...a submission to the Reich president which had been signed by 15 industrialists. They had asked, though without success, that following

[von] Papen's dismissal the new cabinet should contain members of the Nazi movement in leading positions. Apart from Schacht, there were now a number of prominent representatives of heavy industry in the Ruhr, among them Fritz Thyssen, Paul Reusch and Albert Vögler, as well as some other influential bankers and businessmen who, like Schröder, belonged to a growing minority in big business. This minority advised that, in order to stabilise the presidential regime and to put the economy back on an even keel, the leadership in the cabinet should be left to the Nazis.[145]

It would be a mistake to think that big business support of this kind directly catapulted the Nazis into power. The connection between the economic power of capitalism and its state was, as already indicated, far more complex than a cause and effect relationship. But the confidence of important sections of the bourgeoisie was essential. It remained for the NSDAP to show it still had the potential to perform its counter-revolutionary duties and its influence had not slipped too far. In mid-January the Nazis poured all their efforts into recovering electoral ground in the tiny state of Lippe with its 90,000 strong electorate. The NSDAP bounced back with a 17 percent increase on its previously low vote. More important was the march against the KPD headquarters in Berlin. Billed as a mass demonstration against 'Red murder', the claim was that 'the brown parade rules Berlin'.[146] The Nazi leaders told their followers that they were engaged in a symbolic struggle not only against the left, but against the establishment. The truth about the 22 January march was rather different, as the *Berliner Tageblatt* explained:

> The Nazis wish to boast that they could march 'unhindered' through even the reddest district. Whoever saw this demonstration knows that that is not true. For the SA were drawn up behind walls of police officers and protected by 1,000 police carbines along empty streets. They 'demonstrated' in front of the police and dead house fronts. They 'conquered' an empty city. They were able to collect in front of the Liebknecht house and march because the square and the streets were empty, because police truncheons and carbines guaranteed the route.[147]

The Nazis had made clear that a Hitler regime would be a counter-revolutionary regime. This does not mean that the circumstances that shaped Nazism's birth (the immediate threat of revolution) were present as it reached maturity. The immediate prospects of workers' revolution that existed in 1923 had long gone. But the solution to capitalism's deep social, economic and political crisis would lie in breaking the bones of working class organisation. In 1933 Hitler's coming to power represented 'a defensive reaction of the bourgeoisie, but a defence against the disintegration of its own system, far more than against any nearly non-existent proletarian offensive'.[148]

Nazism remained counter-revolutionary in two senses. In the ideological arena the tremendous crash of 1929 pointed to the irrationality and destructiveness of capitalism. The NSDAP's crude politics diverted millions from a real understanding of the causes and so from finding a socialist solution. In the practical arena its primary role would be to attack and destroy the organisations of the working class, the only force in society capable of challenging and overthrowing capital. The bosses cannot do without a working class to exploit, and so the Nazis were not out to physically liquidate the class (although individuals could be eliminated). The aim was repression and/or conversion through destroying any offensive or even defensive capability on the part of the class. On the basis of this there could be an intensified level of exploitation.

At this point in time it was already becoming clear that Schleicher's plans were crumbling. They collapsed when Strasser proved unable to bring any sizeable sections of Nazis with him into a Schleicher-led coalition. Hugenberg of the nationalist DNVP abandoned Schleicher and began negotiations with Hitler just three days later. Von Papen came forward with the suggestion of a coalition government. This would give Hitler the coveted post of chancellor and powerful positions to other Nazis; but von Papen himself was to be vice-chancellor with enough non-Nazis to keep Hitler in check (or so he hoped). So here we have von Papen courting Hitler. Incredibly, at this stage, so did Schleicher! On 29 January von Hammerstein, army commander-in-chief, had a conversation with Schleicher which he reported in these terms:

> We were both convinced that the only possible future Reich chancellor was Hitler. Any other decision would generate a general strike, if not a civil war, and thus to a totally undesirable use of the army against the National Socialists as well as against the left.[149]

Note that it was only 'totally undesirable' to use the army against the Nazis. Hitler, who was staying with his piano manufacturing friends, the Bechsteins, nervously watched developments. His own testimony on the final outcome is clear. Some months later he praised 'the part played by our army, for we all know well that if, in the days of our revolution, the army had not stood on our side, then we should not be standing here today'.[150] This then was a 'revolution' with the support of a key section of the state, the army. But this is surely a clear indication that far from being a revolution, it was a counter-revolution.

The next day, 30 January 1933, has been called the 'midnight of the century'. It was the day that Hitler was appointed chancellor by Hindenburg. The *Deutsche Allgemeine Zeitung*, representing heavy industry, banking and shipping interests, enthusiastically interpreted Hitler's promotion as its own victory. Its front page headline was, 'To Power!' It then reminded the NSDAP of its task:

> The forces of disruption do not remain inactive. Mass poverty is the breeding ground of revolution… The German left ruled and has been ruling for a decade. The German right has been standing for years on the threshold of power. Finally it has entered.[151]

The relief was palpable: 'It must be said openly—the takeover of power by Hitler, Seldte and Hugenburg spared us potentially serious conflict in February'.[152]

The above account shows unequivocally that Nazism did not come to power through the ballot box or the will of the people. Though backed by the middle class, it was supported by industrialists and bankers and courted by both the previous and incumbent chancellor plus the army. Behind this tiny ruling class grouping was an enormous social process played out in a capitalist context.

Every time the capitalist system breaks down the ruling class expects workers to pay the price in jobs lost, poverty and exploitation. Sometimes the sacrifice can be negotiated with the cooperation of reformist movements. Sometimes, when the level of sacrifice is too great to be accepted, or the defensive institutions of the working class too strong, more aggressive measures are adopted. After three fruitless years searching for an alternative, the key sections of the German ruling class came to the conclusion that an open physical offensive was the only way out.

Chapter 4

The Nazi machine

Although the NSDAP came to power through ruling class intrigue, its mass support gave it crucial bargaining power. The combined vote of the SPD and KPD was greater than that of the NSDAP in every free election except one (July 1932). Yet in that election the popularity of Nazism was undeniable:

> With a voting strength of 13,700,000 electors, a party membership of over a million and a private army of 400,000 SA and SS, Hitler was the most powerful political leader in Germany, knocking on the doors of the chancellery at the head of the most powerful political party Germany had ever seen.[1]

Is there not a contradiction in our argument? How could the Nazi Party reflect the interests of a tiny minority of the German population but also have the support of vast numbers of ordinary Germans? Many historians deem this impossible, writing that the Nazi Party was 'something unique in German political culture, a catch-all party of protest'.[2] Even Ian Kershaw, who usually has a sound instinct in these matters, describes the NSDAP as a 'super-interest-party'.[3] Others go further, describing it as a 'combination of middle class formation…and working class protest' or even a 'workers' party'![4]

This is dangerous nonsense. If parties were a simple reflection of the people who joined them or voted for them, then no capitalist policy would ever be enacted anywhere. All mass parties in every country would be 'people's parties', and, since workers vote for them, they would also be 'workers' parties'. It would be pointless pondering the causes of mass unemployment, the gulf between rich and poor or why thousands are homeless and social services are starved of cash. After all, according to this logic, the victims of capitalism have voted for it! But Lenin explained, 'Whether or not a party is really a political party of the workers does not depend solely upon a membership of workers, but also upon the men that lead it, and the content of its actions and its political tactics'.[5]

To make sense of the Nazi Party it is necessary to distinguish 'between the class composition of the movement and the class interests it served'.[6] The contradiction was particularly sharp in the NSDAP and it did not suddenly emerge when the Nazis came to power. In this it differed from many reformist parties. Reformist leaders often gain office genuinely intent on change only to then confront the objective contradictions between the system they accept and the aspirations of their supporters which they eventually betray. The Nazi leaders' elitism, respect for bosses as 'of a higher race', adulation of property and hatred of any challenge to German capitalism meant that, while it might be inaccurate to suggest a large scale conspiracy to dupe its supporters, the NSDAP was undoubtedly one of the most consciously manipulative ruling class parties in history.

So the Nazi Party did indeed reflect the interests of a tiny minority but had the support of vast numbers of ordinary Germans. Such a paradox can exist because under capitalism exploitative relationships are disguised. Marx explained, 'The ideas of the ruling class are in every epoch the ruling ideas: ie the class which is the prevailing material force of society is at the same time its ruling intellectual force'.[7] In this situation, mass voting for pro-capitalist policies, even of the extreme counter-revolutionary kind espoused by the Nazis, is a sign of the influence of capitalist ideology rather than a reflection of freely developed wishes.

However, ruling class ideology is only one influence. Marx also argued that 'social being determines consciousness'.[8] The daily experience of life under capitalism mediates the impact of capitalist ideology. It can reinforce it, contradict it, or have still more complex results, partially reinforcing some points of the ideology and negating others. The general pattern is that with capitalists their life experience serves to reinforce belief in the system; the life experience of workers tends to clash with the received ways of thinking and cause it to be questioned either partially or totally. The middle class has a life experience which leaves it vacillating between both these poles.

With these considerations in mind it is now possible to deal with how the Nazis built up their support. The primary means of doing this was through propaganda.

The grand lie: the role of propaganda

The Nazis took an absolutely cynical approach to propaganda which 'though crude and violent in form, utterly unscrupulous in substance, and quite indifferent to truth, was managed with an agility and sophistication'.[9] Goebbels, the master of this art, declared, 'Propaganda has only one aim, to win the masses. And any means that serve this end are good'.[10] Hitler similarly described propaganda as:

> ...a means to an end...propaganda is no more than a weapon...its effect for the most part must be aimed at the emotions and only to a very limited degree at the so called intellect... The receptivity of the great masses is very limited, their intelligence is small.[11]

In particular, Hitler placed great emphasis on the use of the grand lie:

> In the big lie there is always a certain force of credibility, because the broad masses of a nation...more readily fall victims to the big lie than the small lie, since they themselves often tell small lies in little matters, but would be ashamed to resort to large-scale falsehoods. It would never come into their head to fabricate colossal untruths and they would not believe that others could have the impudence to distort the truth so infamously... The grossly impudent lie always leaves traces behind it, even after it has been nailed down.[12]

There were two opposite trends in Nazi propaganda which at first sight appeared to be mutually exclusive, but in fact were complementary. On the one hand there was the attempt to divert attention away from social reality and any rational thought which might lead to a questioning of capitalist ideology. The highest point of this pseudo-religion was the Nazi slogan, 'Hitler is Germany, just as Germany is Hitler'.

On the other hand, there was the reverse approach—'the differentiation of target groups',[13] using carefully judged appeals which, despite all protestations to the contrary, addressed economic interest and class. All sorts of promises were made to a range of groups. The army would throw off the shackles of Versailles, students would have their educational efforts rewarded by well paid jobs, the young would see a dynamic new party in action while the old would witness a return to traditional values. Unmarried women would find a husband and be accorded high status, while men were told women would be put in their place—*Kirche, Küche, Kinder*—at church, in the kitchen and with the children. Civil servants' jobs would be secured yet taxpayers would pay less through reduction of state officialdom. Farmers would be able to charge higher prices, while consumers would get cheap food. These disparate groups each had a Nazi section dedicated to cultivating their support, from the Hitler Youth to the Nazi Physicians' League, National Socialist (NS) Society of German Jurists, NS Students' League, NS Teachers' League and so on.

Wooing the workers

Great efforts were made towards winning the working class. It is even claimed that 'contrary to previous assumptions, the working class rather than the middle class was the chief target group of NSDAP propaganda until 1932'.[14] The initiative for this propaganda effort towards workers came in the mid-1920s from north German Nazis operating in an area much more industrialised than Bavaria. An example of such propaganda was this statement of Strasser's:

> We are socialists, we are enemies, deadly enemies of the present economic system with its exploitation of the economically weak, with its unjust means of reward, with its immoral valuation of people according to their possessions and money...and we are resolved to destroy this system in all circumstances.[15]

Goebbels went still further: 'We want to make a socialistic national state out of Germany... We want justice. We are no charitable society but a revolutionary socialist party'.[16] Stennes, an SA leader who eventually fell out with the NSDAP, published a newspaper called *Workers, Soldiers, Peasants*, in direct imitation of the Russian soviets.[17] One Nazi factory bulletin had the inexplicable title *The Revolutionary* and the subtitle 'The Militant Voice Against Fascism'![18] During April 1932, in the important Prussian Landtag election, the Nazis' slogan was 'Work, Freedom, Bread'. This was also the motto of the SPD. In 1924 it had been used by the KPD and was obviously reminiscent of the Bolshevik slogan 'Peace, Bread, Land'.[19]

In July 1928, in Goebbels' Gau of Berlin, the National Socialist Organisation of Factory Cells (NSBO) emerged. This claimed to stand for 'the genuine trade union idea for which the National Socialists must prepare the way'.[20] By 1929 the NSBO had been officially adopted as an NSDAP affiliate and in 1931 the '*Hib-Aktion*' or 'into the factories' strategy was launched. As part of this NSBO members participated in strikes. When 40,000 metal workers were locked out in Bavaria in March 1931 one of its leaders declared, 'If we German workers want to see our strike efforts really crowned with success, then the only way is through a general strike'.[21] Between April 1932 and January 1933 the NSBO claimed to have participated in 117 different strikes.[22]

Before getting the impression that the Nazis had suddenly been converted from fundamental counter-revolution, Hess's fundraising tour of businessmen, at the very time the NSBO was being established, provides the necessary antidote:

Hess had less to say that he had to show. He pulled two sets of photographs out of his pocket: one set consisted of turbulent revolutionary scenes (red flags, mass demonstrations of Communists); the other showed marching Stormtroopers, SA men falling in for roll call, the SS with their select 'human material'—in short, formations of 'discipline and order'.

He passed these two sets around among the assembled businessmen, waited patiently until they had all seen them, and then spoke. He uttered at most ten sentences, along the lines of: 'Here, gentlemen, you have the forces of destruction, which are dangerous threats to your counting houses, your factories, all your possessions. On the other hand, the forces of order are forming, with a fanatical will to root out the spirit of turmoil… Everyone who has must give lest he ultimately lose everything he has!'[23]

Turner makes great play of the way businessmen were frightened by Nazism's radical rhetoric. But this was relative. It did not prevent the NSDAP being invited to be part of the 'National Opposition' or the Harzburg Front of right wing pro-capitalist forces. It did not prevent the donation of millions of marks or the friendship of the bourgeois press. Clearly sections of the upper class were either able to see through the smokescreen and ignored the radical rhetoric or were calmed by Hitler's periodic assurances of his real counter-revolutionary intentions.

The shallowness of the Nazi pro-worker orientation was shown by the way the NSBO was manipulated for propaganda ends. It was turned on when the Nazi leadership required mass support in its bid to be taken seriously by the Hindenburg clique, but switched off when the negotiations for chancellorship began. So the NSBO backed 74 strikes between September and November 1932, but only two in December when the talks began.[24] In spite of this cynical attitude, ordinary Nazi supporters inevitably took some of the fraudulent rhetoric seriously. This would have consequences when the party came to power.

The unscrupulous dishonesty of the Nazis and their promises of absolutely conflicting policies to different target audiences could have curious results. This was illustrated by the clash between the NSBO, which claimed it was not a strikebreaking organisation, and the SA, which clearly was. On more than one occasion NSBO members themselves became victims of the strikebreaking activities of the SA,[25] while an employer at a striking AEG factory described the behaviour of Nazi employees in this way: 'One group showed itself more radical than the Communists and perfectly prepared to smash the machines— the other group by contrast acted as strikebreakers'.[26]

Nazi radicalism, even when directed towards workers, was given a particular twist. It started with genuine grievances as the hook, but reeled supporters in to reactionary politics. Ordinary members might get involved in strikes, but the leaders' aim was to blunt workers' action. For example, during the Berlin transport strike of late 1932 the *Völkische Beobachter* declared:

> The strike today is the last resort of men who wrestle for their lives and the lives of their families. Only when those responsible for the system of impoverishment…have been dismissed, is the way free for the National Socialist Reich under the leadership of Adolf Hitler… And under this state the strike will have become superfluous as a means of struggle.[27]

By means of incredible contortions and downright lies, Nazi counter-revolutionary propaganda was dressed up in radical garb:

> Class struggle is the aim of the RGO [the Communist trade union movement]. The Marxist outlook demands that the masses are constantly stirred up and opposed to the ruling social order. But Marxism, as a materialist viewpoint, can only achieve this aim if the masses are impoverished. Impoverishment must continually be felt and hence must be encouraged all the more. Marxism strives for this using all available means… Yet we must also differentiate ourselves from the anti-revolutionary and anti-social standpoint of Herr Hugenberg [DNVP leader]. We do not accept his statement that, 'He who thinks in socialist terms is a Marxist.' No. Whoever does not think and behave in a socialist way supports Marxist class struggle.[28]

Supporters of the notion that Nazism was somehow pro-worker offer as proof such efforts to win the working class (and even partial successes in doing so). The conclusion is not borne out by the evidence. Capitalist ideology is always presented as standing for the 'common' or 'national' interest, which is said to include the working class. Plans to give labour its 'rightful place' in a socially harmonious society including capitalists can mean nothing other than prolonging the existing exploitative relations—with the owners and controllers of capital on the one hand, and workers having only labour to sell on the other.

It might be asked, why would a counter-revolutionary current bother to appeal to workers at all? Apart from the Nazis' sheer opportunism there was a deeper reason. Capitalism cannot wish for the abolition of the working class as a whole since it is vital to production. It may, in certain circumstances, even advocate improvements in conditions, or a not too great deterioration, since the working class must be maintained at a certain productive level. This 'concern' should not be misconstrued. As the mass conversions of West Indian slaves to Christianity showed, the slave owner who takes an apparent interest in the condition of his slaves and tries to control them ideologically is an intelligent exploiter, not a philanthropist.

The middle class in Nazi propaganda

Despite its heterogeneous and self contradictory character, there was a reactionary core appeal to be found in much Nazi propaganda. Guerin describes it as a form of petty bourgeois anti-capitalism 'quite different from socialist anti-capitalism':

> Fascism thus kills two birds with one stone: on the one hand it flatters the middle classes by becoming the faithful interpreter of their most reactionary aspirations; on the other, it feeds the working masses, and particularly those categories of workers lacking class consciousness, with a utopian and harmless anti-capitalism that turns them away from genuine socialism.[29]

Trotsky's analysis of the 'class nature' of Nazi mass appeal in the period leading to its assumption of power reinforces this argument. First he locates its centre in the middle class:

> [The Nazis] did not quite find an approach to the working class. On the other side, the big bourgeoisie, even those who supported Hitler with money, did not consider his party theirs. The national 'renaissance' leaned wholly upon the middle classes, the most backward part of the nation, the heavy ballast of history.[30]

The attack on Marxism was an attack on the working class itself. Whatever the failings of the SPD, KPD and the unions, these bodies were the organised expression and the defensive bulwark of labour:

> [The Nazis'] political art consisted in fusing the petty bourgeoisie into oneness through its common hostility to the proletariat. What must be done in order to improve things? First of all, throttle those who are underneath. Impotent before big capital, the petty bourgeoisie hopes in the future to regain its social dignity through the ruin of the workers.[31]

Finally, the middle class utopia which would replace class consciousness with national consciousness was to be based on:

> Recollections of the 'happy' days of free competition, and hazy evocations of the stability of class society…an envious hostility to inequality in the person of a proprietor in a car, and animal fear of equality in the person of a worker in a cap and without a collar.[32]

Does this perhaps mean that the Nazis were a middle class movement, by dint of their propaganda? As we shall see, core support was found among the middle class, and the bulk of members and leaders were drawn from this source. But while it might have been possible to talk of such a middle class dominated project having some coherence at the birth of capitalism (such as Jacobinism in 1790s France), in 20th century Germany the reality of social relations was that mass parties of whatever stripe could only carry through policies which reflected the interests of a key social class, workers or capitalists.

Whatever the Nazis and their supporters believed they stood for, a middle class utopia never stood any chance of coming to fruition. The NSDAP could only play into the hands of the capitalists. Class 'harmony' of the Nazi type could only be aspired to by eliminating the existence of one of the antagonistic forces—working class organisation. Rendering such assistance to capitalism could only accelerate evolution towards monopolistic concentration, which would seriously damage the middle class.

Nazi propaganda involved more than posters and meetings. One important feature which was necessary to mould the disparate and unconnected mass of middle class supporters (or 'human dust' as Trotsky called them) was the street demonstration. Lacking the workplace as a collective focus, it was, in Hitler's words, 'parades of hundreds of thousands of men which burned into the small wretched individual the proud conviction that, paltry worm as he was, he was nevertheless a part of a great dragon'.[33]

The fact that the Nazis put out 'catch-all' propaganda does not mean the party was a non-class institution, for two important reasons. Firstly, the Nazis privately admitted that their propaganda did not reflect their actual nature. 'As Goebbels himself remarked with cynical candour, even the German people would never have voted for the Nazis if it had known what they intended to do'.[34] Secondly, Nazi propaganda could not ignore the reality of class. Much propaganda was framed with specific class groupings in mind, even if the cumulative aim was to win maximum votes overall, and even that which claimed to be above class in reality targeted mainly the middle class.

Anti-Semitic propaganda

We have already considered the link between anti-Semitism and counter-revolutionary thought in Nazism. However, another issue arises. To what extent did the Nazis gain a mass following through anti-Semitism? If this was the vehicle by which the NSDAP won support from other parties, then the view of Nazism as primarily a racist rather than a social/class phenomenon would be justified.

In fact, the role of Nazi anti-Semitic propaganda before 1933 was surprisingly restricted. This does not mean that there were not disgusting publications, such as Streicher's grotesque and pornographic *Der Stürmer*. However, until after the assumption of power, when its circulation soared to almost 500,000,[35] it was a minor publication, which even provoked opposition among Nazi ranks.[36] A survey of NSDAP members and their reason for joining found 60 percent of respondents making no reference at all to anti-Semitism, while 4 percent openly expressed disapproval of it in terms such as this: 'Only their statements about the Jews I could not swallow. They gave me a headache even after I had joined the party'.[37]

Analysis of Nazi posters in the period from 1928 to 1932 has revealed the following.

Enemy groups targeted by NSDAP posters, 1928-32[38]		
	No of posters	Percentage
the 'system'	15	12.1
'November parties'	25	20.1
SPD/Marxism	39	31.5
Centre Party/allies	10	8.1
KPD	6	4.8
Jews	6	4.8
miscellaneous	23	18.6

The subjects chosen for front page headlines in the official daily, the *Völkische Beobachter*, between the crucial July 1932 election and Hitler's installation in power, confirm the picture.

Subject matter of lead headlines in *Völkische Beobachter* (Berlin edition) 1 August 1932 to 30 January 1933		
	Total no	Percentage
failure of present government and/or reasons why NSDAP should rule	75	51.7
threat of Marxism/Marxist violence	35	24.1
poverty and unemployment	20	13.8
German foreign policy/national status	6	4.1
anti-Semitism	5	3.4
miscellaneous	4	2.8

Ian Kershaw argues that 'anti-Semitism was quite secondary to Nazism's electoral success',[39] and 'the main appeal of the NSDAP [lay] in its claim to be the most powerful adversary of Marxism and the most radical and forthright exponent of the belief in national and social renewal (the "national community" idea, which was itself of course in essence outrightly anti-Marxist)'.[40]

The majority of *Völkische Beobachter* headlines crudely combined the demand for power with counter-revolution: 'Von Papen's Cultivation Of Bolshevism Alarms The World';[41] 'The Government Fails To Take Seriously Action Against Bolshevisation Of Germany By The Bully-boys Of The SPD And KPD';[42] 'Where Bourgeois Reaction Rules, Marxism Thrives. Where Marxism Thrives, The People Are Ruined'.[43] Others insisted that 'We Hunger While The Bankers Earn Millions'[44] and stressed the Nazi plans for job creation.[45] The emphasis was very much on contrasting the government, portrayed as a 'posh gentlemen's club' with 'the will of the people'.[46]

The Nazis may have claimed that they were a protest movement against society. In fact, class hatred against organised workers was the central pivot of Nazi propaganda and counter-revolution its goal. The aspects of 'society' they protested against were the high level of workers' organisation and consciousness and the fact of capitalist crisis, not capitalism itself. The crisis itself was blamed on the workers and the 'November system' which their revolution had inaugurated.

It is now necessary to ask how important Nazi propaganda was to its success. One view emphasises the 'incredible success of this conglomerate of ideas' and their 'astonishing effect'. This showed 'inspired handling of new techniques of opinion making. But at the same time, it was a truly religio-psychological phenomenon'.[47] If such statements are correct, Nazi success was not class based but due to media manipulation.

The 1930 Reichstag election, which saw the NSDAP emerge from obscurity to become the second largest party, is a good test of whether such an assessment is accurate. A study of the Swabian district of Günzburg has shown that 'despite the limited propaganda effort in this locality, the NSDAP made massive gains'. Indeed, the party 'scored its greatest successes in the small communities which had been relatively neglected in its campaigns as far as meetings, marches, and the usual propaganda razzmatazz was concerned'.[48] The impression that propaganda played a less than decisive role is echoed by several historians: 'In the agrarian-rural regions the NSDAP succeeded more than the average without having a particular organisational and propaganda presence... Although there was practically no party organisation in the South Hesse Dreieich District, the NSDAP achieved peak returns of up to 28 percent'.[49]

If propaganda was not always instrumental in mass conversion to Nazism, this suggests that the ideological groundwork for the movement was prepared within German society rather than being won by the brilliance of media technique: 'It was not that the NSDAP won over their voters, but rather that the voters sought out their party'.[50] Further reinforcement for this view comes from the fact that the Nazis did not begin using their lying propaganda in 1930 but long before, yet they had remained a marginal sect. It was social crisis and consequent class polarisation that was the driving force behind growth, not a sudden display of propagandist genius.

Nazi voters

So the focus must shift to the question of who was susceptible to Nazism and who was resistant. This is vital for any strategy that opposes fascist resurgence today. In the 1930s it was generally agreed that Nazism reflected class influences. Recently, however, oceans of ink have been spilt trying to deny this viewpoint and to argue that as a 'catch-all' party there was no class pattern to Nazi support. Complex computer calculations have been performed on election results and membership data; local studies, regional studies and analyses of individual groups have been devised to justify this position. To approach this issue it is first of all necessary to draw a sharp distinction between two positions. One is the idea of the catch-all, non class based party. The other is that presented by Trotsky which insists on the class character of fascism but recognises that it 'is a form of despair in the petty-bourgeois masses, who carry away with them over the precipice a part of the proletariat as well'.[51] Far from disproving the relevance of class the evidence confirms it.

Let us begin with national election results. To clarify matters party support has been grouped under four major headings—firstly, the left parties, mainly supported by workers; secondly, the Catholic parties, backed by a cross-section adhering to that religion; thirdly, the parties with mainly middle class support excepting the NSDAP; and fourthly, the bourgeois and petty bourgeois votes plus the NSDAP.

Given the extraordinary upheavals that rocked German society from the 1918 Revolution, through the roaring twenties, to the depths of the Depression, these voting patterns are far less volatile than might have been expected. There were three great political blocs—workers, Catholics and the middle class. Let us consider each in turn.

National parliamentary elections, 1919-33 (in percentages)[52]							
	1919	1920	1924	1924	1928	1930	July 1932	Nov 1932
Left								
KPD	-	2.1	12.6	9.0	10.6	13.1	14.5	16.9
USPD	7.6	17.9	0.8	0.1	-	-	-	-
SPD	37.9	21.7	20.5	26.0	29.8	24.5	21.6	20.4
Total	45.5	41.7	33.9	35.1	40.4	37.6	36.1	37.3
Catholic								
Centre	15.9	13.6	13.4	13.6	12.1	11.8	12.5	11.9
BVP	3.8	4.2	3.2	3.8	3.1	3.0	3.7	3.4
Total	19.7	17.8	16.6	17.4	15.2	14.8	16.2	15.3
Middle class								
DDP	18.6	8.3	5.7	6.3	4.9	3.8	1.0	1.0
DVP	4.4	13.9	9.2	10.1	8.7	4.7	1.2	1.9
DNVP	10.3	15.1	19.5	20.5	14.2	7.0	6.2	8.9
other	1.6	3.3	8.6	7.5	13.9	13.8	2.0	2.6
Total without the Nazis	34.9	40.6	43.0	44.4	41.7	29.3	10.4	14.4
NSDAP	-	-	6.5	3.0	2.6	18.3	37.4	33.1
Total with the Nazis	-	-	49.5	47.4	44.3	47.6	47.7	47.5

For the left parties, hopes aroused by the revolutionary period 1918-23 produced radicalisation of sections of white collar workers and broke down barriers between the social groups. But when hope of radical change evaporated, support was reduced to the core working class. From then on the vote remained fairly constant at a little over one third of the total. Though voting is a highly passive expression of views, given the almost unbelievable ineptness of the SPD and KPD leaders (the subject of the next chapter), this resilience is remarkable testimony to the dogged determination of millions of workers to stay loyal to their class. Indeed, the actual number of left voters increased by 800,000 between 1928 and July 1932 (although the left's percentage share declined because of a larger poll).[53]

The Catholic parties, gathering votes across the social spectrum, retained an almost unchanging level of support of just under one fifth because of the durability of religious affiliation.

The third group of parties, which embodied varieties of middle class supporters, showed the most internal fluctuation. Once the revolutionary wave of 1918-23 had passed, its share of the popular vote stood in the middle to upper 40 percent region. However, the portion going to the non-NSDAP segment plummeted from a total share of 41.7 percent to just 10.4 percent between May 1928 and July 1932. Where did the 30 percent or so of votes go? Barring the improbable scenario that masses of these voters suddenly veered to the SPD or KPD at the same time as equal numbers of KPD and SPD voters switched to Nazism, the evidence for a redistribution of votes within the bloc is overwhelming. It supports the view that from 1930 'the National Socialists were, as representatives of middle class political demands, flesh of flesh of the German middle class movement'.[54] The NSDAP was the beneficiary of an electoral movement away from traditional middle class parties.

A tendency in this direction was visible even before the Nazi electoral breakthrough in 1930 with the growth of the 'others' category shown in the above table. Since the hyper-inflation, traditional middle class loyalties were crumbling. 'Others' included bodies such as the Real Estate and Homeowners Party, the Reich Association for Revalorisation, the Tenants Party and the Reich Party of the Middle Class whose titles betray their class character. Childers writes that:

> Individually these splinter parties were small and insignificant, but together they had outpolled the two liberal parties and almost matched the conservatives... These parties spoke for a sizeable segment of the bourgeois electorate which had been alienated by the traumas of the inflation and stabilisation period... Without the destabilisation of traditional voting allegiances within the middle class electorate, the spectacular rise of National Socialist fortunes after 1928 is hardly conceivable.[55]

At this point it is necessary to briefly discuss the concept of class. The voting pattern shown in the above table arises from class identification, something which is subjectively determined. This in itself does not fully settle the nature of Nazi support. Historians who describe Nazism as a 'catch-all people's party' use different criteria to prove their point on the grounds that it is not possible to determine class simply by party allegiance. They employ an alternative perspective, considering class in its objective aspect.

This is a valid approach. Marx himself employed both subjective and objective aspects though he stressed they were dialectically linked: 'In the course of historical development and precisely through the inevitable fact that in the division of labour social relationships assume an independent existence...personality is conditioned and determined by very definite class relationships'.[56] But the objective fact of class is not the same as subjective class consciousness. Giving the example of the workers in this context Marx wrote that if this consciousness is not yet fully formed, 'The proletariat is not sufficiently developed to constitute itself as a class...so long as the struggle itself between proletariat and bourgeoisie does not yet have a political character'.[57] In using both perspectives Marx drew a distinction between the working class as a class 'in itself' and the class 'for itself':

> The domination of capital has created for this mass a common situation, a class against capital, but not yet for itself. In the struggle...this mass becomes united and constitutes itself as a class for itself.[58]

Working class voters

Returning to the statistics for Germany, while the evidence for the NSDAP being a mainly middle class electoral force is irrefutable from the point of view of 'subjective' political identification by its voters, it remains to be seen whether the same is true when the alternative approach is applied. The popular view today has been promoted by Falter who suggests that 'contrary to received beliefs...a particularly marked resistance by workers in general or industrial workers in particular towards National Socialism does not seem to have any empirical foundation'.[59]

If Falter is correct, then the thesis of this book would have serious flaws. However, his evidence disproves his own case. First there is his definition of a 'worker' which is that of the census and was extremely wide. Consequently, as he admits:

> The range of living and working conditions concealed behind the collective term 'worker' was huge... The foreman who had worked in the same Württemberg family firm for 30 years was as much a 'worker' according to the census as the young labourer in an Upper Silesian ironworks, the home worker...or the daily help in a villa in Berlin-Zehlendorf.[60]

The definition is so broad that it cannot produce valid conclusions about the working class. As Manstein observes, 'To proceed with the theme "the NSDAP was backed by the workers" almost amounts to a clumsy conjuring trick: attention is focused on the industrial working class, while the rest are concealed from the analysis'.[61]

If a Marxist understanding of class is used to break Falter's statistics into meaningful categories such as 'agriculture', 'handicrafts', 'industry' and the 'service sector' a clear pattern emerges: 'The higher the proportion of agricultural workers in the electorate the better the NSDAP's performance'.[62] With workers in crafts and industry 'the position is exactly the reverse',[63] while the service sector occupies a middle position. Out of the broad definition of 'worker' the group least likely to vote Nazi was the industrial worker, the most likely the agricultural worker.

Other influences can be observed: the larger the town, the smaller the proportion of NSDAP votes.[64] Unemployment gave 'a remarkable degree of immunity from the NSDAP'.[65] Falter finds it 'quite astonishing' that 'in all elections after 1930 the NSDAP fared, on average, significantly better where unemployment was lower and vice versa. The contrary is true for the Communists'.[66] The mass unemployment of the early 1930s struck workers with much greater force than white collar employees. Those classified as workers constituted half of the population but made up over four fifths of the unemployed.[67] So how did the mass unemployment of the crash influence support for the Nazis? Falter continues, 'Voters for National Socialism must have been mainly people who felt threatened by unemployment and the radicalisation of many unemployed to the left'.[68]

The only significant factor that cuts across the class issue is Catholicism. The Catholic vote, much of which was centred in southern Germany, had been hardened into mistrust of the centralised German state in Bismarck's day. Consequently 'the NSDAP had a much harder time of it [in] Catholic areas'.[69]

Alas, Falter concludes from this evidence that Nazi 'electoral successes were nourished by so many different sources, that the NSDAP [was] socially balanced'.[70] Apart from Catholicism (which offered a cultural allegiance resistant to external challenge), is there not a distinct class pattern in Falter's figures?

There was a spectrum of responses to Nazi appeals. The strongest rejection came from industrial workers, living in larger towns and most prone to unemployment. In between were those working in the craft or service sector, in medium sized towns and less affected by unemployment; finally come the least resistant—agricultural or rural labourers living in small communities.

Surely this pattern cannot be coincidental. It is, in fact, entirely bound up with the character of the working class in the Marxist sense. The workers' situation under capitalism pushes both in the direction of rebellion against exploitation and towards submission to the pressure to earn a living. The balance between these two facets is influenced by many factors. The conditions of the industrial worker tended to generate a greater sense of a distinct and collective interest due to the assembling together of workers in collectively related units. Similarly, big cities tended to have geographical concentrations of workers with more homogeneous class communities, less inter-mixing with other social groups, and therefore more possibility of developing an independent class consciousness. Experience of being sacked by the boss who, 99 times out of 100 was not Jewish, meant that anti-Semitic propaganda about the causes of unemployment would be seen as a lie. The factors encouraging resistance to capitalist ideas by the industrial worker grew progressively weaker as the unit size of production declined and geographical dispersal increased.[71]

How big was the core working class, that group which fitted the pattern of most resistance to Nazism? Official figures from 1925 show that 17 million people (or 53 percent of the economically active population) were officially classified as 'workers' using the very broad census definition. Of these 11 million (or 34 percent of the population) were wage workers 'in capitalist enterprises'; seven million of these (21 percent of the population) were in enterprises employing more than 50 people.[72]

It would be ridiculous to say that every industrial worker withstood Nazi propaganda and voted SPD or KPD. Much depended on the actions of those parties as to whether they could retain worker loyalty; and, as we shall see in the next chapter, it is difficult to imagine that either the SPD or KPD could have pursued worse strategies than they actually did. Trotsky believed that 'counter-revolutionary despair embraced the petty-bourgeois mass with such force that it drew behind it many sections of the proletariat'.[73] Even so, it is not unreasonable to suppose that the consistent mid-30 percent of the electorate which supported workers' parties roughly coincided with a core of industrial workers (employed and unemployed) identified above. Equally, while there will have been many Nazi voters classified as 'workers' by official data, these will have tended to come from groups on the margins, at points where working class shaded into the middle class, or from isolated sections with little or no contact with labour organisation and therefore more subject to ruling class ideological influence.

Middle class voters

Here too a class pattern was visible. It has commonly been assumed that the Nazis 'gave the most blatant expression to the fears and prejudices of the middle and particularly the lower middle classes',[74] while leaving the most respectable pillars of society relatively untouched. The reality was different. Just as the pattern in the working class could not have been deduced from prestige or income (after all, agricultural workers were the worst paid with the lowest incomes, yet more prone to voting Nazi than industrial workers), so with the middle class the determining factor was not general social standing but actual class relations.

Childers' 'catch-all' thesis is based on a sophisticated analysis, but his evidence actually points to a definite class pattern. He considers three groups: an old middle class of artisans (often self employed), shopkeepers and farmers; a rentier group living off petty investments and pensions; and, finally, a new middle class of white collar workers (including civil servants).

With regard to the old middle class, he notes that 'well before the onset of the Depression' there were signs of an NSDAP electoral advance at the expense of middle of the road parties.[75] This was the first group to show Nazi sympathies. By 1930 the Nazis had also broken through into the 'rentier' vote—those who had lost their petty investments during the hyper-inflation.[76] This group overtook the old middle class in strength of commitment to Nazism to become 'the strongest predictor of the National Socialist vote in July 1932'.[77]

The 'lower middle class thesis' would predict that the old middle class with its firm social status and relative job security would be less prone to Nazism than the 'new middle class' of white collar employees, many in firms crippled by the Depression. The opposite is true:

> Instead of rallying to the National Socialist banner, white collar employees appear to have scattered their votes across the rich and varied spectrum of Weimar politics... A much stronger relationship [with] National Socialist voting...is found when one turns from the white collar population to the traditionally conservative civil service.[78]

Even in the turbulent and changing situation of 1932:

> There is little convincing empirical evidence to support the traditional view that white collar employees flocked to the NSDAP in 1931-32... Support appears to have been far more concentrated in the traditionally elitist civil service than in the socially heterogeneous but largely lower middle class.[79]

The pattern is once more based on the social relations of capitalism. The rentier group lived off the profits (however petty their share) made by exploiting the working class and so the solution to their problems did not appear to be an alliance with the working class, but the strengthening of capitalism which Nazi counter-revolution seemed to offer. Civil servants had an indirect relationship to capitalism, but, as bureaucrats who ran the capitalist state, they saw in the Nazis the means of self preservation against disruption of career patterns and hierarchies.[80]

White collar workers were in a different position. Before the war, as a commentator in the 1920s put it, compared to industrial workers:

> White collar employees dressed better, lived in nicer homes, possessed higher quality household goods, pursued educational opportunities, attended lectures, concerts, or theatrical performances, and read good books. Their standard of living approximated to that of the propertied class, not perhaps in range and freedom but in type.[81]

However, this golden age disappeared even before the 1929 crash. Exploitative capitalist relations of production wrecked a once cosy existence through unemployment and 'the enormous intensification and mechanisation of white collar work [which] results in a doubling of the energy output required'. The writer added that this brutal reality clashed with 'the wishful dreams of bourgeois ideologues'. However, white collar workers did not automatically see how much they had in common with the industrial working class: 'Obviously this comparison has not yet taken hold among the majority of white collar employees'.[82]

The white collar worker, as a victim of capitalism (rather than a mourner at its ineffectiveness) could have found common cause with the industrial working class. A sign of this was the level of white collar union organisation which, in 1932, stood at 43 percent of all employees, outstripping even the industrial labour force with its union density of 34 percent.[83] However, the peripheral advantages of white collar employment over manual labour encouraged an ideological gulf which was not instantly overcome. That it could have been overcome is proved by the evidence given earlier of trade union organisation and left wing militancy in 1919 when socialist revolution seemed an immediate prospect. Failure to carry this through meant that the AfA-Bund, the socialist affiliated trade union federation, declined from its 48 percent share of the unionised white collar workers in 1920 to 33 percent by 1930. By contrast the DHV, which was closer to the Nazis, expanded from 32 percent to 41 percent of the total.[84] Class development meant that the vote of the white collar workers was disputed territory.

The same could not be said of the classic petty bourgeoisie in farming. Here the Nazis scored their most striking successes. The Depression cut farm sale proceeds by 35 percent while the cost of servicing debt rocketed. In 1932 a wave of rural riots against evictions swept Schleswig-Holstein. Tax offices and town halls were burnt down or blown up.[85] Once again, detailed examination reveals a class pattern. Heberle's contemporary study of this area found that industrial villages and working class communities 'on the outskirts of the larger cities…show low Nazi and high Socialist and Communist percentages'.[86] The agricultural areas divided into two basic types—rich farms (operating in a highly commercial context or on landed estates), and the Geest, consisting of small peasant family farms. In the former there was a tradition of class hostility and consequent class political organisation that kept both workers and rich farmers locked into their political allegiances (SPD and DNVP). In July 1932 the Geest voted by a staggering 78.7 percent for the Nazis. Heberle puts this down to a weak tradition of political organisation among these middle class voters.[87]

Before concluding this section it is important to note the change in the number of individual electors voting in Reichstag elections. These increased from 37 million in 1919 to 44 million in 1932. The Nazis did particularly well in attracting the new voters. This qualifies, but does not undermine, our general argument. The SPD and KPD followed disastrous and self defeating policies and therefore often failed to attract those who were unorganised, new to politics, and looking for a dynamic way out of the crisis.

To sum up, while no class was bound hand and foot to a particular party, the fundamental pattern of electoral support for the NSDAP was set by the development of class relations under capitalism. Hamilton's work on the social composition of different party votes lets us locate support quite precisely within this pattern. Even using a broad definition of 'worker', the position is clear when a comparison between the different parties is made—the SPD/KPD bloc showed a marked working class preponderance; the liberal DDP/DVP parties had a disproportionate share of new middle and old middle class support; the NSDAP occupied roughly the same social territory as the reactionary, traditionalist DNVP, inheritor of the German conservative tradition dating back to Bismarck's time.

Social composition of votes of different parties (in percentages) in the July 1932 election		
	Workers	New middle class	Old middle class
general population	48	18	32
SPD	57	28	15
KPD	81	13	6
Catholic	38	18	43
DDP/DVP	33	30	37
DNVP	38	27	35
NSDAP	39	19	42

In *Who Voted for Hitler?* Hamilton concludes, 'Support for the National Socialists in most towns varied directly with the class level of the district. The "best districts" gave Hitler and his party the strongest support'.[88]

Nazi organisations

Electoral statistics show who voted for Nazism. What about those who actually joined the NSDAP and its affiliated organisations? A current academic fashion insists on the significance of workers in the party. This probably has much more to do with Blairite politics than history, as the conclusion to a book on the subject illustrates. It criticises Marxist attempts to categorise parties along class lines, and adds, 'That major parties of whatever political hue should transcend class interests has become increasingly common currency in the post-1945 world. To that extent National Socialism was a peculiarly German anticipation of future developments'.[89]

In an essay entitled 'A Workers' Party or a "Party Without Workers"?' Mühlberger estimates the proportion of 'workers' in the NSDAP to be '40 percent of members in the period between 1925 and the end of January 1933'.[90] The notion of the NSDAP as a workers' party is ludicrous. Even if the NSDAP had been a democratically organised body, which it was not, the nature of the party would still not have been determined by its social composition. The ideology, the policies of the party, reflected capitalist counter-revolution from beginning to end. Those workers who joined it were either ignorant of its character or accepted the ideology of capitalism in one form or another. Yet arguments like those of Mühlberger lead another historian to the grotesque notion that the NSDAP:

> Enhanced [workers'] self esteem and legitimised their desire for social mobility... The NSDAP emerged as a viable choice for many German workers...largely by virtue of its ability to generate a set of innovative ideas to redress the economic problems confronting labour.[91]

Physically smashing the trade unions, banning strikes and terrorising workers may have been 'innovative' but they hardly solved the problems facing labour.

Of course there were workers in the Nazi Party, as there were in all the other parties; but this does not mean that the party had a working class character or offered workers a real political home. The testimony of the Gauleiter of Hamburg, though impressionistic, brings this out. He writes that despite the 'socialist' elements the NSDAP put to the German worker:

He wouldn't buy it. Even in the public meetings he was hardly to be seen…except when he showed up as a part of the heckling squads organised by both Marxist parties. And among the actual party membership, workers played no role at all down to 1930-31, except for a few rare instances.[92]

If social composition does not directly determine political character, it does tell us about the sort of person a party tends to attract, an important issue in itself. Many different historians have considered Nazi Party membership,[93] and while the criteria used vary, the pattern conforms to that seen in the electoral statistics. Kater provides information for 1933, comparing those who joined the NSDAP that year and the general population:

Percentages of NSDAP joiners in 1933 and general population[94]		
	NSDAP	*Population*
Lower class		
unskilled workers	12.6	37.25
skilled workers	18.1	17.31
Total	30.7	54.56
Middle class		
master craftsmen	8.9	9.56
teachers	4.2	1.79
white collar	10.6	12.42
lower civil servants	11.7	5.18
merchants	12.8	6.0
farmers	8.9	7.7
Total	57.1	42.65
Elite		
managers	2.3	0.53
higher civil servants	2.8	0.48
lecturers	3.0	0.96
students	1.7	0.48
entrepreneurs	2.4	0.34
Total	12.2	2.78

So compared to the general population, workers were underrepresented by almost half (44 percent), the lower middle class was overrepresented by one third, while there was a fourfold over-representation of the elite (438 percent).

As with the electorate, factors such as the distinction between industry and agriculture or urban size play a part. In Germany as a whole those employed in industry and crafts outnumbered those in agriculture by a ratio of eight to five.[95] Yet within the NSDAP (in July 1932), the ratio was three to five.[96] Again, the larger the town, the weaker the Nazi membership.[97] One striking feature was the very low proportion of women who joined the NSDAP. Between 1925 and 1932 they formed just 7.8 percent of all joiners, falling to just 5.1 percent by 1933.[98] This was partly due to the extreme male chauvinism of the NSDAP which never allowed women to occupy any position of leadership. Another feature was the young age of many of those who joined, a factor linked both to the party's dynamic image and the lack of previous attachments amongst this section.[99]

If workers were under-represented in the NSDAP, the fact remains that some were present. Who were they? Mühlberger provides valuable information despite his intention to deny the Marxist approach. His study shows immediately that within the broad definition of 'worker', the NSDAP's membership was skewed. In the general working population the unskilled outnumbered the skilled by two to one, yet, 'Unskilled blue collar workers were a comparative rarity within the Nazi Party, accounting for less than one fifth of the total blue collar membership'.[100] In addition, there 'is the consistently strong over-representation within the Nazi Party of workers associated with traditional artisanal occupations such as tool makers, painters and decorators, bakers, butchers and shoemakers'.[101] The most strongly over-represented element of all were 'workers in food preparation and processing industries…in the ratio of three to one'.[102] By contrast, 'in every region' the consistently under-represented groups were likely to be in larger units more divorced from employer influence such as miners.[103] Once again the real basis of class (rather than the bureaucratic census definition) is revealed. What counts in resisting Nazism are the chances of collective organisation and consciousness and freedom from the direct influence (and intimidation) of the employer.

Though limited in the size of its sample, Fromm's survey of German workers conducted in 1931 suggests a fundamental gulf in attitude separated the NSDAP worker and that of the left wing parties. To the question, 'Who in your opinion, has the real power in the state today?' the following answers were given (in percentages):[104]

	SPD	KPD	NSDAP
capitalists, industrialists banks, bourgeoisie, landowners	68	83	26
Jews alone or with freemasons and Jesuits	1	1	50
other	31	16	24

Another question raised the issue of individualism versus social influence on ordinary life: 'Do you think the individual has only himself to blame for his own fate?' Here is the response (in percentages):[105]

	SPD	KPD	NSDAP
yes	27	22	59
no	42	67	35
other	33	11	6

'How do you get on with your colleagues at work (in comparison with superiors)?' provided interesting answers. Nazis were more than three times more likely than Communists to have a better relationship with their superiors than their own workmates.[106]

Nazis and left wing workers held an entirely different world view on a whole range of issues; the key difference being that the former demonstrate an almost unquestioning acceptance of individualistic and racist capitalist ideology, while the latter held an anti-capitalist collectivist viewpoint. If workers joined the NSDAP because they thought it was a 'party of protest', it would seem clear from this evidence that their protest had little to do with a genuine rejection of capitalist values.

This is borne out by the fact that it was not those who were the worst victims of the economic crisis who joined the NSDAP. This is not to say that the capitalist crisis did not influence the growth of the party. Hitler held membership number 55 when he joined in 1919. Before the Depression the figure stood at 96,918, but by 1933 it had reached 849,000.[107] However, it was:

> Those least affected by the Depression who were attracted to the NSDAP. And among the workers it was those living in country areas, where dislocations were least likely to occur, who joined the NSDAP in greatest strength… The workers, who suffered most from the Depression, continued to be under-represented; the lower and upper middle classes, which suffered less, continued to be over-represented.[108]

How is this paradox to be explained? It was fear of the disruptive consequences of the crisis for capitalism (and their place within that system) that seems to have motivated those who joined after 1929, not a rejection of the system which caused the crisis. This was qualitatively different to, and indeed opposed to, the arguments of the left parties and the organised working class which backed them.

Before concluding this study of Nazi membership, two specific organisations are worthy of attention—the SA and the NSBO. The SA was a vast organisation and, by the early 1930s, on occasion actually outnumbered the NSDAP's membership.[109] Due to its function the SA was different in key ways from its parent. It was overwhelmingly composed of young men. Four fifths of its members were under 29 years of age, the biggest single group (41 percent) being aged between 20 and 24.[110] Further, although precise figures are lacking, the bulk of the SA were unemployed, the proportion nearing 70 percent.[111] Part of its attraction for the young unemployed, many of whom failed to qualify for any unemployment benefits, was its provision of soup kitchens, clothing (uniforms and boots) and hostels. In 1932 its units were described as being 'composed solely of unemployed. For these men in particular, the creation of SA hostels was especially fortuitous. For many…these hostels became their real home'.[112]

In terms of social composition the SA was quite different to the NSDAP. Its paramilitary character meant that many of its leaders were noble ex-officers clearly distinguishable by the 'von' in their names; from the overall chief (until his replacement by Röhm), Captain von Pfeffer, to deputy leaders respectively for west, central and south Germany—von Ulrich, von Killinger, von Obernitz. Its leading ranks also included the Kaiser's son Prince August-Wilhelm, Prince Friedrich-Christian of Schaumbeurg-Lippe, Prince Philipp of Hesse, Duke Euard of Saxe-Coburg—and the list goes on.[113] Among the lower ranks the situation was reversed, the presence of workers being far more significant than in the NSDAP itself. A comparison of SA members with the overall population of the same age shows the following:

Occupational background of stormtroopers and for male working population, 1929-30 January 1933 (in percentages)			
Social groups	SA	Population	20-30 age group
workers	64	53	63
white collar, civil servants	26	19	20
independents	10	22	7
others	0.1	6	10

To a certain extent the character of the SA can be explained by the circumstances of the time and its role. Unemployment affected manual workers more severely than other sections, and many SA unemployed were attracted by food, warmth and a roof. The life of an active street fighter (as opposed to aristocratic 'commanders of men') may have been a less acceptable choice for those from 'genteel' backgrounds. One difficulty in tracking the social composition of young people just entering the labour market is that immediate economic circumstances may distort the picture. Although not conclusive, it is interesting to note that 'many more Stormtroopers' parents were apparently middle class than were the Stormtroopers themselves'.[114] Finally, while a gulf separated Nazi workers from those of the organised left, it seems that the SA was sometimes an exception to this, with examples of KPD members crossing over to join the SA, transfers also taking place in the opposite direction.[115]

So the SA was more working class in composition than the NSDAP. If the general argument about the Nazis being an all-class movement were correct, then we would not expect social distinctions between the SA and the parent body to cause tension between the two. In fact there were a multitude of differences which culminated in the bloody slaughter of the SA leadership by Hitler's SS henchmen in the 'Night of the Long Knives' of 1934. Interestingly, the SS was, in social terms, largely drawn from elite social groups.[116] However, dissent between the SA and NSDAP was developing much earlier than 1934.

First of all, fewer than half of the Stormtroopers actually belonged to the Nazi Party.[117] This suggests a lack of commitment to the party's aims and outlook. Secondly, the SA's ideology was rather different from that of the parent body. In one sense it is a mistake to dignify the ragbag of ideas circulating in the SA with the term ideology. If there was a greater emphasis on socialism, this amounted to little more than:

> A series of passionate, radical, and often pugilistic remarks by various leaders on the necessity of smashing Marxism, the republic and Jews and of creating some sort of ill defined egalitarian *Volksgemeinschaft* [people's community]... It was a force designed to capture and dominate the streets. Ideology mattered little in these circumstances, and the socialism it is supposed to have possessed amounted to little more than the ability to organise soup kitchens, shelter, and clothing for sections of the working class unemployed.[118]

There does seem to have been a vague common attitude amongst SA members: 'Most were convinced that as long as the Weimar Republic's political institutions survived, and as long as the socio-economic order remained the same, they would never work again. The "system", as they described it, had to be destroyed'.[119] If the first part of this statement accorded with the aims of Hitler and his circle, the second part, which apparently challenged the 'system', did not.

The political tensions between the SA and the NSDAP led to a number of high profile disputes. In April 1931 there was the so called Stennes Revolt. Stennes was leader of the important Berlin SA who resented that the policy of 'legality' prevented his men from fighting on the streets. When he was sacked he declared that 'the revolutionary force of the SA has been saturated with bourgeois liberal tendencies',[120] and led a forcible occupation of the offices of the newspaper *Der Angriff*, Goebbels' Nazi daily. The police were called in and Hitler sarcastically dismissed Stennes as a buffoon of 'salon Bolshevism and salon socialism...who played the role of socialist revolutionary against the capitalistically thinking [Nazi] party bosses'.[121] The difficulties did not stop with the defeat of Stennes. The Boxheim documents caused embarrassment. Two days before the November 1932 Reichstag election an East Prussian SA leader announced, 'We are ready with a million rifles. We will see a revolution after 6 November which we shall launch together with the Communists'.[122] In April 1933 disappointment with Hitler even led to an open gunfight between SA members. The KPD was wrong to imagine that such events meant that 'the proletarian elements are in revolt against the capitalist leadership of the NSDAP'.[123] They were mainly expressions of impatience and wishful thinking; yet the SA, with its unusual social composition, caused more headaches for the NSDAP leaders than any other grouping under its umbrella.

If the SA was, in a sense, the exception that proved the rule of Nazism's class character, then what of the NSBO—the Nazi factory cells organisation which claimed to be closest to the working class? One writer accurately sums up the sort of workers who were attracted to Nazism in these terms:

Those industrial workers who did find their way to Hitler were invariably located, for one reason or another, outside the mainstream of working class organisational and ideological development, and in some instances were drawn from the lumpenproletariat. A small labour aristocracy of skilled workers, dependent craftsmen, and workers with responsibility, such as foremen, were as likely to end up voting for Hitler as not... They were joined by another set of workers who did live in small towns or the countryside and who, if employed, were not subject to the supervisory control of a trade union or other kind of workers' group. Most of them were employed in a semi-skilled or non-skilled capacity in small businesses and family concerns, such as handicrafts, where the influence of the master/owner and his family was often decisive. These workers lacked, therefore, a developed proletarian consciousness, which prevented them from identifying with the traditional working class movement.[124]

The notion that there was no qualitative difference between Nazi workers and the rest of the class was rejected by the unions which certainly thought there was. The NSBO's members were expelled during 1931.[125] Yet it has recently been claimed the NSBO was more representative of the working class than mainstream unions: 'The NSBO had been founded as a general union, unlike the socialist unions, which had traditionally concentrated on one profession or branch of industry'.[126] This rubbish is no more than an echo of NSBO rhetoric which claimed that it would create a union movement independent of politics, expressing 'genuine trade union thinking'.[127]

NSBO leaders were compelled to raise wage and other issues and pose as a 'genuine trade union organisation' to retain membership.[128] In this limited sense it is true that to a degree 'it was unavoidably driven in the direction of classical trade unionism',[129] or rather had to pretend to be so driven. Like the SA it was prepared to use left wing phrases, such as, 'Struggle for German socialism' or 'Only Hitler will bring you real socialism'.[130] But the Nazis' cynical use of radical phraseology to win support should not be underestimated, and there were other sides to the NSBO. It was conceived as a means of hitting at the root of genuine proletarian workplace organisation. In 1932 Goebbels launched the slogan, 'No workplace without a Nazi cell'.[131] The target was the trade unions, not the employers, as proved by the fact that bosses' organisations, often anti-union in the extreme, requested that the NSBO recruit the unorganised.[132] The *Arbeitgeber* (*Employer*) journal, writing shortly after Hitler's assumption of power, bemoaned the fact that the NSBO, as 'a quite new weapon of the movement...has still to be rewarded with the full fruits of its work... The bulwark of Marxism in the workplace has been shaken, but it is still not annihilated'.[133]

How much support did the NSBO enjoy in the working class? Though slow to take off, by the beginning of 1933 the membership figure had risen to 294,000.[134] Despite claims to the contrary,[135] this was fewer than the Communists' union wing, the RGO, and a mere fraction of the SPD affiliated ADGB:

Comparative size of trade union movements[136]			
	ADGB	RGO	Christian	NSBO
1930	5,220,018	106,000	1,273,096	-
1931	4,798,548	145,380	1,190,023	39,000
1932	3,932,947	322,000	1,100,000	170,000

The puny size of the NSBO was also reflected in elections to factory councils. At a time when the Nazis had gained 18.3 percent of the vote in Reichstag elections, in factory council elections the NSBO won just 710 of the 138,418 representatives (or 0.51 percent).[137] In Berlin, where Goebbels, the propaganda wizard, was Gauleiter, in 1931 the ADGB won the election of 6,583 stewards, the RGO 733, and the NSBO just 36.[138] In the metal industry the NSBO took just 1.74 percent of the mandates.[139] The NSBO counted the Ruhr among its 'successes'. In 1931 it managed 4.1 percent of the mandates, compared to the RGO's 29 percent and ADGB's 36.4 percent.[140] Even after the Nazi government was formed, the factory council elections of early 1933 gave the NSBO a derisory 7.7 percent of the total vote.[141]

However, if the NSBO had failed to make major inroads into the organised working class, it is notable that its few successes confirm the class dimensions of Nazi support already described. Firstly, the NSBO found it easier to build among white collar sections than industrial labour forces, taking a 30.2 percent share of the vote in workplace elections in early 1933. Secondly, among blue collar workers it influenced those who lacked a tradition of organisation. The Ruhr collieries were an example. Here there was a low union density with only 60,000 of the 415,000 miners in the ADGB (in 1927) and just 2,000 Communists. By March 1933 the NSBO was scoring up to 55 percent in pits like the one at Dinslaken.[142] The fact that the pit was owned by Thyssen, the pro-Nazi businessman, was probably a factor.

Conclusion

To avoid a repetition of the German experience today, knowledge of where resistance was greatest is vital. A clear class pattern pervaded every aspect of Nazism. The greatest vulnerability to it was found amongst the middle and upper classes; the greatest degree of immunity was amongst the workers.

The reason for this pattern lay with the nature of Nazism as a pro-capitalist counter-revolutionary movement (however confused and deluded some of its supporters may have been) on the one hand, and the degree of anti-capitalist consciousness of workers on the other. This does not mean that workers had some kind of genetic immunity to Nazism. They withstood Nazism because of the daily experience of exploitation and the lessons it taught, plus their traditions of union and political organisation.

If the working class was the point of departure for resisting Nazism's rise to power, then the obvious question has to be asked: how was Hitler able to take control when Germany was home to one of the most powerful labour movements in the world?

Chapter 5

The failure of the German left

The working class was the social force most able to prevent fascism, and its best opportunity was in the period 1918-23. A revolutionary movement and leadership adequate to the task could have drawn behind it the bulk of the middle class (at that time moving rapidly leftwards). Destroying the capitalist system would have removed the breeding ground for Nazism. A revolutionary socialist Germany linked up with Soviet Russia could have spearheaded world socialist revolution, thus banishing the spectre of fascism forever.

However, this was not to be, and Russia's workers' state was left isolated in a backward country devastated by poverty and war. The result was to be the withering of Soviet democracy under the hammer blows of civil war and foreign intervention and its eventual replacement by Stalin's state capitalism. This in turn had repercussions in Germany where, on the advice of Moscow, the KPD pursued suicidal policies. Thus, as Chris Harman puts it, 'Social democracy in the West begat Stalinism in the East. The blood spilt by Stalin, as much as the blood spilt by Hitler, lies also at the door of the...social democrats'.[1]

With the ending of the German revolutionary period in 1923 attention shifts to the period 1930-33 and a narrower question: could the working class have prevented Hitler coming to power at that time? Many historians answer 'no'. Quite apart from the depressing conclusion that would follow—that the triumph of Nazism was inevitable (and given the character of capitalism, must be so in the future)—this ignores the evidence both within Germany and internationally.

Fascist movements were active across Europe in the inter-war period, but many faced fierce resistance. This does not mean that workers' opposition was guaranteed to triumph in all circumstances. The disaster of Hitler coming to power in Germany rang alarm bells in Austria where a heroic revolt against rising fascism occurred in February 1934. The socialist 'Schutzbund' battled for four days and was defeated. Yet the resistance had positive international repercussions:

The attempt, however unsuccessful, of the Viennese workers contrasted strongly with the meek capitulation of both Communists and Socialists in Germany. It was after all possible to fight; the workers were not hopelessly delivered into the hands of the fascists. The Vienna rising did more to restore the spirits of the labour movement than many a brilliant success could have done.[2]

In France the fight against fascism was outstandingly successful. On 6 February 1934 an attempted fascist coup caused 20 deaths and the replacement of the government by a more right wing one. Six days later the country was gripped by a general strike involving one million in the Paris region alone.[3] The strength of this movement lay in the attitude adopted by both Socialist and Communist demonstrators in uniting their action:

> In one unforgettable moment the two columns joined together to cries of 'Unity! Unity!', and then proceeded in tightly-packed rows along the whole width of the Cours de Vincennes. For the first time for years Socialist and Communist workers were marching side by side.[4]

The rank and file compelled the leaders of both political currents to overcome factional strife in the face of fascism. July 1935 witnessed an 'unforgettable' demonstration of 500,000 whose 'songs and slogans gave voice to their hopes and their confidence in the triumph of social justice and their faith in the eventual emancipation of the workers'.[5]

The powerful torrent of hope undermined the current of counter-revolutionary despair which gripped the middle class during the Depression and so undercut the fascists. By June 1936 a strike wave swept through France. Le Temps reported:

> The folly of 6 February [1934] is gone forever: the shop workers, the technicians who announce that they have no special demands to lodge but simply want to demonstrate their solidarity with their worker comrades, the women, the young girls so full of fight, the staffs of the insurance companies, the stock exchange and the banks, they all now understand that there is only one fight.[6]

What began as an effort to resist fascism developed into something much greater, raising union membership from one million to five million, bringing in a left wing government and crippling the fascist movement. Fascism would come to France, but it had to be imposed by Hitler's tanks from outside.

In Spain during the summer of 1936 General Franco's fascist-backed offensive won support in almost every army garrison. It was initially met by passivity and resignation on the part of the Popular Front government. However, the Nationalist advance was halted when workers seized arms and began resistance: 'Without so much as a by your leave to the government, the proletariat had begun a war to the death against the fascists'.[7] In five of Spain's seven largest cities the military revolt was extinguished by such action.[8] One of the participants described the atmosphere:

> It was incredible, the proof in practice of what one knows in theory; the power and strength of the masses when they take to the streets. Suddenly you feel their creative power; you can't imagine how rapidly the masses are capable of organising themselves. The forms they invent go far beyond anything you've dreamt of, read in books.[9]

The initial military successes were striking:

> The revolution's armed expression, the militias, organised by the trade unions and political parties, set out with great rapidity to defeat the enemy. Hastily formed and poorly armed, they took the initiative in rushing from Madrid to conquer and hold not only the passes of the Guadarrama but the neighbouring provinces. From Barcelona, thousands of men, many of whom had never handled a rifle in their lives, poured westwards to liberate Aragon.[10]

What began as a fight against fascism soon developed into a full-scale workers' revolution. Its failure and the victory of Franco was due not so much to the power of the Nationalists but the internal politics of the Republican side which stifled popular initiatives.

In Britain MI5 reported the 'great resonance' of Mosley's British Union of Fascists in the summer of 1936.[11] However, the rising fascist movement was halted at the 'Battle of Cable Street' on 4 October 1936. This was a defence of an area of working class east London mainly organised by the Communists. One of those involved writes that despite the denunciation of anti-fascists by Labour's leadership, the appeal to stop the Mosleyites' march 'was responded to by thousands of Labour Party members and supporters... Never was there such unity of all sections of the working class as was seen on the barricades at Cable Street'.[12] Fascism in Britain was dealt a mortal blow. Still further examples could be cited.[13]

Was Germany doomed to be different? In fact the same pattern of workers' organisation as the focal point for actively resisting Nazi growth can be discerned here. One does not need to go all the way back to the 1920 general strike against Kapp and his swastika-bearing Freikorps units. In a fascinating study of Saxony, Szejnmann shows that 'the better the network of Social Democratic organisations, the more problems the Nazis faced in gaining mass support'.[14] He contrasts Leipzig with Zwickau, the former 'the SPD's greatest bastion in the last Weimar elections', while in the latter the party 'nearly disintegrated' and its vote collapsed.[15] One significant difference between the two areas was the density of SPD membership. Between 1926 and 1931 in Leipzig it increased from 2.9 percent to 3.4 percent of the population. In Zwickau it fell from 1.8 percent to 1.4 percent of the population.[16] The number of public meetings held by local SPD branches was another indicator of the likely strength of resistance to Nazi growth.[17] In Freital:

> The local SPD organisation organised 13 educational courses and 92 single lectures... The town remained one of the most solid SPD bastions and a wilderness for the Nazis until the end of the Weimar Republic. In the July 1932 Reichstag elections the SPD scored 43.8 percent of the vote, the NSDAP only 21.6 percent. In Bautzen, where the Social Democrats only organised four educational courses and 33 lectures...the NSDAP received 42 percent of the vote in July 1932, compared with 24.4 percent for the SPD...[18]

Leipzig and Freital were, alas, exceptions. The fact remains—Hitler was appointed chancellor in a country which had one of the best organised and most class conscious workers' movements in the world.

There are two possible explanations—one is that the strength of the working class was simply an illusion; the other is that this strength was never used. Geary and Kershaw, like the SPD deputy Hilferding before them,[19] insist that, political problems notwithstanding, the working class was in a powerless condition. Geary writes, for example, that the working class could not stop Hitler because of:

> ...the most profound disaster of all, namely the Depression. The Depression robbed labour of its industrial muscle; it compounded the division between Social Democrats and Communists, which increasingly became a social as well as a political divide; it set worker against worker, the employed against the unemployed; and it demoralised many of those without work.[20]

To mechanically relate unemployment to paralysis of the working class is false. Of course, years of Depression after 1929 were debilitating but this does not mean that the class was impotent or broken. In fact, there were significant workers' struggles on the economic front. The first week of 1932 saw strikes in the Ruhr, Berlin engineering, among Hamburg sailors, chemical workers in Halle and ballots supporting strikes in the gas and water industries, among others.[21] Between mid-September and mid-October 1932 there were 500 disputes.[22] These were mainly in response to von Papen's austerity measures and were launched against union advice. Officials argued that due to unemployment, scabbing was likely. However, 'the unemployed did not undermine those involved in the struggle, but in many cases actively supported them'[23] and the great majority of strikes were successful.[24] In November von Papen expressed his perplexity at 'how much power the workforce was able to wield', seeing this as potentially 'a very serious danger'.[25]

Unemployment did not abolish the powerful tradition of political, social and trade union organisation accompanied by a developed sense of working class consciousness. The decline in the German trade unions' membership was not dramatically worse than Britain's and they 'were, with remarkable success, able to keep up the wages of those still in work in the years of crisis and heavy unemployment'.[26] Of course, unemployment damages workers' confidence but it can lead to an individual or a collective response. The fact that the unemployed tended to turn to the KPD rather than the Nazis demonstrates that a collective understanding that it was caused by capitalism was common. Thus, there were many ways in which the working class retained considerable defensive potential. Just as it would be a mistake to mechanically relate unemployment to political impotence in the face of fascism, it would be wrong to see an automatic connection between a degree of resilience in the workplace and effective struggle against fascism. It was only one potential element if the working class was to be mobilised in a proper campaign.

What of the situation outside the workplace? Hitler's SA projected an image of strength and the Brownshirts were indeed a large organisation, but the fact remains that the SPD's paramilitary wing alone, the Reichsbanner, outnumbered it significantly.[27] To this number could have been added the KPD's equivalent, the League for Anti-Fascist Struggle, which claimed over 100,000 members in the early 1930s.[28]

Furthermore, the fighting power of the SA was greatly exaggerated. It was often dependent on the police in its efforts to intimidate workers. In Berlin 'the SA never appeared *en masse* in a working class neighbourhood without police protection'.[29] As late as 22 January 1933 it required a massive police presence to guarantee the safety of a Nazi demonstration at the KPD's Berlin HQ.[30] Even in Nazi strongholds like Marburg the SA found it difficult to operate. In 1931, for example, the SA decided to invade the 'totally Red nest' of Ockershausen, a working class district of this predominantly middle class university town. They were met by residents who shouted:

'Now you're going to get it… You Nazi swine.' An hour before the assembly Social Democrats and Communists gathered in the Welhelmsplatz to march to Ockerhausen, where they quickly disrupted the Nazi assembly with catcalls and insults. When the leader of the assembly, an NSDStB [Nazi student] member, began to yell back, Reichsbanner members shouted, 'Social Democrats to the fore!' and charged. As fighting began, the police official Diederich immediately dissolved the assembly and had his men use rubber truncheons to restore order. Police then detained Nazi Party members in the hall and escorted them out of town while Ockershausen residents shouted, threw rocks, and finally prompted police to pull their guns.[31]

From within the Nazi Party, Krebs, the Hamburg Gauleiter, saw through the phoney claims of the Nazi leadership, as he later admitted:

What was completely misguided was to think that the SA and SS constituted something like a potential civil war army. Despite all their willingness to fight and be sacrificed, their combat power would have been utterly insignificant… You could fight meeting-hall battles with them but not an armed uprising. Yet it was remarkable how officials and high ministers seemed to have believed in such a danger… I do not doubt that it still would have been possible, even in 1931 and 1932, to eliminate the Nazis as a party organisation.[32]

This challenges Hitler's claim that the Nazi movement could only have been stopped if it had been ruthlessly crushed in the very earliest stages.[33]

This does not mean that the working class was yet in a position to mount a revolutionary overthrow of the capitalist state, as the KPD suggested at the time. Trotsky judged the balance between working class and Nazi forces when he wrote in 1931:

The main strength of the fascists is their strength in numbers. Yes, they have received many votes. But in the social struggle, votes are not decisive. The main army of fascism still consists of the petty bourgeoisie and the new middle class… On the scales of election statistics, 1,000 fascist votes weigh as much as 1,000 Communist votes. But on the scales of the revolutionary struggle 1,000 workers in one big factory represent a force 100 times greater than 1,000 petty officials, clerks, their wives, and their mothers-in-law. The great bulk of the fascists consists of human dust.[34]

It is a myth that all citizens have equal power and influence due to the franchise. The reality in Germany was that power was determined by social relations. On one side were the capitalists and their state, with control over the means of production and repression. In the centre were the petty bourgeoisie. These middle class masses were composed of isolated individuals incapable of maintaining a social force able to seize power. Hitler had learned this lesson in 1923 and his political strategy thereafter rested upon cajoling and blackmailing his way into power through ruling class channels.

When mobilised as in 1918 or 1920 the power of the working class to influence the situation and thwart ruling class intentions had been amply demonstrated. Even in the Depression it was this section who had, as Trotsky argued, 'the powerful means of production and transportation in their hands, who have been bound together by the conditions of their work into an army of iron, of coal, of railways, of electrical wires [and so would] prove to be immeasurably superior in the decisive struggle to Hitler's human dust'.[35] Until the Nazis were in possession of state power their lack of real social leverage remained a considerable weakness. Despite unemployment workers still were at the heart of production. There should have been no cause for despondency, because 'the organisational solidarity of the German workers...has almost altogether prevented until now the penetration of fascism into their ranks.' And this 'opens the very greatest possibility of defensive struggle'.[36]

What would this defence consist of? We have seen how progress was made in other countries when workers united together to combat the fascists. In Germany, with its high level of organisation, it was less likely that this would occur spontaneously. An organised united front of the key workers' institutions was needed. This did not imply the ignoring of political differences. If Germany's revolutionaries had dropped their principles to unite behind the crass parliamentarism of the SPD, the outcome would have been worthless. The arguments Trotsky directed at the KPD are worth quoting at length on this subject:

> Assuming a defensive position means a policy of closing ranks with the majority of the German working class and forming a united front with the Social Democratic and non-party workers against the fascist threat.
>
> Denying this threat, belittling it, failing to take it seriously is the greatest crime that can be committed today... The Communist Party must call for the defence of those material and moral positions which the working class has managed to win in the German state. This most directly concerns the fate of the workers' political organisations, trade unions, newspapers, printing plants, clubs, libraries etc. Communist workers must say to their Social Democratic counterparts: 'The policies of our parties are irreconcilably opposed; but if the fascists come tonight

to wreck your organisation's hall, we will come running, arms in hand
to help you. Will you promise us that if our organisation is threatened
you will rush to our aid?' This is the quintessence of our policy in the
present period.[17]

No united front was built in Germany. To see why we need to look
at the two dominant forces in the German labour movement, the
SPD and KPD.

The SPD and parliamentary fetishism

As a party deeply committed to reformism, the SPD sought to work
through the institutions of capitalism to deliver reforms beneficial for
its working class supporters. While the Social Democratic leaders and
ordinary members shared this common starting point, they were not
in the same social position. The rank and file regarded capitalist institutions such as parliament as a means to an end—the improvement
of their lives. For the leaders it was different. They were inside these
institutions themselves and derived their status from them. The massive commitment of the SPD to the structures of the German capitalist
state is shown by its position in 1928. It had 152 Reichstag deputies,
419 provincial deputies, 353 aldermen, 947 burgomasters, 1,109 village presidents, 4,278 sub-provincial deputies, 9,057 town council-
lors and 37,709 village deputies.[18]

In conditions of a stable and booming capitalism, a reformist strategy might serve the aspirations of the leadership in local and national
government and provide the reforms expected by the members. But
in Weimar Germany, racked as it was by crisis, revolution and counter-
revolution, what started out as a strategy to extract reforms through
capitalist institutions rapidly degenerated into a defence of these institutions, often from the very workers whom the SPD claimed to represent. This was evident from the earliest days when the SPD in
government used Freikorps troops not just against Communists and
revolutionaries but against strikers and ordinary SPD members. Still,
many workers continued to support the SPD out of loyalty and hope
of reforms in the future.

For the middle class, which was only beginning its move to the left
after the 1918 Revolution, the initial attraction of the SPD was rapidly
eroded. As one Nazi explained, 'We had all heard of liberty, peace, and
democracy, only to find that under Marxist rule reality differed from
these slogans'.[19] Of course, there was no Marxist rule at this time, but
the SPD's politics, which made it the principal proponent of Weimar's

capitalist state structure, allowed this slander to appear plausible. Thus Saxon Nazis were able to gloat over the fact that:

> The belief in the Reich, more specifically in the government, was eroded in the years after the November Revolution amongst the people... They too had heard the promises which were made at that time and...many even followed the Marxists because their agitators made most promises. Year after year [they] waited in vain for the promises of the various parties to be fulfilled. However, they saw with their own ears and eyes that things increasingly got worse...[40]

The problem did not disappear when the SPD was out of government, as was the case for most of the Weimar period, because the hope that the party would one day regain office was always present. Thus reformist leaders put defence of the existing order before that of the working class.

A tragic example of what this could lead to was seen in Berlin during May Day 1929 when the SPD police chief, Zörgiebel, banned the traditional workers' demonstrations. When the KPD defied the ban the police reacted brutally. Confrontations spread into the heart of workers' districts. The final death toll was over 30 people. None of them was a policeman, while at least six of the victims had been shot in their own homes. This was 'a concerted campaign to isolate and subdue particular sections of working class Berlin'.[41] Not long before the same police had protected a Nazi meeting from anti-fascist demonstrators when the SPD Prussian government lifted the speaking ban imposed on Hitler as a result of the Beer Hall Putsch.

Such harsh treatment was not meted out to Hindenburg or the chancellor he appointed when the SPD-led Grand Coalition was toppled in 1930. The SPD decided that Brüning's vicious deflationary policies, which clearly meant cuts in living standards of 10 to 15 percent, had to be 'tolerated'[42]: 'the SPD's post-1930 policy of always supporting the "lesser evil" was no tactical blunder; it was at the core of a party whose raison d'être depended on saving whatever was saveable of the parliamentary system'.[43] If the SPD was to be the doctor of an ailing capitalism the cure would be at the expense of its own supporters in the working class.

The effect on workers of putting the enemy first was deeply damaging and demoralising. After all, Brüning was appointed to dismantle the very democratic institutions which, though incapable of transforming capitalist society, provided the SPD with a platform and allowed the working class to exercise some pressure upon the system. An effective defence of the republic therefore depended on mobilising the working class against Brüning and his capitalist backers, not appeasing them. Therefore Winkler puts things the wrong way around by arguing that 'to be able to combat National Socialism effectively' the SPD had 'no alternative to the policy of toleration'.[44]

Party tactics were centred on defending its key power base—Prussia's SPD government; but far from protecting it, the toleration policy put it in jeopardy. Chancellor von Papen's coup against this stronghold on 20 July 1932 was a key event in the development of Nazism. A serious resistance would have made the ruling class think twice about accepting Hitler as chancellor because of the risk of revolt and civil war it might arouse. Goebbels was conscious of this when he wrote in his diary just afterwards, 'The Reds are overthrown. Their organisation put up no resistance. [They] have missed their great moment. It will never return'.[45]

The SPD leader's reaction to the coup revealed a pattern of submission and blind faith in parliamentarism that would characterise its action up to and beyond the Nazi assumption of power. On the day that von Papen acted, its newspaper, *Vorwärts*, carried the headline: 'Martial Law In Berlin! Our Answer—31 July!' (the date of the Reichstag election).[46] It continued:

> The struggle for the re-establishment of proper legal order in the German republic is henceforth to be pursued with all energy by electoral means. Through the ultimate decision of 31 July the German people can prepare to end the current situation which has arisen due to the collaboration of the Reich government and the National Socialists.

Then came the first of many calls for order and discipline which was really directed at preventing any action that might go beyond electoralism:

> Organisations are to be made ready for the highest level of struggle. More than ever the strongest discipline is demanded. Wild slogans from unauthorised sources must be resisted. Now concentrate all force on the victory of Social Democracy on 31 July.[47]

The 31 July 1932 Reichstag election witnessed the doubling of the Nazi vote. The 'highest level of struggle' that the bastions of Social Democratic organisation were permitted to take was to make a complaint about von Papen's action at the Supreme Constitutional Court!

As the year wore on the SPD made it clear that the Nazis, whose contempt for the republic's democratic institutions was notorious, would not be physically opposed as long as they played by the rules: 'The NSDAP obviously has the right to form a government if it can establish a majority in the Reichstag, as it hopes to do. That Social

Democracy will mount its strongest opposition to such a majority is also self evident'.[48] If the wolf 'obviously' has the right to control the flock, then it is 'self evident' that the sheep's 'strongest opposition' will be ineffective when it runs amok. The Nazis were not like any other party, but openly planned to smash and destroy any democratic structures, using the power of the state to do so. They could not be accorded equal rights to take over the state, but had to be opposed by every means at the disposal of the working class.

Despite its official statements, many in the SPD were alive to the terrible threat. By the end of 1931 pressure from below compelled the assembling of the Iron Front to coordinate the efforts of the Reichsbanner, SPD sporting organisations and trade unions. One activist told an Iron Front rally, 'The Socialists deserve to end up in the madhouse if they confront the fascists with democratic means alone,' while a shop stewards meeting heard that, 'if the others threaten civil war, we can't wave the peace palm; if the others spray bullets, we can't toss candy'.[49]

Among the rank and file the response to the new initiative was enthusiastic and thousands inscribed their names in the 'Iron Book'. Disillusioned former activists shook off their apathy, 'provincial ADGB officials described with wonder the drawing power of the new movement. Excitement gripped SPD districts of all political orientations'[50] and dozens of meetings were held to counter Nazi propaganda in the factories. Breitscheid, who led the SPD in the Reichstag, even proposed a united front against Nazism with the KPD. For reasons that will be clear further on, it was contemptuously rejected.[51]

The SPD leadership had its own ideas about the Iron Front. They insisted that it should be merely another arm of electoral propaganda and maintain the 'disciplined order' of the graveyard imposed on all its other organisations. Wels, the chair of the SPD, even questioned the idea of painting slogans and graffiti on walls because of its dubious legality![52] Very soon the SPD was tied up in the 1932 presidential election promoting the slogan 'Smash Hitler. Vote Hindenburg!' If an old reactionary general who had overthrown Reichstag democracy was sufficient to smash Hitler, then who needed the Iron Front? Given what would occur in January 1933, a more accurate slogan might have been 'Appoint Hitler chancellor—vote Hindenburg!'

Although the leadership's tactics were disastrous, they were sincerely worried about the Nazis coming to power, not least because of the clear threat this posed for the democratic structures of the republic. But if electoralism and relying on Hindenburg or the judges was the route to salvation there was no need for a united front of all the workers. Indeed, the SPD was frequently as hostile to the KPD as to the Nazis, seeing extreme left and extreme right as equally evil. The KPD did little to earn the SPD's friendship, but this did not justify the hostile attitude of the Social Democratic leaders.

In the run-up to the 1930 election *Vorwärts* denounced the 'National Communists'[53] and declared that 'a bosses' alliance has arisen —Nazis and Communists. Whoever votes for the Communists on 14 September serves the interests of the employers and helps reaction... A united front of Hitler-Thälmann-Goebbels-Heinz Neumann is thus established' (Thälmann and Neumann were KPD leaders).[54] Whatever disagreement there might have been between the SPD and KPD they both had everything to lose from the triumph of the Nazis. The SPD line was short sighted stupidity.

In spite of this the degree of shared existence and experiences that workers from both parties had at work and in the community meant that the policy of unity against the Nazis could have prevailed. As one ordinary SPD member put it, 'Of course we had our debates and our aims diverged... But the feeling remained that, by God, we are workers, you and I'.[55] In Berlin the Socialist Youth (SAJ) leader Schmidt argued that the KPD and SPD had much in common because, 'Just as the Sermon on the Mount stands at the centre of every Christian's beliefs, so for us does *The Communist Manifesto*'.[56] SAJ branches called themselves after Liebknecht and Luxemburg and in the summer of 1931 SAJ opposition to the right wing line of the SPD leadership led to its dissolution.[57]

However, the leadership line held sway to the bitter end. As late as 22 January 1933, when the KPD called for a united front, the SPD denounced it as a 'manoeuvre', and affirmed that 'only a genuine united front helps'.[58] The next day the paper said, 'Unity is needed! Unity, not united front manoeuvre.' In other words, the SPD and its supporters should remain united in inaction, rather than bring the working class together for active resistance to Nazism; and this one week before Hitler was appointed!

The tragic fate that awaited the SPD was not due to its inherent weakness. It had a vast and well organised structure with millions of adherents which compared favourably to Hitler's unstable and fractious movement. Its chief failure was to see scraps of paper cast into a ballot box as more important than real class activity. This error was not made by either the ruling class or the Nazi leadership. Both saw the Reichstag as merely one factor, and not the decisive one, in the overall class struggle. Unfortunately, it is often the case that reformists make exactly the same mistake when faced with Nazi movements today.

It was unlikely that the SPD leadership would willingly have entered into a united front, but they could have been pressurised into accepting one. For this to happen influence from outside the party was necessary. This ought to have been forthcoming from the Communist Party.

The KPD

In contrast to the SPD, the Communist Party was an avowedly revolutionary organisation and in theory should have been unencumbered by reformism when opposing Hitler. It was the only mass organisation that confronted Nazism directly. After 1929 the KPD membership threw itself into physical resistance to the SA. Street battles were fought all over the country with many dying or wounded. Thus Trotsky believed that 'the German Communist Party is governed by a sincere and burning aspiration to conquer the fascists, to break the masses away from their influence, to overthrow fascism and to crush it—of this, it is understood, there can be no doubt'.[59]

There were, however, severe problems with KPD tactics which were increasingly determined by Stalinist control exercised through the Communist International.[60] This process had involved the destruction of inner-party democracy and the establishment, at the 1929 party congress, of what one writer says amounted to a Communist version of the Führer (leader) cult. The appearance of the party leader, Thälmann, was greeted with a prolonged ovation and thrice repeated 'Heil Moskau!' while banners proclaimed him 'Führer of the German Proletariat'.[61]

The key element at the 1929 KPD congress was the concept of the 'Third Period'. According to this, following the initial revolutionary wave of 1918-23 and the 'stabilisation period' of 1924-28, world capitalism had entered a third and final stage of terminal crisis which would inevitably lead to its overthrow. Stalin adopted this line as left cover for his launching of the Five Year Plan of state capitalist industrialisation. Russian workers and peasants were asked to tolerate massive exploitation to help 'catch up and overtake' the West. The idea of revolution around the corner was useful in maintaining popular enthusiasm for this process.

Thälmann's address spoke of 'a new powerful revolutionary wave [which] was the fundamental characteristic of development at present'.[62] A congress resolution stated that 'the question of armed uprising has unavoidably entered on to the agenda'.[63] This judgement had very little to do with an objective assessment of the situation. Take the

KPD's reaction to the 1930 election which had catapulted the Nazis from obscurity to become the second largest Reichstag party. The KPD declared, 'The only victor in the September elections is the Communist Party'.[64] At the same time, the number of strike days was plummeting. By 1931 these were one tenth of the 1928 figure.[65] Yet a revolutionary offensive continued to form the basis of all policies.

If revolution was in prospect it followed that any party opposed to immediate uprising was objectively counter-revolutionary. While the Nazis were open counter-revolutionaries (or 'national fascists'), by this logic they differed little from the SPD who were hidden counter-revolutionaries, or 'social fascists'. The SPD were actually held to be more dangerous than the Nazis and the numerous Communists who dared to suggest the SPD was a 'lesser evil' were vigorously denounced, because 'Social Democracy is the main social support of the bourgeoisie' and plays 'an active role in the carrying through of the fascist dictatorship'.[66] By the same token 'a Social Democratic coalition government standing against a disarmed, divided and confused proletariat would be 1,000 times worse than an open fascist dictatorship which would be confronted by the proletarian masses united in class consciousness and determination to struggle'.[67] For the KPD, Remmele declared, 'We are not afraid of the fascists. They will shoot their bolt sooner than any other government'.[68]

In vain would Trotsky warn of the true consequences of Nazism: 'The coming to power of the National Socialists would mean first of all the extermination of the flower of the German proletariat, the destruction of its organisations'.[69] With chilling accuracy he prophesied that fascism 'will ride over your skulls and spines like a terrific tank'.[70]

This did not impress Thälmann. In November 1931 he explained that 'fascism will not begin when Hitler arrives; it began a long time ago'.[71] The KPD was 'the only anti-fascist party'[72] and those not of the KPD were fascists of one stripe or another. The more left wing they sounded, the more likely they were to divert the masses and so 'the most dangerous representatives of social fascism' were Trotskyists and other left groups such as the SAP (Socialist Workers' Party) or KPO (Communist Opposition).[73]

If fascism was everywhere, then it was impossible to find meaningful partners for a united front or distinguish where the real danger lay. The result was that the Communists adopted some positions that can only be described as lunatic. At first glance it might appear that these were blindly irrational and arbitrary; but on closer examination it becomes apparent that the key determinant of the twists and turns in policy was the attitude of Moscow.

Establishing this fact is important because there is a theory that the German working class was incapable of stopping Nazism and that 'the claim that there was a "left" alternative...has more to do with wishful thinking than historical analysis'.[74] Proponents of this suggest that the KPD's line was largely the result of 'social fragmentation of the working class'[75] and the 'general social historical nature of the republic [which] had substantially shaped the political culture of German Communism'.[76] While Third Period thinking may have made sense to some members, it is a mistake to portray its dominance as inevitable. It was not the inescapable consequence of the murder of Luxemburg and Liebknecht. Neither was it the result of the preponderance of desperate unemployed workers and 'a hardening of the division between the respective constituencies of the SPD and of the KPD' at a time when 'the Depression set worker against worker not simply in the political arena but in everyday life'.[77]

There were indeed political differences between the parties. Yet in the mid-1920s the KPD showed itself capable of cooperating where necessary with the murderers of Luxemburg and Liebknecht over issues like opposition to compensating German royal houses for loss of property. The benefits of joint KPD/SPD committees to prosecute this campaign were shown when 14.5 million people voted with them at a time when the parties' votes in elections added up to only 11 million.[78] As late as November 1928 four SPD cabinet ministers broke ranks to vote with the KPD in the Reichstag over arms spending.[79]

The grounds for stressing social divisions in everyday life appear to be stronger. At the height of the Depression the proportion of KPD members who were unemployed reached between 85 and 90 percent![80] The figure for the SPD is not known, but was probably closer to that affecting workers as a whole, which peaked at 44.4 percent in 1932.[81] Yet if the class background rather than immediate employment status is considered, the social composition of both parties was not so dissimilar.[82] The failure to create a united front against Nazism was fundamentally due to the respective leaderships: 'Political choices were not determined by social location within the working class'.[83]

Of course, unemployment produced potential conflicts in the class and 'conditioned Communists to accept "Third Period" policies...and militated against the success of a policy that relied on mass action and the exercise of economic pressure'.[84] However, the driving force for the KPD's ultra-left policies did not originate from the ordinary membership, and a different political leadership could have linked the struggles of employed and unemployed together against the common fascist enemy. Neither can the SPD's position be ascribed to its supporters' social situation. After all, the gulf separating the ordinary SPD member from Hindenburg's clique could not have been greater, yet this did not preclude Socialist toleration of the chancellors he appointed.

Above all, social composition cannot explain the actual fluctuations in KPD policy in the years between 1929 and 1933. This becomes clear if they are considered in a little detail. Weber notes seven distinct changes of tactic in the period and concludes that direct intervention by the Comintern accounts for no less than five of them.[85] The first phase of policy, which lasted until the end of March 1930, consisted of a blistering attack on the SPD, extending even to the factory committees, where the shop stewards were described as 'social fascists just like the bloodhounds Noske, Severing and Zörgiebel'.[86] Moscow feared in these, the last days of the Grand Coalition, that an SPD-led government would effect an alliance with France which would weaken its international position.

A change in line occurred when the Grand Coalition fell, and not before time; damage caused by the social fascist line had contributed to a decline in membership from 135,000 at the end of 1929 to 120,000.[87] The new position was still scarred by Third Period thinking, though it was now considered mistaken to describe ordinary members of the SPD as 'little Zörgiebels'. There was even talk of the need for a united front. However, it was to be a 'united front from below': 'We turn to the Social Democratic workers. They themselves may put our policies to the test, comparing our action within parliament and outside with the treacherous policies of their own party and their own leaders'.[88] Posing a united front as 'from below' rendered it meaningless. If SPD members had rejected the SPD leadership, then there was no need for a united front; they would join the KPD.

When the Communist International had elaborated the concept of the united front in the early 1920s it had been understood that a united front involved both reformist leaders and the reformist masses:

> Does the united front extend only to the working masses or does it also include the opportunist leaders?
>
> The very posing of this question is a product of misunderstanding.
>
> If we were able simply to unite the working masses around our own banner or around our practical immediate slogans, and skip over reformist organisations, whether party or trade union, that would of course be the best thing in the world. But then the very question of the united front would not exist in its present form.[89]

The KPD's united front 'from below' against fascism was bound to appear, to both reformist leaders and rank and file, as a cynical ploy to win members rather than unite the class, especially when couched in slogans like 'with the SPD workers against social fascism'[90] (ie their own leaders). In the Baden parliament the Communist deputies put theory into practice, moving a bill to ban the Iron Front, Reichsbanner and all Social Democratic organisations![91]

The next shift occurred when Moscow sought Russian-German cooperation to counter any potential German-French alliance. Now Germany was to be portrayed as a victim of Western powers and in need of 'national liberation'. At the very moment that the Nazis were making their electoral breakthrough, the KPD was adopting jargon not dissimilar to theirs. This was combined with attacks on 'corrupt Social Democracy' in language which would not have looked out of place in the *Völkische Beobachter*.[92]

Time and again the *Rote Fahne* claimed that it was a truer defender of the national interest than the Nazis, even coming close to anti-Semitic innuendo:

It is pointless the *Völkische Beobachter* complaining that the KPD steals National Socialist slogans. We are the mortal enemies of the NSDAP leaders who betray the people... Our programme is for the smashing of the Young chains [a scheme for paying war reparations] and the shameful Versailles Treaty. It is the programme of...the sharpest revolutionary struggle directed against Kirdorf and Thyssen and against Goldschmidt and Warburg [Jewish businessmen].[93]

Hitler was criticised for backing Mussolini in 'the national oppression of the Germans in South Tyrol... The Communist Party is the only party which struggles for national liberation'.[94]

It was not long before KPD leaders began thinking that they might win over NSDAP supporters. For example, on 18 May 1932 the KPD held a meeting which a Nazi speaker and 300 NSDAP supporters attended. In the debate Nazi arguments were countered in this way: 'The Nazis only want to overthrow a section (the Jewish section) of capitalism and leave the rest in existence, but Communism would uproot every last vestige of capitalism'.[95] Soon the slogan of *Volksrevolution* was being proposed. In German 'Volk' is a term which can mean people, nation or race. The Nazis saw themselves as part of a 'Völkisch' movement. So the KPD's slogan was deeply ambiguous. One outcome of this new approach was that the KPD won over a few Nazis, some even prominent, like Scheringer. An open letter appeared in *Rote Fahne*, the KPD daily, addressed to 'Working National Comrades' of the NSDAP and SA. It recorded that 'as honest fighters against the hunger system, the proletarian supporters of the NSDAP have joined the United Front of the proletariat and carried out their revolutionary duty'.[96] A KPD newspaper argued that due to the crisis the party would soon be 'enrolling the Nazi voters who belong to us in class terms in the anti-fascist, anti-capitalist front'.[97]

This was a serious mistake. Having rejected trade unions and the largest workers' political organisation, the SPD, as fascist, the KPD could no longer tell the difference between the partial class consciousness expressed in reformism and the rootless, deadly rage of SA boot boys which served counter-revolution. These latter would not be won by debate but by proving in practice that workers' interests could be defended and indeed advanced through socialist struggle. Instead, the KPD made repeated appeals to 'Nazi proletarians' who 'were sold out and betrayed by the SPD leaders'[98] and who 'could not be for the bootlickers of the international finance magnates... Your place is at the side of the KPD'.[99]

The worst example of this strategy came on 9 August 1931 in what the Nazis called the 'Volk's Referendum', but the KPD called the 'Red Referendum'. The idea of a vote to topple the SPD-led government in Prussia came from the Nazis and DNVP. At first the KPD Politburo voted unanimously against participation. Then Stalin and Molotov weighed in and forced the KPD to reconsider. Soon after, the party threw its efforts into the campaign, working alongside the Nazis and claiming that a big vote would 'be a great victory against fascism'.[100] But few would have believed Thälmann's defence that this was 'not a united front with the mortal enemies of the working class'.[101]

Trotsky was appalled by the KPD's action. In a conflict between the SPD and Nazis, revolutionaries could not be neutral or, still worse, support the Nazis! While he stressed that the reformist SPD helped protect capitalism from revolution, in no way did that mean that it was equivalent to the Nazis:

> These two systems: the one parliamentary-democratic, the other fascist, derive their support from different combinations of the oppressed and exploited classes; and they unavoidably come to a sharp clash with each other.
>
> Social Democracy, which is today the chief representative of the parliamentary-bourgeois regime, derives its support from the workers. Fascism is supported by the petty bourgeoisie. Social Democracy without the mass organisations of the workers can have no influence. Fascism cannot entrench itself in power without annihilating the workers' organisations. Parliament is the main arena of Social Democracy. The system of fascism is based upon the destruction of parliamentarism.[102]

Only 37 percent voted to overthrow the Prussian government and so the job was eventually carried out by von Papen's decree instead.[103] It is not the case that the KPD leadership's line was popular with the rank and file. The vote of 37 percent represented considerably fewer people than the 47.5 percent combined vote of the pro-referendum parties in the Reichstag election, and it is likely that the main abstentions came from the Communists. As a KPD official admitted, in the party's key strongholds:

> A comparison with the last Reichstag election shows that on no occasion did the Communists on 9 August bring out even half of their supporters. Only in the mainly agricultural districts—classic electoral deserts for the KPD—did the pro-referendum parties exceed their September 1930 results.[104]

The leadership might denounce those Communists who saw the SPD as 'the lesser evil' when compared to the Nazis, but as one ordinary member from Brandenburg put it, 'We will do what we want here'.[105]

By April 1932 the pendulum was swinging back towards what this time almost amounted to a genuine KPD appeal for a united front: 'We are ready to work with any organisation which has workers backing... in a common struggle'.[106] Thälmann added, 'A united front from below and above [with the SPD] is not excluded'[107] and an 'Anti-Fascist Action' movement was launched. Soon the Comintern was becoming afraid that the enthusiasm was going too far and warning against this 'opportunist excrescence'.[108] As the July 1932 Reichstag elections approached the KPD leaders wanted to sharply differentiate themselves from their SPD rivals and so Anti-Fascist Action was converted into a propagandist platform for the KPD: 'Anti-Fascist Action means untiring daily exposure of the shameless, treacherous role of the SPD and ADGB leaders who are the direct filthy helpers of fascism'.[109]

On the day von Papen's coup against Prussia occurred the KPD's newpaper wrote of a united front 'from Wels [of the SPD] to Hitler'.[110] It did call for a general strike but Thälmann simultaneously warned against the 'dangerous...tendency towards unity in the working class [and] dangerous ideas such as "unity above all leaders".'[111] The July 1932 Reichstag election was reported as 'magnificent electoral victory of the KPD'.[112] No mention was made of the NSDAP's doubling of its vote to 13 million.

In the autumn of 1932 a Comintern plenum announced yet another 'new turn' which produced 'a sort of united front from below' with Nazis![113] In November 1932 this took practical shape in an unofficial pay strike among the 22,000 strong Berlin transport workforce.[114] While the strike had considerable support, the KPD wanted to use it to discredit the trade union officials. This played directly into the hands of the Nazis who, at this time, were keen on posing as radicals in order to bully their way into power. The strike committee included four NSBO members out of 22.[115]

Eventually, after three deaths, 60 injured and 500 arrests[116] the dispute was called off, but the KPD celebrated it as 'a real united front in which the Revolutionary Trade Union Opposition (RGO) managed to forge together Communist, Social Democrat, National Socialist and non-party workers'.[117] For its part, the NSBO saw the strike as:

> National Socialists and Communists struggling in comradeship, united in a belief in their own power, inspired by the will to save their homeland and people under the leadership of Adolf Hitler.[118]

In his diary, however, Goebbels gloated, 'We have broken the Berlin transport strike'.[119]

Not only had the KPD contributed to paralysing the whole working class, it had, despite numerical growth, seriously undermined its own strength. It is true that the party's share of the Reichstag vote rose from 11 percent in 1928 to 17 percent in November 1932,[120] but in terms of the party's implantation and influence in the working class, decline had been dramatic. This was not only the result of unemployment but of a disastrous attitude to organisation and activity in the workplace.

In 1930 the Communist RGO, which represented around 18 percent of the ADGB membership,[121] adopted the slogan, 'Out of the Free Unions'. *Rote Fahne* published a series of five articles on 'German trade unions on their way to becoming Mussolini's syndicates'.[122] If the revolutionary tide had been rising, as predicted, then masses of workers would flood from the SPD-dominated ADGB to the RGO. Of course, the reverse was the case, with the hammer blows of the Depression making workers cling to the organisations they already had. The net result was to cripple KPD activity within the trade union movement. In the 1931 ADGB congress not a single Communist delegate was present among the 307 who assembled,[123] while the RGO could only claim 4 percent support in factory committees as against 84 percent for the ADGB.[124] In mid-1932 a less ultra-left tone was adopted in line with the Anti-Fascist Action policy. RGO members were enjoined 'not to give up posts of struggle'.[125] It now emerged that far from enthusiastically following the Third Period insanity ordinary KPD members had mostly ignored the earlier call to quit the unions.[126] Fortunately, as Merker of the RGO complained:

Numerous Communists see the social fascist factory committees and trade union officers as comrades who are fighting for the same goal— socialism… Numerous Communists do not see the social fascist functionaries, and in particular the 'honourable' reformists as the main enemy.[127]

Despite the sense shown by some members on the ground, the ultra-left Third Period line inevitably led to adventurist tactics. One example was the Ruhr miners' strike the KPD called in early 1931. At its height the RGO succeeded in getting only 15 percent of miners out. To hold a minority strike would be disastrous at any time. It was particularly misguided in the middle of a Depression. At the Hibernia mine, for example, just 177 miners struck—15 were immediately sacked, including seven shop stewards. At Concordia the Communist convenor managed to win 22 percent support for the strike, at the cost of his job. After one day just 7 percent, or 1,500 people, were still off work and all of these were sacked.[128] On the national scale the KPD called for general strikes no less than seven times between 1929 and 1932.[129] The first time this was done a single factory came out. After this not even that level of response was forthcoming.[130] This was a classic case of crying wolf; for when Hitler came to power the general strike call which, with a different history, might have been taken up, was simply ignored.

Adventurism on the industrial field was accompanied by adventurism in the streets where the mass of Communist members were now concentrated as a result of unemployment. The KPD which had 2,000 street cells in 1926 had 6,200 by 1931.[131] Sectarian politics meant that there was little attempt to relate this force to the still functioning collective organisation in the workplaces. Instead it became focused on tit for tat street fights with the SA. At the height of the Anti-Fascist Action campaign the slogan 'Strike the fascists wherever you meet them' meant that activity degenerated quickly into 'squadism'—individualistic acts which failed to involve the organised working class. This generated its own momentum and when the leadership criticised those involved, the response was, 'We do not only want mass struggle, but individual terror!'[132]

In the case of both the SPD and KPD the respective leaderships had adopted utterly disastrous policies which prevented an effective response to the growth of Nazism. It is clear that when the opportunity was opened up for a positive way forward, for example with the launching of the Iron Front by the SPD, or a less ultra-left attitude on the part of the KPD, the memberships of both organisations had been enthusiastic.

On the political level too there were analyses of fascism which clearly went beyond the sterile viewpoints of the SPD and KPD leaders and pointed out the mortal danger of Nazism. This account has concentrated on Trotsky's arguments, but Thalheimer of the Brandlerites, the Austro-Marxist Bauer, and Togliatti of the Italian Communists all made contributions to an understanding of fascism.

There were also sporadic efforts to overcome the fatal division of active forces in the face of Nazism. In Brunswick the murder of a young worker by Nazis led to mass strikes and a demonstration of 10,000 in January 1932.[133] In July 1932 there were brief stoppages in the suburbs of Berlin against fascist murders and in Düsseldorf transport workers struck against the presence of SA men.[134] The Communist leader Münzenberg wrote that 'this united front will spring up all at once, elementally, under the pressure of increased fascist terror and fascist attacks'.[135] An example of this potential was the proposal by the Zehlendorf Reichsbanner for a united defence of workers' organisations and individuals. Alas, it was dismissed because 'it did not include measures against capitalist exploitation and fascism, but only technical measures for defence against Nazi terror. The key task in the present struggle against fascism is to fight the Brüning dictatorship and the [SPD] Prussian government'.[136] This meant that no precedent was set by these examples.

Other left wing groups lacked the influence necessary to break the logjam. Trotskyists, who numbered only 230 nationally[137] managed to encourage united front defensive organisation in two tiny German towns—Bruchsal and Klingenthal.[138] Alas, these examples could have minimal impact on the mighty structures of the SPD and KPD. Although on a different scale and in a different period, in Britain the Anti Nazi League showed, during the 1970s and more recently, that a small organisation of a few thousand such as the Socialist Workers Party could forge a united front with much larger organisations and involve numbers stretching into the hundreds of thousands in the process.[139] Alas, even such a small core was lacking for the German Trotskyists.

Reactions to Nazism in power

When Hitler was appointed on 30 January 1933 the die had still not been cast. The enemy, wrote Trotsky, had occupied 'an entire series of commanding posts...but there has been no battle as yet. The occupation of advantageous positions decides nothing by itself—it is the living forces that decide'.[140] Workers' organisations were still intact, with millions in left wing parties and trade unions. Even the Nazis were unsure of how quickly they could attack:

> Much evidence suggests that the new government of the Reich wanted to proceed with caution in this conflict and was concerned above all to avoid a general strike or civil war. At the beginning of March, for example, Reich labour minister Franz Seldte had drafts of laws prepared with the aid of which the power of the independent economic organisations of the working class was to be gradually reduced... These measures reflected views which had been current in conservative entrepreneurial circles for a long time, but they did not entail the immediate destruction of the working class movement.[141]

The reaction of the labour movement in the critical hours and days after 30 January was therefore critical. The left parties and unions did slowly awake to the true horror of their situation, but the political dogmas which had paralysed them did not dissolve easily. As a result there was what Trotsky called 'undoubtedly the greatest defeat of the working class in history'.[142]

The SPD

The SPD executive and Reichstag deputies met on 30 January and the following surreal exchanges took place:

> Breitscheid: 'The greatest difficulty comes from the Communists. It seems impossible to undertake any common political work with them because after two or three days they will again denounce us as traitors.'
> Braun: 'The people have elected a parliament the majority of which is disposed to anti-parliamentarism. We stand for the idea that in a democratic state the will of the people must decide...'
>
> It seemed to him that the East Elbian [Junker] ruling class, which was very influential, will not let the house painter [Hitler] hold power.

Aufhäuser alone injected a sense of urgency into the proceedings:

> It would be impossible to assemble the Iron Front and instruct it to bide its time. We have already done that for too long.

He rejected waiting any longer.

> The 20 July [coup against Prussia] had already been a great disappointment and we dare not let things go so far that we missed the critical moment when we had to act. We must now set out the line for defensive struggle.

But Hilferding replied that the only correct slogan was 'dissolution of parliament and new elections':

> He was surprised an argument against waiting had been advanced: 'If we carried out a defensive strike the SA would certainly be incorporated into the army and the result would be an armed revolt [against us]. Extra-parliamentary action is still not on the agenda'.[143]

The next day Breitscheid took the argument for passivity further:

> It is conceivable that in initial discussions people will talk of extra-parliamentary actions and air the question of mass strikes, individual strikes and marches of one sort or another to 'demonstrate in public'.
>
> We put the issue the other way around. Is this the moment for great extra-parliamentary action?... People talk of the possibility of undertaking a brief general strike. Could we expect success?... It could only open us to the danger when we and the unions call for a return to work, that the Communists would fall on our backs and say that the revolution must be carried forward. A section of our supporters could let itself be influenced by this; and then a movement would exist that would be confronted by both state power and the army which would drown the workers in blood... We stress the need for unity of the working class, but there should be no talk of unity with the Communist Party and their people.[144]

One speaker warned that if the KPD was banned its members might seek refuge in the ranks of the SPD. The way would have to be barred to them.[145]

The SPD strategy was summed up by Wels: 'Our foes will perish through our legality'.[146] With Hitler poised to destroy parliament, parliamentary cretinism of this sort was absolutely disastrous and the repression could not be ignored.[147] A united front to resist this onslaught was becoming unavoidable and tentative indirect negotiations were held with the KPD. On 28 February, the day the two parties were scheduled to meet face to face, the KPD was violently suppressed as a result of the Reichstag fire; discussions ended indefinitely. At the same time the SPD press was closed down, never to legally appear again.[148]

In his diary entry of 1 February 1933 Goebbels recorded a conversation with Hitler who said that 'for the moment we will abstain from any counter-measures against the Red terror'.[149] But after a week of SPD grovelling it is no wonder that he could write:

> A group of Red bosses have been taken out by Goering, amongst whom is the Chief President of Hanover, Noske. How small these pygmies are, whom a mocking fate has set up as our opponents. They present no

resistance and hardly seem ruffled, only asking if one will pay the costs of their change of residence.[150]

That this ignominious rout was not inevitable but due to appalling leadership is brought out in Allen's excellent account of a small town he called Northeim. No doubt the same story would apply to countless other places in Germany.

> One has to ask the question, what happened to those who had sworn resistance?... The Reichsbanner was destroyed without a single blow struck in its defense. The Reichsbanner, with all its plans for instant mobilisation, had its members struck down one by one, its leaders imprisoned, beaten, hounded from their jobs and their homes without any resistance from the organisation as a whole... The Northeimer Reichsbanner itself was ready to fight in 1933. All it needed was the order from Berlin. Had it been given, Northeim's Reichsbanner members would have carried out the tested plan they had worked on so long—to obtain and distribute weapons and to crush the Nazis. But Northeim's Reichsbanner would not act on its own... They felt that their only hope was in common action, all together, all over the Reich... So they waited and prayed for the order to come but it never did. And while they waited the Nazis began tracking them down, one by one.[151]

Elsewhere too the movement waited for a lead. Just the day before Hitler's appointment a huge SPD rally had proclaimed that 'Berlin remains Red!' and symbols of the Iron Front were worn.[152] Although the Socialist Youth were expressly forbidden to organise underground activity, they resorted to stealing duplicators and typewriters from SPD offices to avoid their seizure by the Nazis.[153] Rejecting the sectarian attitudes of the leadership, rank and file SPD and KPD members formed mixed underground groups in Hanover, Hildesheim, Leipzig, Magdeburg, Rostock, Stuttgart and at least ten other towns.[154]

Overall, however, the central leadership prevailed. All efforts were directed towards the 5 March election which the party had wished for, and which, obligingly, Hitler proposed. However, he made sure this was no ordinary election. The full force of Nazi violence was hurled against opponents in order to intimidate and put them in awe of state power. Given the harassment meted out to the SPD and its supporters the party performed well, losing only 70,000 of the votes it had had in November and gaining 18 percent of the total.[155] Yet even in parliamentary terms this was a totally inadequate result. The SPD had vainly hoped that the NSDAP's loss of two million votes seen in November 1932 would be repeated: 'The Nazis believe that in a flag-waving atmosphere they can drag their vote up. Are they not deceiving themselves?'[156] Alas, no. The deception was on the other side. The rigged Nazi vote rose to 44 percent, though this was still short of an absolute majority.

On 23 March Hitler rammed through an Enabling Act granting dictatorial powers. This was achieved by excluding the 81-strong KPD contingent and threatening dire consequences for any Reichstag deputy who voted against. Only the SPD opposed, although many of its deputies were arrested, in hiding, fled abroad or were hospitalised by the SA. It fell to Wels to present the only expression of resistance to Nazis plans: 'No Enabling Act will give you the power to destroy ideas which are perennial and indestructible'.[157] Maybe so, but the proponents of passivity personally paid for their policy of trusting the constitution to defend them. Thus Hilferding died in a Gestapo prison, allegedly by his own hand, while Breitscheid was killed at Buchenwald.[158]

Even Wels's stand over the Enabling Act was atypically bold. The SPD leaders hoped to survive by submitting to Nazi pressure. So when Goering complained about 'false' stories of Nazi violence in the foreign socialist press, Wels begged these papers to stop their reports. They refused and the SPD quit the Socialist International (the international organisation of social democratic parties).[159] On 17 May 1933 Hitler, ever the audacious hypocrite, put forward a 'peace resolution' designed to cover his warlike intentions. Although Nazi Minister of the Interior Frick said, 'We don't care if the Social Democrats agreed to the resolution or not',[160] the SPD Reichstag fraction voted for the motion, declaring this 'was no vote of confidence in the Hitler government'.[161] Only three deputies, including Pfülf refused to vote.

> When the Social Democratic deputies rose as a body to vote with the bourgeois parties, the chamber, including Hitler, broke into a storm of applause. The German Nationalists burst into 'Deutschland, Deutschland, über Alles', and many Social Democrats joined in. Hoegner later reflected, 'It was as if we Social Democrats, ever cursed as the prodigal sons of the fatherland, for one eternal moment clasped Mother Germany to our hearts.' Three weeks later, unable to bear the collapse of her party, Toni Pfülf committed suicide.[162]

On 23 June 1933 the SPD was banned in perpetuity.

The KPD

The KPD's reaction was the mirror opposite of the SPD's fatalism. While the larger party held its forces in reserve for the call that never came, the KPD cried out for 'ceaseless mass action of all types, in all areas...an unbroken chain of mass resistance and mass struggle, the one flowing into the other'.[163] Though there was a call for a united front 'from above and below',[164] its tone was guaranteed to produce a rejection: 'We'll whip the masses who are still in the ranks of the class enemy parties, and stir them up against their leaders and enrol them in the revolutionary freedom front'.[165] Those who demanded an end to sectarianism were expelled.[166] Third Period politics ensured that these strategies came to nothing. The call for for a general strike fell on deaf ears. Meetings and demonstrations in Stuttgart, Frankfurt and Lübeck soon petered out, as did dockers' strikes in the north.[167] It seems that the largest general strike movement led by Communists occurred in a tiny town of just 4,000 inhabitants—Mossingen.[168]

The party leadership suffered from a sort of political schizophrenia. On the one hand it was convinced that Hitler coming to power 'would ripen the working class for higher struggle',[169] and the Comintern reinforced this optimism: 'The workers would realise that Nazism offered Germany no way out of its difficulties, and would then turn to the KPD—"after Hitler, our turn"'.[170] The very appointment of Hitler was taken as a sign of the KPD's growing power: 'Our strength forced the bourgeoisie's hand, so they got rid of [von] Papen and brought in Hitler. This positive judgement must be the starting point for our higher revolutionary struggle'.[171] However, harsh reality sometimes broke through the dogma. On 2 February the Nazis marched up to Karl Liebknecht House, the KPD's headquarters, and police occupied it. Two days later a decree on the 'defence of the German people' began an all out offensive. The number of murders multiplied. By 7 February, at a secret conference, Thälmann admitted, in the midst of a speech full of bravado, that 'the party is threatened with extinction',[172] and 'we don't underestimate the terrible danger'.[173] But since revolution was an immediate prospect the policy must be to use 'all forms of political and economic daily struggle and activities—partial struggle, partial strikes, etc—to set a decisive course to the political general strike. Our slogan: strike, mass strike, general strike'.[174]

This was tragic posturing. It had no effect on the Nazi terror machine whose programme was set out by Goering, now Prussian Minister of the Interior:

> Fellow Germans, my measures will not be crippled by any judicial thinking... Here I don't have to worry about justice, my mission is only to destroy and exterminate, nothing more... Certainly, I shall use the power of the state and the police to the utmost, my dear Communists, so don't draw any false conclusions; but the struggle to the

death, in which my fist will grasp your necks, I shall lead with those down there—the Brownshirts.[175]

On 17 February Goering issued explicit orders for a police shoot-to-kill policy against Communists, warning that 'whoever misguidedly fails in this duty' faced 'disciplinary action'.[176] The last legal KPD assembly was on 25 February. Two days later the Reichstag building was burned down. A Dutch Communist was held responsible on dubious evidence, and that very night an order to arrest 4,000 leading Communists was issued. The KPD had called everyone from Brüning to the Social Democrats and Trotskyists 'fascists'. It was discovering the truth the hard way.

In vain did Trotsky, with practically no supporters in Germany, criticise both the KPD and SPD approach: 'The unhappy fact of the matter is that the proletariat is not on the defensive, but in a retreat which tomorrow may be turned into a panicky rout. We summon the proletariat not to the offensive but to an active defence'.[177]

Trade unions

As disaster followed upon disaster it was left to the trade union officials, who still led 5.5 million workers,[178] to create the ultimate cataclysm. They hoped to escape the bloody fate of the left parties by passivity and by turning their backs on politics. 'Organisation, not demonstration—this is the slogan of the hour,' said Leipart, ADGB leader.[179] Capitulation was absolute. There was some resistance to this on the ground, with some 160 strikes occurring between March and early April, usually in response to the arrest of shop stewards.[180] However, this was far too limited to have any real impact, or even to slow the pace of the betrayal.

The joint trade union council comprising all the key union federations drew up a draft statement which said:

> The national revolution has created a new state. This fact makes it necessary that every German of every rank define their attitude to this state. In wrestling with the new situation parties and one-sided interest groups are of no account. Only that which has inner health, which is rooted in nationhood, can survive. It speaks for the vitality, for the healthy nationhood of the German unions, that their life force remains undiminished.
>
> The German trade unions are conscious that the new structure of race and nation puts demands on them. They consider that by consciously integrating into the new structure they can have a decisive influence on the future of the German people... Due to this racial unity and will to power there can be no toleration of class-based hostility nor distracting internationalism.[181]

The ADGB, the main trade union federation, had been created and sustained by the SPD for 50 years. Yet it too abased itself: 'The trade unions realise that their own movement for freedom must recognise that it is limited by the higher right of the state as representative of the whole folk community. The state must have the right to intervene to order and regulate the economy'.[182] This grovelling had little effect. By the beginning of April 1933 at least 160 union offices had been wrecked by the SA, the SS and the police.[183] Worse was to come. When, in a cynical move, the Nazis made 1 May a national holiday, the official ADGB journal carried this disgusting article:

> There is really no need to admit to 'capitulation' when we say that the vic-tory of National Socialism is also our victory, even if it occurred through struggle against a party which we regarded as the bearer of socialism...
>
> ### From The International Day To The National Holiday
>
> We believe we have shown that the promotion of May Day, the proletarian workers' holiday, into a national holiday is no defeat, but means a victory of proletarian thinking. But has there been a basic his-torical change if 1 May no longer has an internationalist character? ... That might be so for a small group of utopian internationalists who have not been influenced by the plain reality of the German labour movement... An anti-national internationalism has never had a foothold in the mass of the German working class.
>
> ### From Proletarian Socialism To German Socialism[184]

The ADGB presented the 1 May holiday as a concession to labour, a day on which 'the German people will unconditionally show its sol-idarity with the workers'.[185]

A description of the march in Gagganau shows how May Day was really 'celebrated':

> The morning of the holiday was particularly impressive at the Daimler-Benz Company... Director Baron von Jungenfeld stepped up to the platform which was flanked by two NSBO flags. Obviously moved, grasping the meaning of this moment, he made a speech to the folk comrades [the Nazi term of greeting]...about how the meaning of May Day had been quite wiped out and faded away before the solemn creed of the nation... Baron von Jungenfeld ended his speech with a 'Sieg Heil' to the new Germany of labour, and the strains of 'Deutschland, Deutschland über alles, über alles in der Welt' joyously rang out from over 3,000 throats as they sang the oath to the fatherland.[186]

The very next day the combined forces of the state and the Nazi

Party smashed their way into every trade union office in Germany, assaulting officials and dragging many off to concentration camps. Half a century of work wiped out in 24 hours!

The working class in Germany had the potential to stop the 'human dust' of the Nazi Party from gaining state power and destroying its institutions. Although the Depression meant struggle had to start at the level of defence, uniting forces around the issue of combating fascism, it was above all political failures within the SPD, KPD and unions that caused the damage. Not only was there no defence, the major setback represented by Hitler's appointment as chancellor rapidly turned into a catastrophic rout of world historic proportions. This would make the arduous job of rebuilding the labour movement and generating a resistance to Nazism incredibly difficult.

Chapter 6

1933-34: a Brown revolution?

Nazism was a class phenomenon that within the framework of capitalist society represented a counter-revolutionary force. Today this has become an unpopular view. For example, Schoenbaum's book on Nazi society is called *Hitler's Social Revolution*.[1] Recently Zitelmann has gone even further. In his book, entitled *Hitler: The Self Consciousness of a Revolutionary*[2] he declares that 'his violent hard line position was not simply directed against Jews and Communists, but above all against bourgeois forces'.[3] Such an emphasis matches the Nazis' own insistently repeated claims. In 1937, for example, Hitler declared:

> Surely nobody will doubt the fact that during the last four years a revolution of the most momentous character has passed like a storm over Germany... For the National Socialist revolution was in itself a revolution in the revolutionary tradition.[4]

There are those who rightly reject the notion that Nazism brought about a social revolution, but suggest instead that it initiated a 'third way' or 'racial revolution':

> The Nazi period in German history was a unique phenomenon which, though containing both traditional and modern elements in chaotic relationship, must nevertheless be seen primarily as a racial revolution of an entirely new kind...it does not seem to me very helpful to trivialise it as a mere 'abortive' revolution or as a 'counter-revolution': it should be regarded as an alternative revolution to the existing Marxist-Leninist project.[5]

Others believe Nazism created a 'revolutionary thrust into the modern'.[6] This 'modernisation thesis' receives broad support. It states that 'Nazism represented a distinct mode of dealing with and instrumentalising modernity [through] terror, progress and upward mobility'.[7]

The argument about the character of the Nazi takeover of power is not simply a dispute about how the word 'revolution' is defined but much more. It can only be resolved by looking at the historical evidence.

What was the character of the actual policies that the Nazis carried out at this time? In contrast to the above, this chapter will argue that the Nazi takeover certainly constituted a major transformation, but one that served to buttress existing social relations rather than to undermine them. While leading Nazis followed a unique path to reach this goal and feathered their own nests in the process, the goal itself was essentially the defence and promotion of German capitalism by the most brutal and systematic methods imaginable—counter-revolution at home and, later, world war abroad.

This does not mean that after 1933 Nazism was simply a tool of the direct economic interests of the capitalist class. It was distinguished from other pro-capitalist parties by its direct counter-revolutionary methods and by the fact that it was a mass movement. Consequently its leaders had relative, but by no means absolute, autonomy.

The practice of counter-revolution

The NSDAP's counter-revolutionary zeal did not diminish once Hitler became chancellor in January 1933. On 1 March Goering claimed that 'to exterminate Communism…will be my noblest task',[8] while Goebbels vowed that 1933 would strike the French revolutionary year of 1789 out of history.[9] In May Hitler said, 'I regard it as my task before posterity to destroy Marxism, and that is no empty phrase but a solemn oath which I shall perform as long as I live'.[10] By new year 1934 he claimed, 'The great life task which I had set before myself was completed in barely six months! Marxism was destroyed and Communism laid in the dust. Fourteen years long have I preached the necessity of conquering this doctrine of madness'.[11]

On the international scale there have been many examples of dictatorships attacking and destroying labour movements. In the strict sense of the term, many such dictatorships are not fascist, though they may use violent methods popularly identified with fascism. The manner by which the suppression of the labour movement was accomplished in Germany revealed the unique nature of fascism—it was carried out with a thoroughness in both breadth and depth which set it apart from almost any other counter-revolutionary process. This was due to the Nazi Party's mass roots, its millions of supporters and huge activist core.

Direct repression involved the destruction of the KPD, SPD and trade unions. At the opening of the first official concentration camp at Dachau, Himmler explained that it was designed for 'the entire Communist and—if necessary—Reichsbanner and Marxist functionary groups'.[12] Parallel to this was the process called *Gleichschaltung*. This is an untranslatable word, but is often rendered in English as 'coordination'. 'Nazification' might be more appropriate. Looked at superficially, *Gleichschaltung* appears to have been directed at bringing under full Nazi control all sectors of society outside of itself—whether local government, social institutions or rival political groups.

This has given rise to the notion that Nazism was independent of, and hostile to, all the existing social forces, that it was bent on founding a totalitarian system opposed to both communism and capitalism. This is incorrect. Totalitarianism might be a useful shorthand term to describe a certain form of state rule; it does not explain the social content or driving force behind that rule. Today there are many totalitarian states where all parties, bourgeois ones included, are violently suppressed, and yet these states co-exist perfectly happily with capitalism. The same applied in Germany where the creation of the one party Nazi dictatorship was, in fact, a necessary element in its counter-revolutionary defence of capitalism, not a challenge to it.

In appointing Hitler, the conservative elite around von Papen and Hindenburg had planned to co-opt his supporters in order to stabilise their rule and, through controlled counter-revolutionary action, to tilt the social balance still further against the working class. To this limited end, the Nazis received just three posts in an 11 strong coalition cabinet—chancellor (Hitler), minister of the interior (Frick) and minister without portfolio (Goering). Key posts such as foreign minister and defence minister (with control of the army) were given to Hindenburg's own nominees—von Neurath and von Blomberg. The main economic post was handed to Hugenberg of the DNVP. Von Papen boasted that 'it is we who engaged him... In two months we'll have pushed Hitler so far into the corner that he'll squeal'.[13] This proved entirely wrong. Hugenberg later admitted that participation in Hitler's cabinet was 'the greatest stupidity of my life'.[14]

The swift establishment of the Nazi monopoly of power has been portrayed as almost a historical accident, the result of duplicity by Nazis and weak characters like von Papen. It is true that, 'Hitler and his supporters were to demonstrate a cynicism and lack of scruple—qualities on which his partners particularly prided themselves—which left von Papen and Hugenberg gasping for breath',[15] but it is mistaken to conclude from this that the key issue was that 'the history of National Socialism from beginning to end is the history of its underestimation'.[16] Though personalities played a role, the problem lay with deeper social forces.

Taylor's eloquent analogy explains the process rather better:

In January 1933 the German upper classes imagined that they had taken Hitler prisoner. They were mistaken. They soon found that they were in the position of a factory owner who employs a gang of roughs to break up a strike: he deplores the violence, is sorry for his workpeople who are being beaten up, and intensely dislikes the bad manners of the gangster leader whom he has called in. All the same, he pays the price and discovers, soon enough, that if he does not pay the price (later, even if he does) he will be shot in the back. The gangster chief sits in the managing director's office, smokes his cigars, finally takes over the concern himself.[17]

It was the counter-revolution that sidelined von Papen and Hugenberg. The wiping out of all bourgeois political rivals to Nazism was a necessary by-product since total political subordination to the Nazi project was essential to its success.

The first thing to go would be the last vestiges of democracy. Goering, as Reichstag president, declared that the 5 March election was 'bound to be the last in ten years, and presumably in 100'.[18] The campaign itself was bloody, with 69 political murders taking place.[19] The neutering of the Reichstag by the Enabling Act immediately deprived the electoralist parties of their principal field of activity. The way it was passed was typical of the Nazis' style. The deputies (minus the outlawed KPD) had to push their way through crowds of SS men to reach the chamber. When they arrived they were confronted by a platform draped with a huge swastika flag and a gallery filled with Stormtroopers. As the debate proceeded, Nazis outside could be heard chanting, 'We want the bill—or fire and murder'.[20]

The bourgeois parties were not allowed to wither away peacefully. Dating from the Weimar period, these groupings had shown themselves unwilling or incapable of physically liquidating the labour movement, preferring to contain it through negotiation or manoeuvres in the Reichstag chamber and local parliaments. This would no longer be tolerated so, to ensure there would be no space for any resistance, the DNVP, DVP, DDP and Centre were leant upon by the SA.

It might be argued that these parties perished because the Nazis feared them as rivals for state power; there may be some truth in this. However, in 'normal' parliamentary politics there is often intense rivalry between competing parties, but elimination of individual contenders is not the result. As Broszat points out, it was as a by-product of wiping out the left (ie counter-revolution) that the bourgeois parties succumbed:

The violent elimination of the left would inevitably give expression to the superior numerical and physical power of the Nazi movement against the remaining middle and right wing parties and so prepare their capitulation.[21]

So it was that the smashing of the left immediately preceded the demise of the old right. The main blows against the KPD followed the Reichstag fire of 27 February. In the next two and a half weeks there were 7,784 arrests under emergency laws in the main districts of Prussia alone. Some 95 percent of these were Communists.[22] On 20 March, Himmler announced that the SS was opening the first official concentration camp at Dachau. 'Wild' concentration camps in the cellars and basements of buildings had been operated from the very first by the Stormtroopers. On 31 March hanging was restored for 'crimes against public security'. On 4 April this became applicable to 'political crimes'.[23] On 8 March the SA and SS occupied SPD and union buildings. Goering seized all of the SPD's assets on 10 May and by 22 June it was officially obliterated. The ADGB unions had already been destroyed on 2 May. They were replaced by the German Workers' Front (the DAF). On 20 June collective bargaining was declared defunct and four days later the Christian trade unions were terminated.

No sooner was the labour movement destroyed than the other political parties came under pressure, though, in stark contrast to the labour movement, they dissolved themselves voluntarily. The former DDP began the process on 28 June, the DVP following the next day. At the same time the DNVP, after vain attempts to bolster its position by identifying itself with the 'national movement', declared a 'pact of friendship' with the Nazis which involved self dissolution; members entered the NSDAP 'with full and equal rights and were recognised as part of the common struggle for German nationalism'.[24] At the same time the DNVP's paramilitary allies, the Stahlhelm (Steel Helmets), were gradually absorbed into the SA. The Centre Party was the last to succumb, deciding on its own dissolution on 5 July. Its position had become untenable when the pope began negotiating a concordat with the Nazis which would protect church property but which also agreed to 'remove priests from party politics'.[25] On 14 July Germany officially became a one party state and anyone who contemplated forming an alternative to the NSDAP would face three years in prison.[26]

The process of coordination was not limited to political parties. Institutions were to be purged as well. A civil service decree of 11 April required the sacking of all with Communist or Jewish connections. One month later the prohibition was extended to judges, notaries, school and university teachers and the police. Communists and Jews had already been excluded from law, medicine, journalism, dentistry and so on.[27]

Gleichschaltung was applied to the local state governments which, under Weimar, enjoyed some degree of autonomy.[28] For the Nazis there could be no crack in the state edifice that might offer any space for opposition, because any opposition could quickly assume a class form. Repression must be monolithic and inescapable. Within state institutions the grip of counter-revolution must be absolute. The nature and purpose of coordination was expressed by Württemberg's freshly installed dictator: 'The government will brutally beat down all who oppose it. We do not say an eye for an eye, a tooth for a tooth. No, he who knocks out one of our eyes will get his head chopped off, and he who knocks out one of our teeth will get his jaw bashed in'.[29]

There has been much debate about whether the Nazi Party swallowed up the state machine or, conversely, whether the state machine swallowed up the Nazis. Both viewpoints are largely misplaced. The key issue was that all the repressive powers at the disposal of the state and the Nazi Party (as a mass movement) were now committed to the cause of unbridled counter-revolution. Ideological resources—radio, newspapers etc—were also coordinated. Interestingly, some newspapers were allowed to continue because the Nazis did not wish to interfere with private property (although, naturally, such considerations did not apply to the left wing press). However, even the bourgeois press was extensively purged. Attempts to coordinate the churches proved problematical. While a Protestant Reich church was set up, a minority Confessional church led by Martin Niemöller put up resistance. The Catholic church could not be destroyed or coordinated, but was largely neutralised by the July 1933 concordat with the pope.

So far this description of the building of the Nazi dictatorship has been one sided, because it has concentrated on action being taken at the top of the state. However, the secret of the Nazis' effectiveness lay in the fact that moves from the top were matched by violence from below. The takeover of local states was a good example. On 7 April, Nazi Reich governors were installed at the head of all of Germany's 18 states: 'Developments in Württemberg, Baden, Saxony, Hesse, Hamburg, Bremen and Lübeck followed a similar pattern. Threats of violence (from below) and telegraphic intervention by Frick [Nazi interior minister] intermeshed, until governments were replaced'.[30] Key to this had been the 'auxiliary police' established on 22 February —50,000 Brownshirts and Blackshirts who had donned white armbands to enforce official 'law and order' by means of the street thuggery they knew so well.

It was this combination that enabled the counter-revolution to take place at the molecular level in a way that no exclusively state-sponsored repression could have done. To appreciate this point it is necessary to look at detailed local examples of the process. The best account has been given by Allen for the town he calls Northeim. He describes the process of coordination from the moment that power was seized:

> Control of the city government was one thing; absolute power in the town was another... It involved control over the local police. But that was not enough. The Nazis had to prove in the first months after the appointment of Hitler as chancellor that they were willing to use the power apparatus in a ruthless and effective way [so that] Northeimers came to believe implicitly that they might expect no mercy from their new Nazi rulers.[31]

One means of terrorising the population was the threat of the nearby Moringen concentration camp which was quickly filled to bursting point. A Communist-led hunger strike was broken by turning off the water and force feeding the leaders. Arrest could be for the slightest of reasons, such as the odd oppositional comment.[32] Rumours of a Nazi hit list abounded. The secrecy of the Gestapo led people to imagine there were agents everywhere, when Northeim had only one.[33] Socialists were sacked and those that were not arrested were offered backbreaking work in a stone quarry.[34] The completeness of the Nazi takeover reduced the left to 'poverty, terror...social isolation [and] what might have been the most significant factor of all: the sense of futility'.[35]

Alongside repression in Northeim came mass propaganda and activity. The Nazi movement did not just include the young thugs of the SA. Respectable middle class citizens staged public events, sang Nazi songs, celebrated Hitler's birthday, and so on. Northeim had a 'major celebration' every three weeks:[36] 'Thus in the first six months of the Nazi regime, Northeim was subjected to a veritable barrage of propaganda. While the NSDAP took the lead, all the various nationalistic and militaristic elements in the town were brought into play to support and generalise the Nazi appeal'.[37]

As campaigns began against Jews:

> The Nazis undertook their most Herculean task: the atomisation of the community at large. Though the methods differed, the result was the same, and by the summer of 1933 individual Northeimers were as cut off from effective intercourse with one another as the Jews had been from the rest of the townspeople... Eventually no independent groups were to exist.[38]

The lengths that the Nazis went to were extraordinary. The chess club was 'coordinated' and renamed the National Socialist Chess Club, with a Nazi in charge. The same happened to the bowling club.[39] The public library followed, one quarter of its books being burned as 'un-German'.[40]

The town Allen describes did not have a particularly strong working class presence. Offenbach, on the other hand, was a place where the unity of employed and unemployed had generated exceptionally strong resistance to Nazism before 1933. A left wing activist returning to the town reported:

> I could not recognise the town. Offenbach under the swastika! Swastika flags everywhere... They were hanging so thick in the narrow Biergrund that it was almost impossible to get through. And that was the main stronghold of the KPD.[41]

Allen explains the corrosive effect of Nazi rule:

> People began to distrust one another. What was the value of getting together with others to talk if you had to be careful what you said? Thus to a great extent the individual was atomised. By the process of Gleichschaltung individuals had a choice: solitude or mass relationship via some Nazi organisation.[42]

In his conclusion Allen notes that in this process:

> The critical figures were the local Nazi leaders. Hitler, Goebbels and the other Nazi leaders provided the political decisions, ideology, national propaganda, and, later, the control over the government that made the revolution possible... But it was in the hundreds of localities like Northeim all over Germany that the revolution was made actual. They formed the foundation of the Third Reich.[43]

While taking issue with the use of the word 'revolution' in this context it is clear that major changes in the structure of political and daily life were occurring at this time. So far, however, what has been discussed has been no more than an open counter-revolution with the necessary political and institutional adjustments required to make it thoroughly effective. The working class could not be atomised without atomising the middle class too.

The limits of change written in blood

By the summer of 1933 the 'National' element within National Socialism had largely obliterated the internationalist enemy. Was the path now clear for the 'Socialist' element to come to the fore? Was the Brown revolution (as opposed to the counter-revolution) about to begin?

To approach this issue it is essential to remember the fundamental contradiction discussed previously, that 'the Nazi Party reflected the interests of a tiny minority of the German population but also had the support of vast numbers of ordinary Germans'. Whether the leading Nazis like Hitler or Goebbels were conscious that their function as protectors of capitalism was incompatible with the expectations of the masses is an unresolvable and largely irrelevant question. What was in their heads mattered less than the reality, and this was that counter-revolution immeasurably strengthened the very system which would frustrate the petty bourgeois aspirations of the Nazi rank and file.

The takeover had given a sense of empowerment to hundreds of thousands of ordinary Nazis. They had not only been allowed to indulge their petty hatreds against the labour movement, but had occupied public buildings, expelled state and local governments, and seized control of the full gamut of social and recreational bodies. While anti-Marxism had been a motivating force it was thoroughly mixed in with expectations deriving from the party propaganda that had been pumped out over the previous years. The middle class shopkeeper hoped to see the end of the department store, the debtor the abolition of the 'slavery of interest', the NSBO supporter the introduction of 'German socialism', and so on. If Hitler's victory was to amount to more than a maintenance of the existing system through counter-revolution, it would arise from carrying out these promises.

The fact that millions of middle class people shared a collective hope does not make it any less a collective delusion. The fundamental classes in a capitalist society are the capitalists and the workers; the notion of a middle class alternative became ever more utopian as capitalism developed. In Germany, one of the most advanced industrial states, the smashing of the labour movement meant that the ruling class was immensely strengthened and the chances of its meeting the demands of any other section of society, whether workers or middle class, dramatically reduced. Individual members of the middle class might have the chance for personal advancement by becoming tinpot dictators through *Gleichschaltung*; as a class there was none.

The clash between the Nazi leadership and the 'human dust' of its supporters reached its symbolic climax in the blood purge of 1934, the so called 'Night of the Long Knives'. During this the SS eliminated the leaders of the SA, but the trend was evident earlier. One of the first signs was Goering's defence of non-Nazi civil servants. He rebuked Nazi zealots and 'gave his full approval to those civil servants who because of their character and sense of decency had certain inhibitions about joining the party at this particular moment.' These were preferred to party members who 'threatened gradually to undermine and shatter the authority of the state'.[44] Thus relatively few individuals were purged from the civil service in what was 'a cosmetic rather than a surgical operation'.[45] If the Nazis were truly interested in revolution rather than counter-revolution, why did they draw back from pressing their advantage at the most favourable moment?

The same reticence to drive through full coordination applied to the key organisation of industrialists, the RDI. Changes here have also been described as 'cosmetic'. Jewish members had to resign 'but it escaped a long term presence of Nazi commissars'.[46] Hitler's views on industrialists were identical to Goering's on civil servants: 'We must therefore not dismiss a businessman if he is a good businessman, even if he is not yet a National Socialist; and especially not if the National Socialist who is to take his place knows nothing about business'.[47] The proposition that Nazism was primarily a racial revolution rather than a counter-revolution is also thrown into doubt by a curious debate in the cabinet shortly before the 5 March election. Hugenberg, DNVP leader and Reich economics minister, proposed hitting Jews by a special tax on department stores. On this occasion Hitler's desire to draw the line at smashing the left and thus protecting property took precedence over his anti-Semitism. He rebuked Hugenberg for going too far.[48]

The same generosity was not extended to the shopfloor. As mentioned above, the destruction of the trade unions led to the creation of a new body, the DAF, under Robert Ley. At first sight this seems a strange development. The Nazis already had the NSBO, which had been preparing for years to fulfil precisely this role, with leaders skilled in appealing to workers and a mission to 'be the framework for all other trade unions'.[49] Ley himself admitted, 'I was a greenhorn when I arrived on the scene and was probably more surprised than anyone else as to why I was given this job… I simply got an order from the Führer to take control of the unions, and then I had to work out what to do next'.[50]

The NSBO's claims were overlooked because it had taken Nazi propaganda too seriously in some places, blocking the closure of a mine, threatening a director with the concentration camp, and so on.[51] Goebbels accused the NSBO of having been infiltrated by Marxists.[52] In April, Hess banned NSBO demonstrations 'against any economic enterprise, industrial firm, bank or union without the party's permission'.[53] The NSBO was then swallowed up by the DAF. To enforce 'Hitler's first priority in social and economic policy [which] was to forbid any interference with private ownership', employers were invited to join the DAF to ensure its internal balance was not favourable to the NSBO.[54]

On 19 May an important law on the organisation of German labour was introduced, one of its functions being to transfer responsibility for setting wages out of the reach of the NSBO and into the hands of 12 'Trustees of Labour'. They were 'largely a mixture of officials from the federal states and lawyers associated with employers' organisations'.[55] In 1934 one trustee reported his work in the early phase of the Nazi dictatorship:

> I rarely met a workers' leader who did not demand the arrest of his employer right at the start of negotiations, the moment after he had greeted me. During night long negotiations in the Ruhr area I often had to threaten the NSBO agents and works council chairman with the Gestapo in order to achieve peace and order in the labour sphere.[56]

Like the NSBO, the SA was one of the Nazi organisations closer to the working class than most; many of its members were duped into thinking that the party stood for something more than counter-revolution. In 1934 the leadership of the SA was butchered to teach it that, in Hitler's words, 'The purpose of a revolution can be only…to crush resistance.' He added that 'recurrent revolution must lead to the destruction of the life of the people, and of the state, and also of economic life.' Therefore, 'in the next 1,000 years there will be no other revolution in Germany'.[57]

The chancellor claimed that the Night of the Long Knives was a preventative strike against 'the outbreak of a second revolution'.[58] This is doubtful. We have seen that the SA was capable of very radical rhetoric before 1933, and the feeling of power gained in the excesses of counter-revolution strengthened that mood. A speech at an SA meeting illustrates the point: 'Our revolution…has only begun. They talk about a national government, a national awakening… What is all that? What matters is the socialist part of our programme… We have only one more enemy to conquer: the bourgeoisie!'[59]

However, the hollowness of Nazi 'left' rhetoric should also not be forgotten. Until 1933 it had been a tool in the hands of the Nazi leadership, but if it became an obstacle, it would be dispensed with along with those credulous enough to believe in it. This did not appear to be an easy matter. By the summer of 1934 fear and opportunism had swollen SA membership to nearly four million, and its leader Röhm was impatient to record some real gains. He hoped to convert his paramilitary force into a proper army. A merger between the SA and the 100,000 strong Reichswehr would, in effect, mean the former swallowing the latter. When Hitler objected, Röhm declared:

> Adolf is rotten. He's betraying all of us. He only goes around with reac-
> tionaries. His old comrades aren't good enough for him. So he brings in
> these east Prussian generals. They're the ones he pals around with now...
> Where the hell is the revolutionary spirit to come from afterwards?[60]

Hitler saw things differently. Nazism's counter-revolutionary content would have to be made abundantly clear. After the Night of the
Long Knives he admitted, 'It had not simply been a matter of snuff-
ing out the revolt...but instead to make it clear to every single leader
and SA man that he risked his neck if he conspired in any way what-
soever against the existing regime'.[61] The preparations for the blood
purge were carefully disguised. First, Hitler wrote to Röhm to thank
him 'for the imperishable services which you have rendered to the
National Socialist movement and the German people, and to assure
you how very grateful I am to fate that I am able to call such men as
you my friends and fellow combatants'.[62] Then, in April 1934, Hitler
met military leaders to assure them that he put their interests before
those of his own supporters. Soon Himmler's SS was involved in plot-
ting the downfall of its Brownshirt comrades and death lists were
drawn up.

On 4 June Hitler asked the SA to stand down and take a 'holiday'
in July. Between 30 June and 2 July the blood purge was carried out.
The SS hunted down Röhm and his SA allies as they slept in their Bad
Wiessee hotel retreat. Elsewhere they settled old scores with people
like Kahr (for opposing the Beer Hall Putsch, 1923) and Schleicher
(for blocking Hitler's path to the chancellorship).

The SA offered no resistance, succumbing incredibly easily and
quickly. Exact numbers of those killed (both SA leaders and others)
have never been established. At the time it was believed to be around
400.[63] The smashing of the left had been a staged operation lasting five
months, with mass arrests, torture and murder. The battle to crush
any resurgence of the labour movement would occupy the authorities
until the very end of the regime. While the brutality of the Night of
the Long Knives was real, the removal of a few dozen key figures completely broke the SA which henceforth served only ceremonial functions. After Hindenburg died on 2 August Hitler combined the roles
of chancellor and president. In gratitude for preserving their independence from the SA, the generals had their troops swear a personal
oath of allegiance and 'unconditional obedience to Adolf Hitler, the
Führer of the German nation and people [and] supreme commander
of the armed forces'.[64]

The purge completed the establishment of the Nazi system. It had accomplished a counter-revolution but ensured, by persuasion, pressure and ultimately murder, that not only was it free from any obligation to its supporters, but that any notion of fundamental change in the balance of power between the classes was blocked. The list of those who received official protection from the demands of rank and file Nazis—businessmen, department store owners, media bosses, senior civil servants and army generals—is highly indicative. The sole victims of Nazi oppression to be found amongst the elite were either Jewish or found in the political field where they might obstruct the engine of counter-revolution from carrying out its gruesome task.

The tide of Nazi activity flowed in one direction—towards the devastation of the labour movement. As soon as there were signs it might reverse direction to challenge aspects of capitalist rule it was dammed up. A regime, even one as apparently powerful and autonomous as Hitler's, does not exist in a social vacuum. With the working class organisationally smashed and atomised, rank and file Nazis and the middle class neutralised but the ruling class substantially intact, the dictatorship was bound to be fundamentally shaped by the demands of capitalism.

Chapter 7

The Third Reich:
a fusion of state and capital

Most non-Marxist histories of the Third Reich assume that Nazism and capitalism had widely divergent aims. They accept the Night of the Long Knives symbolised a compromise with the establishment, but view this as merely a temporary halt on the road to Nazism's own and unique goal of world domination and conquest. There was, it is argued, a turning point around 1936-38 which was marked by an accelerated rearmament programme and the removal of military leaders Fritsch and Blomberg, along with Schacht as the guide of economic policy. This episode is described as 'the country's rapid and final restructuring into the total leader state'.[1] Thus, 'At a single blow Hitler succeeded in removing the few checks which remained upon his freedom of action'.[2]

As a leading Marxist historian of Nazism, Tim Mason has made an excellent contribution to an understanding of the relationship between the Nazi regime and the workers. However, his treatment of Nazi-capitalist relations is much weaker because it insists on treating the political sphere of the state and the economic sphere of capitalist production as entirely separate. Mason argues that in the late 1930s the Nazi regime became 'increasingly independent of the influence of the economic ruling classes, and even in some essential aspects ran contrary to their interests'.[3] The Third Reich therefore exhibited the 'primacy of politics'.[4] This ignores the notion of state capitalism and by default ascribes to the Nazi regime an autonomy which almost freed it from the social and economic basis of the capitalist mode of production. It flies in the face of Marx's fundamental idea about the relationship between the economic base and the political superstructure of societies. This recognises the connection between both spheres and their dialectical interplay, and it fits the facts of the Third Reich much better than Mason's analysis.

Trotsky argued that there was a relationship between the Nazi state and capitalism:

Today, the German bourgeoisie does not rule directly; politically it is placed under complete subjection to Hitler and his bands. Nevertheless, the dictatorship of the bourgeoisie remains inviolate in Germany because all the conditions of its social hegemony have been preserved and strengthened. By expropriating the bourgeoisie politically, Hitler saved it.[5]

The relations of autonomy and interconnection were summed up in this analogy: 'The sabre by itself has no independent programme. It is the instrument of "order",[6] and that order was capitalism. This analysis relied on the concept of Bonapartism. While Trotsky recognised that 'there is an element of Bonapartism in fascism', he also insisted that fascism in 'the epoch of imperialist decline...is qualitatively different from the Bonapartism of the epoch of bourgeois rise...imperialism finds it indispensable to mobilise the petty bourgeoisie and to crush the proletariat under its weight'.[7]

There is another way in which the term Bonapartism (as developed from 19th century examples) needs modification. While it holds good at the level of a formal division of labour between state (politics) and capital (economics), by the 20th century state capitalist structures which incorporate both elements had become increasingly common. Just as Nazism served capitalism in the political sense even though it was apparently autonomous, so there was an emerging symbiosis which eroded the political/economic division of labour. A fusion occurred which, if anything, accelerated after 1936.

As pointed out in Chapter 2, Nazi ideology was already an extreme variant of capitalist thought, being an element of the ideological superstructure of that system. The distinction between the economic motivations of big business and the political aims of the Nazi state was the difference between the base and superstructure of capitalism. Hitler was not unaware of the connections, even if his understanding was flawed. In a passage previously quoted he explained his belief that 'it was not German business which conquered the world and led to the development of German power, but...the power state which created for the business world the general conditions for its subsequent prosperity'.[8]

This was not a startlingly original idea. Although the first industrial revolution in Britain was an economic phenomenon, it owed much to state action through the acquisition of cotton producing colonies and the wealth generated by slavery. Capital, as Marx wrote, comes into the world 'dripping from head to foot, from every pore, with blood and dirt'.[9] The explosive expansion of German capitalism as a result of the forced unification through 'blood and iron' of Bismarck's armies was a tribute to the role that the state could play in promoting capitalist interests by force of arms. The drive to war of imperial Germany had been encouraged by the obstacles that native capitalism faced to further development and, as the 20th century progressed, the links between state and capital became progressively stronger.

As early as 1915 the Russian Marxist Nikolai Bukharin, building on Hilferding's concept of 'finance capitalism', had explained that there was a tendency towards the fusion of the state and capital. Although earlier states had been committed to the interests of the economic system, their relations with the economic ruling class had been shaped by the existence of a large and disparate mass of small capitalists. Now concentration and centralisation meant that more and more 'combines in industry and banking syndicates unite the entire "national" production, which assumes the form of a company of companies, thus becoming a state capitalist trust'.[10] The links between the state and prominent blocks of capital had thus become far more direct. Before the 20th century, the state had emphasised its role of neutral arbiter between competing capitals within the country (passing laws to regulate contracts, printing money and so on). Now the size of capital units meant that competition often took place between firms in different countries and so the state took on the additional role of energetically defending its capital from foreign rivals.

Competition to win markets and supplies of raw materials through trade gave way to new and dangerous methods: 'In the epoch of finance capitalism...the centre of gravity is shifted to the competition of gigantic, consolidated and organised economic bodies possessed of a colossal fighting capacity in the world tournament of "nations".'[11] This had implications for internal relations within states:

> The more strained the situation in the world sphere of struggle—and our epoch is characterised by the greatest intensity of competition between 'national' groups of finance capital—the oftener an appeal is made to the mailed fist of state power... If state power is generally growing in significance, the growth of its military organisation, the army and the navy is particularly striking... The immensely growing state budget devotes an ever larger share to 'defence purposes', as militarism is euphemistically called.[12]

Bukharin's account expresses perfectly the pattern of development which took place not just in Germany but in state capitalist Russia, and in most of Western Europe during 1930s rearmament.

However, Nazism's drive to war was especially pronounced. Its domestic political method was counter-revolution—war to the death against working class organisation; its approach to foreign policy was equally extreme. As Tasca put it in the 1930s, 'For fascism, war is not a possibility that the state must take account of, but a certainty and a necessity to which everything must be subordinated... The fascist economy is a war economy'.[13] Hitler's pursuit of German capitalist interests would take a particular form, due to the the difficulty that a dynamic yet crisis ridden German capitalism faced in world competition. This was illustrated by its declining share of world trade. Before the First World War this had stood at 13 percent. Even before the crash the figure was only 9 percent and in 1932 it was down to 8 percent.[14]

Hitler's approach would be to solve the economic problem through state sponsored economic self sufficiency, or autarchy, in combination with aggressive expansionism for what he called called *Lebensraum*, or living space. These would simultaneously furnish ever greater quantities of manpower, markets and raw materials and exclude foreign competition.

Nazi state capitalism and the working class

It has been seriously argued that 'the Nazi economy was neither socialistic nor capitalistic...it was a curious hybrid of both systems'.[15] One author suggests:

> When the Nazi government, actively supported by Labour Front [DAF] leaders, stepped up efficiency and exploitation in the interest of rearmament and preparation for war, this was experienced by many workers as an objective improvement of their income, their personal prosperity, and even their working conditions. More important still, at least according to their idealised reminiscences, were the symbolic compensations: the new esteem of physical labour and of the labouring classes.[16]

Smelser suggests that the DAF 'mounted a major, sustained psychological and cultural campaign to raise the self image of the worker, to underscore the value of work, whether manual or otherwise... In short, the DAF tried to bring both the virtues and the amenities of the middle class to the worker'.[17] Its long term plans were 'astonishingly progressive and far-sighted'.[18] Schoenbaum says that Third Reich policies 'can scarcely be called anti-labour'.[19] Indeed, 'Equality of status was to extend to equality of opportunity, the distinction between employer and employee would disappear in the fluidity of free competition in which all liberated energies were concentrated on the achievement of national goals'.[20] Labour Service (compulsory work to get dole) was the 'ultimate manifestation of "German Socialism" and *Kameradschaft* (comradeship), the irresistible solvent of existing class differences'.[21]

It would be laughable, if not so dangerous, that these authors have virtually taken Nazi claims about the creation of a 'national' or 'folk' community (*Volksgemeinschaft*) at face value. The distinguishing feature of fascism, as opposed to traditional reaction, was its ability to pose as a friend of the masses while pursuing its counter-revolutionary aims, and such duplicity did not diminish under the Third Reich. As individuals many leading Nazis were outsiders to the ruling class and often resented or envied their power. They still would rhetorically articulate the middle class desire to remove obstacles to upward mobility (and used the party's control on power to make this possible for a privileged few). But demanding the right to share in the fruits of exploitation does not abolish it. This is brought out in the following declaration by a leading Nazi: 'In this state only one monopoly was to rule: achievement! Unceasingly and unconstrained, the best and eternally young elements were to emerge from the people...in order to safeguard not only the stability of the state, but also to guarantee its constant advance and greatest possible degree of development'.[22]

The absolute nonsense written by the above historians about the *Volksgemeinschaft* is exposed by an analysis of the regime within the factories. Hitler expressed the official line on this. Under Nazism, 'The German labourer will be the mainstay because he is susceptible to that feeling...which consecrates itself to an idea in blind faith and obedience'.[23] Thus the 'esteem' of Nazis for the workers was that in their blind faith and obedience they would be the mainstay of the economy, in the same way that cattle are the mainstay of an abattoir.

The 'Law on the Organisation of National Labour' of 20 January 1934 defined the government's position. It declared that the factory regime 'proceeds directly from the nature given, destiny determined community in the enterprise, the works community, in which the entrepreneur as the born leader of the enterprise is bound together with his workers and employees, the followers'.[24] The workforce or 'retinue' had therefore to swear 'fealty and obedience'.[25] The leader, on the other hand, 'alone makes the decisions'.[26] Ley of the DAF added that he 'need not be lenient to his followers... If conditions in the establishment or higher economic considerations should demand it, then the leader should also be firm and the followers must then acquiesce to a just refusal of their wishes'.[27]

The Law on the Organisation of National Labour replaced the Weimar compromise of factory committees with 'Councils of Trust', bodies nominated by the 'factory leader' (though workers were supposed to vote their approval). Their functions were to discuss matters 'pertaining to the improvement of efficiency, the establishment and supervision of working conditions [and] the strengthening of the bonds of factory members'.[28] They had no power to negotiate on pay or conditions but could be consulted on these. The only formal check on the power of the boss was the system of Trustees of Labour established in May 1933. Civil servants responsible to the ministers of labour, trustees were 'supposed to interfere as little as possible in the internal affairs of the industrial community [with their] duties confined to checking the need for any proposed mass redundancies, ensuring that minimum working conditions conformed to the existing agreements... and keeping the Reich government informed of developments on the social policy front'.[29]

Official statements, however, are not sufficient. The role of the DAF on the ground must be investigated. Established through the physical liquidation of the trade unions it was forced, in order to exercise an influence, to pose as genuinely representative of workers' interests. Having taken over all trade union property, and backed by the risk to an individual's employment of non-membership, the DAF became a vast organisation, standing at eight million members shortly after its foundation and 16 million by 1935.[30] It had 30,000 functionaries, and rapidly expanding subsidiary organisations like the 'Strength through Joy' and 'Beauty of Labour' movements.

Robert Ley's vast bureaucracy acquired its own institutional momentum and interests in competition with other sectors of the Nazi state like Himmler's SS. As such it was part of the so called 'polycratic' system of competing bureaucratic empires that formed the chaotic internal administration of the Third Reich. To bolster its claims it had to make demands which would simultaneously enhance its prestige amongst the workers and increase its power. As fear of unemployment receded in the 1930s the danger of losing control of the workforce increased, and so did the DAF's need to deliver some concessions from the employers.

This meant that there was a tension between the DAF's stated 'lofty goal...to instil in all German working people the National Socialist way of thinking',[31] and its actual practice. One concession it obtained was that the employers' associations agreed to dissolve themselves.[32] This was assisted by the employers realising they needed no special organisations of their own when the Gestapo and other Nazi institutions were available.

It was Hitler's determination that 'the German Labour Front is not the place to decide the material questions of workday life'.[33] Instead it was to ensure that 'every individual…is capable of their maximum performance and thus of guaranteeing the greatest benefit for the folk community'.[34] In practice the DAF had to go beyond this limited remit. As the deputy leader of the economy reported soon after, DAF functionaries 'have arrogated to themselves the power to inspect factories at any time, to examine the possibility of improving their social amenities, to negotiate on hours of work and wages, and to investigate every complaint'.[35] In March 1935 the 'Leipzig agreement', involving economics minister Schacht and Robert Ley, sought once again to regulate the Labour Front's operation and restrict its interference in the economy.

But soon Ley was back proposing draft laws which would have made membership compulsory, given the DAF independence from the NSDAP and direct access to Hitler, and increased its economic functions to the point of influencing directly the Ministry of Labour.[36] It would be a mistake to exaggerate how radical these proposals were. They were made in a context where not only was the right to strike abolished, but any attempt by workers themselves to improve conditions might be brutally repressed. Action by the DAF was designed to strengthen its position as a Nazi institution, not to undermine the regime or its capitalist allies, and, in any case, none of these proposals was enacted.

Another proof offered of the 'socialistic' side of Nazi labour policies is the Courts of Honour. Here transgressors of the 'harmonious working relations' sought by the 'folk community' could be brought to book. Schoenbaum reports that in 1935, 205 court cases were led against employers or their representatives and only 18 against employees.[37] He omits to mention that these were mainly against small firms, less than half resulted in any penalty and these were all the cases raised in a labour force of 20 million.[38] The Courts of Honour system was obvious window dressing.

To really judge the aims of Nazi labour policy Ley's speech before industrialists is noteworthy: 'A few words about the Labour Front… Many were probably asking, "Why are they doing this?" Well, there were two ways to go. Either we could have smashed the unions completely at the time, outlawed them and left 12 million people without a home in our state; or we could have gone down the path that I did… Nothing is more dangerous for a state than people without a home'.[39] The genuine tension generated by the DAF's struggle for legitimacy in the eyes of the workers and the demands for untrammelled power by business was not an example of class versus class, but of friction between the political and economic requirements of capitalist stability. Thus, as one study concludes, 'The competition for control never resulted in the exclusion of any of the dominant groups, but rather to a growth in co-operation between the DAF, employers and state institutions'.[40]

The situation of labour under the Nazis revealed an important difference between revolution and counter-revolution. Great revolutions such as France in 1789 and Russia in 1917 were aimed at the overthrow and abolition of particular classes. The French bourgeois revolution abolished the feudal landowners. In Russia the revolution not only abolished landowners but individual capitalist owners. (After 1929 capitalism would return in the form of the Stalinist bureaucracy establishing state capitalism.) Nazi counter-revolution could not aim at the abolition of the working class on whose exploitation the system depended. Its goal was therefore that of minimising its challenge to the system.

One feature of the Labour Front which has led to confusion is the activities of its subsidiary organisations—Strength through Joy (Kraft durch Freude or KdF) and Beauty of Labour. The former provided entertainment and holidays for the workers, while the latter helped improve workplace facilities such as washrooms. It is suggested that the goal of the DAF and of the Nazis generally could not have been maximum exploitation, since they promoted leisure activities and a better working environment. This is to misunderstand the nature of the drive for capitalist exploitation which even in the 19th century, Marx pointed out, was not achieved only through extension of working hours. An alternative was 'increased expenditure of labour in a given time, heightened tension of labour power, and closer filling up of the pores of the working day'.[41]

To achieve such intensification of labour, employers needed new methods of controlling and directing workers. In the early 20th century these were provided by F W Taylor, the creator of 'scientific management'. For Taylorism to function, 'Control over the labour process must pass into the hands of management, not only in the formal sense but by the control and citation of each step of the process, including its mode of performance. In pursuit of this end, no effort is excessive'.[42] The smashing of the trade union movement and the factory committees was the ideal preparation for the application of such methods, and there was 'an almost explosive extension' of Taylorism under the Nazis.[43]

Added to this was an ambitious plan, first pioneered by heavy industrialists in 1926 under the auspices of the German Institute for Technical Education and Training. It had an explicitly counter-revolutionary purpose: 'Socialist ideas are directed towards a definite aim, the close unity of the workers [and] the collapse of capitalism.' To counter this 'the sociologist sees things clearly—what is important is to divide and rule!'[44] Its method was 'to take in hand leadership of all from earliest child-hood to the oldest man in order, not—and I must emphasise this once more—for social purposes, but from the point of view of productivity'.[45] The grand ambition of controlling every aspect of the worker's life was summed up by Ley: 'The only person still leading a private life in Ger-many today is someone who sleeps'.[46] This has often been interpreted in terms of a totalitarian Nazism which distinguished it from capitalism, but this is false. Braverman, writing about post Second World War US capitalism, shows that this approach was the consequence of capitalist development:

> It is only in its era of monopoly that the capitalist mode of production takes over the totality of individual, family, and social needs and in subordinating them to the market, also reshapes them to serve the needs of capital.[47]

This illuminates the meaning of the Orwellian sounding Strength through Joy (KdF) movement. Like battery hens serenaded with music, German workers' productivity was to be raised by DAF organised hol-idays and outings, and even the KdF-wagen (or Volkswagen, which was never delivered because of the war). The scale of the operation was enormous and compared well with restricted opportunities for holidays in previous times.[48] While only 8,000 wealthy Germans out of a work-force of 20 million could afford the cruise to Madeira in 1936,[49] by 1939 some seven million had taken some sort of holiday with the KdF, with 35 million on day trips.[50] The KdF was clearly popular, but, as Mason argues, this 'popularity had absolutely nothing to do with spreading the nation's cultural wealth among the masses or reinvigorating the *Volk*. Rather it was rooted in the desperate need for fun and diversion, a need which was continually being created by the regime itself'.[51] The 'des-perate need for fun and diversion' is the product of modern capital-ism and was not unique to Nazi Germany. Braverman, again, suggests:

> In a society where labour power is purchased and sold, working time be-comes sharply and antagonistically divided from non-working time, and the worker places an extraordinary value upon this 'free' time, while on the job time is regarded as lost or wasted. Work ceases to be a natural function and becomes an extorted activity... But the atrophy of community and the sharp division from the natural environment leaves a void when it comes to the 'free' hours. Thus the filling of time

away from the job…develops to an enormous degree those passive amusements, entertainments and spectacles that suit the restricted circumstances of the city and are offered as substitutes for life itself.[52]

The Beauty of Labour movement had a similar productivist goal. By 1936 it claimed to have improved working conditions by decorating 26,000 workshops, 24,000 changing rooms and 18,000 canteens.[53] The aim was to give the workers the impression, as Ley put it, that, 'The workplace is yours, and you must learn to love the machine like a bride'.[54] In practice, as one disgruntled worker put it, 'What it means in reality is that we have to clean up the machine and tidy the working area in work time which means less time for us to be earning. The result is a cut in wages of two to three marks per week'.[55]

Did either of these movements demonstrate a commitment to socialism, or a distinction between Nazism and capitalism? This extract from a textbook on management techniques in Britain today could have been written by any DAF official or boss:

> Managers have continuously sought a legitimation of their work role by subordinate employees and a degree of employee commitment to the processes of work, consistent with high output, low costs and the absence of industrial conflict… The welfare approach, for example…is concerned with the comfort and attractiveness of working conditions, canteen facilities, employee counselling, sports and social clubs.[56]

The KdF and Beauty of Labour schemes reached their highest expression in the plans Ley was called upon to draft for Nazi society after it had won the war. These promised full employment, a broad social security system, health service and housing, which Smelser says 'amounted to a German "Beveridge Report".'[57] He is aware that these measures 'were deeply and inextricably embedded in a destructive racial ideology' and so, 'Attractive as they might be alone or in a very different context, [they] lose much of their validity',[58] but this is still an understatement. The intention was that, without eating into the profits of German capitalists, the welfare of German workers would be paid for by both foreign slave labour and migrant German workers subject to:

> General compulsory labour up to 65 years and over; exclusion from the system for 'malingerers' and 'strikers'. The model was based on cost calculations which had place neither for the 'rearing of inferior humans' nor the 'building of institutions for idiots'.[59]

Nevertheless, the comparison with Beveridge, despite the great differences between Nazi Germany and parliamentary Britain, is not entirely misplaced. Advanced capitalism in the mid-20th century was entering a period of boom which required the organised reproduction of labour power and a means of buying off discontent at a time when full employment gave workers strong bargaining power. The Third Reich's treatment of the working class was not fundamentally different from any other capitalist country's, except in the crucial area of its counter-revolutionary destruction of organised labour. It is true that the rector of Heidelberg University marched alongside workers on the May Day demonstration preceding the liquidation of the unions and claimed this was 'the unity of the workers of the mind and fist'.[60] A Nazi coal boss professed to real proletarian solidarity by donning a miner's uniform, while the *Völkische Beobachter* enjoined the 'brother in gold and silk' to shake hands with the 'brother in fustian'.[61] The great material sacrifice the Nazis demanded of the rich was that one Sunday each month they consume a simple 'one pot meal' (the usual fare for many workers every day), donating the money saved to Nazi charities like the 'Winter Help', which had replaced the extensive Weimar system of social benefits. But to believe that these made the 'folk community' anything more than a sick joke (as Zitelmann does, for example) is contemptible.

Did the arrival of full employment show the real sympathy of the Nazi leadership for the working class? Between 1932 and 1939 official unemployment fell from 5.6 million to 100,000 (or 0.5 percent). Over the same period the number in employment rose by ten million.[62] In the early days the Rheinhardt job creation scheme provided over one billion marks. It was an extension of work begun under previous chancellors though it quickly outgrew the previous plans.[63] It was certainly designed to head off worker discontent and there can be little doubt that in this the Nazis were partially successful. However, the ending of unemployment must be kept in perspective.

Despite the massive publicity given, progress was comparatively modest during 1933-34. At this stage some one million of the 3.5 million new jobs were generated by compelling youths and 'relief workers' to work for a pittance on farms or in backbreaking projects which paid little more than the dole.[64] This was the Labour Service (compulsory from 1935) that, it is claimed, was 'the irresistible solvent of existing class differences'.[65] Jews disappeared from the statistics while marriage loans and social pressure meant many women gave up work. With an expanding state bureaucracy, Mason suggests that 'finding employment for veteran party members was doubtless the most successful aspect of the Nazis' employment creation policy'.[66] Nevertheless, as the figures on total numbers employed show, new jobs did also materialise and, while European employment rates recovered generally, the rate first fell in Germany.[67] The main reason for this was the drive to war.

As early as 8 February 1933, Hitler announced to his cabinet, 'The next five years in Germany must be dedicated to the rearming of the German race. Every public effort towards job creation measures must be judged from this viewpoint—whether it is necessary from the standpoint of the rearmament of the German race'.[68] This consideration shaped employment policy fundamentally. Most of it was designed to assist heavy industry and involved infrastructure that assisted military aims indirectly—*Autobahns* (motorways), airfields—or directly through armaments.[69] Up to 1936 some 80 percent of all additional government spending went into rearmament and expansion of the army.[70] Herbst suggests spending on military projects was twice that of civilian projects in the same period and that many of the latter had military uses.[71] The consequences were visible in the way employment growth was distributed. By 1936 employment in heavy industry exceeded 1929 levels by almost 6 percent yet was still 15 percent lower for light industry.[72] Apart from buying off trouble, job growth in Nazi Germany was primarily driven by the competitive military drive of the government and its capitalist allies. Employment was a by-product of a process that would end in death and destruction.

There was nothing especially Nazi about this. Capitalist economies that are heavily committed to war and its preparation enjoy low levels of unemployment. Thus Japan achieved full employment in 1938 as a result of its war with China. The US, with ten million unemployed, solved the problem in 1942.[73] If Nazi Germany was unusual it was that job creation was intimately linked with rearmament from the start. Other countries expanded arms production in response to Germany's growing military only in the later 1930s so that initial 'job creation and rearmament were in two clearly separate phases'.[74] So, far from disproving the link between Nazism and capitalism, the decline of unemployment under Nazism reinforced it.

As this account has already shown, relations between the regime, capitalists and the workers were not those of early capitalism but of the modern technocratic variety and the same holds true for wages. Viewed on their own, figures for real wages do not suggest a downward trend after 1933:

Index of weekly real earnings				
(after deductions and cost of living adjustment—1932 = 100)[75]				
1929 118	1932 100	1933 104	1934 109	1935 110
1936 112	1937 110	1938 114	1939 118	

These figures only give a partial view of the situation of workers under Nazism. It is important to note that capitalists are not concerned so much with an absolute reduction of wages as much as a relative reduction of wages as compared to profits. If low wages were the chief focus for capitalism, today the Third World would be the prime target for investment. Capitalists are primarily interested in the rate of exploitation, or the relative level of wages compared to output. Here the evidence is unambiguous. In the decade after 1929 wages had gradually returned to their previous level, but workers had to labour an average three hours extra per week to earn them.[76] Pay increases did not halt the increasing rate of exploitation because productivity rose much faster—by 34.4 percent between 1934 and 1939.[77] Thus the share of total national wealth going to wages fell consistently.

Wages as a percentage of national income[78]				
1932 57.0	1933 56.0	1934 55.5	1935 54.6	1936 53.5
1937 52.7	1938 52.4	1939 51.8		

Rising productivity was achieved through a mixture of repression and persuasion. Alongside the Gestapo was the more conventional means of upping the tempo of work—the incentive scheme. The two should not be seen as entirely distinct, the one associated with Nazism and the other with something different—capitalism. The smashing of organised labour dovetailed with methods of persuasion:

> Piecework bonuses and suchlike served to increase productivity and made it possible to differentiate more acutely between individual workers and between specific groups according to their qualifications and importance. A finer gradation of wage groups and an ingenious system of assessing the value of individual jobs kept the total wages bill low and at the same time created effective incentives to higher productivity. Even with limited additional recruitment of labour a company could thus achieve considerable increases in productivity— and strengthen the conviction amongst the workforce that hard work was always rewarded.[79]

The system depended on the fact that bosses could deal with 'individual workers' and assess payment for 'individual jobs' only because trade unions had been crushed, collective bargaining abolished, and the workforce reduced to a commodity comprising atomised individuals.

There were many other signs of rising exploitation. Work related accidents and illnesses increased one and a half times; occupational diseases tripled and fatalities rose two and a half times.[80] The emphasis on heavy industry meant that vital consumption needs were ignored. Perhaps the most important of these was housing, where by 1937 the number of homes built by the government fell to half the level of 1929.[81]

So far the emphasis has been on the similarity between capitalism in Nazi Germany and the system generally. However, if the aim everywhere is to maximise the rate of exploitation, the unique 'contribution' of the counter-revolution should not be ignored. The most striking feature of the period 1933-39 is that at a time when Germany was reaching unparalleled levels of employment and a labour shortage, workers were not able to take advantage of this. A comparison with Britain and the US, where employment levels recovered much later, brings this out. Despite the demand for building workers, German wage rates did not rise much above Depression levels while in Britain they increased 10 percent and in the US over 20 percent. The equivalent increases for coal miners were—Germany, 18 percent; Britain, 31 percent; and the US, 72 percent.[82] The German ruling class may have had to give up its political freedoms, but this had been more than compensated for by increased exploitation.

A remarkable letter of 1936 in the Nazis' own daily newspaper sums up the reality of Nazi rule perfectly:

> Nobody concerned with economic questions will believe the capitalist system has disappeared. Although it is true that methods of public financing have assumed a different character—a character of coercion—capital, or at least what is generally understood by this word, has never been so powerful and privileged as at the present time... The economy accumulates enormous profits and reserves; the workers are invited to wait... One group is making immense profits at the expense of the rest of the population. That is what used to be called capitalist exploitation.[83]

The destruction of labour organisation had opened the way for a massive increase in exploitation, but not even triumphant counter-revolution could abolish the working class, so the regime continued to fear its revolutionary potential. In conversation with his architect, Speer, Hitler spoke of his fear of 'riots' and 'disturbance' and requested that a fully motorised regiment armed with the most modern equipment be located near his palace, which itself was guarded with a huge steel gate.[84] He indicated that 'after the experience of 1918 one could not be cautious enough'.[85]

Nazism and the middle class

The middle class did not evoke the same fear in the Nazi leadership as the working class and so it was largely ignored and abused by the regime. One author goes so far as to argue that 'the petty bourgeoisie, traditional and new, was the main economic victim of fascism, together with the middle and lower middle peasantry'.[86] This seems odd when so much of the core support and ideological structure of the NSDAP was bound up with the middle class. It becomes comprehensible, however, as soon as it is remembered that Nazism was not a 'Third Way' distinct from capitalism. The middle class had served its purpose by helping Hitler to power and was no longer required as a counterweight to the labour movement.

In almost every respect the regime betrayed its promises. Middle class organisations had turned to the government immediately after the Hitler's appointment with high hopes,[87] but they were soon 'coordinated' and lost all autonomy. And that was it! When a group of Bavarian shopkeepers sympathetic to the Nazis decided to cash in on their 'victory' by raising their prices, the government used 'the sharpest police measures' against them. Some 200 were rounded up, their shops closed, and signs hoisted outside saying that 'the owners were under protection in Dachau'.[88] One of the key promises of the NSDAP had been to restrict and break up department stores. However, in July 1933 Hess announced, 'The membership of the NSDAP is hereby forbidden to undertake any further action against department stores or similar enterprises'.[89] At the same time the diatribes against foreign capital were forgotten. When Hitler was approached by the New York based ITT company about investment opportunities in Germany he 'energetically' informed them that 'there would be no discrimination against legitimate foreign capital'.[90] In August the middle class Kampfbund was dissolved in a move similar to the ending of the NSBO; the more pliable 'NS-Hago' organisation replaced it.[91] As the economy gathered pace and capital became more concentrated, the very fate which middle class Nazi supporters had dreaded—descent into the proletariat—came to pass. Between 1936 and 1939, 180,000 small craft enterprises (10 percent of the total) went out of business.[92] The same happened to shop assistants whose numbers fell by 9 percent (1933-39) at a time when the number of workers increased by seven million.[93]

The same reversal of expectations occurred in agriculture, despite the May 1933 law which made hereditary farms inalienable and so not subject to mortgage. Darré of the Reich Food Estate had stressed, 'The inexorable tie between blood and soil is the indispensable prerequisite of the healthy life of a people',[94] yet the proportion of those with livelihoods dependent on farming fell from 29 percent in 1933 to 26 percent at the outbreak of war.[95] The overall result of Nazi rule was:

> The exact opposite of what had been its original ideological intentions…not the self confident and independent 'free peasant farmer' who served the good of the 'national community' as artists faithful to the regime were wont to portray on canvas, but an agricultural producer caught in a web of regulations… Instead of the establishment of new farms there was a massive flight from the land. Peasant Teutons, supposedly so true to the soil, were rushing into the metropolitan conurbations.[96]

The capitalist class

While the working class got the knout and the middle class the cold shoulder, the bonds between capital and the Nazis were made of gold. On 20 February 1933 a meeting of leading German businessmen gathered to be addressed by Hitler and Goering. After hearing that the Nazis planned the 5 March election to be the last, they contributed three million marks to the campaign funds.[97] In June the industrialists went further, deciding to pay the NSDAP one five thousandth of their total wage and salary bill. 'This was intended as a mark of gratitude for the elimination of the trade unions, the prospect of a rearmament led boom and the departure into economic autarchy [self sufficiency], which promised big business outstanding profits and possibilities for development'.[98] Business was not disappointed. A 390 million mark loss on net earnings of large corporations in 1932 was converted into a 120 million mark profit the next year, and by 1936 the figure had risen to 520 million, a 433 percent expansion in just three years![99]

Nazi solicitude for capitalist affairs differed sharply from the hostility meted out to workers and the middle class. Firstly, the industrialists wanted the anti-capitalist strivings of the Nazi radicals to be restrained and, as we have seen, this was carried out. While the working class had Ley (who admitted he knew nothing about trade unions) foisted upon it, Nazi economic policy was set directly by prominent capitalists themselves. Once Hugenberg had been removed (because of his links with the DNVP) the Minister of Economics was Schmitt, Director General of the largest insurance company (Allianz). He was later replaced by Hjalmar Schacht, President of the Reichsbank, whose Social Democrat past was forgiven and forgotten.[100]

Secondly, the Nazis ensured that the process of 'coordination' or Gleichschaltung, which wiped out the trade unions and neutered independent middle class organisations, left the representative organs of industry and capital virtually untouched.[101] The main change was the expulsion, at the hands of the SA, of Kastl, a Jewish member of the RDI. There was a re-organisation which put the pro-Nazi Krupp von Bohlen in charge. Soon after, some 50 bankers and industrialists met to replace this with a 'General Council of the Economy', while individual branches had their own self governing Specialist Groups, who were simultaneously an arm of the civil service.[102] This process of reorganisation was undertaken by the industrialists themselves.[103]

A process of fusion of state and capital was taking place. At a meeting of military officers, landowners and industrialists in early 1933 Himmler called for a 'merging of everything genuine which had survived from the past and shown itself capable of confronting the future' so that his SS would reflect the 'bearing and breeding of the German nobility, and the creative efficiency of the industrialist'.[104] The banker Schröder expressed the same view from the other side of the fence. In 1945 he was asked how strong an influence he and his colleagues had had. He replied:

> Too strong!… The influence of the big banks was, in my view, much too strong!… The influence of the big banks on German industry reached such a level that there was hardly a section of German industry that was not under its control… [Also] they had a quite powerful influence on the party and the government. The big banks were *de facto* almost a second government. The party and the government which it controlled consulted the big banks on every financial and economic question which arose.[105]

Schröder was the leading member of Himmler's fan club, setting up a special account to channel big business donations into the coffers of the Reichsführer SS.[106]

Fusion did not stop after 1936. Far from there being a break in the later 1930s, links between business and government actually became even closer during the drive to war organised under Goering's 'Four Year Plan' office:

> Any remaining illusions about a proper demarcation between the state administration and private business were finally dispelled. The aim was the closest possible alignment between the regime and big business. This was particularly clearly expressed by the increasing number of industrial managers who, without being removed from the payrolls of their companies, occupied posts in the Four Year Plan organisation alongside Wehrmacht [army] officers.

> The most blatant example of the increasing interlacing of politics

and the economy was the appointment in 1938 of Carl Krauch as 'General Plenipotentiary for Chemicals'. A member of the board of IG Farben...he saw to it that the Four Year Plan was effectively turned into an IG Plan... Thanks to a quasi-monopoly in central areas of production, and Krauch's own energy, the company succeeded in extensively 'privatising' a good part of the economic policy of the Third Reich.[107]

Until 1933 IG Farben had been castigated by the Nazis as an 'international Jewish organisation'.[108] No such scruples troubled relations now because in 1937 IG Farben became 'almost completely Nazified... Almost all of the members of the IG managing board who did not already belong now joined up [while] all Jewish officials were removed, including a third of the supervisory board.' Another prominent businessman, Flick, of the Flick Concern, was proposed for 'Führer' of armaments production in 1937 by his friend Goering.[109] Even foreign businesses could be honoured, with Mooney, a General Motors director, receiving the Grand Cross of the German Eagle for 'distinguished service to the Reich'. This was richly deserved. The GM subsidiary Opel produced the 'highly profitable' Blitz truck for the invasion of Eastern Europe.[110]

The flow of influence was not always from the economic side of capitalism into its state machine. The reverse pattern was seen in the appointment of Goering's brother to an Aryanised bank.[111] Meanwhile the Hermann Goering Works was established. This was a huge steel concern which private industrialists were encouraged to fund. Thus, 'The steel industry had to pay protection money to the state by financing its own competitor'.[112] This indicates the complexity of Nazi-capitalist relations. The relationship between the Nazis (as fundamentally a wing of capitalist politics) and those capitalists in charge of production was not always harmonious. There is nothing unusual about this. In its commercial dealings capitalism is already riven with hatred and rivalries due to the nature of competition. It is therefore no surprise that the division of labour between politics and economics also causes tensions in even the most conventional capitalist societies. Nonetheless, any strains expressed within the ruling class family were qualitatively different to the treatment meted out to other classes and oppressed groups.

One example of contrasting interests within an overall community of purpose was the expense of the state machine and its Nazi hangers-on. For example, in 1937, industrialists submitted a memorandum to Hitler which complained that prior to the Nazi takeover the ratio of functionaries to the workforce was one to 12. Now it stood at only one to eight.[113] However, tensions could appear in other spheres such as the question of large versus small capital. Despite the bulk of its supporters being middle class or small capitalists, the Nazi regime supported concentration of capital from the very first, on the grounds that it would be more efficient for the waging of war. Schacht has been portrayed as a defender of capitalism (and by inference peaceful economic competition) as opposed to Nazi militarism, yet in 1935 he had this to say on the matter: 'Guns, aeroplanes, submarines, and anything else that may be necessary for defence in modern times are unthinkable in the absence of the highest development of capitalist industry'.[114] As early as July 1933 a cartel law was passed imposing this concentrated form on wide sections of the economy. Here was 'one of the first examples of the harmony of interests between the Nazi regime and monopolistic big business which itself represented a form of "organised capitalism".'[115]

The number of individual enterprises shrank as the individual units of capital grew. Between 1933 and 1939 the total of limited companies fell from 9,148 to 5,353.[116] The process of concentration was driven by government investment, which saw the proportion of funds from private sources drop from 36 percent to 29 percent of the total.[117] However, not all sections of capitalism benefited equally. While investment in heavy industry increased twelvefold up to the war, in consumer industry it only expanded three and a half times.[118]

It was already clear in the rise of Nazism that not all sections of the ruling class regarded the NSDAP in the same way, because the commercial conditions of capitalism varied, in particular between heavy industry and light industry. While the common interests of the class would always come first, there were doubts about what was the best policy for the state to pursue. Nazism had always attracted a particular wing of ruling class thinking. In the early days of the regime, when the emphasis had been on counter-revolutionary repression, Schacht, as economics minister, had been left to pursue a fairly conventional approach, emphasising a mix of foreign trade and internal economic reconstruction with fairly minimal government direction. However, from the mid-1930s the state wanted more emphasis put on preparations for war, and so a different approach was required.

It has been argued that the Third Reich 'cannot be properly described as state capitalism...for often it was hard to tell where the autonomy of private interests ended and the system of state orders began. In Hitler's armament programme there was no hard and fast division between state control and private initiative, between the regime and the economy'.[119] Surely that is the whole point. There was no break between them in what amounted to a fusion of capitalist state and capitalist economics where at other times there is a division of spheres.

It is interesting to note that even after 1936 the features that marked Nazism out were overshadowed by those it shared with other capitalist regimes between the wars. All showed a trend towards state capitalism, even if Stalin's Russia is left out of the picture. As Germany moved towards an autarchic block (involving its own territory, plus south east Europe where the share of German trade more than doubled between 1929 and 1938),[120] Britain was increasingly dependent on its Sterling Block of vast imperial territories. Japan was establishing similar hegemony in the far east.[121] State regulation of farming was observed in practically all Western countries,[122] German government intervention to stimulate the economy (including Labour Service) was paralleled in the New Deal and 'Civilian Conservation Corps' in the US.[123] In the early 1930s Japan's finance minister 'fully realised that the strain imposed by deflation on the social and economic structure of the country was too great for it to bear. He proposed a 'full employment' policy, launched four years before Keynes's General Theory provided him with a theoretical justification'.[124]

The drive to war

The German drive to war is often represented as something that was external to German capitalism and imposed from without by the politically motivated Nazis. The Four Year Plan of 1936 openly prepared for war and showed once more the government's militaristic intentions. Arms spending increased from 2 percent of national income in 1932 to 16 percent by 1936; by 1938 it stood at 32 percent.[125] However, there were also compelling economic reasons for the change in policy which saw Schacht resign as economics minister in 1937:

> Economic expansion inside Germany depended upon imports—especially of raw materials—which could not be financed by exports because of the stagnation of the rest of the world economy.
>
> The problem made itself felt within a year of the Nazis taking power. A surplus of exports over imports of 1,000 million marks in 1932 turned into a deficit of 316 million marks in the first six months of 1934. As Germany's gold and foreign currency holdings fell dramatically, the regime imposed very tight controls over foreign trade... The result was 'the economic insulation of Germany' as 'price connections with other countries were severed or greatly modified'. At the same time, the government unilaterally cancelled interest payments on Germany's foreign debts. All these measures constituted a powerful drive towards 'autarchy' (economic self sufficiency) within the German economy... But such expedients

could provide only an interim, stopgap relief... The only way to overcome such instability in raw material sources was to expand the boundaries of the German Reich so as to incorporate neighbouring economies, and to subordinate their industries.[126]

Evidence for the dynamism of the German state capitalist economy is the fact that by 1938 its industrial production was 37 percent above its 1925-29 average. Comparable figures for the US were minus 11 percent, France minus 10 percent, and Britain plus 29 percent.[127] By 1938 a labour shortage was manifest: 'There were no more reserves to be found among the registered unemployed... In December 1938 the minister of labour estimated that the economy was short of about one million workers'.[128]

If aggressive militarism gave a boost to the economy through rearmament, the dynamic economy gave a boost to aggressive militarism. As internal resources became exhausted, the desire for expansion, intrinsic to capitalism, imposed the need for an immediate solution. Given Germany's lack of empire this soon took a militaristic turn. As Hitler put it, 'What India was for England, the territories of Russia will be for us'.[129] The demand of industry for labour and raw materials encouraged military expansion, and the needs of military expansion sharpened the shortages of labour and raw materials. It was impossible to see where politics ended and economics began—they were fused in a state capitalist whole.

The much vaunted 'turning point' of 1936-38 was therefore the result of quantitative development rather than a qualitative change in class/state relations. The notion that '1936 marked the transition from "partial fascism" to "full fascism" ' can be rejected.[130] It is true that when Goering became head of the Four Year Plan office he effectively took charge of economic policy and, in 1937, this led to Schacht's resignation and replacement by Funk. This was not a clash between Nazism and capitalism, but a disagreement about the degree the economy should opt for autarchy and its capacity for rapid rearmament. Schacht's ingenious 'Mefo-bill' system had financed the military budget till then, and he did not disappear from the government, but continued as a minister without portfolio, being quickly reappointed as president of the Reichsbank. As one newspaper put it, 'Schacht goes out and stays in'.[131] Schacht feared that too rapid a rearmament was starving Germany's export industries, and so he proposed measures to slow its pace.[132] In opting for the Four Year Plan instead, Hitler was choosing a different form of competition—autarchic and militaristic—not a different social goal.

After Schacht's change of post, two senior military figures were made to retire due to sex scandals; 14 other generals also left at this time and the Hitler salute was adopted.[133] This too is represented as proof of Nazism's radical anti-establishment character. However, the decline of the traditional nobility at the head of the army was a long drawn out process which had seen a fall in the proportion of aristocratic generals from 61 percent in 1920 to 25 percent *before* the Nazis' purge. There were disagreements between sections of the army leadership and Hitler's circle, but, as with the economy, they were of a tactical nature, regarding the pace of rearmament and the strategic possibilities open to Germany.

One thing that was not in dispute was the ambition to recover ground lost at Versailles and to pursue a general war of conquest. In the early 1920s the general who blocked Hitler's Beer Hall Putsch, von Seekt, had set the overall aim: 'We must become powerful once more, and, naturally, as soon as we have such power we will take back all that we lost'.[134] Schleicher, the chancellor who preceded Hitler and who was put to death in the Night of the Long Knives, had called for, '(1) The strengthening of state authority; (2) The reorganisation of the economy; (3) The rebuilding of our defence capability: all the preconditions for a foreign policy which aims at a Greater Germany'.[135]

Now the most significant military commentator was Ludwig Beck, chief of the general staff from 1935. He was replaced at the same time as Fritsch and Blomberg (and would later be titular head of the officers' plot against Hitler in 1944).[136] Beck had been the first senior military figure to embrace Nazism, welcoming the Third Reich in 1933 'as the brightest ray of hope since 1918',[137] and he believed, like the Nazis, in 'total war' which 'for Germany would be a struggle for its very existence'.[138] However, Beck feared that Hitler's policies were reckless and might jeopardise the nationalist goals they both shared. During the Czech crisis of 1938 his slogan was 'For the Führer! Against the war!' because at that time 'a war on Czechoslovakia must lead to a world war and the destruction of Germany'.[139]

Beck was not alone. An article supported by 100 anonymous Wehrmacht officers published in Switzerland in 1938 predicted that a too rapid commencement of world war would confront the Berlin-Rome-Tokyo Axis powers with the combined economic might of Britain, France, the USSR and the US. A war would be lost because it would 'demand enormous sacrifice and be of long duration'.[140] The judgement of these officers was prophetic, but there was no sign that they disagreed with the overall imperialistic aims of Nazism.

The 1936-38 disputes were not a symbol of a fundamental break between Nazism and the capitalist establishment (in this case, in its military aspect), but the opposite. The changes 'did not disturb...the officers' corps unduly',[141] and:

> Since February 1938 the balance had indeed shifted in favour of Hitler, but this was unthinkable without the active assistance of the military leadership itself. What occurred was a stronger identification of the military with the political goals of Hitler in the direction of a German imperialism that strove for a 'New Order' of Europe.[142]

Once again there was a fusion of the aims of Nazism and capitalism. The view that Nazism created a unique kind of society which was neither capitalist nor socialist is utterly false. There were indeed special characteristics—its location in one of the most advanced and dynamic capitalist states in combination with a regime of extreme counter-revolutionary character and intense anti-Semitism. Hitler's rule was a unique brand of ruling class politics, not a distinct item standing on its own. As Trotsky put it, 'Fascism in power is least of all the rule of the petty bourgeoisie. On the contrary, it is the most ruthless dictatorship of monopoly capital'.[143] The Nazis' policies, which involved the fusion of state and capital, did not represent a takeover of the latter, but a cooperation of the two. Such collaboration between the state and the capitalist economy was a characteristic trend in all advanced industrial societies in the period between the wars.

Chapter 8

War and the Holocaust

It is often argued that the Second World War originated from Hitler's programme, as 'stated, as clearly as possible, in 1924, in *Mein Kampf*'.[1] In this view, 'The initiator and motive force of everything that happened was Adolf Hitler'.[2] But gigantic wars costing millions of lives did not begin in 1939, nor have they ceased since 1945. It is the system of capitalism, where all too often competition through trade turns into competition through armed conflict, that is ultimately responsible for the prevalence of wars in the 20th century, while modern technology makes them more destructive.

Yet the system is not driven always and everywhere to military action, so it is not enough to deny Hitler's sole responsibility with the notion that capitalism in general caused the Second World War. Taylor offers a neat analogy: 'Wars are much like road accidents. They have a general cause and particular causes at the same time. Every road accident is caused, in the last resort, by the invention of the internal combustion engine; but it is also important to seek a specific cause for each accident... So it is with wars'.[3] The Second World War was certainly no accident, and Hitler cannot be exonerated from blame, but, like the First World War, it grew out of imperialist competition:

> A considerable part of the world divided into two groups, one led by Germany, Italy and Japan, the other by France and the Soviet Union... The first group was, for varying reasons, dissatisfied with the territorial settlement of the world made in 1919—a settlement which the second group desired to maintain. The fundamental division was between those who were in the main satisfied with the existing international distribution of the world's goods and those who were not.[4]

The trigger for war was the German invasion of Poland on 1 September 1939. Explanations for this tend to fall into two schools—the intentionalist and structuralist/functionalist. The former stresses Nazi ideology as the most important factor, while the latter puts emphasis on the role of institutions and society generating a dynamism towards conflict in a process that has been described as 'cumulative radicalisation'. Both sides have convincing evidence for their claims, but the dispute is essentially a false one. In its pure form the intentionalist argument implies that Nazism had to deliberately push the structures of capitalism in a direction they were not going in themselves. The functionalist claim underplays the Nazi leadership's consciously imperialist policies. In fact, there was an inner relation between both facets. The Third Reich was, however unusual, a product of capitalist development. Yet as part of the superstructure it was relatively autonomous and its actions reflected back on society. This interplay was brutally demonstrated in Hitler's straightforward justification for the Second World War: 'What we need but do not have, we must conquer'.[5]

The political/ideological dimension up to 1939

The Nazis believed war was virtuous. Hitler told his dinner companions in 1941, 'For the good of the German people, we must wish for a war every 15 to 20 years'.[6] He considered the conflict in 1939 a re-run of the 1914-18 war. On the day it erupted he declared, 'A November 1918 shall never repeat itself in German history'.[7] But a counter-revolutionary twist was added, as Goebbels' diary indicates:

> The Führer is gloriously convinced of victory. He shows how different the situation is from that in 1914, and declares that our defeat then was a result of treachery alone. Today he does not intend to spare the lives of traitors.[8]

Yet the early stages appear to contradict this counter-revolutionary intent. On 23 August Hitler signed a non-aggression pact with Stalin, and hostilities actually began against Britain (which was supposed to be a 'racial ally' of Teutonic Germany) and France. Conventional imperialist motives were therefore an important component. However, the Nazis still saw the war as an ideological crusade against Bolshevism. While a Marxist analysis shows Russia in 1939 to have been state capitalist for a decade, Hitler and his circle still regarded it as the embodiment of Communism, as well as the region for Lebensraum. The Nazi-Soviet pact was a strictly temporary expedient. Just days before it was signed, he said in private:

> Everything I do is directed against Russia; if the West is too stupid and blind to grasp this, I shall be forced to reach agreement with the Russians to attack the West and then, after its defeat, turn against the Soviet Union with my combined forces.[9]

Goebbels saw Operation Barbarossa (the invasion of Russia) as 'our one great duty to history'.[10] For Hitler, the Russian campaign was a struggle 'of ideologies and racial differences and will have to be conducted with unprecedented, merciless and unrelenting harshness... The commissars are the bearers of ideology directly opposed to National Socialism'.[11] Perhaps the most chilling comment was Goering's: 'Between 20 and 30 million persons will die of hunger in Russia. Perhaps it is well that it should be so, for certain nations must be decimated'.[12] This prediction came horribly true, with over 20 million dying in the Soviet Union (13.6 million of them soldiers).[13] In September 1944, with defeat staring him in the face, Hitler confessed his perplexity about being opposed by what he regarded as the 'wrong' enemies:

> I can't understand the stupidity of these people. They just can't see how dangerous Bolshevism is, or that they're sawing off the branch they're sitting on. I'd like to see these two powers [the US and Britain] realise, before it's too late, that they're fighting on the wrong side... Providence has shown me that there's no coming to terms with Bolshevism, and I shall never offer my hand to Russia.[14]

The background to 1939—the economic dimension

Though Nazi Germany was impelled to challenge the existing international balance of capitalist power in the late 1930s, world war was not inevitable. If its capitalist rivals had given Germany the competitive space Hitler craved, world war could have been avoided. At first this seemed likely as Britain adopted the policy of appeasement. It had various reasons for doing this, such as the popular opposition to war (after the horrors of 1914-18) and the fear that Britain was not ready militarily. A further motive was expressed by Lord Halifax when he met Hitler in 1937:

> He and other members of the English government were convinced that by smashing Communism in his own country the Führer had done a great service not only to Germany but had blocked its way in Western Europe. Thus Germany could rightly be seen as the bulwark of the West against Bolshevism.[15]

On the strength of this information Hitler chose to act ever more boldly on the international scene, reoccupying the demilitarised Rhineland, annexing Austria (1938), and, in spite of promises made at Munich, occupying the Czech lands of Bohemia and Moravia in 1939.[16] However, foreign powers would not allow piecemeal German expansion indefinitely. At a certain point a general conflict would erupt. In 1937 Hitler discussed a preferred date for a large scale war. With rearmament still incomplete he picked the years 1943-45 because after that, 'Our relative strength would decrease in relation to the rearmament which would by then have been carried out by the rest of the world'.[17] Yet the war did not begin in 1943 but 1939 when 'the military estimates were unequivocal. The German armed forces were unprepared'.[18] Why?

Part of the explanation might be that Hitler underestimated the seriousness of Western pledges to defend Poland, but, more importantly, there was an internal dynamic driving the regime to ever more reckless action. As Hitler said ten days before the invasion of Poland, 'Because of our restrictions our economic situation is such that we can only hold out for a few more years. Goering can confirm this. We have no other choice; we must act'.[19] Mason suggests that there was a 'general economic crisis' caused by labour shortages on the land and in industry.[20] In this view, the key 'restriction' was the German working class which was therefore the force that drove the Nazis into starting a war long before they wanted.

This thesis has caused great controversy. A critic of Mason argues that in 1938, 'After six years of repression and party rule and propaganda, the working class was demoralised, powerless and fearful'.[21] This may be correct, but it is also also true that the Nazi regime feared the working class's potential for fighting back. Boosting armaments output required a significant squeeze on living standards, yet time and again the regime baulked at this:

> In 1938 Hitler categorically refused to agree to a plan for priorities in the national economy; a year later he refused even to discuss...let alone accept, food price increases. Evidently it was Hitler's and Goering's attitude that lay behind the refusal to increase taxes. When in 1939 a coupon system for food rationing was introduced, Hitler was angry and disturbed to think of the effects on popular opinion... In November 1938 [Goering] told the assembled Reich ministers, commanders of the armed forces and secretaries of state that shutting down part of the consumer sector for the benefit of the armaments industry was simply impracticable. Even in cases where the political leadership had attempted to promote rearmament by introducing an element of overt compulsion, the results, owing to a less than rigorous enforcement, fell far short of what was required. The clearest example of this is the effect of the state wages policy introduced in June 1938. The first year of would-be stabilisation and cutbacks saw the average hourly and

weekly wage in industry rise significantly faster than in the previous 12 months. The introduction of civilian labour conscription produced similar results.[22]

Even when demand for labour intensified still further the Nazis refused to mobilise women workers for fear of the effect on morale. The number of women workers in the labour force actually fell by 300,000 after the outbreak of war. Only in 1941 did women's employment surpass 1928 levels, and in April 1942 Hitler still rejected the idea of conscripting women. This contrasted with Britain, where the government campaigned for women's involvement in the war economy.[23] Foreign labour was imported instead, but this required the very military expansion which led to premature world war. Perhaps Mason's argument about the role of the working class is not the complete explanation for the Second World War beginning when it did, but it was certainly a crucial element in Nazi calculations.

The outbreak of the Second World War did not find Nazism deviating from the naturally peaceful path of capitalism. There was still a continuing and indeed intensifying overlap of capitalist economic and political interests. The rearmament boom had shifted the balance within the capitalist economy from one in which profits were predominantly made through trade to one in which profits were made through fighting. Towards the end of the war the heavy industrialist Krupp would look back nostalgically and conclude, 'For the employer, unlike virtually every other occupational category, the National Socialist upheaval represented a thoroughly new, startlingly favourable situation'.[24] Goering had kept his promise of 1936, that returns on capital speculated in a military adventure would far outstrip conventional investments: 'All that matters is victory or defeat. If we conquer, the business world will be fully indemnified... We are playing for the highest stakes. What can be more profitable than rearmament orders?'[25] Industrialists, both German and non-German, were enthusiastic. Röchling, an iron and steel industrialist, told Hitler in 1936, 'War is almost inevitable...so we must use every means to fight this very struggle for existence', while the General Motors director in charge of overseas operations discussed prospects with Hitler face to face just two weeks before the outbreak of the Second World War.[26]

Profits did not stop with preparations for war. Conquest would offer all manner of exciting commercial opportunities in the most disgusting but lucrative ways. So before the war began IG Farben planned how to swallow up foreign chemical firms (both Jewish and non-Jewish owned).[27] As the fighting developed, excitement grew:

On 18 May 1940 Krupp, a partner in Henkel, the detergent manufacturers, and two other industrialists spent hours listening to the radio while seated round a table covered with a map of north western Europe. As news flashes of the Wehrmacht's advances into the Low Countries came in, they grew increasingly agitated and started waving their hands about to jab at the map: 'This one here is yours, that one there is yours, we shall have that man arrested, he has two factories.' In the midst of the hubbub one of the four industrialists got up to telephone his office staff and ordered them immediately to request Wehrmacht permission for two of their number to proceed to Holland the following day.

Further phone calls over the next few months and years procured for Krupp's Dutch shipyards, Belgian metalworks, a large slice of the French machine tool industry, Yugoslav chromium deposits, Greek nickel mines, iron and steel plants in the Ukraine and so on.[28]

Balance sheets soon told the tale. IG Farben's profits rose from 363 to 822 million marks between 1939 and 1943, Krupp's rose from 57 to 111 million (1935-41), AEG's from 598 to 1,200 million (1939-45).[29] Industry was not ungrateful. Even as the first army divisions advanced in 1938 the IG Farben boss wrote a letter saying, 'Profoundly impressed by the return of the Sudetenland to the Reich which you, my Führer, have achieved, the IG Farben industrie AG puts a sum of half a million Reichsmarks at your disposal'.[30]

The actual conduct of the war owed a lot to the economic restrictions on the German state. The army had no choice but to use the strategy of *Blitzkrieg*—short limited engagements to provide labour and raw materials for an expanding, yet still inadequate, war machine. Thus Goebbels saw Poland as 'an enormous reservoir of labour. From there we can get people for the menial jobs, where there is a great shortage. After all, we have to get them from somewhere'.[31] However, the respite offered by Poland was only temporary:

Other economic problems became more serious and encouraged a broadening of the conflict. German imports and exports suffered a sharp fall, largely because of Germany's inability to pay for imports. The occupation of Denmark, Norway and the Benelux countries was largely designed to put the resources of these countries at Germany's disposal. Hitler also ordered an immediate attack upon France, partly because he believed that Germany's economic position must worsen in comparison to the Anglo-French allies, and because he feared continued dependence upon Soviet supplies.[32]

At first, *Blitzkrieg* tactics proved remarkably successful. The Polish operation lasted just four weeks, the Norwegian eight weeks. Holland fell in five days, Belgium in 17. France took six weeks, Yugoslavia 11 days and Greece just three weeks.[33] However, in the 20th century military success is linked to overall capitalist strength, where once it mainly depended on manpower. Germany's frenetic military expansion could succeed against isolated competitors with inferior strength. The Russian campaign turned out differently (despite Stalin's disastrous purge of his best generals and the massing of troops on the western border because he doubted the German army's manoeuvrability). In 1941, Operation Barbarossa failed to reproduce the early success of a *Blitzkrieg*.

Without minimising the anti-fascist motivation and heroic self sacrifice of the resistance movements and many in the Allied armies, the war was ultimately fought as an imperialist conflict rather than as a struggle for social and economic liberation. So its result ultimately depended on the size of capitals being thrown onto the scales of competition, as this table illustrates.

Economic and military statistics of warring states in 1939[34]		
	National product (billion dollars)	*Population* (millions)
US	68	130
USSR	31	167
GB	24	48
France	10	42
Poland	3	35
Germany	33	68
Italy	7	44
Japan	6	71

The course of the war was dictated by the laws of capitalist competition as translated into guns, bombers and tanks.

The prominent role of the state in promoting German capital dated back to the 19th century. Hitler's speech to the Industry Club in 1932 had stressed this point and now, in 1939, it was being put into practice. The war was not just the product of ideology but followed from the logic of capitalist expansionism, where the interests of the capitalist state and the economy overlapped.

The Holocaust is commonly held to be an event which stood outside this pattern. This is inaccurate, for it was an element in the creation of the *Grossraumwirtschaft*—the macroeconomic space which Nazi hegemony over Europe through war was supposed to bring.

The Holocaust

The organised mass murder of civilians and prisoners of war carried out by Nazism during the Second World War is rightly counted as the greatest single crime against humanity in history. It included two elements in a hitherto unique combination, the decision to 'kill off, as completely as possible, a particular group of humans, including old people, women, children, and infants',[35] and elimination 'on an assembly line basis',[36] using the most advanced scientific and organisational methods available. The enormous scope and coldly calculated prosecution of the barbaric plan seem almost to defy rational analysis. However, with Nazi movements today springing up all over Europe, we cannot limit our reaction to expressions of horror and revulsion. To prevent a repetition, the gruesome event must be understood.

This account will not dignify with a lengthy discussion the lies of so called 'historians' who deny the fact of the Holocaust or, like David Irving, pretend that Hitler was ignorant of what was happening.[37] When Hitler declared that, 'The discovery of the Jewish virus is one of the greatest revolutions that has taken place in the world', and, 'We shall regain our health only by eliminating the Jew',[38] it is not necessary to have a signed decree authorising mass murder. Eichmann, the chief administrator of the extermination process, reported under interrogation, 'I never saw a written order... All I know is that Heydrich said to me, "The Führer has ordered the physical extermination of the Jews".'[39] As for the evidence, the murder of millions is all too present in the blighted families, the memories of survivors, and the camps themselves. To give just one example, the six storerooms (out of 35) that the Nazis failed to destroy at Auschwitz disgorged 368,820 men's suits, 836,255 women's coats and dresses, while in the tannery seven tons of human hair were found.[40] Eichmann put a rough figure of six million Jewish non-combatant victims of genocide.[41] These were part of the larger process of the Holocaust, to which must be added some ten million others:

> Greeks, Poles, Yugoslavs, Czechs, Russians, and men, women and children of a dozen other nationalities, all of them civilians who had taken no part in military action... Among those murdered were as many as a quarter of a million Gypsies, tens of thousands of homosexuals, and tens of thousands of 'mental defectives'. Also murdered, often after the cruelties of torture, were several million Soviet prisoners of war.[42]

There are also more 'respectable' and 'eminent' figures who accept the reality of the Holocaust but who try to explain it away.[43]

Serious students of the Holocaust sometimes explain it in the following way: 'Hitler's calculations were the sole determining factor as regards the inception, development and planning of the extermination policy'.[44] So the Holocaust fulfilled an idea 'adumbrated by apocalyptic minded anti-Semites during the 19th century' which Hitler transformed 'into concrete political action'.[45] This approach simply cannot explain the vast machinery of destruction which involved large numbers in its complex organisation. Of course fanatical racists were involved at every stage, but they encountered practically no objections to their plans from the rest of the establishment; the close cooperation of party, state and capitalism did not decrease during the extermination, it grew.

Finally, there is the perspective which argues Hitler merely responded to the wishes of ordinary people: 'German society...enthusiastically pursued genocide because of a culture-wide phobia against touching Jewish flesh'.[46] Goldhagen argues in a similar vein: 'Germans' anti-Semitic beliefs about Jews were the central causal agent of the Holocaust'.[47]

Rejecting the above three approaches, this account will try and locate the murder process in its political and social context.

The development of anti-Semitism after 1933

The early days of the Third Reich were characterised by SA mass terror in which Communists were the main victims. Although Jews also suffered, in April 1933 there were less than 100 Jews out of the 1,000 inmates in the first concentration camp, Dachau.[48] During that first year up to 45 Jews were beaten to death in so called 'wild actions'.[49] At first the regime was happy to unleash the SA to smash left wing opposition, drive through Gleichschaltung (coordination), and generally atomise society. Anti-Semitism played its part in this. However, as we have seen, once the bloodhounds had served their purpose they were reined in, and during the Night of the Long Knives, neutralised. The same applied to their uncontrolled anti-Semitic violence.

The 1 April 1933 boycott of Jewish businesses was the first centrally organised anti-Semitic action of the government, but it did more than serve the fanatical hatred of leading Nazis. It was above all designed to placate the Nazi radicals in the SA by showing state commitment to their cause. It also channelled their excesses in a centrally controlled and 'safer' direction. This was necessary to avoid damaging international reaction, and to calm the fears of the elite and middle class regarding uncontrolled grass roots Nazi rowdyism. Thus anti-Semitic policy had both an ideological and functional role.

If the causes of the 1 April boycott were complex, it was not a response to the pressure of the mass of German people. Bankier writes:

> Not only did sizeable parts of the population severely condemn the persecution, but even Nazi sympathisers did not fully endorse it. Sometimes there were animated discussions in front of Jewish shops and fighting broke out between the public and party men. Even generals wearing medals came to stores owned by Jews in Berlin to demonstrate their disapproval of the Nazi policy.[50]

This does not mean that racist attitudes were absent in the population, but that aggressive tactics were disapproved of. This is important because it means Nazi policy was marked out as qualitatively different to the 'normal' racism endemic in capitalist societies. Reprehensible though the latter is, it does not produce the organised violence of fascism.

A barrage of measures followed the 1 April boycott, such as the previously mentioned ban on Jewish civil servants (11 April). The next targets were 'non-Aryan doctors' (22 April), school and college students (25 April), assistant judges (28 April), and so on.[51] The vindictive spiral of discrimination continued over the years. It was directed at separating Jews from the rest of the population, not exterminating them.

The infamous Nuremberg decrees of 1935 have been seen as a dramatic escalation in the Nazi leadership's drive towards extermination. These laws for the 'Protection of German Blood and Honour'[52] made important decisions in terms of excluding Jews from citizenship, defining who was a Jew, and banning sexual relationships between Jews and 'Aryans'. Yet these laws were inspired by the same motives that animated the April 1933 boycott. Even the most rabid anti-Semite of all, Streicher, argued, 'We don't smash any windows and we don't smash any Jews. We don't have to do that. Whoever engages in single actions of that kind is an enemy of the state, a provocateur, or even a Jew'.[53] It may be the case that 'the vast majority of the population approved of the Nuremberg laws because they identified with the racialist policy', but they also welcomed the laws as providing a framework 'that would end the reign of terror and set precise limits to anti-Semitic activities'.[54]

The intense anti-Semitism of the leading Nazis was moulded by political considerations:

> That Hitler was able to contain the rivalries and maintain his position at the top of this tangled and shifting hierarchy is testimony to his political

acuity and charismatic power. It was the Jew who helped hold Hitler's system together—on the practical as well as the ideological level. The Jew allowed Hitler to ignore the long list of economic and social promises he had made to the SA, the lower party apparatus and the lower middle classes. By steering the attention of these groups away from their more genuine grievances and towards the Jew, Hitler succeeded in blunting the edge of their revolutionary wrath, leaving him freer to pursue his own non-ideological goals of power and cooperation with those whose influence he had once promised to weaken or even destroy.[55]

In 1938 came the anti-Semitic pogrom of *Kristallnacht* (night of broken glass). On 9-10 November an orgy of violence was unleashed in which 100 Jews died. The US consul described events in Leipzig:

> A barrage of Nazi ferocity as had had no equal hitherto in Germany, or very likely anywhere else in the world since savagery began. Jewish buildings were smashed into and contents demolished or looted. In one of the Jewish sections an 18 year old boy was hurled from a three story window to land with both legs broken on a street littered with burning beds and other household furniture... Ferocious as was the violation of property, the most hideous phase of the so called 'spontaneous' action has been the wholesale arrest and transportation to concentration camps of male German Jews.[56]

Kristallnacht was not the result of popular hatred, nor even a concerted government policy. The pretext for the pogrom was the assassination by a Jew of a German diplomat in Paris, yet a similar assassination in 1936 produced no such reaction. Although authorised by Goebbels, Hitler himself appears to have been ignorant of the intended pogrom.[57] Goebbels planned it as a means of enhancing his influence in the power struggle of the various Nazi factions. He was roundly attacked by his competitors. Himmler denounced his 'craving for power' and 'empty headedness'; the economic minister asked, 'Are you crazy, Goebbels? To make such a mess of things',[58] and Goering said, 'I have had enough of these demonstrations! It is not the Jew they harm but myself, as the final authority for coordinating the German economy'.[59]

Kristallnacht was supposed to be a spontaneous popular protest but, as a secret party report admitted, Goebbels' 'oral instructions' were 'that the party should not appear outwardly as the originator of the demonstrations, but that in reality it should organise them and carry them out'.[60] Ordinary Germans were not fooled:

> For the first time, all Germans were personally confronted with anti-Semitic violence. For this reason there is no trace of indifference. All

sections of the population reacted with deep shock. The public was po-larised on the handling of the Jewish question: party circles and their periphery gave full support, while the large majority condemned it.[61]

Loud arguments occurred between the Brownshirts and ordinary people, who tore up their leaflets, and working people demonstra-tively shopped in Jewish businesses.[62] It is significant that *Kristallnacht* was the very last occasion that the Nazis attempted a public demon-stration of violence against Jews within Germany. The 'Final Solution' was therefore clothed in euphemisms and secrecy.[63]

Once *Kristallnacht* was launched, more conventional capitalist considerations came into play. The political costs could be offset by plunder. Since 1933 anti-Semitism had walked hand in hand with sound business principles. One example was the 'Haavara Agreement' between Nazis and Zionists which, between 1933 and 1938, helped some 170,000 Jews emigrate to Palestine while the German economy gained valuable exports and foreign currency.[64] Then came 'Aryani-sation'—the seizure of Jewish assets which gathered pace when Go-ering sought funding for the armaments programme.[65] Due to the November 1938 pogrom 35,000 Jews were bundled into concentration camps as a lever to force emigration and expropriation. They were released if they promised to abandon their wealth and emigrate.[66] The number of Jewish owned businesses plummeted by 80 percent within one year.[67] This procedure 'combined deportation with extortion'.[68]

One example of Aryanisation was the takeover of the Kreditanstalt bank (a concern of the Jewish Rothschild family) and associated chem-ical plants in Austria. In the days before the annexation the commer-cial negotiations were conducted from the Austrian end by two Jews—Rothenberg and Pollack. When Austria was incorporated into Germany, Rothenberg 'was taken for a ride by uniformed Brownshirts …and thrown out of a moving automobile' while Pollack 'was tram-pled to death. In the meantime, the German businessmen went about their business. The Kreditanstalt was gobbled up by the giant Deutsche Bank, and its subsidiary, the Pulverfabrik, fell to IG Farben'.[69] With its heart set on the giant Petschek Group in Czechoslovakia, the Flick Concern encouraged Goering to pass an Aryanisation Law and picked up its rival, valued at 16 million dollars, for a mere six million.[70]

Could it be that these events merely camouflaged a 'racial revolu-tion' bent on mass Jewish extermination? The barbarity of the Nazis' policies until then cannot be minimised, yet they ran counter to any goal of extermination. The policy was to drive Jews out (and thus beyond the reach of the Nazi butchery), if necessary by instilling panic.

In 1938 Hitler formally declared for emigration 'by every possible means',[71] and a year later Goering used exactly the same expression.[72] Even in private there seem to have been no discussions of the 'Final Solution'. In December 1939, for example, Goebbels noted after a discussion with Hitler that despite the anti-Semitic policies the Jewish issue 'will return in a few generations. There is no panacea against it'.[73]

In 1940 and 1941 Hitler prohibited the entry or re-entry of Jews into German controlled territory,[74] since expulsion was the aim. One idea, posed in late 1939, was to create a Jewish 'reservation' (in imitation of Native American models) in the Polish region of Lublin. When that proved impractical, in June 1940 Hitler opted to use Madagascar 'to harbour the Jews'.[75] Eichmann claimed the idea for such a 'Jewish homeland' came from Herzl, the father of Zionism.[76] The scheme came to nothing because British sea power made transportation impossible. Such plans for expulsion would have destroyed many lives, but they did not amount to genocide.

Counter-revolution or racial revolution? The initial phases of the Holocaust

So far this account has used the term racism in an undifferentiated form. To understand the Holocaust, however, it is important to note that the racism of the regime was not the same as that to be found in the population. Without the evidence of extensive social surveys it is impossible to say how far ideas of racism penetrated the various strata of German society, though reactions to events like *Kristallnacht* suggest it was far less intense than in the Nazi Party.[77] Nevertheless, given the silencing of opposition views and the massive propaganda efforts of Goebbels, Streicher and others, it would not be surprising if racism was widespread. Even so, racism at the base of society, while influenced by ideology from above, tends to be driven by fear, anger and frustration generated within society. To the extent that these emotions fail to find an outlet in challenging their real cause, capitalism, they can be channelled against scapegoats, an 'out-group' (such as Jews). Although this is utterly misguided and ultimately self defeating, such racism is conceived as a defence of the 'in-group'. Thus it was that the SA was both the most emotionally anti-capitalist but also the most actively anti-Semitic section of the NSDAP.

Ruling class racism is different. Whether deliberate or not it is used to divide and weaken opposition forces, justifying the contemptuous treatment by the upper class of all other human groups in a hierarchy running from the 'superior' boss, to the 'inferior' worker, and the still more 'inferior' minority 'race'. Ruling class racism is thus a component in the broader notion of superiority and inferiority. It is not motivated by deluded defence of the 'in-group' as a whole, but defence of the ruling class interest. A society that sees human beings as factors of production, commodities to be bought and sold, used or thrown on the unemployment scrapheap, produced the Holocaust. Today the same driving force can take less violent forms, such as the destruction of food while millions starve, or the rationing of the poor's survival chances (through healthcare) while the rich enjoy maximum life potential.

Nazi racism in this context took the form of eugenics, a racism directed towards producing a 'healthy' (ie fully exploitable) population. This had a respectable capitalist pedigree, for a Reich sterilisation law was drafted in July 1932 before Hitler was made chancellor.[78] It had been motivated by the crash. In order to cut government spending welfare programmes were slashed and cheaper 'biologically conceived remedies replaced political solutions to social problems'.[79]

This motivation is important in explaining why the first victims of the Holocaust were Germans, non-Jewish and Jewish alike. Compulsory sterilisation began as early as 1933,[80] and by 1939 had been applied to 200,000 people including the 'feeble minded', 73,000 schizophrenics, 57,000 epileptics and 30,000 alcoholics.[81] Although 20 percent of Germans were reckoned 'unfit' to reproduce,[82] the total sterilised by 1945 was only(!) 360,000, or almost 1 percent of the population.[83] Compulsory abortion was introduced in 1935, the number performed reaching 30,000.[84] In selection for sterilisation, women 'were tested as to their capacity and inclination for housework, for childrearing...as well as to their capacity and inclination for employment. Men were assessed mostly for their work behaviour'.[85]

In October 1939 a qualitative leap took place with the introduction of 'Action T4', the so called euthanasia campaign against 'lives not worth living'. People falling into this category were condemned because, as a meeting of all German mayors was told, they 'are nothing but a burden—their care creates endless expense'.[86] To prove the point, careful calculations were made on potential savings. The money 'wasted' on marmalade, for example, was computed at 7,083,504 marks.[87] A senior official in Hitler's chancellery affirmed that 'since the problem is mainly an economic one, it will have to be tackled from an economic perspective'.[88] Children under three were the first targets, with 3,000 dying. In general the criteria for Action-T4 selection paralleled the sterilisation campaign. 'There was one ground for exemption—the ability to work'.[89] Later groups selected for elimination included, 'asocials' (defined as 'the group of failures...the workshy and slovenly...and criminals').[90]

Action T4 exposed the difference between the ruling class version of racism and that of even the rank and file Nazis. One judge explained:

> Great agitation prevails in wide circles of the population, and not only amongst those national comrades who count someone who is mentally ill within their family. [The fear is that] all life that is of no more use to the community as a whole, but rather—seen in purely material terms—is a burden upon it, would be declared, through administrative channels, to be no longer worthy of life and eliminated accordingly.[91]

In August 1941, after some 70,000 deaths, Action T4 was apparently stopped. In fact it continued covertly. The Nazis had discovered that secrecy was required and operations were moved east.[92] It was immediately replaced by the more secretive 'Special Treatment 14f13' which eliminated many more, non-productive concentration camp prisoners and others.[93] Grounds for selection included 'persons with criminal records', alcoholics 'no longer capable of successfully handling their economic and domestic relationships', 'prostitutes', 'the remaining widows and children of persons liquidated', 'shirkers who persistently refuse to do physical labour', and 'persons who are completely degenerate or particularly inferior in appearance'.[94] The extermination method developed would later be used in the death camps: 'Undressing the victims, or making them undress, and leading them into a room rigged with dummy showers where they were gassed... After the removal of their gold teeth, the corpses were burned in a crematory oven'.[95]

The other side of the equation to exterminating those not useful to production was the enslavement of those who were. In January 1938 Himmler launched a 'single, comprehensive and surprise swoop' on 'workshy elements...who can be proved to have rejected offers of work on two occasions without just cause or have accepted work only to abandon it again shortly afterwards'.[96] Henceforth concentration camps were not only for political suspects but for the removal of those who were 'a burden to the community'. According to Heydrich, the aim was to force the 'employment of every able-bodied person and not permit anti-social individuals to avoid work and thus to sabotage the Four Year Plan'.[97]

The developing mentality of mass murder among the Nazi leaders

The outbreak of war gave a particular twist to the Nazi leaders' thinking. Hitler made the following sinister prophecy in January 1939:

If the international Jewish financiers in and outside Europe should succeed in plunging the nations once more into a world war, then the
result will not be the Bolshevising of the earth, and thus the victory of
Jewry, but the annihilation of the Jewish race in Europe![98]

The implied anti-capitalism of denunciations against financiers
can be ignored. We have seen the central role that Aryan German financiers had in Nazi planning for world war. But the link between
threats to Jews and the outbreak of war was real enough.

The Second World War seemed a fulfilment of Hitler's prophecy,
and in 1942 he pointed this out by publicly referring to his 1939
speech over and over again.[99] However, despite the immense brutality of late 1939, the 'final solution of the Jewish question' in terms of
wholesale extermination had not commenced. Terrible acts were still
committed though, principally in Poland. In Hitler's view Poland was
'of use to us only as a reservoir of labour' and his instructions called
for the eradication of the 'Polish intelligentsia', many of whom were
Jewish.[100] Himmler, addressing concentration camp commandants,
added that in due course 'all Poles will disappear from the world... It
is essential that the great German people should regard it as its chief
task to destroy all Poles'.[101] Thus in the first six weeks of war the primary targets were the Polish intelligentsia. Some 16,000 civilians
were murdered, 5,000 of whom were Jewish.[102]

While no decision for genocide against the Jews had yet been taken,
the Polish war produced a sequence of events that made it far more
likely. Although policy towards Jews was based on expulsion, every advance only increased the number of Jews under Nazi jurisdiction. In
June 1940 the number had risen to 3.25 million.[103] When the notorious
Wannsee Conference (December 1941) convened, Heydrich explained
that, while the half million strong German Jewish population of pre-1933
had dwindled to 131,000, annexation of Austria had added 44,000 and
the Czech seizure (Bohemia and Moravia) 72,000, while the predicted
Nazi hegemony of Europe would result in 'about 11 million Jews to be
considered'.[104] With the failure of the Lublin and Madagascar plans a decision was made to concentrate Jews within ghettos. Overcrowded and
underfed, life for the populations of ghettos in places like Warsaw and
Lodz was hell on earth and the death rate phenomenal, with 20,000 dead
by starvation and disease by the summer of 1941. Yet, by contrast with
what would follow, 'in no Jewish community had more than two or
three percent been murdered'.[105]

The deliberate decision to conduct genocide was not made until
1941 at about the time of the invasion of Russia. These two events did

not coincide accidentally. A delusion had burnt into Hitler's mind—defeat in the 1914-18 war was caused by revolution; the revolution caused by Bolshevism and inspired by Jews was to be avenged. At the beginning of his political career Hitler had imagined a clear link between the Jews and the 'stab in the back' of revolution, writing in *Mein Kampf*:

> If at the beginning and during the war, someone had only subjected about 12,000 or 15,000 of these Hebrew enemies of the people to poison gas...then the sacrifice of millions at the front would not have been in vain.[106]

As war approached the same obsession returned:

> The last thing world Judaism wants to see is the Jews disappear from Europe. On the contrary it looks on the Jews in Europe as the advance troops for the bolshevisation of the world (November 1938).[107]

> We are going to destroy the Jews. They are not going to get away with what they did on 9 November 1918. The day of reckoning has come (January 1939).[108]

This view had fateful consequences for the planning of Operation Barbarossa. In March 1941 Hitler's speech preparing his commanders for this was summarised as follows: 'Struggle between two *Weltanschauungen* [world views]. Devastating assessment of Bolshevism... It is a war of extermination... The struggle will be very different from that in the West'.[109]

Hitler was not alone in holding such attitudes. Innumerable other examples could be cited. Here are a few. Heydrich explained in June 1941 to the Einsatzgruppen (the squad which carried out the first mass exterminations) that 'Judaism in the east was the source of Bolshevism and must therefore be wiped out in accordance with the Führer's aims'.[110] General Keitel insisted in September 1941 that 'the struggle against Bolshevism demands ruthless and energetic measures above all against the Jews, the main carriers of Bolshevism'.[111] Field Marshal von Reichenau told his troops in October 1941 that the nature of the Russian war was 'against the Jewish-Bolshevik system' and so must 'go beyond the conventional... Therefore the soldier must have complete understanding of the necessity for the harsh but just atonement of Jewish sub-humanity. This has the further goal of nipping in the bud rebellions in the rear of the Wehrmacht which, as experience shows, are always plotted by Jews'.[112] The most explicit discussion of the Holocaust would be made by Himmler in 1943. His motivation is absolutely clear:

This is a page of glory in our history which has never to be written and is never to be written, for we know how difficult we should have made it for ourselves if, with bombing raids, the burdens and the deprivations of war, we still had Jews today in every town as secret saboteurs, agitators, and troublemongers. We should now probably have reached the 1916-17 stage.[113]

The change in policy was soon evident. Within five weeks of the German offensive in Russia 'the number of Jews killed exceeded the total number killed in the previous eight years of Nazi rule'.[114] The Einsatzgruppen had followed the advancing army into Soviet territory, rounding up Jews in their thousands, herding them into huge pits where they were shot, and the bodies piled up one upon another. There were scenes of indescribable cruelty such as befell the Jews of Kiev at Babi Yar in September 1941. Along with these must be numbered at least 140,000 Soviet POWs who were selected for extermination by the Einsatzgruppen.[115]

Had the Final Solution begun? While decisions relating to it were deliberately not written down, it is possible through the actions taken to piece together the process of decision making, though in the end the evidence is circumstantial. In doing so the fundamentally counterrevolutionary calculations behind it become clear. It has been argued that there was a time lag between the invasion of Russia on 22 June 1941 and the resolve to carry out the Holocaust. Streit and Burrin believe the deliberate full scale annihilation of Jews occurred after the failure of the Blitzkrieg tactic. Others think the 'euphoria of victory' in the early stages led the way to adopting the Final Solution.[116] Whichever view is correct, Hitler had designed Operation Barbarossa as a Blitzkrieg 'to crush Soviet Russia in a quick campaign even before the conclusion of the war against England'.[117] Any campaign longer than a few weeks would leave Germany facing war on two fronts, a situation Hitler had long vowed to avoid.

The war against Russia brought about a terrible revenge for those supposed 'allies of Bolshevism' within Nazi reach. Thus up to five million Russian prisoners of war were murdered (mainly through starvation and ill treatment) during the war.[118] They were also the first foreign victims of mechanised mass murder in a concentration camp. In Sachsenhausen between September and mid-November 1941 at least 6,500 were killed, while at Auschwitz it was Soviet POWs who were the guinea pigs for Zyklon B (the chemical that would later be used on a mass scale in the extermination camps).[119]

We have seen that the road to the Final Solution was a tortuous as well as a tortured one. The progressive escalation from the 1933 boy-cott of Jewish shops, through the Nuremberg laws, *Kristallnacht* and forced emigration to the ghettos does not suggest an early decision to organise mass extermination, although extreme racism and contempt for human life were already manifest. Counter-revolution was upper-most in the Nazi leaders' minds. Burrin's view that the decision for genocide was made weeks after the start of Barbarossa might explain why the method changed from mass shootings to death camps. Mass shootings often attracted public attention for a process that the Nazis wanted to keep secret; and, while the murderers deserve no sympathy, this method proved highly stressful for them and hard to maintain: 'If Himmler and Heydrich had known in the spring that their men would be killing women and children in large numbers a few months later, they would have devised less arduous methods than shooting'.[120]

The statistics of death point to the conclusion that the murder was improvised at first, rapidly escalating into a organised form when 'Bol-shevism' did not crumble:

> A rough estimate would show about 50,000 Jews killed up until mid-August, in nearly two months of activity. An impressive figure, ten times higher than the one for Jewish victims of the Polish campaign; but a modest figure compared to the total, ten times higher still, that would be achieved by the end of the year, in four more months.[121]

It was not long before alternatives to mass shooting were tried, such as mobile gassing vans. These proved 'unsatisfactory' and so vast factories of destruction were created. There were six 'killing centres', to which three million Jews as well as many others would be shipped. Chelmo, Belzec, Majdanek, Treblinka, Sobibor and Auschwitz were in isolated areas of Poland and constructed between the end of 1941 and 1942. As Hilberg puts it, 'They were unprecedented. Never before in history had people been killed on an assembly line basis'.[122]

The motivation of the lower echelons

If the decision to enact the Final Solution is partly explicable by refer-ence to a narrow leadership group, the smooth functioning of the murder process, which necessarily involved hundreds of thousands in various ways, still needs to be clarified. Goldhagen suggests a mass pathologi-cal hatred of Jews but his case is not borne out by the evidence.[123]

Burleigh and Wippermann argue that the chief aim of the Nazis was 'the creation of a hierarchical racial new order. Everything else was subordinate to this goal' making the Third Reich 'a singular regime without precedent or parallel'.[124] One problem with this approach is that the Holocaust was also perpetrated by a much larger group of people that was not in the grip of some demonic possession and who occupied a lowly place in the hierarchy.

Browning's *Ordinary Men*, a study of the murderous police battalions which shot many tens of thousands of Jews face to face, gives two main reasons for their behaviour: 'Everywhere society conditions people to respect and defer to authority'; and, 'Everywhere people seek career advancement.' He adds that 'within virtually every collective, the peer group exerts tremendous pressures on behaviour and sets moral norms'.[125] Deference to an externally imposed authority coupled with competition for career advancement in a hierarchical structure are not features of every society but peculiar to capitalism. It was the smashing of working class collective organisation and consciousness that allowed the external imposition of the Nazis' abhorrent 'moral norms'. Browning may be right to affirm that 'ordinary men' are capable of horrific deeds, but they committed genocide because of the externally imposed social structure in which they were located.

The death camp system also worked through the usual institutions of capitalist society:

> Thus the civil servant set the course and the direction of the entire process… The foreign office negotiated with Axis states for the deportation of Jews to killing centres; the German railways took care of the transport; the police, completely merged with the party's SS, was engaged extensively in killing operations. The army was drawn into the destruction process… Industry and finance had an important role in the expropriations, in the forced labour system, and even in the gassing of the victims.[126]

There was thus a ghastly capitalist normality about wartime Germany's shift from production of goods to production of death. Thus Trotsky wrote of Hitler, 'This German epileptic with a calculating machine in his skull and unlimited power in his hands did not fall from the sky or come up out of hell: he is nothing but the personification of all the destructive forces of imperialism'.[127]

Take, for example, the arrangements for transporting Jews to the death camps. Carried in freight cars, railway regulations stipulated the authorities pay the third class fare of four pfennigs per kilometre. Children under ten paid half, those under four went free. There was even a group discount for convoys over 400. The victims were paid as a one way trip and the guards got a return ticket![128] It was this very normality that explains how it was carried out. The death camp was simply one part of a huge productive machine constructed on hierarchical lines, with the difference that, at a certain point, the range of the raw materials processed was extended to encompass human life.

The relationship between destruction and production

The genocide against the Jews cannot be understood in isolation from the wider decision making processes of the Third Reich and of German imperialism in the war. This generated a push-pull effect between the competing motivations of destruction and production. For this reason the explanation for what happened simply cannot be reduced to racism or the actions Hitler or Himmler.

One factor was the immediate need of industry for labour. This was the subject of intense debate. Heydrich thought that, 'though the economic perspectives that must be taken into account have been clearly recognised as having immediate pertinence, any attempt to postpone the issues of race and integrity of national culture until the post-war period should be resolutely opposed'.[129] However, Goering argued, 'It is more important that we win the war than carry through our racial policy. Whether Poles or Jews suit us or not is irrelevant. The only important thing is that they are used in the service of the German race'.[130] So even as the war in Russia generated a furious determination to wipe out Jews because of their alleged Bolshevik connections, a greater need for labour arose. The consequences became obvious when Himmler told the Auschwitz commandant he had 'modified his original Extermination Order of 1941, by which all Jews without exception were to be destroyed, and ordered instead that those capable of work were to be separated from the rest and employed in the armaments industry'.[131]

In 1944, when non-Jewish slave labour supplies had dried up, Hitler himself decided to obtain '100,000 necessary men from Hungary by provision of large contingents of Jews'.[132] As Herbert points out, 'This was in strict contradiction with the principle that had been adhered to until then of keeping the Reich Judenfrei [free of Jews]'.[133]

A second factor pushed in the opposite direction—towards mass extermination. Here racism teamed up with imperialist economic planning in a long term strategy of the Nazis and big business to construct a Grossraumwirtschaft (or macroeconomic space). This idea was common currency among a range of people. In Hitler's view, 'It is inconceivable that a higher people should painfully exist on a soil too narrow for it, whilst amorphous masses, which contribute nothing to civilisation, occupy infinite tracts'.[134] Concrete propositions were put forward by experts at the foreign office,[135] by private industrialists, academics[136] and by the state's economists. For Poland the latter decided the 'main problem lay in rural overpopulation. A third of the population would be deemed surplus to requirements should modern means of cultivation be adopted' making over-population effectively 'a barrier to capital formation'.[137] When the Ukraine fell into Nazi hands it was thought that 'to skim off the rural surplus so as to meet the food supply goals of the Reich is only conceivable through...the removal of superfluous eaters (Jews, populations of the big cities of the Ukraine such as Kiev...)'.[138] Pulling these ideas together the agricultural experts of 'Economic Organisation East' added their advice: 'Millions of people will become superfluous... Attempts to save the population there from starvation by bringing in surpluses from the fertile farmlands could only be carried out at the expense of supplies needed for Europe'.[139] Not to be outdone IG Farben was busy at this time drawing up plans for its chemical *Grossraumwirtschaft*.[140] It is difficult to know how far the concept of a *Grossraumwirtschaft* conditioned immediate actions, but one author suggests, 'The basic Nazi concept of a *Grossraumwirtschaft* was already being realised in wartime, though initially it had been planned as the crowning touch after final victory'.[141]

Another area where the politics of racism and the economics of exploitation interconnected was the employment of foreign labour. The previous chapter considered the class relations within German industry before the war. In essence these did not change after 1939, but the workforce was extended to include a vast army of additional labour peaking at 7.7 million in 1944. At that time it provided half of agricultural labour, one third of the entire armaments workforce and one quarter of all those employed in Germany.[142] A complex hierarchy of pay, housing, food, working conditions and personal freedom was created both to divide and rule, and to exploit at minimum cost.

It is important to note the functional use of racism here. Herbert explains its development in the first phases of the war. The initial position of the Reich Labour Ministry was to guarantee to foreign labour 'the same wages, salaries and other working conditions' as Germans.[143] But, as numbers increased, initiatives for discriminatory regulations for Polish workers were justified by 'race': 'Prior to 1939, there had not been a strict line on racial policy vis-à-vis Polish labourers... For that reason, the national head office of the NSDAP intensified its efforts to provide an ex post facto [after the event] racial and political basis for discrimination against the Poles'.[144] The same thing happened when Germany invaded Russia. At that very moment a leading 'scientist' made the obliging discovery that 'Bolsheviks were, like Jews, a distinct degenerate species'.[145]

As the foreign workforce expanded to encompass the new conquests, five separate 'racial' groups were identified and a strictly hierarchical structure of pay and conditions was imposed:

> Relatively best off were the West European workers and Czechs...
> Below them came Western prisoners of war; then 'Eastern workers'
> viewed as 'capable of Aryanisation', particularly Ukrainians; then the
> mass of civilian 'Eastern workers' and Poles; and below them, in turn,
> Russian prisoners of war who eked out an existence on, or often below,
> starvation level. Further down the scale still came the inmates of penal
> camps, to which foreign workers could be committed for disobedience
> or 'idling' at work... The lowest position in the hierarchy was held by
> the inmates of concentration camps.[146]

One consequence of this policy was shown at the mundane level in a Krupp cast steel plant where 'Western' male workers received 91 percent of the wages of German males; 'Eastern' males got 41 percent and 'Eastern' females just 37 percent.[147]

However, racism was not simply about savings on the wages bill but control. Höss, the commandant of Auschwitz, explained this vital function. Having a relatively small number of guards in charge of a vast camp, he wrote that:

> Enmities were keenly encouraged and kept going by the authorities, in order
> to hinder any strong combination on the part of all of the prisoners...
> The greater the number of antagonisms, and the more ferocious the strug-
> gle for power, the easier it was to control the camp. *Divide et impera!*[148]

As one historian has written, behind the structure of racism was:

> The open acknowledgement that Nazi society was in fact, and ought in
> the future to be, constructed upon this very inequality of treatment, em-
> bracing prosperity at one extreme and destruction at the other. The
> internal hierarchical structure within the 'works community'... here ap-
> peared writ large.[149]

Alongside mass extermination there were profits to be had. Private companies would contact the camp authorities and labour would be supplied. In the 'Dora' rocket project labour was brought in to dig tunnels before housing was available and 3,000 out of 17,000 labourers died within six months, the total death count reaching 60,000.[150] Together with the main camps were sub-camps dedicated to slave labour. Their number rose from 82 in 1942 to 662 by January 1945, at which time 600,000 people were still incarcerated.[151] Who used these camps?

> The list of the beneficiaries reads like a guide to German industry. To name but a few: Siemens leased some 7,400 concentration camp prisoners for its plants in Bobrek near Auschwitz, Ravensbrück, Nuremberg, Berlin, Neustadt, Ebensee and Jungbuch. AEG-Telefunken employed 1,500 Jews in Riga... From 1941 to 1944, some 35,000 prisoners were deployed in the Buna plant of IG Farben in Auschwitz-Monowitz. They were selected from the extermination transports and exploited as labourers; invalids were sent back to Birkenau to be gassed. The life expectancy of a Jewish prisoner at Buna was three to four months, and just one month in the nearby coal mines.[152]

Even the monstrous medical experiments of Dr Mengele at Auschwitz become comprehensible when one realises that the camp was virtually run by a drug and chemical conglomerate which would profit enormously from any discoveries made on human guinea pigs. The SS became greatly excited at the prospect of marketing a hormonal treatment for 'curing homosexuality' developed during experiments conducted at Buchenwald.[153]

Goldhagen makes a great deal of the fact that, in the case of Jews, exploitation of labour (which is regarded as rational) usually gave way to 'the staggering irrationality of destroying a talented, unusually productive labour force'. He concludes that the explanation must be 'pathological'.[154] However, in the grim calculus of death it should be remembered that leading Nazis were looking to a *Grossraumwirtschaft* and from this point of view, as Hitler put it, 'Since Germany ruled over a population of 250 million people in Europe, the very notion of labour shortages was a contradiction in terms'.[155]

Does the wastage of a valuable human resource sever the links between the Holocaust and the operation of capitalism? The system often wastes labour through unemployment and ill health. It also wastes resources through, for example, weapons or land left untilled while millions starve. It is not 'rational' in that general sense. Furthermore, the pointless wastage of Jewish labour was not an isolated instance. Of 3,350,000 Soviet POWs held between June 1941 and March 1942 only 166,881 (5 percent) were deployed as workers. Part of the explanation for this is that with a death rate of up to 25 percent over just two months, only 5 percent of the prisoners were physically capable of labour.[156]

Similar contradictions applied to the treatment and deployment of

Jews. An 'expert' discussing the Warsaw Ghetto before its elimination brings this out:

> The ghetto in its present structure is like a besieged stronghold. The siege currently has the aim of forcing the Jews to deliver up their goods, gold and cash supplies. Once this is done, then the economic task of exploiting the labour power that is available in the ghetto moves to the foreground.[157]

But there was a contradiction. In order to extract all the wealth in this way the labour power of the Jews was drastically degraded, as the authorities noted. There was a 'lack of physical capability as a result of months of continuing malnutrition which has also led to a reduction in the will to labour of a large portion of the Jews'.[158]

Is there an explanation that can tie all these disparate threads together? It is not pathology. It lies with the evaluation of human beings as mere objects. This operated from the very bottom to the very top of the Nazi system. Take the fate of the children of Eastern labourers torn away soon after birth and placed in special homes:

> Here there is only a situation of 'either/or'. Either there is no desire to keep these children alive—and then they should not be allowed to slowly starve to death, siphoning off many litres of valuable milk... Or the intention is to raise the children in order to be able to make use of them later on as workers.[159]

The results were that from the autumn of 1944 every newborn taken to the Volkswagen factory children's 'home' at Rühen died.[160] At the top there is this sickening document by Thierack, the justice (!) minister, which managed to combine every abominable motive of Nazism into one statement:

> With the aim in mind of ridding the German people of Poles, Russians, Jews and Gypsies, and of opening up the Eastern territories to be added to the Reich as a settlement area for German culture...I am proceeding here on the assumption that the justice system can contribute only in a minor way to the extermination of these ethnic elements... There is also no point in incarcerating such people for years on end in German jails and prisons—not even if their labour is exploited for the war effort as is usually the case today.[161]

The Nazi hierarchy was a grotesque radicalised version of capitalism, both in its economic and security needs. In this individuals had no intrinsic worth as human beings. Political considerations of worth or risk sat alongside economic ones. From the Führer at the top to the Jews at the bottom there was a spectrum of utility. Politically important

German workers were objects of exploitation but allowed to reproduce their labour; Soviet POWs were of lower utility, to be exploited yet also starved to death; Jews were regarded as a positive threat and so many were not held to deserve even exploitation.

If Thierack gave theoretical expression to the barbarous aims of Nazism, Auschwitz gave them practical form. It was not only the biggest camp by far, but the ultimate Nazi monstrosity. In four and a half years it consumed the lives of 3.5 million people, of whom one third were Jews.[162] Here 'the two objectives (extermination and use of Jewish labour) competed on the spot'.[163] The result was the selection process. A few healthy individuals were saved, at least temporarily for exploitation. Others were doomed. The symbiosis of private capitalism and Nazi state was absolute:

> While the IG [Farben] built the barracks, the SS supplied the 'furnishings'—bunks. The SS provided the guards, and the IG added its factory police. The IG requested punishments for inmates who violated its rules, and the SS administered the punishments.[164]

A worker described what this meant:

> We worked in the huge Buna plant, to which we were herded every morning about 3am. At midday our food consisted of potato or turnip soup and in the evening we received some bread. During work we were terribly mistreated. As our workplace was situated outside the chain of sentry posts, it was divided into small sections of ten by ten metres, each guarded by an SS man. Whoever stepped outside these squares during working hours was immediately shot without warning for having 'attempted to escape'. Often it happened that out of pure spite an SS man would order a prisoner to fetch some given object outside his square. If he followed the order he was shot for having left his assigned place. The work was extremely hard and there were no rest periods. The way to and from work had to be covered at a brisk military trot; anyone falling out of line was shot.[165]

Operating from late 1941 this mixture of selection for work and extermination of the less productive coincided with an attempt to redesign the German armaments industry for the long war that was now inevitable. However, as long as the Jews were seen as the power behind the Bolshevik enemy, the demands of ideology always risked overwhelming the requirements of economic expediency. As the war dragged on, ideology gained the upper hand and efforts were made to replace Jewish labour wherever possible. Yet 'normal' economic calculations were never entirely suspended.

Even in death some profit could be extracted. The IG Farben chemical combine could exploit labour in its Buna plant while its DEGESCH subsidiary could make 200 percent annual profit from production and sale of Zyklon B to gas those who broke down.[166] Gold teeth could be extracted and melted down. Human hair could be shorn and woven for profit. Meagre belongings could be looted and sold on, furs distributed back to Germany, and so on.

Auschwitz, the giant among death factories, had a capacity to 'process' 24,000 persons every day.[167] It was a miracle of modern capitalist methods, not of pathology, but of time and motion study and human resource management:

> On a 24 hour basis, victims were murdered, their corpses disposed of. Kommandos of prisoners collected the belongings of the dead and brought them to the sorting sites. Mass annihilation was organised on the basis of a division of labour. The process was integrated into a kind of assembly line, its stations coordinated in temporal sequence... The death factory was an apparatus that functioned smoothly, virtually trouble free, working at a high capacity and speed. A death train arrived at the ramp in the morning; by the afternoon the bodies had been burned... The death factory rationalised killing, transforming it into labour that required no internal involvement—not even cold-bloodedness. All it asked was for one to be matter of fact, efficient and exacting.[168]

Looked at in this light, Sofsky concludes that:

> Not everything in the system of the German concentration camps was unique. The camp system evinced features that also appear elsewhere. The German executioners and their accomplices were not unusual individuals. The overwhelming majority of perpetrators were so ordinary and average that, if they were not specifically called to account, they were later accepted without difficulty by civil society... For their part, the victims only became so for one reason: because they were made into victims, labelled outsiders, enemies, superfluous human beings, so that they could be persecuted, tormented, and killed. And many practices of camp power are reminiscent of other well established practices in modern society, procedures long since tried and tested.[169]

At one level the Nazi Holocaust was a unique event produced by an exceptional combination of circumstances stretching back to the destruction of the working class movement in the counter-revolution of 1933 and the evolution of the wartime regime. In this sense the word

'Holocaust' should not be used loosely, in the same way as the term 'fascism' can be too broadly deployed. Nevertheless the ingredients for the Holocaust were not some accident of history or the product of Hitler's pathology, but arose from capitalist society, a society which is still with us.

Conclusion

One interpretation of Nazism that has become very popular among historians recently is the view that it was a 'modernising' movement which, by centralisation and rationalisation (such as the wiping out of many small farms and businesses, and weakening of the traditional aristocratic elite), brought about a 'social revolution'.

> Hitler was a revolutionary *par excellence* in both home and foreign affairs…a revolutionary motive force of German (and European) history—one who, at the price of admittedly disproportionate sacrifices such as genocide and the destruction of the *kleindeutsch* [literally 'small German', ie the unit created in 1871 by Bismarck] national state, introduced or set in motion a political and social revolution whose effects were felt far outside Germany and are still active in our day.[170]

In one sense a more 'modern' society did emerge from the ruins of the Third Reich. However, what is meant by 'modern' in this context is nothing more than that which Marx and Engels already noted in capitalist society of the mid-19th century:

> The bourgeoisie cannot exist without constantly revolutionising the instruments of production, and thereby the relations of production, and with them the whole relations of society.

They went on to give telling examples:

> [Capitalism] has agglomerated population, centralised means of production, and has concentrated property in a few hands. The necessary consequence of this was political centralisation… Modern industry has converted the little workshop of the patriarchal master into the great factory of the industrial capitalist. Masses of labourers, crowded into the factory, are organised like soldiers. As privates of the industrial army they are placed under the command of a perfect hierarchy of officers and sergeants. Not only are they slaves of the bourgeois class, and of the bourgeois state; they are daily and hourly enslaved by the machine, by the overseer, and, above all, by the individual bourgeois manufacturer himself.[171]

If Nazism can be said to have modernised Germany in any way it was by updating its capitalism. This, however, is no step forward. 'Modern' methods of exploitation are no real advance. In the scale of history this system has outlived its usefulness and anything which preserves and strengthens it holds back human progress as a whole.

War and the Holocaust cannot be wholly attributed to the insanity of a small group of Nazis, or the mentality of an entire population. They were, above all, the product of a definite historical development —the development of capitalist society in general and in Germany specifically, a place where the powers of resistance to untrammelled exploitation had been wiped out by counter-revolution. Not every capitalist crisis leads to a Holocaust, but contained within every capitalist crisis is the potential for a Holocaust if the system that treats people as objects, numbers, to be used or disposed of, is not overthrown.

Chapter 9

Resistance and opposition

When the war turned against Germany, Hitler, with incredible mono-mania, decreed the country's self destruction:

> If the war is lost, the people will be lost also. It is not necessary to worry about what the German people will need for elemental survival. On the contrary, it is better for us to destroy even these things. For the nation has proved the weaker [and] only those who are inferior will remain after this struggle for the good have already been killed.[1]

In spite of this policy, the regime was not overthrown. It was only on 30 April 1945, as the Russians closed in on his Berlin bunker, that Hitler committed suicide, the European war ending one week later. Some 55 million people had been killed and 90 million wounded.[2] The destruction of Nazism came from outside. This poses a difficult question. How did such a regime endure shattering blows and avoid overthrow by internal forces?

One common explanation is that it enjoyed universal popularity among the German population. This quotation from a book called *German Resistance to Hitler* is typical: 'On the whole, at all times from 1933 to 1945 the majority of German voters, indeed of the entire population, supported the government, albeit with varying degrees of willingness.' But in the same breath it admits, 'There were no reliable methods in Germany for measuring popular approval of the government during the period from 1933 to 1945'.[3] There was a visibly high level of compliance with the regime, but compliance cannot be equated with general support for Nazism.

Like most Western accounts, *German Resistance to Hitler* recognises there was struggle against Nazism, but stresses the role of conservatives which culminated in the officers' bomb plot of 20 July 1944. If the Nazis' chief opponents were from the ruling elite, then the thesis of this book would need serious revision. In fact, after 1933, as before, the working class continued to be the force most resistant to Nazism within Germany. Yet Tim Mason, who does most to reveal labour's resilience under the Third Reich, notes that even when the regime was crumbling:

The years 1944-45 saw no mass movements of discontent in the German working class. As long as they had factories to go to, most German workers continued to clock in and to perform whatever production tasks they could, in the midst of collapse of the supply of raw materials and power... When their factories were bombed, many German workers were soon on the spot to clear up the rubble and to try to get production going again.[4]

To understand the paradox this chapter will look at varieties of resistance and opposition to Nazism. It begins by setting these in context.

Repression in Nazi Germany

A distinction can be drawn between resistance (in the sense of political struggle against Nazism) and opposition (defined in terms of economic protests, obstruction or non-compliance with Nazism).[5] Neither can be understood without appreciating the massive repression the Third Reich exercised from the very start. By July 1933 almost 27,000 people were in 'protective custody'[6] and by April 1939 numbers had escalated to 163,000 political inmates of concentration camps with another 140,000 in the prison system. Over this period 225,000 people had been sentenced to 600,000 years of servitude for political resistance.[7]

The ultimate aim of all this was, in Heydrich's words:

The total, permanent registration of all the people of the Reich and the associated possibility of a permanent overview of the situation of individual persons [for] not only the securing of law enforcement, but also ideological security and that relating to everyday life.[8]

In the remit given to the political police 'Communism and other Marxist groups' came first on the list[9] and the organised working class bore the brunt of the attack. The situation at Dachau, the first concentration camp, was described in 1937 by a report smuggled to the SPD organisation in emigration (known as SOPADE). Prisoners were divided into nine companies (firstly, political functionaries; then, asocials, such as beggars or alcoholics; political prisoners; Jews; political prisoners, gays, criminals; and finally, invalids and sick). While the Jews were badly treated, 'the first company [of political functionaries] is reckoned in the camp to be hell. They are almost exclusively former political functionaries of the workers' movement. They are pitied by the other Dachau prisoners'.[10]

While every left wing group was hit, in terms of sheer numbers the SPD and KPD suffered the most. The SPD's formal organisation disintegrated rapidly and so its membership largely managed to avoid arrests on the scale of the KPD which opted for open resistance:

> By the end of 1933 somewhere between 60,000 and 100,000 Communists had been interned by the regime. By 1945 fully half of the 300,000 party members in 1932 had endured Nazi jails and concentration camps. About 20,000 Communists were killed by the Nazis, some under the most brutal circumstances... Of the functionary corps in 1932, almost 40 percent were dead by 1945.[11]

The attack was constant and never ending. Although organisations were disintegrating and the numbers of arrests were falling in the mid-1930s (only to climb again with the war), Gestapo arrest rates for Communists were still phenomenal and calculated to demoralise the most hardened activists. A typical report was this one from Halle-Merseburg in 1934:

> Dear friends!...in Halle the Gestapo once against found its way to the party functionary corps. As a result, the previous leading man, friend H, was murdered by the fascist executioners. According to reliable reports with him 150 to 180 friends of our organisation have been arrested.[12]

The impact of such repression can easily be imagined. In early 1934 one person described how appalling things were even at that early stage:

> One year only after the collapse, most of the remnants of the old organisations have largely been annihilated. I am not suggesting that their members have given up their faith or that all organised connections have ceased to exist. But it does mean that the movement and its activities have been reduced to microscopic size... [Communist] central as well as district and local headquarters have been hunted down by the police time and again... Many, only too many, are caught—as recently in the Chaussee Strasse in Berlin—in the course of surprise raids on the huge working class tenements. In that case as in most, every single person present, men, women and children, were questioned and searched by the police.[13]

It would be a grave mistake to imagine that members of political organisations were the only target, and that a classless 'people's community' somehow existed for everyone else. A brief sample of the secret reports published in the SPD's bulletin *SOPADE* shows how any manifestation of working class independence could be ruthlessly dealt with. The data here are from July/August 1937. At the Braunsdorf colliery a number of miners refused to go down the shaft because wages had been cut. The Gestapo were sent for and five people were arrested. Interestingly, three of these were SA and considered to be the ringleaders. The strike collapsed.[14] At a 400 strong engine works 20 night shift workers struck and, rather than risk arrest outside, stayed by their machines, to no avail: 12 Gestapo arrived, arrested the four 'spokespeople' and the rest gave up the fight.[15] A Berlin bus factory was at this time suffering repeated Gestapo raids even though it had been 'purified of all "Marxists" in 1933'. The targets for arrest here were often long standing Nazi Party members.[16] From north west Germany it was reported that 'in the workshops they have grown accustomed to see a Gestapo car draw up to fetch one or more workmen out of the premises'.[17] The Junkers Dessau Works in central Germany saw 115 workers arrested in 1933, 107 in 1934, 63 in 1935 and 95 in 1936.[18]

A disturbing report, showing the overlap of business and state interests, came from the giant chemical works at Leuna, a plant with a long history of working class struggle:

> Everything is watched and controlled. For every three workmen there is a supervisor. With stop watch in hand supervisors ascertain that by quicker running so much percentage more can be done; that through too frequent visits to the toilet so much more percentage of waste material arises, etc…and so hardly a week passes without ten to 20 people being arrested. The concern has its own arrest cells which adjoin the invalid station, so that this can be used, without attracting attention, as a sort of transit junction. There is room for 80 arrested people at the same time.[19]

Later on, during the war, the blending of business and state in managing the factories intensified. At Volkswagen, for example:

> Surveillance of the workers, designed to obstruct any form of political activity, was carried out by informers who reported to the Gestapo and the representative of military intelligence. The factory guard or Werkschutz, consisting of SS men, patrolled the factory corridors and floor with guns and dogs, arresting workers for the slightest infraction of rules; they were then beaten, confined in the factory cellars and taken to a special workers (punishment) camp at Hallendorf near Salzgitter. Those who were not killed there returned to their workplaces in a desolate condition or were sent to hospitals to recover from their injuries.[20]

Returning to the 1937 period it was clear that repression was not confined to group activities at work such as striking. Individuals were just as much a target. At a single sitting of the Bamberg special court the following sentences were handed down:

One year for 'speaking against the Leader in vulgar language'.

Ten months for posting a letter 'brimful of calumnies against the government'.

One hundred mark fine for 'abusing the government and everything else whilst in a drunken state'.

In Nuremberg a picture of the Nazi film maker Riefenstahl was found defaced by graffiti. A 54 year old workmen was given eight months after experts examined the handwriting. A 60 year old refused to do the Hitler salute. The verdict—one year.[21] Within 24 hours a Kiel woman who grumbled to her grocer that 'Hitler hasn't made anything better' got ten months hard labour.[22] Such formal sentences were preferable to the 'protective custody' of the concentration camp which was of indeterminate length. In Silesia a woman was arrested for complaining about the scarcity of meat and saying the rich could get anything. It was believed that the police had handed her over to a concentration camp.[23]

Information about detainees was hard to come by, as this example from 1936, written by the friend of a man arrested on suspicion of homosexuality, demonstrates:

One day people from the Gestapo came to his house and took him away. It was pointless to enquire where he might be. If anyone did that, they ran the risk of being similarly detained because he knew them, and therefore they were also suspect. Following his arrest, books and address books were confiscated... All those who figured in them, or had anything to do with him, were arrested and summoned by the Gestapo. Me too. For a whole year I was summoned by the Gestapo and interrogated at least once every 14 days or three weeks... After four weeks my friend was released... Hair shorn off, totally confused, he was no longer what he was before... We had to be very careful with all contacts. I had to break off relations with my friend. We passed each other by on the street...[24]

The years 1936 and 1937 were actually a period of relatively light repression! When the war began, 'protective custody' often turned into large scale summary executions, the first victim being a Communist from the Junker workers who refused to carry out air raid protection work.[25] By 1943 German civil courts passed some 5,500 death sentences, and this figure excludes court martials and murder in police stations, concentration camps and death camps.[26]

The destruction of workers' organisation erected massive barriers to resistance in a vast number of ways. Since organisation had declined beyond a critical point and atomisation had set in, the universal Nazi assault did not rally the working class to collective defence. Instead the basic bonds of trust and solidarity essential to such action were gnawed away at the root. Fear of spies meant those arrested and then released would fear coming into contact with their organisations once more. Since former prisoners were often 'turned' by the Gestapo through torture or other methods, they themselves became objects of suspicion.[27] One KPD 'instructor' trying to re-establish organisation complained that the local members would not talk to him because they 'don't trust the agents from abroad and prefer to work with people from their own ranks'.[28]

Relations between left organisations which had been strained before 1933 were also thoroughly poisoned. In response to proposals for a local united front with the SPD, Communists asked, 'Who knows whether the rascals are genuine?'[29] The Edelweiss Pirates, an anti-Nazi youth movement that reached mass proportions during the war, had little connection with adult workers' political organisations because the latter feared it contained Gestapo spies.[30] A sad example of the effect of mistrust was reported in a Westphalian enterprise where some workers apparently wanted to rouse anti-Nazi activity. Since anyone who did this might well be an agent provocateur they were not believed. When they attempted to distribute oppositional literature 'the workmen warned each other not to accept the material and, in the end, appealed to the Council of Trust [the Nazi works committee]' and the men were removed.[31] Perhaps these men were sincere militants. Perhaps they were, as suspected, SS agents. It was impossible to be sure.

Atomisation was the most potent weapon in the Gestapo's armoury. Its staff was surprisingly small in number—just 32,000 in 1944 when repression was at its height. Thus Essen, a city of 650,000 inhabitants, had just 43 officials.[32] So their undoubted effectiveness did not rely on their being everywhere. It came, above all, from the extent to which members of the population informed on others.[33] A case study of the Düsseldorf Gestapo (1933-44) brings this out. In their card index Communists made up over a fifth of all entries, and the largest single factor in initiating proceedings against individuals was reports from the population (26 percent of the total). 'Own observation' accounted for only 13 percent.[34]

It is true, as Grunberger argues, there was a 'widespread readiness of Germans to exercise unpaid surveillance over their neighbours and workmates'. But this evidence can be read a number of ways. It might show the presence of corrupting Nazi ideas in the mass of the population; it might reflect the struggle for survival when the best way to avoid suspicion was to betray someone else; or it could indicate private motives where collective advance was blocked. In all these cases the vital importance of workers' organisation and the disastrous consequences of its destruction were underlined. One thing the evidence does not do is demonstrate the existence of a 'people's community' in which, 'no matter how humbly stationed in life, every man enjoyed equality of opportunity for laying information against his social superiors'.[35] The Düsseldorf sample showed only a quarter of denunciations were motivated by loyalty to the Third Reich, while fully two thirds were linked directly or indirectly to the resolution of private conflicts.[36]

The Gestapo itself was not staffed mainly by committed Nazis but by the German police, with their traditional 'fixation upon the authoritarian, nation state [and their] mentality of the "unpolitical" civil servant'.[37] And far from undermining class barriers, the structure of repression was bound up with class. Some 18.7 percent of the top SS rank, Obergruppenführer, were aristocrats[38] and the Gestapo came almost exclusively from the middle and upper class backgrounds. Workers, though 50 percent of the population, provided just 12 percent of recruits.[39] Yet victims of the Gestapo through secret condemnation were almost never from the upper class and the 'denunciators belonged to the same social milieu as the denounced'.[40]

The conservative resistance

Opponents of Nazism who came from the traditional conservative elite are well known because they were (literally) within inches of blowing Hitler up when Stauffenberg's bomb exploded on 20 July 1944. The plotters paid dearly for their attempt, many being hanged with piano wire from butchers' hooks (an event which Hitler had recorded on film).

However, the character of their stand, courageous though it was, must also be considered. The army officers who formed the core of the conservative resistance had an advantage. Given the massive apparatus of repression, only those 'within the system' stood a chance of reaching figures like Hitler. This produced a deeply contradictory situation, a 'convergence of resistance and compliance'. Even a sympathetic observer of the conservatives' effort has had to admit:

> In many instances continued service to the Nazi state seemed justified
> by the calculation that it might be effective in causing obstruction and

averting the worst excesses of the regime. In many cases, staying in office served as a necessary cover for conspiracy... But alas, by virtue of their tradition, these very groups were little predisposed to rebellion against state and authority. They had in the past displayed a marked indifference, if not hostility, to the Weimar Republic and towards democracy in general. All too long they had been satisfied with fending off the new regime's intrusions into their own respective spheres rather than facing up to the comprehensive threat of Nazism to the nation as a whole.[41]

Industrialists were notably absent from the resistance, and domestic policies were not the officers' key concern.[42] The main point of divergence with Nazism seems to have been conduct of foreign policy. A glance at the people who were linked with it shows the fine line between their collaboration and their resistance. If the 1944 bomb plot had succeeded, Beck would have been made regent.[43] We have already seen his pro-Nazi attitude in the early 1930s and that his disillusionment was due to doubts about the effectiveness of Hitler's military plans.

Von Hassell was to be foreign minister. He had been a Nazi Party member since 1933 and ambassador until 1938. Seeking support from Britain he wrote a note opposing the war because it would lead to the Bolshevisation of Europe. He wished for Germany to retain its conquests in Austria and Czechoslovakia, plus the ceding of Polish land to restore Germany to its 1914 borders.[44]

The key thinker of the group and would be chancellor was Carl Gördeler, who was Hitler's price commissioner in 1934. Yet he opposed assassinating the Führer and rejected democracy—'The active military man has the right to determine which statesman shall have his confidence'.[45] He added that 'a hereditary monarchy is the form of state for...our fickle, unpolitical people'.[46] His peace proposals matched Hassell's, demanding in addition South Tyrol from Italy and 'colonial territory as far as possible interconnected and as far as possible capable of development which Germany will administer'. Finally, Germany and England should jointly seek 'the restoration of a reasonable order in Russia and...removal of the pestilence of Bolshevism'.[47]

Sympathisers of the conspirators included Canaris, head of military intelligence who 'developed close ties with Franco and in fact hung a large, inscribed portrait of the Caudillo on the wall of his office'.[48] He performed his job for the Third Reich diligently until his dismissal in 1944. Only the tiny Kreisau Circle, which included conservatives and socialists went beyond such far right wing politics, but it was a discussion group and little more. Its key figure von Moltke protested that

'We only thought... We are on the outside of each practical action; we get hanged because we have thought together'.[49]

The conservatives focused their efforts on winning support from Western governments and the German Army High Command. In both they were unsuccessful. The British government decided that it was 'better off' that the bomb plot failed so that Allied plans for full conquest were not compromised.[50] However, amongst the High Command things seemed more promising: 'The opposition to Hitler's war plans was virtually unanimous', at least early in the war.[51] It is this that explains and defines the nature of the conservatives' resistance—the defence of German 'national interest' as the military saw it, from the arbitrary and fanatical raving of Hitler and his crew. Such activity had little to do with democracy or social justice, and it waxed and waned according to foreign developments. There were three phases of activity—1938, early in the Second World War, and 1944.

In 1938 it was believed that Hitler's threats to Czechoslovakia would cause a war for which Germany was 'not prepared'.[52] When Hitler seized the country without a shot, plans for a mass resignation of the generals or a coup were shelved. The same process was repeated in the run up to the conquest of France. Once again Hitler's success paralysed the resistance, one of its leaders noting, 'Even those generals who before 10 May 1940 had misgivings about an offensive against the West are now convinced of its appropriateness, talk disparagingly of the enemy, and do not like to be reminded of their previous judgements'.[53] The final effort was the 1944 bomb plot launched once the suicidal nature of Hitler's strategy was plain to see.

So, while there were a variety of opinions in the conservative resistance, it is fair to conclude that, 'preoccupied with questions of national restoration, the conservative resisters remained relatively indifferent to the human crimes committed by Nazis',[54] and many 'objected more to Hitler's methods than to his goals'. In a situation of autocratic rule, political disagreements within the ruling class were bound to take the form of sedition, since major changes of policy were only possible through the removal of the dictator. In fact, the conservative resistance was part of a spectrum of ruling class dissent from Hitler which, in its mildest form, included the highest ranking Nazis. Hess, Hitler's deputy, was the most famous. He flew to Scotland in a vain attempt to broker peace with the Western Allies before it was too late. Goering put out diplomatic feelers via Sweden to see if an alternative policy to Hitler's would prove viable.[55] Even Himmler seems to have kept Gördeler alive for a time so that he might concoct plans for a possible 'Hitler-Himmler-Schacht-Gördeler' government.[56]

The churches

The conservative resistance had links with individual Protestant churchmen such as pastor Dietrich Bonhoeffer. Martin Niemoeller would also become well known with his imprisonment from 1937 to 1945. However, even the breakaway Confessional church (from the Nazi-dominated Reich church) objected mainly to Nazi interference with the churches' area of competence—religion: 'The totality of the demands made by this philosophy of life brings innumerable religious persons into a sharp conflict of conscience'.[57] As Niemoeller's famous poem hinted, much to his later regret he himself welcomed the victory of the NSDAP in 1933. From his prison cell he even offered to rejoin the navy and fight for 'a motherland that we loved'.[58] A study of German Protestant resistance concludes:

> True resistance designed to overthrow the Nazi regime was undertaken by a tiny minority of Protestants in Germany. Contrary to the early post-war picture, Christian support for Hitler was broad and enthusiastic, with Christians and Nazis mixing more easily than has generally been thought.[59]

Catholic opposition did not have a promising start. In 1933 Cardinal Faulhaber wrote to Hitler, 'What the old parliamentarians and parties did not accomplish in 60 years, your statesmanlike foresight has achieved in six months'.[60] However, discontent was roused by Nazi interference in religion. The pope's encyclical protested, 'We have no greater wish than the restitution of a true peace between church and state in Germany,' but warned of the 'Old Germanic, pre-Christian ideas [which] deny God's wisdom and providence'.[61] The churches objected to the euthanasia campaign, but even here motives were complex. Cardinal von Galen's sermon was that 'if you establish and apply the principle that you can kill "unproductive" fellow human beings then woe betide us all when we become old and frail!' It was a violation of the commandment, 'Thou shalt not kill'.[62] However, a key argument the church used against the murder of mental and physical 'defectives' was that it was up to the Creator who should live or die, and in contrast to eugenic theories 'no one except God had control over the genetic possibilities inherent in procreation'.[63] It is notable that defence of human life was not extended to a campaign against the racist attacks and murder of Jews; 'The church had become too enmeshed in its support for the existing socio-political order'.[64] The papal nuncio in Berlin raised the question of the Holocaust just once, and this was to ask for information, which was denied. No protest followed.[65]

One religious group which deserves mention is the Jehovah's Witnesses, who, refusing to put state laws above their beliefs, rejected military service or support for anything connected with the war. One writer gives this sect 'pride of place' in the opposition: 'None had more of its members incarcerated and killed in proportion to its size, none was more efficient in illegal propaganda, none produced more "martyrs" willing to suffer for their faith.' He adds a significant rider: 'Yet the large majority were humble men and women either from the working class or domestic servants or white collar workers, while the higher social ranks were hardly represented among their ranks'.[66]

Jews, partisans and the struggle of the oppressed

Some of the most inspiring pages in the history of resistance were written by the most oppressed—the Jews. Their achievement has been eloquently expressed in these terms:

> In practically every ghetto and in every labour and concentration camp there existed a Jewish underground organisation which kept up prisoners' morale, reduced their physical sufferings, carried out acts of sabotage, organised escapes, collected arms, planned revolts, and, in many instances, carried them out.[67]

The variety of forms resistance took was enormous. In Berlin Herbert Baum's group operated from 1936 until 1942 when, in a symbolic act, they firebombed an anti-Soviet exhibition.[68] Struggle for survival in the face of an enemy who wants to destroy you is a form of resistance in itself. In Galicia, for example, tens of thousands evaded the Nazis and for a time eked out an existence in the woods and forests.[69] Sometimes the opposite action was a form of resistance. When 60 year old Leyb Goldszteyn realised that his coughing would give away the hiding place of his family and Ukrainian protector, he went to the local Gestapo/Ukrainian HQ and set off two grenades, killing himself and 12 others.[70] Very often Jews did not fight in separate groups, but as members of partisan detachments:

> We find Soviet Jews wherever there were partisans fighting the Germans... We come repeatedly across the names of Soviet Jews, many of them Red Army officers who had avoided capture or escaped from German camps. They invariably distinguished themselves as fighters and commanders and a number impressed the Polish Jews with their

fearless reactions to all manifestations of anti-Semitism in their Russian superiors or subordinates.[71]

Where Jews were isolated into ghettos they also fought. To the famous Warsaw Ghetto uprising must be added resistance at Minsk, Vilno and Bialystok.[72] When the Nazis tried to clear the Warsaw Ghetto in April 1943 they arrived with 2,100 soldiers equipped with 69 machine guns, 135 submachine guns, howitzers and 1,358 rifles. The Jewish resistance had just 17 rifles and some worthless pistols. They faced certain death.[73] Yet with incredible courage they fought for every inch. A Polish general noted that:

> The insurgents toppled the Germans from their pedestal of omnipotence and proved to Poles the effectiveness of armed resistance. Thus the blood of the ghetto defenders was not shed in vain. It gave birth to the intensified struggle against the fascist invader and from this struggle there came victory.[74]

The death camps also saw extraordinary acts of resistance. In June 1943 Treblinka inmates managed to acquire weapons, burn down many of the buildings and destroy gas chamber equipment. Of the 1,000 prisoners some 500 escaped.[75] In October 1943 a Jewish Red Army soldier organised a revolt and mass break out from Sobibor.[76] At Auschwitz a Combat Group was formed which regularly smuggled information to the outside world about what was going on, including this message to the Allied airforces: 'Next to our block in the camp area an enormous factory is being built... As regards us, don't hold back because we are living here. The firm of Krupp must be destroyed and razed to the ground'.[77] Alas, despite this and much aerial photographic information, the Allied bombers failed to bomb Auschwitz or even the rail tracks leading there.

Other resistance among the oppressed came from slave labourers. They organised the 'Fraternal Cooperation of Prisoners of War' which hoped for a mass uprising but was smashed by the Gestapo in 1943.[78] According to official reports groups were later organised in 38 different cities.[79]

Youth movements

The Nazi attitude to youth was set out by Hitler:

> These young people learn nothing but how to think as Germans and behave as Germans... And if, after a year and a half or two, they have not become fully National Socialist, then they will be put to Labour

Service…then the army…and straight away into the SA, or SS and so on, and they will never be free for their whole life![80]

The Hitler Youth (for boys) and League of German Maidens (for girls) set out to make this horror a reality with a law of December 1936 enrolling 'the entire youth of Germany in the Hitler Youth'.[81] The striving of many young Germans to escape from this straitjacket was inevitable and ultimately irrepressible. It blossomed across Germany in innumerable gangs with exotic names: OK Gangs, Charlie Gangs, Bush Wolves, Loafers, Swingers, Bear Gangs, Club of the Golden Horde, the Shambeko Band, Snake Club, Blue Miasma, Dreadful Stones, Dusters, and even Municipal Bath Broth.[82]

Youth opposition to Nazism affected different classes, and the variety of forms it took are interesting. Middle class youth protest was usually channelled towards the 'swing' movement—listening to the forbidden music of jazz and dressing in a particular casual style. To indulge in such pastimes required money, gramophones and homes large enough for 'jitterbugging'. This middle class protest was 'not anti-fascist in a political sense—their behaviour was indeed emphatically anti-political'.[83] Even so, every deviation from the Nazi cultural norm was regarded as a challenge to the authorities. Thus a single jazz session in Hamburg resulted in 408 arrests.[84] An exception to middle class youth's mainly cultural opposition was the 'Society of the White Rose', a tiny student group at Munich University, that sacrificed itself by openly distributing leaflets addressed to 'the German intelligentsia' in 1943.[85]

For working class youth, both male and female, there was no escape from the streets, and gangs were formed usually composed of a dozen or so boys and a few girls.[86] Any non-conformist behaviour here meant an inevitable clash with Hitler Youth (HJ) patrols, and since the very mixing of the sexes was thought seditious, fights were inevitable. Working class youth opposition was therefore far more physical and direct, and the title of 'Pirates' adopted by many of the gangs shows this. A typical HJ denunciation of some Babcock Works youth with suspected KPD connections was sent in 1941. The HJ member recognised them by the badges worn in their buttonholes, 'a typical sign': 'I approached several of them and they used filthy language to insult me, expressions like "traitor to the workers" and "bloodhound", followed by threats, we'll bash your brains in'.[87]

These gangs often went beyond mere words. Pre-war Gestapo reports talked of roaming Leipzig 'packs' which altogether involved 1,500 working class youth and which clearly had links with the KPD.[88] Kittelsbach and Edelweiss Pirate gangs of 60 to 70 armed with brass knuckles toured the streets of Duisberg during the early 1940s.[89] The level of repression of such activities could be high: 'In a single day, on 7 December 1942, the Düsseldorf Gestapo broke up groups in Düsseldorf, Duisburg, Essen and Wuppertal, including the Cologne Edelweiss Pirates'.[90] By 1943 Himmler was having to establish special youth concentration camps.[91] Such action ensured that only a minority of working class youth ever became involved in such oppositional activities.

The most spectacular example of youth resistance occurred in Cologne in late 1944 in the midst of the rubble of a bombed out city full of deserters and of anger at the continuing futile war. The Edelweiss Pirates had working class backgrounds, often with anti-fascist connections, and the group itself developed some contact with the KPD. The nominal leader was 23 year old Heinz Steinbrück whose father had been a Communist Red Fighter.[92] The Pirates went beyond cultural protest and even gang fighting to plan the blowing up of bridges. They successfully derailed a train and killed the chief of the local Gestapo. The Edelweiss Pirates financed their activities by robbery and the black market, and, through raids on military depots, acquired an armoury of machine guns, grenades and pistols.[93] Shortly after having freed a Jewish woman from captivity a number of them were captured.[94] In 1944 on 10 November 13 were hanged without trial, five aged just 16 or 17.[95] The Gestapo congratulated themselves for stopping a Communist group bent on killing Nazis, encouraging Cologne to revolt, and 'thereby bringing the war to a quicker end, to our disadvantage'.[96]

Factors weakening workers' resistance and opposition

The working class, young and old, was the only section of German society to offer fundamental opposition and resistance to Nazism on a mass basis. However, it is important not to sow illusions in this regard. It is not true that workers everywhere and at all times took a stand, or even that toleration or acceptance of the Third Reich was not widespread on occasion. Apart from repression, several factors undermined the position.

The shameful manner in which the trade unions, the SPD and the KPD failed to counter the Nazi assumption of power must have done incalculable harm to class confidence and led to widespread disorientation. While many in the parties' core memberships remained loyal, for the millions on the periphery of the labour movement, the validity of working class politics must have been sorely tried. Writing in June 1933 Trotsky put the consequences for workers of the left's failure in these terms:

> Hating and despising the Nazis, they are least of all inclined, however, to return to that policy which led them into the noose of Hitler. The workers feel themselves cheated and betrayed by their own leadership. They do not know what must be done, but they know what must not be done. They are unspeakably tortured, and they want to break away from the vicious circle of confusion...[97]

Trotsky predicted mass political apathy would be the result, and this seems to have occurred on a huge scale. The problems facing workers were so great that 'grand' political concerns were replaced with the daily struggle for existence, which intensified during the war years when working class districts bore the brunt of bombing raids on civilian targets.

Another factor was the creation of full employment which was bound to be welcomed by the unemployed. Of course, it was only possible because of preparations for a horrific war that would destroy almost seven million German lives (2.8 million of them civilians);[98] but that lay in the future and was not foreseen by many.

When the war began the Nazis were careful to sow divisions between German workers who enjoyed superior pay and conditions to a foreign slave labour 'underclass'. Goering insisted that foreign workers should have 'no contact with the German population, in particular no "solidarity". German workers always basically the boss of the Russians'.[99] In a situation where the collective strength of the labour movement had been smashed and it seemed to be a situation of 'everyone for themselves' such tactics could be effective. Thus, when food rations to the German population were reduced in April 1942, instead of resentment being turned against the government and the war, many complained about the 'exceptionally good' food given to foreign workers![100]

Within the workplace there were many reasons to hate the Nazis. However, the government, while intent on maximum exploitation of the workers, was also conscious of the potential revolutionary danger that they could pose. This meant that vicious repression was accompanied by extreme caution in handling any issue that might generalise discontent. An example was the War Economy Decree of 4 September 1939 to reduce wages and abolish various bonuses. Reaction was so hostile that soon Gauleiters were insisting that the cuts be reversed. In vain did ministers complain that 'if the ban on bonus rates, the only sacrifice the workers had had to make so far, was cancelled, the workers would be exceptionally favoured, they would even profit from the war'.[101] The cuts were withdrawn and Ley invented this pathetic story to explain it:

> At the beginning of the war, the severest sacrifices, the tightening of belts; after ten weeks' life back to normal... That was not because the leadership yielded to your demands, workers, but because everything had been so well prepared that these sacrifices were unnecessary.[102]

It was only in 1942, under the leadership of Speer, that armaments production expanded rapidly (the 1941 total being exceeded by 44 percent in 1942 and 226 percent in 1943).[103] Speer wrote:

> It remains one of the oddities of this war that Hitler demanded far less from his people than Churchill and Roosevelt did from their respective nations. The discrepancy between the total mobilisation of labour forces in democratic England and the casual treatment of this question in authoritarian Germany is proof of the regime's anxiety not to risk any shift in the popular mood... Hitler and the majority of his political followers belonged to the generation who, as soldiers, had witnessed the revolution of November 1918 and had never forgotten it.[104]

Speer's programme of rapid expansion had to depend on a mass of foreign labour so that German workers would not be hit too hard. Output of consumer industries dropped by up to 15 percent during the war but by 1943 had actually recovered to 90 percent of its pre-war level.[105]

Blows to workers' resistance to the Third Reich were also delivered from abroad. The visit of the British foreign minister to see Hitler and to pursue appeasement was one example. The *SOPADE* report noted:

> In the ranks of the opponents of Hitlerism a deep depression is noticeable, increased by Lord Halifax's journey. Nothing has been more dampening upon the opponents of Nazism than the visits of serious politicians and statesmen from foreign countries to Hitler. These visits give the impression that little by little the chief powers are preparing to come to terms with Nazism, and that there is no means left in the world for combatting fascism.[106]

Misery must have turned to despair with the signing of the Hitler-Stalin pact and the start of the Second World War. If Stalin and Hitler were allied, then for the KPD the enemy must again be the SPD who 'work as agents in the pay of English and French imperialism'. For their part, the SPD brought back their old hatreds: 'We have always known that one day the brothers will get together'.[107]

Repression disrupted channels of communication. A *SOPADE* correspondent showed the result:

> The most shocking thing is the ignorance of wide circles about what is actually going on... They are completely convinced that there are no longer concentration camps... It is always happening that even in the case of arrests of opponents of the regime only a few families hear about it and even the neighbourhood remains completely in the dark.[108]

The KPD found that 'many members are active but they have no contact with the centralised organisation'.[109]

Lack of organised counter-propaganda created an opening for Goebbels' lying media. While these could not disguise the reality of life in the factories, they could spread confusion about general issues and make workers susceptible to influence. An example of this is given in the *SOPADE* reports: a miner's wife said that she knew that in the Spanish Civil War, then a year old, the Bolsheviks were creating chaos and raped children.[110]

Some 60 percent of the Reserve Police Battalion 101, which committed horrific mass shootings of Jews near Lublin in 1942, were from working class backgrounds.[111] The German army also contained millions of workers. As a result of the First World War it had experienced large scale mutinies and eventual dissolution. In the Second World War it maintained its cohesion until the very end (although the execution of 20,000 soldiers for offences like cowardice or desertion must also have been a powerful deterrent to rebellion).[112] There is little doubt that the corrupting influence of Nazism penetrated right through society.

It was impossible to present a generalised or effective rebuttal of Goebbels' poisonous propaganda, especially where the lies could not be checked against personal experience. And when the class was blocked from taking any action, the generation of class consciousness was impeded. However, where propaganda did not match known reality it had less influence. This often produced a split consciousness which was revealed starkly in the contrast between the plebiscites on general questions and Councils of Trust elections in the factories. There was a vote in August 1934 over Hitler's merger of president and chancellor roles. Even though Gestapo reports suggested a degree of working class hostility or abstention,[113] the combined efforts of Communists and Social Democrats apparently could not prevent 90 percent plus voting for Hitler's policy.[114] It might be objected, quite rightly, that such votes were rigged. For example, 99.5 percent of Dachau inmates were recorded as voting for Hitler![115] Unfortunately the same reservations cannot be applied to the results of the January 1935 Saar regional plebiscite. This was over whether to give up the existing arrangement, imposed by the Versailles Treaty, of rule by the League of Nations in favour of control from Berlin. It was a genuinely free election in which both the SPD and KPD could openly plead for a no vote; but still 76 percent voted in favour, not because Hitler was so popular, but because, as Trotsky said, the population there felt the Versailles Treaty made them third class citizens and 'in Germany, at least, they will be oppressed on the same basis as the rest of the population'.[116]

The opposite pattern occurred in workplaces. In March 1933 and in 1934 there were shop stewards elections. In early 1933 these were still called 'works councils' and all union tendencies were represented. In spite of Nazi repression the NSBO managed only to attract 25 to 30 percent of the mandates.[117] The 1934 elections were for 'Councils of Trust', bodies designed to replace the old union shop stewards committees. Four different forms of opposition developed. In many places repression meant it was too dangerous to stand against the candidates nominated by the bosses and/or the Nazis, so voting no was the means of showing disapproval. Examples of this were the Wolfsbank pit in the Ruhr where only 241 of the 1,300 miners approved the list presented. Seventy percent refused to vote for the Nazis in the printworks of Ullstein and Scherl.[118] Many other examples could be cited. Abstention was another tactic. Some 4,200 out of 6,000 refused to vote in a Rhenish metal works.[119] Ley eventually had to admit that overall barely 40 percent participated in the 1934 Council of Trust elections. The no votes and abstentions combined made up about three quarters of those entitled to vote.[120] In a few cases the names of Nazi nominees were struck out and former stewards or known left wingers substituted.[121] In one Krupp factory and a Silesian mine it seems that alternative councils were set up, though how long these lasted is not clear.[122] Soon afterwards Council of Trust elections were abandoned altogether for, as a *SOPADE* report put it:

> The attempt to replace organisations of the labour movement which had grown up throughout decades, by means of artificial formations, has failed. Comparisons made between the former voluntarily recognised people of trust and those now thrust upon them are always and everywhere in favour of the former.[123]

So a contradiction existed in many workers' minds between generalised attitudes based on lack of alternatives to government propaganda and workers' own experience.

Another example of the contradiction was revealed by the contrast between Hitler's public image and that of the regime in general. Before 1933 the Führer, as leader of a hierarchical movement, acquired an aura of invincibility and genius. The charisma of individuals (politicians, stars, royalty and so on) in capitalist society is a function of alienation and lack of control in the mass of people who are made to feel that their lives are worthless. The lower the self confidence, the greater the fascination exercised by the famous. Trotsky argued that 'the leader is always a relation between people' and that Hitler's middle class background, war record and expressive powers made him a focal point of a relationship between a powerless middle class and their search for a saviour: 'Not every exasperated petty bourgeois could have become Hitler, but a particle of Hitler is lodged in every exasperated petty bourgeois'.[124]

After 1933 the regime built upon his image to attract new layers. Ian Kershaw's book *The Hitler Myth* refutes the assertion of one historian that 'at the peak of his popularity nine Germans out of ten were "Hitler supporters, Führer believers"'[125] and argues that 'the working class remained the social grouping least impressed by the "economic miracle" and relatively immune to the image of Hitler'.[126] Nevertheless he stresses that 'the adulation of Hitler by millions of Germans who may otherwise have been only marginally committed to the Nazi ideology, or party, was a crucial element of political integration in the Third Reich'.[127] With class politics banished from sight Hitler claimed to represent the 'national interest' of all Germans, and so, along with full employment, his successes in foreign affairs raised his status to new heights.

SOPADE reports from the mid-1930s show worker attitudes were split between Hitler's high status and discontent with Nazi policies on the ground. Workers would say things like, 'Hitler did not know anything and therefore cannot remedy anything...' So 'people do not criticise him, whereas, for example, Goebbels is almost universally loathed even among the Nazis'.[128] Gestapo reports confirm this: 'The recognition of the Führer's great successes in the field of foreign policy...goes parallel with discontent of wide sections about economic events... Confidence in the Führer is unlimited and criticism of many subordinate authorities is as strong as ever'.[129]

Attitudes to the outbreak of the Second World War give a clear example of personal experience (the memory of 1914-18) conflicting with the generalised propaganda. Speer described the atmosphere in Berlin as:

Noticeably depressed; the people were full of fear about the future.

None of the regiments marched off to war decorated with flowers as they had done at the beginning of the First World War. The streets remained empty. There was no crowd on the Wilhelmsplatz shouting for Hitler. It was in keeping with the desolate mood that Hitler had his bags packed into the cars one night to drive east, to the front... Not a soul on the street took notice of this historic event: Hitler driving off to the war he had staged.[130]

Yet the spectacular military successes of the period before the Russian campaign probably raised Hitler's standing to its peak level.[131]

Workers against Nazism

In spite of all the difficulties facing the working class, a significant minority mounted an extraordinary resistance to Nazism. The best tribute paid to this is the reports of the Gestapo itself. The KPD figured most prominently. A report of October 1934 said:

> We employ the expression 'Communist danger' with all seriousness. This danger lies less in the approximately 50,000 paid up members enlisted in the KPD, less in the number of inflammatory leaflets that are handed out, less in the rebuilding of almost entire Communist satellite organisations like the RGO, Red Aid, Red Veterans' League and Young Communist League, as in the long-term threat that the authority of the National Socialist state will crumble among ever wider circles of the population and in the great danger of the re-emergence of partial political strikes, public demonstrations and active resistance to state measures.[132]

The Gestapo admitted the 'self sacrificing readiness of all the supporters of the illegal KPD, who were on every occasion ready to fill any gap which occurred in the ranks... Convinced Communists again and again sacrifice their lives to avoid having to betray their comrades'.[133]

Left wing literature was produced and distributed on a large scale. In 1935 a report on KPD activity in Berlin spoke of 62,000 copies of Communist literature being published in June alone. There was 'no end of material being circulated. There are newspapers for cells, city districts, sub-districts and factories. In the last period it is reckoned that on a monthly basis there are about 60 new issues that are successfully circulated. When one considers that [probably] 200-300 copies of each are produced, it is possible to imagine how widely Communist propaganda is spread here in Berlin'.[134] It was reckoned that the SPD's *Socialist Action* had a national readership of between 200,000 and 300,000.[135]

In 1936 some 1.6 million copies of illegal literature were seized.[136] The year 1937 saw the seizure of 900,000 copies of illegal literature.[137] Some extraordinary distribution methods were employed such as the balloon that floated into Cologne carrying the leaflets subtitled 'KPD Central Rhine Balloon Post'.[138] The written word carried dangers and much agitation was by word of mouth. The Gestapo found that 'the KPD enjoys a political influence which appears to extend beyond the limits of its organisational work. Unfortunately their subversive oral propaganda has spread widely on account of the unfavourable economic situation'.[139]

All of this was possible because many tens of thousands remained committed to active resistance to the Nazis. It is not true that, as one writer suggests, 'Character, not...class origin, made people into resisters'.[140] For there can be no comparison between the workers' mass resistance and that of the tiny conservative groupings. While many of the latter welcomed Hitler's accession and became concerned only when his policies looked likely to fail, the left's rejection of Nazism began immediately and was root and branch in character. Evidence for this was *Young Guard*, issued by the Communist youth wing in May 1933:

Against fascism and war

Barracks drills, military exercises led by fascist officers, uniforms—isn't that preparation for war? Labour service is not job creation, it is the new form of general conscription adapted to current circumstances—a great and widespread preparation for war. On poverty wages, performing fascist drills, you young worker, are being trained to be cannon fodder.

The Hitler government is not only a regime of brutal violence, it is a government for imperialist war.

You, young trade unionist, young Socialist, young Christian worker, young anti-fascist, you ask what can we do about it? Can we bring fascism down?... We feel the terror in our own bodies, we are being drilled to be cannon fodder. To wait will mean hunger, prison and death for thousands.

WE will bring fascism to ruin![141]

Goldhagen implies that the left were silent about Nazi treatment of the Jews, but the KPD warned that 'race hatred' and the passing of the 'inhuman' Nuremberg laws 'were preparing the masses for being drawn into the slaughter of the "less worthy" people'.[142] After *Kristallnacht* it stated that:

Before all mankind the honour of Germany has been covered with the deepest disgrace... Help our tormented Jewish fellow-citizens in whatever way possible. Wall into isolation the deeply despised anti-Semitic rabble from our people!... Show solidarity through sympathy and help for our Jewish comrades...[143]

The SPD, after a period of internal turmoil, also expressed its determination to combat Nazism in this famous declaration of 18 June 1933:

Break The Chains

The victims of today will be the victors of tomorrow.

A cry is rising up, the cry of the raped and gagged German working class. Though it may be suffocated—it will be heard. We will be its mouthpiece.

Hitler announces that 'Marxism is dead. Social Democracy exists no more!' We answer, 'Marxism lives, democratic socialism cannot be killed off!'

We do not deceive ourselves over the gravity of the defeat that we have suffered, nor over the sharp struggle that lies before us. But if anyone expects us to accept the defeat or relinquish the struggle, we answer: 'Never!'...

There is no real democracy without socialism!...

We want strong, true, rule by the people—battling democracy, which will overthrow all supporters of despotism and all violent organisations that oppose freedom...[144]

Despite the bravery of these statements and the self sacrifice of many, it was exceedingly difficult for resistance to be effective. Indeed, in the case of the KPD, tremendous damage was inflicted on the organisation by the crazy policies of the leadership and its mentors in Moscow. With the slogan of 'Forward with the Red Offensive!'[145] and the belief that 'the tempo of revolutionary development is accelerating',[146] Communists were encouraged towards suicidal actions. In June 1934 a call went out for mass non-payment of rent, tax, gas and electricity bills. Workers were advised to march on the town halls.[147] Anyone who took this call seriously was inviting an immediate visit by the Gestapo. Following Stalinist bureaucratic practices, the KPD insisted on maintaining its elaborate command structure which meant that the arrest of key individuals could bring entire districts to a halt. And far from learning from the defeat of 1933, the KPD continued to pursue the 'social fascist' line, arguing that the SPD was only banned to prevent its leadership exposing its bankruptcy and thus driving workers over to the KPD![148]

In August 1934 the disastrous consequences of the KPD's policy of frontal assault led to a re-evaluation of strategy[149] which, alas, compounded past mistakes with deeper confusion. Along with tentative moves towards a popular front (in line with Comintern's new policy) came the idea of the 'Trojan Horse' approach.[150] Communists were told to infiltrate the Nazi bodies and subvert them from within. This tactic immediately aroused the suspicion of a great many Social Democrats as well as many rank and file Communists. By the mid-1930s, despite herculean efforts, mistaken tactics, repression and the booming economy meant that not only had the KPD failed to dent the Third Reich in any way, but political indifference was weakening its position in the working class.

Popular front policies replaced the 'war to the knife'[151] approach to the SPD of 1933. In a complete reversal of policy the call was for an alliance with 'the SPD, leading Catholics and the freedom-loving bourgeoisie'.[152] The goal was no longer socialism but 'a democratic republic with democracy of a new type'.[153] The only difference with the Weimar Republic 'would be that there will be no room for fascism, the fascists will be made illegal'.[154] In the new perspective socialism was never mentioned. To cover this move to the right there was a ferocious attack on so called 'Trotskyist murderers in league with the Gestapo'.[155]

While never fully extinguished, KPD resistance stumbled on at a low level after this. Demoralisation at the Hitler-Stalin Pact broke KPD spirits that even the Gestapo could not humble, one sign being the decline in underground leaflets from 15,922 in 1939 to just 1,277 in 1940.[156] In spite of these incredible difficulties Communist resistance continued.

The SPD, as noted previously, tried to avoid repression in the early days by quoting the constitution and so it did little to prepare for working underground. However, the SPD's massive organisation was internally divided and in certain places maintained active cells. In 1936 the authorities still described Leipzig, one of the strongest centres of the SPD pre-1933, as 'a bastion of the workers' movement, as always'.[157] In Berlin left Socialists organised the 'Red Shock Troops' movement.[158]

Factional strife within the SPD leadership was at times severe; initially between those leaders who trusted to legality and avoidance of confrontation and an emigre leadership in Prague who openly denounced the Third Reich. Ordinary members were also bitter, some commenting that 'none of us wants to hear any more of that parliamentary stuff'. Others 'did not want to know any more of the Weimar Republic' or 'to hear the name Social Democracy. They only laugh about it'.[159] This attitude did not necessarily mean a move to the left (though the organisation adopted a far more radical tone). It could also be the prelude to apathy.

Active resistance to Nazism was far less pronounced among the SPD than the KPD. Its basic line was that of the 'long perspective'—to maintain what little remained of links between members—but to avoid mass resistance. Social networks often took the place of formal political ones. A SOPADE report put the situation like this:

> The good old root of the organised workmen has remained intact. Also the younger generation of workmen…has made a good stand, with some few exceptions. All know each other, all know who can be trusted and keep in touch with each other in those forms which today are possible. To be sure, that is wanting which once made us strong: the mental life in the organisations.[160]

One of the few examples of SPD activity on the mass scale was a silent anniversary visit by thousands to the graves of the old leaders Wilhelm Liebknecht and Hugo Haase on a day in 1934. Even this proved risky, for the 18 who laid flowers were arrested.[161]

In the trade unions attempts were made to retain contacts even though activity itself was virtually impossible. It is no surprise, therefore, that it was railway and transport workers that had the most success in this. Backed by Edo Fimmen's International Transport Workers' Federation, Jahn of the railway union claimed to have 137 area centres, 284 centre leaders and 1,320 officials operating in 1936. But this network was smashed a year afterwards.[162]

Neither the frontal assault of the KPD nor the relative passivity of the SPD proved effective against Nazi terror, although the former was more costly. In 1935 between June and December 9,517 people were arrested for 'Marxist sedition in the wider sense', of whom 8,269 were Communists.[163] In 1936 11,687 Communists and 1,374 Social Democrats were seized. Marxists arrested in 1937 totalled 8,068 people.

There was a third strategy that was put forward by a group which became known by its manifesto's title—*Neu Beginnen!* (*Begin Anew*). This organisation actually went underground as early as 1929 and stressed the importance of a carefully selected, tightly disciplined cadre organisation trained to survive under fascism. When the Third Reich eventually fell the 500 or so members of the organisation were supposed to emerge and lead the way to socialism. But the authorities' pursuit of every trace of workers' organisation was relentless. No group was immune. Even Neu Beginnen was infiltrated by the Gestapo and destroyed in 1938.[164]

Other left groups were swept away too. The German Socialist

Workers' Party, a left split from the SPD, had 17,000 members in 1933. This shrank to some 5,000 by 1937 and in that year it was smashed by arrests.[165] The anarcho-syndicalists claimed between 6,000 and 10,000 members at the end of the Weimar Republic, but their organisation collapsed under the weight of police pressure in the spring of 1937.[166] The militant International Socialist League (ISK), which also tried to build a cadre organisation against Nazism, was crushed in the late summer of 1938.[167] The Communist Opposition retained some 1,200 members until 1936. In February of the next year it was broken by mass arrests.[168] The Left Opposition of the KPD, in which the Trotskyists also worked, benefited from a short lived influx of disillusioned KPD members after 30 January 1933, but was snuffed out by 1936. Tragically, much of the information required by the Gestapo to achieve this was obtained by the seizure of KPD records, since the latter had itself sought to suppress Trotskyism.[169]

There was no obvious means for workers' political organisations to withstand the Nazi onslaught. If it was from the German working class generally that the main internal opposition to fascism came, it must also be recognised that that opposition was totally inadequate as a means of toppling the regime. Only in the long term might Nazism's own contradictions have weakened it internally and allowed a left wing revival; but that was no comfort to the victims of the 1933-45 period. The bitter lesson has to be that *Hitler's movement needed to be stopped before it had control of the levers of state power.* Nevertheless, though defeat followed defeat, workers' political organisations fought on to the very end of the war in underground organisations like the 'Red Orchestra' and the Robert Uhrig Group. The bravery, heroism and anti-fascist commitment of so many different women[170] and men should never be forgotten.

Overt political activity was only one aspect of workers' opposition under the Nazis. Equally important was the spontaneous struggle of the working class, especially in production. This could be far more diffuse and less consciously anti-Nazi, frequently centring on economic issues like wage rates. A KPD survey of 100 disputes in the mid-1930s recorded 47 percent as concerning wages, 26 percent conditions and just 3 percent 'for democratic rights and against the presence of spies'.[171]

The Nazis themselves 'always acted on the supposition that, behind every strike, etc, stood a Communist "wire-puller" or a Marxist "agitator".' Much to their astonishment, brutal interrogation rarely discovered political organisations behind such actions.[172] Ordinary workers needed no prompting to hate the enemy regime. However, it would be mistaken to see all such opposition as apolitical.

Once more Gestapo reports bore testimony to workers' struggle. In the months of June, July and August 1935, for example, it recorded 13 disputes and 39 acts of sabotage.[173] An example of sabotage occurred in the Opel works in Rüsselheim where, during the night, fire hoses were turned on machinery, wrecking 200 motors destined for the army.[174] Other diverse forms of recorded opposition included refusal to contribute to the compulsory Nazi charity, the 'Winter Help' and petitioning against arbitration decisions by the Trustees of Labour.[175]

The difficulties of striking and the likelihood of arrest led to many alternative tactics being tried. In a Saxon machine factory of 500, a petition was circulated against wage deductions—80 people signed:

> When the works leader allowed the list to go round once more with the explanation that it would be in the interests of the people's community if the 80 would cross out their names, another 40 men added their names.[176]

In the MAN works in Bavaria piece rate cuts meant that while 'the workmen had not the courage to strike, each gave notice singly'. The piece rate was restored.[177] Full employment made this type of pressure particularly effective, in spite of regulations to prevent job changing.

Absenteeism was another form of protest, as one writer shows:

> In August to September 1939 up to 20 per cent of the workforce were absent in Berlin armament factories on the day after payday... At the Ruhr mines the [Trustee] in the first seven months of 1940, pronounced 2,135 warnings on account of absenteeism and in 261 cases proposed the imposition of 'protective custody'... In a single factory in Bremen 36,000 working hours were missed in 1940...[178]

The destruction of trade union rights affected the character of workers' struggle deeply. Under normal circumstances strikes are most effective when they involve the majority of a workforce. This is still more the case under conditions of a repressive regime where safety resides in numbers. Yet very often only a tiny minority were involved. At Christoff and Unmack, a factory of 1,500 workers, 40 struck over a piece rate cut, and the strike failed.[179] In the same month a motor works of 400 had a strike of 20.[180] The DAF registered 192 stoppages in the 18 months between February 1936 and July 1937. Yet in only six of these stoppages did more than 80 participate.[181] With virtually no possibility of generalising individual struggles, these incidents were not a springboard to a higher level of action. Stoppages had to be short and succeed before the Gestapo arrived. It was often the case that one workshop would be involved while the rest of the plant continued to operate unaware of what was going on.

So although such open opposition was rare and involved only the most determined or exasperated workers, this is not proof of general contentment with Nazism but evidence of the tip of a large iceberg—resentment that dared not show itself. This is brought out by a *SOPADE* report from 1938:

> He who is disappointed in the attitude of the workmen must reflect what they would risk. Every show of insubordination is threatened with the punishment of dismissal. Following upon such a dismissal there is no unemployment relief and no prospect of obtaining a new job. Each attempt to do something by means of joint action is threatened with the concentration camp.[182]

To estimate precisely what proportion of the working class was opposed to the regime is impossible. The poison of racism and other regressive ruling class ideas had filtered into sections of the workers.[183] This *SOPADE* report from central Germany indicates the complexities:

> Ninety percent of the workers beyond all doubt are convinced anti-Nazis. That they are members of the DAF, of the Air Protection Union, of the [Nazi] Worker Sports Association and what not, cannot alter this fact one jot… But apart from a firm block of former [labour movement] functionaries there is also no conscious adoption of a political position, no active attitude against the ruling conditions.[184]

The coming of war did nothing to increase the room for manoeuvre of the workers' resistance. Firstly, Hitler's pledge to avoid any repeat of the 1918 Revolution by dealing with 'traitors' meant the redoubling of repression after years of unbroken assaults. This continued to the very end. In the last days and hours, with the fronts crumbling and many people wanting to surrender, Goebbels insisted that 'this rabble must be shot down'.[185]

Secondly, attempts to maintain German workers' living standards prevented life from becoming unbearable until quite late on (although it became so for foreign labour). Eventually living standards for German workers began tumbling and hours (for the working week) were pushed up to 60 (and 72 hours in the aircraft industry).[186] But depression and apathy were as likely a response as anger by this stage.

Thirdly, Allied tactics, far from encouraging revolt against the Third Reich, seemed calculated to produce a sullen loyalty. Indeed, the whole Allied approach to Germany, including the demand for an unconditional surrender, only makes sense against the background of their own fears of a repetition of revolution as in 1918-19. The Commander in Chief of Bomber Command, Arthur Harris, won no converts to his cause by dropping an address to the German people with an 'Open discussion of whether to attack military targets or whole cities'. It reached this chilling conclusion: 'Our bombs fall on your homes and on you... You can't stop us, and you know it. You have no hope'.[187] Massive aerial bombardments of civilian targets culminated in the Dresden fire storm which killed many tens of thousands in one night.[188] The response was actually to generate rising productivity in the cities that had been bombed.[189] In a grotesque and tragic way this reaction combined with a growing awareness of the enormity of Nazi crimes against Jews. As one soldier who had witnessed the Holocaust put it, 'God forbid we lose the war. If revenge comes upon us, we'll have a rough time'.[190]

Ian Kershaw gives a balanced summary of workers' resistance and opposition:

> The glimpses of worker attitudes which we have extracted from a mass of documentation suggest strongly that workers not only were unfree in the Third Reich, but that most of them felt they were unfree, exploited, discriminated against, and the victims of an unfair class-ridden society in which wealth and opportunity were unevenly divided.[191]

That feeling expressed itself in a wide variety of ways—from continued adherence to an illegal political party, to sabotage, strikes, street gangs, refusal to do the Hitler salute and absenteeism. These never linked up to become a coherent force because state imposed atomisation kept each manifestation separate.

However, at the end of the war, for one all too brief moment, the lid was lifted and workers were given a real chance to express themselves. What was revealed was amazing. A gigantic movement of Anti-Fascist Committees, or 'Antifas', swept across Germany as each new area was liberated from Nazism. There were well over 500 of these committees. They were overwhelmingly working class in composition but free of the dead hand of the discredited SPD and KPD leaders.[192] Alas, they could only exist for a few weeks (during the period between late March and mid-May 1945) after which the new military occupiers banned them. With Stalinism holding revolution back on an international scale, from Greece through to Italy and France, the real revolutionary potential of the Antifas would not be realised.

Yet in their short lifetimes the Antifas grew explosively. In Leipzig there were 38 local committees claiming 4,500 activists and 150,000 adherents. Despite the distractions caused by the devastation of war (the population had fallen from 700,000 to 500,000 for example), up to 100,000 people turned out on their 1945 May Day demonstration.[193] In Bremen, a city where 55 percent of the homes were uninhabitable and one third of the population had fled, there were 14 local groups just two weeks after liberation with 4,265 members. A fortnight later the figure was 6,495.[194] Many Antifas were organised in the workplaces. In the central Ruhr, soon after the ending of Nazism, an assembly of workplace representatives included 360 delegates from 56 pits and many other enterprises.[195]

Such expansion was only possible through the efforts of worker activists who had gained experience in the pre-1933 period and who were linked, however loosely, to networks of like-minded anti-Nazi sympathisers. As one leader put it, 'We are responsible for representing the workforce which we have led illegally for 12 years'.[196]

The Antifas were determined to rip out Nazism. Strikes were launched demanding a purge of Nazi activists.[197] In Bremen and elsewhere DAF buildings were taken over,[198] returning concentration camp inmates housed in the spare rooms of Nazi activists[199] and the most notorious of the latter handed over to the authorities.[200] Stuttgart went further and set up its own 'revolutionary tribunals'.[201]

There was an awareness that only by the workers doing the job themselves could Nazism really be banished for good. The Prince Regent mine in Bochum called for a political general strike and issued the slogan 'Long live the Red Army', not in reference to the Soviet forces, but to the anti-Kapp putsch insurrectionary force of 1920.[202] The view was advanced that 'in the future state there will be no more employers as previously. We must all arrange it and work as if the exterprise is ours!'[203] In some places workers took over their factories and management fled.[204] Antifas set up their own factory militias[205] and replaced police chiefs and mayors with their own nominees. The situation in Stuttgart and Hanover was one of 'dual power', the Antifas having set up their own police forces, taken over a raft of powerful local positions and begun to run vital services like food provisioning.[206]

The eyewitness report of a US official is worth citing at length:

In widely dispersed areas under a number of different names and apparently without any connection one with the other, anti-Nazi unity front movements emerged soon after the collapse of the Nazi government... Although they have no contact with each other, these groups show a remarkable similarity in the way they are constituted and their programme. The initiative for their creation appears in each case to come from people who were active during the Nazi period and in some form or another were in contact with each other... Denunciation of Nazis, efforts to prevent an illegal Nazi underground movement, de-Nazification of civil authorities and private industry, improvement of housing and food supply provision—these are the central questions which preoccupy the newly created organisations... The conclusion is therefore justified, that these communities represent the spontaneous coming together of anti-Nazi resistance forces, which, as long as the terror regime remained, were powerless.[207]

The report went on to contrast the activities of the left, which emphasised uprooting all traces of Nazism as the precondition of a new start, and the right which 'concentrated on the attempt to preserve out of the ruins of the Hitler regime anything that might still be usable'.[208]

Although the regime was not brought down by internal revolt, nothing can diminish the heroism or self sacrifice of those who resisted. Within the broad spectrum of resistance in Germany itself it was the working class that distinguished itself as the most important and chief obstacle to the monstrous ambitions of the Third Reich.

Conclusion

The 'Thousand Year Reich' lasted no more than 12 years. In that brief time it committed acts of barbarity on an unprecedented scale. Yet Nazism was not an incomprehensible phenomenon, nor, alas, is it necessarily unique. It was the product of a specific combination of circumstances: an advanced capitalist state; extreme crisis (expressed through war, and economic collapse in 1918, 1923 and 1930-33); and a highly organised workers' movement that half made a revolution and continued to obstruct capitalist ambitions. The NSDAP came forward to offer its solution—counter-revolution at home and imperialist expansion abroad. Although this precise combination of circumstances will not recur, the basic ingredients for a repetition exist.

Today the world is covered by developed forms of capitalism. Crisis in various forms is endemic. In its struggle to resist both exploitation and paying for the crisis, the working class is still the greatest threat facing the system. Although less rapidly than in the inter-war period, politics are being polarised everywhere, with Nazi-type groups growing on an international scale at the same time as worker militancy.

But there is no inevitability of fascist rule. The lessons of the past can be used to create a different future. Some of these lessons are summarised below:

(1) Fascism is not some 'third way'. Its ideas are a grotesque and exaggerated expression of capitalist ideology, with its elitism and contempt for ordinary human beings. Its most pernicious expression is racism.

(2) It works within the context of capitalism to preserve, by the most brutal methods, the dominance of the system and to secure it from internal threats.

(3) Yet fascism is not a ruling class conspiracy. It seeks to create a mass movement out of the misery and despair that capitalism engenders, directing that energy down paths harmless to the ruling class.

(4) The Nazi leadership uses democratic structures in order to build up support; but unlike other parties, its fundamental purpose is to destroy any form of democracy. Therefore, it cannot be treated in the same way as other democratic parties. There must be no platform for fascists.

(5) Constitutional safeguards and parliamentary rules are no defence against fascism. If the crisis is deep enough, and the ruling class sees no other way out, it will allow the Nazis free reign.

(6) Since fascism is rooted in class society, the most effective resistance comes from that class which has the most to lose—the working class. Its life experience and position in society tend to engender forms of solidarity and collective action that are the very opposite of Nazism.

(7) While political differences exist within the working class, the different currents within the movement need to unite in combating the common deadly enemy. An active united front to oppose Nazism is a vital tactic.

The society we live in today is one of tremendous contrasts and tremendous possibilities. Advances in science and technology mean there is the opportunity to banish want and disease in a way undreamt of in previous generations. Yet millions starve and in places like Russia life expectancy is falling. Modern technology gives humanity the means of controlling and improving the life of everyone, and yet we see environmental destruction and grotesque concentrations of wealth on one side and mass unemployment and impoverishment on the other.

This situation is unstable. Capitalism lurches from one crisis to another. In so doing it encourages the rise of fascism which offers easy scapegoats for problems and feeds on the system's elitist ideology to win converts. In the bewilderment many face, fascism offers a false hope. This has been shown by the growth of neo-Nazi groups such as the French National Front. Operating in different circumstances and in the shadow of Hitlerism and the Holocaust, today's new Nazis do not emulate the Nazis directly. However, in the right circumstances they have the potential to match or even surpass their evil forbears. At the same time the growth of the working class on a world scale means that the possibility for a collective solution to the crisis of the system in the interests of all is greater than ever before. In Indonesia, for example, even a vicious dictatorship like Suharto's can be toppled by mass action.

The threat of fascism will remain as long as capitalist society remains. Therefore, the only way to abolish it forever is to overthrow capitalism itself. The choice is: socialism or barbarism!

Notes

Introduction

1   R Kühnl, *Der Deutsche Faschismus in Quellen und Dokumenten* (Cologne, 1975), p477, for war statistics; M Gilbert, *The Holocaust* (London, 1987), p824, on the Jews.
2   D F Crew (ed), *Nazism and German Society, 1933-1945* (London, 1994), p31n.
3   Quoted in R Breitman, 'The "Final Solution" ', in G Martel (ed), *Modern Germany Reconsidered* (London, 1992), p197.
4   W Sofsky, *The Order of Terror: the Concentration Camp* (New Jersey, 1997), pp277, 281.
5   A Hitler, *Mein Kampf* (London, 1969), pxii.
6   T Saunders, 'Nazism and Social Revolution', in G Martel (ed), op cit, p168.
7   D Mühlberger, *Hitler's Followers: Studies in the Sociology of the Nazi Movement* (London, 1991), p203.
8   J P Stern, *Hitler: The Führer and the People* (no place of publication, 1975), p167.
9   P Baldwin, 'Social Interpretations of Nazism: Review of a Tradition', in *Journal of Contemporary History*, vol 25 (1990), pp5-6.
10 L Trotsky, *The Struggle Against Fascism in Germany* (Harmondsworth, 1975), p14.

Chapter 1

1   For a critical analysis of this approach in relation to Germany see J Kocka, 'German History Before Hitler: the Debate about the German *Sonderweg*', in *Journal of Contemporary History*, vol 23 (1988). See also I Kershaw, *Hitler, 1889-1936. Hubris* (London, 1998), pp73-76.
2   E Vermeil, 'The Origin, Nature and Development of German Nationalist Ideology in the 19th and 20th Centuries', in *The Third Reich* (London, 1955), p6.
3   K D Bracher, *The German Dictatorship* (Harmondsworth, 1970), p46.
4   J Kocka, op cit, p3.
5   R Grunberger, *A Social History of the Third Reich* (London, 1971), p13.
6   A J P Taylor, *The Course of German History* (London, 1993), p77.
7   F Engels, *The Peasant War in Germany* (Moscow, 1969), pp12-13.
8   Quoted in G Martel (ed), *Modern Germany Reconsidered* (London, 1992), p12.
9   F Engels, op cit, p17.
10 W Kendall, *The Labour Movement in Europe* (London, 1975), p89.
11 E H Phelps Brown, *A Century of Pay* (London, 1968), p122.
12 P Stearns, *Lives of Labour* (London, 1975), p361.
13 T Childers, *The Nazi Voter* (Chapel Hill and London, 1983), p21.

14   G Eley, 'Bismarckian Germany', in G Martel (ed), op cit, p19.
15   Beetham, quoted in G Steinmetz, 'The Myth of an Autonomous State', in
     G Eley (ed), Society, Culture and the State in Germany, 1870-1930 (Ann Arbor,
     1996), p268.
16   Bismarck quoted in T Childers, op cit, p16.
17   Quoted in F L Carsten, The German Workers and the Nazis (Aldershot, 1995),
     p200.
18   G Martel (ed), op cit, p26.
19   F Thyssen, I Paid Hitler (London, 1941), p62.
20   L Trotsky, op cit, p259.
21   See H Böhme, Deutschlands Weg zur Grossmacht (Cologne, 1966), p9;
     H Böhme, An Introduction to the Social and Economic History of Germany
     (Oxford, 1978), p71.
22   See, for example, H Wehler, Deutsche Gesellschaftsgeschichte, vol 3 (Munich,
     1995), and discussion in R J Evans, Rereading German History, 1880-1996
     (London, 1997), p15.
23   D Groh, Überlegung zum Verhältnis von Intensivierung der Arbeit und Arbeitskämpfen
     im Organisierten Kapitalismus in Deutschland (Heidelberg, 1976), pp1, 5.
24   W Kendall, op cit, p89.
25   See E Lucas, Zwei Formen von Radikalismus in der Deutschen Arbeiterbewegung
     (Frankfurt am Main, 1976).
26   N Poulantzas, Fascism and Dictatorship (London, 1974).
27   R Hilferding, Finance Capital (London, 1981), p370.
28   P Stearns, op cit, p177.
29   H Grebing, History of the German Labour Movement (Leamington Spa, 1985), p71.
30   Ibid, p73.
31   Ibid, p69.
32   D Groh, op cit, p15.
33   H Grebing, op cit, p59.
34   C Harman, The Lost Revolution (London, 1982), p14.
35   Quoted in H Grebing, op cit, p33.
36   E Anderson, Hammer or Anvil (London, 1945), p9.
37   F Engels, op cit, p13.
38   H A Winkler, Mittelstand, Demokratie und Nationalsozialismus (Cologne, 1972),
     p158.
39   Quoted in J C G Röhl, From Bismarck to Hitler (London, 1970), p46.
40   Hartmut Pogge-von Strandmann quoted ibid, p51.
41   According to Philipp Fürst zu Eulenburg-Hertefeld, quoted ibid, pp42-43.
42   H S Chamberlain, Briefe, vol II, p141 onwards, quoted ibid, p53.
43   Details from K P Fischer, Nazi Germany. A New History (London, 1995), p36.
44   D Goldhagen, Hitler's Willing Executioners (London, 1997), p72.
45   Quoted in J Jacobs, 'Marxism and Anti-Semitism: Kautsky', in International
     Review of Social History, vol 30 (1985), p404.
46   L Trotsky, op cit, p258.
47   R Kühnl, in M N Dobkowski and I Wallimann (eds), Towards the Holocaust, the
     Social and Economic Collapse of the Weimar Republic (Westport, 1983), p97.
48   F Fischer, War of Illusions (London, 1975), pviii.
49   J B Drabkin, Die Novemberrevolution 1918 in Deutschland (Berlin, 1968), p71.
50   G A Feldman, Army, Industry and Labor in Germany 1914-18 (Princeton, 1966),
     p519.

51   Ibid, p469.
52   D Thomas and M McAndrew, *Russia, Soviet Union, 1917-1945* (New South Wales, 1995), p83.
53   M Scharrer (ed), *Die Spaltung der Deutschen Arbeiterbewegung* (Stuttgart, 1985), p28; and R Kühnl, op cit, p28.
54   R Luxemburg, *Rosa Luxemburg Speaks* (New York, 1970), p269.

Chapter 2

1   G Ritter, 'The Historical Foundations of the Rise of National-Socialism', in *The Third Reich* (New York, 1955), pp399, 413.
2   'Bericht über eine Beratung Führender Deutscher Industrieller in Berlin über die Finanzierung der "Antibolshewistischen Liga" am 10. January 1919', quoted in R Kühnl, *Der Deutsche Faschismus in Quellen und Dokumenten* (Cologne, 1975), p57.
3   Bernhard Fuurst von Bülow, quoted in A Kaes, M Jay and E Dimendberg, *The Weimar Republik Sourcebook* (London, 1994), p57.
4   F Thyssen, *I Paid Hitler* (London, 1941), p86.
5   G A Ritter and S Miller (eds), *Die Deutsche Revolution 1918-19*, pp210-214, translation in J C G Röhl, *From Bismarck to Hitler* (London, 1970), p94.
6   H J Gordon, *The Reichswehr and the German Republic* (London, 1957), p4.
7   Quoted in F C Carsten, *Reichswehr und Politik* (Cologne, 1964), p24.
8   *Deutsche Tageszeitung*, 25 November 1918.
9   F Tarnow at the SPD Congress, 1 June 1931, in W Ruge and W Schumann (eds), *Dokumente zur Deutschen Geschichte, 1924-1945* (Frankfurt am Main, 1977), p29.
10   W Groener, quoted in J C G Röhl, op cit, p88.
11   Quoted in C S Maier, *Recasting Bourgeois Europe* (Princeton, 1975), p60.
12   H von Raumer quoted in G A Ritter and S Miller (eds), op cit, pp210-214, translation in J C G Röhl, op cit, pp93-94.
13   D Gluckstein, *The Western Soviets: Workers' Councils Versus Parliament 1915-20* (London, 1985), p155.
14   M Scharrer (ed), *Die Spaltung der Deutschen Arbeiterbewegung* (Stuttgart, 1985), pp126-127.
15   Ibid, p129.
16   H A Turner, *German Big Business and the Rise of Hitler* (Oxford, 1987), p9.
17   M H Geyer, 'Munich in Turmoil: Social Protest and the Revolutionary Movement 1918-19', in C Wrigley (ed), *Challenges of Labour: Central and Western Europe, 1917-1920* (London, 1993), p68.
18   C Harman, *The Lost Revolution* (London, 1982), p142.
19   Hitler in N H Baynes (ed), *The Speeches of Adolf Hitler* (Oxford, 1942), vol 1, p74.
20   Account in T Abel, *Why Hitler came into Power* (Harvard, 1966).
21   Testimony delivered on 18 November 1919, quoted in A Kaes, M Jay and E Dimendberg, op cit, p16.
22   A Hitler, *Mein Kampf* (London, 1969), p124.
23   *Hitler's Secret Conversations* (New York, 1976), p33.
24   A Hitler, *Zweites Buch* (Stuttgart, 1961), p70.
25   Quoted in I Kershaw, op cit, p275.
26   R Luxemburg, *The National Question* (New York, 1976), p136.
27   The only part of the plan not followed in the Second World War was the addition of Sweden; see R Kühnl, op cit, p25. This shows the nonsense of

Hillgruber's claims that 'the racial-ideological conclusions drawn in [Hitler's] programme, which were directed to a complete transformation of Europe along racial principles, represented something entirely different', A Hillgruber, *Germany and the Two World Wars* (Cambridge, Massachusetts, 1981), p54. For a discussion of historical continuities between Hitler and pre-war Germany see F Fischer, *Hitler war kein Betriebsunfall* (Munich, 1992), pp174-181, and F Fischer, *From Kaiserreich to Third Reich* (London, 1986).

28 A Hitler, *Mein Kampf*, op cit, p348.

29 Hitler, quoted in V Kratzenberg, *Arbeiter auf dem Weg zu Hitler?* (Frankfurt am Main, 1989), p25.

30 A Hitler, *Mein Kampf*, op cit, pp219-220.

31 Ibid, p220.

32 K Marx, 'Communist Manifesto', in *The Revolutions of 1848* (Harmondsworth, 1973), p69.

33 W Maser (ed), *Hitler's Letters and Notes* (New York, 1976), p211.

34 A Hitler, *Zweites Buch*, op cit, p65.

35 W Maser (ed), op cit, p361.

36 E Jäckel, *Hitlers Weltanschauung, Entwurf einer Herrschaft* (Tübingen, 1969), p97.

37 While generally very good on the role of anti-Semitism, it is therefore wrong of Kershaw [*Hitler, 1889-1936. Hubris* (London, 1998), p410] to relate the anti-Semitism of the middle class to the presence of Jews in middle class professions. The targets of racist movements are often ethnic groups which may occupy the very lowest strata of society. The fact that there were many middle class Jews is incidental. That there were convenient scapegoats for the crisis of capitalism is the key issue.

38 A Leon, *The Jewish Question* (New York, 1970), p74.

39 D Blackbourn, *Fontana History of Germany: The Long 19th Century* (London, 1997), p437.

40 This interpretation is denied in G Fleming, *Hitler and the Final Solution* (London, 1985), p6.

41 Ibid, p10.

42 A Hitler, *Mein Kampf*, op cit, p254. In arguing this I take issue with the generally excellent biography of Hitler by Kershaw. See I Kershaw, op cit, p152.

43 Quoted in W Maser, op cit, p211-212.

44 Ibid, pp212-213.

45 A Hitler, *Mein Kampf*, op cit, p155.

46 Ibid, p474.

47 Ibid, p446.

48 *Hitler's Secret Conversations*, op cit, p17 (2 August 1941).

49 A Hitler, *Mein Kampf*, op cit, p447.

50 Quoted in H Krausnick and M Broszat, *Anatomy of the SS State* (London, 1970), p147.

51 Quoted in W Maser, op cit, p176.

52 J Goebbels, *Diaries, 1939-41* (London, 1982), p415.

53 A Hitler, *Mein Kampf*, op cit, p47.

54 J M Steiner, *Power Politics and Social Change in National Socialist Germany* (The Hague, 1976), p192.

55 M Kater, *The Nazi Party* (Cambridge, Massachusetts, 1983), p229.

56 24 April 1923. Retranslated from N H Baynes (ed), op cit, p61.

57 18 September 1922, ibid, p42.

58   28 July 1922, ibid, p29.
59   A Hitler, *Mein Kampf*, op cit, p355.
60   Ibid, p93.
61   L Trotsky, op cit, p268.
62   Ibid, p268.
63   A Hitler, *Mein Kampf*, op cit, p164.
64   Ibid, p167.
65   B Miller Lane and L J Rupp, *Nazi Ideology Before 1933* (Manchester, 1978), pp42-43.
66   13 April 1923, in N H Baynes (ed), op cit, pp48-49.
67   K Marx, *Revolutions of 1848*, op cit, p90.
68   T Childers, *The Nazi Voter* (Chapel Hill and London, 1983), p77.
69   17 May 1933, in N H Baynes (ed), op cit, p118.
70   *Hitler's Secret Conversations*, op cit, p36.
71   22 May 1930, in N H Baynes (ed), op cit, p111.
72   A Hitler, *Der Weg zum Wiederaufstieg*, quoted in R Kühnl, op cit, p119.
73   28 July 1922, in N H Baynes (ed), op cit, p35.
74   A Hitler, *Zweites Buch*, op cit, pp62-63.
75   T Childers, op cit, p24.
76   H Speier, *German White Collar Workers and the Rise of Hitler* (Yale, 1986), pp124, 130.
77   P Manstein, *Die Mitglieder und Wähler der NSDAP* (Frankfurt am Main, 1989), p69.
78   300,000 or 20.7 percent belonged to the GdA, itself linked to the left wing of middle class politics, the DDP.
79   P Manstein, op cit, p69.
80   H Speier, op cit, p131.
81   W Koenen, USPD deputy, quoted ibid, p130.
82   L Trotsky, op cit, p15.
83   K Fischer, op cit, p92.
84   A Rosenberg, *Selected Writings* (London, 1970), p38. For the origins of these bizarre ideas see N Goodrick-Clarke, *The Occult Origins of Nazism* (London, 1992).
85   A Rosenberg, op cit, p70.
86   Ibid, p59.
87   H A Turner, op cit, p13.
88   J Noakes and G Pridham, *Nazism 1919-1945* (Exeter, 1964), p35. See also I Kershaw, op cit, pp171-172.
89   M Broszat, *Hitler and the Collapse of Weimar Germany* (Leamington Spa, 1987), p4.
90   H A Turner, op cit, p49.
91   Ibid, p56.
92   Ibid, p59. See also I Kershaw, op cit, pp187-190.
93   A Bullock, *Hitler: A Study in Tyranny* (New York, 1962), p97.
94   W Guttmann and P Meehan, *The Great Inflation* (Farnborough, 1975), p30.
95   M Scharrer (ed), op cit, p74.
96   C Harman, op cit, p276.
97   W Guttmann and P Meehan, op cit, p124.
98   See O Flechtheim, *Die KPD in der Weimarer Republik* (Frankfurt am Main, 1976), p437.

99   Ibid, p180.
100 Albert, quoted in C Harman, op cit, p292.
101 M Geyer, 'Professionals and Junkers', in R Bessel and E J Feuchtwanger, *Social Change and Political Development in Weimar Germany* (London, 1981), p99.
102 Quoted in A Bullock, op cit, p102.
103 R Opitz, *Faschismus und Neofaschismus*, vol 1 (Frankfurt am Main, 1984), p82.
104 Ibid, p85.
105 W Ruge and W Schumann (eds), op cit, p28.
106 1 August 1923, in N H Baynes (ed), op cit, p78.
107 Details from A Bullock, op cit, p108.
108 N H Baynes (ed), op cit, p133.
109 Quoted in K D Bracher, op cit, p157.
110 J Noakes and G Pridham, op cit, p35.
111 P Hanfstaegl quoted in K Fischer, op cit, p163.
112 Details from K Fischer, op cit, p193; and W Maser, op cit, p276.
113 For an interesting discussion of the relationship between the rise of fascism and whether it is always connected with the immediate prospect of workers' revolution or whether the relationship is looser, see C Sparks, 'Fascism and the Working Class: the German Experience' in *International Socialism*, autumn 1978.

Chapter 3

1   D Goldhagen, *Hitler's Willing Executioners* (London, 1997), p87.
2   R Neebe, *Grossindustrie, Staat und NSDAP, 1930-33* (Göttingen, 1981), p202.
3   G Feldman, 'The Weimar Republic: A Problem of Modernisation?' in *Archiv Für Sozialgeschichte*, vol XXVI (1986), p26.
4   This was evident in, for example, the military liaison role of *Landesschutz-Angestellten*. Of the 53 that existed in 1933 some 23 had worked directly in industry while 15 others had come from trade, banking and commerce. See E W Hansen, *Reichswehr und Industrie* (Boppard am Rhein, 1978), p207.
5   D Guerin, *Fascism and Big Business* (New York, 1973), p113.
6   L Trotsky, op cit, pp270-271.
7   M Scharrer (ed), *Die Spaltung der Deutschen Arbeiterbewegung* (Stuttgart, 1985), p28.
8   E Hobsbawm, *Age of Extremes* (London, 1995), p98.
9   E J Feuchtwanger, *From Weimar to Hitler* (London, 1984), p329.
10   Ibid, p39.
11   The pre-war monthly average was 815. In the months of the highest inflation, August-November 1923, the figure was just 11. See M Scharrer (ed), op cit, p38.
12   The number of joint stock companies decreased by 25 percent. See M Scharrer (ed), op cit, p39.
13   D Petzina, 'Problems in the Social and Economic Development of the Weimar Republic', in M N Dobkowski and I Wallimann (eds), *Towards the Holocaust, The Social and Economic Collapse of the Weimar Republic* (Westport, 1983), p42.
14   M Scharrer (ed), op cit, p49.
15   Ibid, p17.
16   Ibid, p48.
17   E J Feuchtwanger, op cit, p329.
18   D Petzina, op cit, in M N Dobkowski and I Wallimann (eds), op cit, p42.

19   D Geary, 'Employers, Workers and the Collapse of Weimar', in I Kershaw (ed),
      Why did Weimar Democracy Fail? (London, 1990), p102.
20   D Landes, *The Unbound Prometheus* (Cambridge, 1969), p371.
21   D Petzina, 'Was there a Crisis before the Crisis?' in J von Kruedener (ed),
      Economic Crisis and Political Collapse (New York, 1990), p16.
22   D Petzina, 'Problems etc', in M N Dobkowski and I Wallimann (eds), op cit, p42.
23   R Beckenbach, *Der Staat im Faschismus* (Berlin, 1974), p122.
24   M Scharrer (ed), op cit, p88. The figure of eight million is given by H-J Braun
      in *The German Economy in the 20th Century* (London, 1990), p67.
25   D Peukert, *The Weimar Republic* (Harmondsworth, 1991), p252.
26   *Der DMV in Zahlen* (Berlin, 1932), p182.
27   C Harman, *Explaining the Crisis* (London, 1984), p54.
28   D Landes, op cit, p366.
29   Ibid, p362.
30   Ibid, p391.
31   D Petzina, 'Problems etc', op cit, p43.
32   Quoted by V I Lenin, *Collected Works*, vol 26 (Moscow), p131.
33   M Scharrer (ed), op cit, p71.
34   Ibid, p74.
35   Ibid, p84; F Deppe and W Rossmann (eds), *Weltwirtschafte, Faschismus,
      Gewerkschaften, 1929-33* (Cologne, 1981), p40.
36   Figures calculated from F Deppe and W Rossmann (eds), ibid, p42.
37   Ibid, p41.
38   I Kershaw (ed), *Why did Weimar Democracy Fail?*, op cit, table IIIc.
39   Ibid, table IIIg.
40   R Bessel, 'Why did the Weimar Republic Collapse?', ibid, p134.
41   C Gradmann and O von Mengerson, *Das Ende der Weimarer Republik und die
      Nationalsozialistische Machtergriefung* (Frankfurt am Main, 1996), p14.
42   For full details see I Kershaw, *Why did Weimar Democracy Fail?*, op cit, table II.
43   R Grunberger, *A Social History of the Third Reich* (London, 1971), p16.
44   Translation in A Kaes, M Jay and E Dimendberg, *The Weimar Republik
      Sourcebook* (London, 1994), p48.
45   Wissell quoted in A Rosenberg, *A History of the German Republic* (London,
      1936), pp125-126.
46   E J Gumbel, 'Four Years of Political Murder', in A Kaes et al (eds), op cit, p102.
47   F Neumann, *Behemoth: The Structure and Practice of National Socialism*
      (New York, 1944), p28; and R Kühnl, *Der Deutsche Faschismus in Quellen und
      Dokumenten* (Cologne, 1975), p74.
48   K D Bracher, 'Democracy and the Power Vacuum: The Problem of the Party
      State during the Disintegration of the Weimar Republic', in V Berghahn
      and M Kitchen, *Germany in the Age of Total War* (London, 1981), p195.
49   W Mommsen (1928) quoted in R Bessel and E J Feuchtwanger (eds), op cit,
      p14.
50   K Marx, Introduction to *Contribution to a Critique of Political Economy* (Moscow,
      1981), pp20-21.
51   Ibid, p21.
52   For a discussion of the impact this had on relations with the state machine, see
      A Dorpalen, *Hindenburg and the Weimar Republic* (Princeton, 1964), p149.
53   F Deppe and W Rossmann (eds), op cit, p46. Strike days (in thousands) for
      1926, 1927 and 1928 were 886, 2,869 and 8,519 respectively. Equivalent figures

for number of lockouts were 39, 269 and 451. See also H James, *The German Slump* (Oxford 1986), p218.

54 M Scharrer (ed), op cit, p89.
55 H A Turner, op cit, p43; and H James, op cit, pp219-223.
56 C Köttgen of Siemens, quoted ibid, p166.
57 M Scharrer (ed), op cit, p91.
58 W Brustein, 'Blue-collar Nazism', in C Fischer (ed), *The Rise of National Socialism and the Working Classes in Weimar Germany* (Oxford, 1996), p141.
59 Turner's summary of the Reichsverband manifesto 'Rise or Ruin?' in H A Turner, op cit, p44.
60 Quoted in P D Stachura (ed), *The Nazi Machtergreifung* (London, 1983), p94.
61 RDI meeting of 12 December 1929, in R Kühnl, op cit, pp71-72.
62 M Broszat, op cit, p81.
63 H A Turner, op cit, pp103-104.
64 Quoted in D Guerin, *Fascism and Big Business* (New York, 1973), pp34-35; Siemens on 27 October 1931 in W Ruge and W Schumann (eds), *Dokumente zur Deutschen Geschichte, 1924-1945* (Frankfurt am Main, 1977), 1929-33, p45.
65 *Deutsche Zeitung*, 14 December 1929, quoted in D Abraham, *The Collapse of the Weimar Republic* (New York and Princeton, 1986), p318.
66 L Trotsky, op cit, p266.
67 L Trotsky, op cit, p263. For an interesting alternative Marxist discussion on the relevance of Bonapartism to the German situation, see A Thalheimer, 'Über den Faschismus', in O Bauer, H Marcuse, A Rosenberg et al, *Faschismus und Kapitalismus* (Frankfurt am Main, 1967), pp19-38.
68 K Marx, 'The 18th Brumaire of Louis Bonaparte', in *Surveys from Exile* (Harmondsworth, 1973), p190.
69 M Scharrer (ed), op cit, p97.
70 R Neebe, *Grossindustrie, Staat und NSDAP, 1930-33* (Göttingen, 1981), p200.
71 D Abraham, op cit. For an interesting contemporary account see A Sohn-Rethel, *The Economy and Class Structure of German Fascism* (London, 1978).
72 D Geary, 'The Industrial Elite and the Nazis in the Weimar Republic', in P D Stachura (ed), *The Nazi Machtergreifung* (London, 1983), p92.
73 M N Dobkowski and I Wallimann (eds), op cit, pp100-101.
74 J Noakes and G Pridham, *Nazism, 1919-45* (Exeter, 1964), p37.
75 Ibid, p162. See also I Kershaw, *Hitler, 1889-1936. Hubris*, op cit, pp337-338.
76 Quoted in A Bullock, op cit, p163.
77 *Frankfurter Zeitung*, 26 September 1930.
78 Letter from Hitler to Captain von Pfeffer, SA leader, on 1 November 1926, quoted in J Noakes and G Pridham, op cit, p56.
79 Quoted in J M H Kele, *Nazis and Workers* (Chapel Hill, 1972), p91.
80 *Der Angriff*, 16 July 1928, quoted in J M H Kele, op cit, p132.
81 Quoted in B Miller Lane and L J Rupp, *Nazi Ideology Before 1933* (Manchester, 1978), op cit, pp74-75.
82 W S Allen (ed), *The Infancy of Nazism: The Memoirs of ex-Gauleiter Albert Krebs, 1923-1933* (New York, 1976), p54.
83 Ibid, p209.
84 Ibid, p209.
85 15 February 1926, E Frölich (ed), *Die Tagebücher von Joseph Goebbels*, vol 1 (Munich, 1987), pp161-162. Another account of the disillusionment of the so called left is given in O Strasser, *Hitler et Moi* (Paris, 1940).

86   24 June 1941, in J Goebbels, *Diaries, 1939-41* (London, 1982), p427. See also I Kershaw, *Hitler, 1889-1936. Hubris*, op cit, p276.

87   Details in K P Fischer, *Nazi Germany. A New History* (London, 1995), pp222-223.

88   Ibid, p227.

89   A Bullock, op cit, p185.

90   E J Feuchtwanger, op cit, p327.

91   D Goldhagen, op cit, p85.

92   *Deutsche Allgemeine Zeitung*, 24 August 1930.

93   *Berliner Börsenzeitung*, 14 October 1930, in W Ruge and W Schumann (eds), op cit, p93.

94   H A Turner, op cit, pp142-143.

95   Ibid, p144.

96   Ibid, p145.

97   F Thyssen, op cit, p129.

98   Ibid, p129.

99   Ibid, p133.

100   H A Turner, op cit, p149.

101   Quoted in A Schweitzer, *Big Business in the Third Reich* (Indiana, 1977), p359.

102   Letter of 12 April 1932 in W Ruge and W Schumann (eds), op cit, p62.

103   H A Turner, op cit, p150.

104   Ibid, p156. See also I Kershaw, *Hitler, 1889-1936. Hubris*, op cit, pp357-359.

105   Details in W Ruge and W Schumann (eds), op cit, 1929-33, p89.

106   M Schneider, *Unternehmer und Demokratie. Die Freien Gewerkschaften in der Unternehmerischen Ideologie der Jahre 1918 bis 1933* (Bonn, 1975), p182.

107   D Geary, 'The Industrial Elite and the Nazis in the Weimar Republic', op cit, p98.

108   K Heiden, *A History of National Socialism* (London, 1935), p153.

109   H A Turner, op cit, pp26-27.

110   Quoted in D Abraham, *The Collapse of the Weimar Republic* (New York and Princeton, 1986), p320.

111   A Bullock, op cit, p223.

112   R Bessel, 'Violence as Propaganda: The Role of the Storm Troopers in the Rise of National Socialism', in T Childers (ed), *The Mobilisation of Nazi Support 1918-1933* (Beckenham, 1986), p135.

113   A Kaes et al (eds), op cit, p139.

114   Ibid, p140.

115   Ibid, p141.

116   Ibid, p140.

117   See the examples given by R Kühnl, op cit, pp160, 162.

118   *Deutsche Allgemeine Zeitung*, 26 April 1932, for example.

119   *Deutsche Allgemeine Zeitung*, 18 July 1932.

120   M Geyer, 'Professionals and Junkers: German Rearmament and Politics in the Weimar Republic', in P D Stachura (ed), op cit, p82.

121   This was reported by the French Military Attaché in Berlin on 4 November 1921, quoted in A Bullock, op cit, pp190-191.

122   W Ruge and W Schumann (eds), op cit, p46.

123   O Flechtheim, *Die KPD in Weimarer Republik* (Frankfurt am Main, 1976), p284.

124   Quoted in K P Fischer, op cit, p234.

125   M Broszat, *Hitler and the Collapse of Weimar Germany* (Leamington Spa, 1987), pp120-121.

126 *Deutsche Allgemeine Zeitung*, 25 July 1932.
127 *Deutsche Allgemeine Zeitung*, 29 July 1932.
128 *Völkische Beobachter*, 10 August 1932.
129 Quoted in F L Carsten, *Essays in German History* (London, 1985), p210.
130 See for example the evidence given by the banker von Schröder quoted in G W F Hallgarten, *Hitler, Reichswehr und Industrie* (Frankfurt am Main, 1986), p110.
131 L Trotsky, *The Struggle Against Fascism in Germany* (Harmondsworth, 1975), p339.
132 A Bullock, op cit, p230.
133 E Frölich (ed), op cit, 10 November 1932, p276.
134 Ibid, 11 November 1932, p276.
135 Ibid, 24 December 1932, p314.
136 *Berliner Tageblatt*, 2 January 1932.
137 *Berliner Tageblatt*, 5 January 1933.
138 *Frankfurter Zeitung*, 24 January 1933.
139 *Deutsche Allgemeine Zeitung*, 5 January 1933.
140 R Beckenbach, *Der Staat im Faschismus: Ökonomie und Politik im Deutschen Reich, 1920-45* (Frankfurt am Main, 1964), p73.
141 F von Papen, quoted in J C G Röhl, *From Bismarck to Hitler* (London, 1970), p138.
142 W Maser (ed), *Hitler's Letters and Notes* (New York, 1976), p174.
143 A Bullock, op cit, p236.
144 Details in M Ruck, *Gewerkschaften-Staat-Unternehmer* (Cologne, 1990), p113. For details of the role of Strasser, see also I Kershaw, *Hitler, 1889-1936. Hubris*, op cit, pp396-402.
145 M Broszat, op cit, p130.
146 *Völkische Beobachter*, 24 January 1933.
147 *Berliner Tageblatt*, 23 January 1933.
148 D Guerin, op cit, p284.
149 Quoted in K D Bracher, *Die Auflösung der Weimarer Republik* (Villingen, 1955), p733.
150 Quoted in A Bullock, op cit, p249.
151 *Deutsche Allgemeine Zeitung*, 30 January 1933.
152 *Deutsche Allgemeine Zeitung*, 1 February 1933.

Chapter 4

1 A Bullock, *Hitler: A Study in Tyranny* (New York, 1962), p218.
2 T Childers, *The Nazi Voter* (Chapel Hill and London, 1983), p118.
3 I Kershaw, *Hitler, 1889-1936. Hubris* (London, 1998), p333.
4 J W Falter, *Hitlers Wähler*, partial translation in C Fischer (ed), *The Rise of National Socialism and the Working Class in Weimar Germany* (Oxford, 1996), pp40-41; and J W Falter, 'The First German Volkspartei: the Social Foundations of the NSDAP', in K Rohe (ed), *Elections, Parties and Political Traditions* (Oxford, 1990), p81; and R Zitelmann, *Hitler: Selbstverständnis eines Revolutionärs* (Hamburg, 1987), p145.
5 V I Lenin, *On Britain* (London, 1959), p460.
6 J Caplan, 'The Rise of National Socialism 1919-1933', in G Martel (ed), *Modern Germany Reconsidered* (London, 1992), p119.

7   K Marx and F Engels, *The German Ideology* (London, 1970), p64.

8   K Marx, Introduction to *Contribution to a Critique of Political Economy*, (Moscow, 1981), pp20-21.

9   H Trevor-Roper, Introduction to *Goebbels' Diaries, The Last Days* (London, 1978), pxv.

10 Quoted in D Guerin, *Fascism and Big Business* (New York, 1973), p71.

11 A Hitler, *Mein Kampf* (London, 1969), pp163-166.

12 Ibid, translated in A Bullock, op cit, p70.

13 G Paul, *Aufstand der Bilder* (Bonn, 1990), p92.

14 J W Falter, Introduction to G Paul, op cit, p9.

15 M N Dobkowski and I Wallimann (eds), *Towards the Holocaust, the Social and Economic Collapse of the Weimar Republic* (Westport, 1983), p136.

16 J M H Kele, *Nazis and Workers* (Chapel Hill, 1972), p142.

17 C Fischer, *Stormtroopers* (London, 1983), p193.

18 Ibid, p213.

19 Details from D Harsch, *German Social Democracy and the Rise of Nazism* (North Carolina, 1993), p119.

20 V Kratzenberg, *Arbeiter auf dem Weg zu Hitler?* (Frankfurt am Main, 1989), p103.

21 Ibid, p114.

22 Ibid, p113.

23 W S Allen (ed), *The Infancy of Nazism: The Memoirs of ex-Gauleiter Albert Krebs, 1923-1933* (New York, 1976), op cit, p213.

24 V Kratzenberg, op cit, p113.

25 Ibid, p112.

26 Ibid, p112.

27 *Völkische Beobachter*, 6/7 November 1932.

28 *Völkische Beobachter*, 13 August 1932.

29 D Guerin, *Fascism and Big Business* (New York, 1973), p77.

30 L Trotsky, *The Struggle Against Fascism in Germany* (Harmondsworth, 1975), p409.

31 Ibid, pp412-413.

32 Ibid, p413.

33 A Hitler, *Mein Kampf*, op cit, p430.

34 H Trevor-Roper, op cit, pxxii.

35 C Fischer (ed), *The Rise of National Socialism and the Working Classes in Weimar Germany* (Oxford, 1996), p135.

36 See K Koszyk, *Deutsche Presse, 1914-1945*, vol 3 (Berlin, 1972), p384; and G Pridham, *Hitler's Rise to Power* (London, 1973), p238.

37 Quoted in T Abel, *Why Hitler Came to Power* (Harvard, 1966), pp164-165.

38 G Paul, op cit, p220.

39 I Kershaw, 'Ideology, Propaganda, and the Nazi Party', in P D Stachura (ed), *Unemployment and the Great Depression in Weimar Germany* (London, 1986), p167. See also I Kershaw, *Hitler, 1889-1936. Hubris*, op cit, p330.

40 I Kershaw in P D Stachura (ed), op cit, p168.

41 *Völkische Beobachter*, 9 November 1932.

42 *Völkische Beobachter*, 3 August 1932.

43 *Völkische Beobachter*, 23 November 1932.

44 *Völkische Beobachter*, 3 November 1932.

45 For example, *Völkische Beobachter*, 6 December 1932, 16 December 1932, 23 December 1932 and 12 January 1933.

46 For example, *Völkische Beobachter*, 3 September 1932, 1 October 1932, 11 October 1932, 1 November 1932.
47 K D Bracher, *The German Dictatorship* (Harmondsworth, 1970), pp189-190.
48 I Kershaw in P D Stachura (ed), op cit, p172.
49 G Paul, op cit, pp92.
50 Ibid, pp92-93.
51 *The Writings of Leon Trotsky, 1938-1939* (New York), p19.
52 Source: J W Falter, T Lindenberger and S Schumann (eds), *Wahlen und Abstimmungen in der Weimarer Republik* (Munich, 1986), p44.
53 R Kühnl, op cit, p97.
54 H A Winkler, *Mittelstand, Demokratie und Nationalsozialismus* (Cologne, 1972), p179.
55 T Childers, op cit, pp126-127.
56 K Marx, *Collected Works*, vol 6 (Moscow), p210.
57 K Marx, 'The Poverty of Philosophy', in K Marx and F Engels, *Collected Works*, vol 6 (Moscow), p494.
58 K Marx and F Engels, Collected Works, vol 6 (Moscow), p211.
59 J W Falter in C Fischer (ed), *The Rise of National Socialism and the Working Classes in Weimar Germany* (Oxford, 1996), p21.
60 Ibid, pp10-11.
61 P Manstein, *Die Mitglieder und Wähler der NSDAP* (Frankfurt am Main, 1989), p12.
62 J W Falter in C Fischer (ed), op cit, pp16-17; and J W Falter, *Hitlers Wähler*, partial translation ibid, p205.
63 J W Falter in C Fischer (ed), op cit, p17.
64 Ibid, p31; and J W Falter, *Hitlers Wähler*, op cit, p168.
65 J W Falter in C Fischer, op cit, pp31-32.
66 J W Falter, 'Unemployment and the Radicalisation of the German Electorate, 1928-1933', in P D Stachura (ed), *Unemployment and the Great Depression in Weimar Germany* (London, 1986), p189.
67 *Statistisches Jahrbuch für das Deutsche Reich* (Berlin, 1934), p19.
68 J W Falter, *Hitlers Wähler*, op cit, p206.
69 J W Falter in C Fischer (ed), op cit, p30.
70 Ibid, p40.
71 There are, of course, exceptions to this pattern. For example, large units of unskilled workers may have greater difficulty in exercising collective power than smaller units of skilled workers with the bargaining strength that comes from exclusive craft knowledge. But the general argument holds.
72 M Scharrer (ed), *Die Spaltung der Deutschen Arbeiterbewegung* (Stuttgart, 1985), pp58-59.
73 L Trotsky, op cit, p14.
74 Orlow, quoted in M N Dobkowski and I Wallimann (eds), op cit, p62.
75 T Childers, op cit, p157.
76 Ibid, pp165-166.
77 Ibid, p227.
78 Ibid, pp172, 175.
79 Ibid, pp240, 243.
80 Weisbrod in R Bessel and E J Feuchtwanger, *Social Change and Political Development in Weimar Germany* (London, 1981), p31.
81 H George, 'Unser Stand vor dem Abgrund', in A Kaes, M Jay and E Dimendberg, *The Weimar Republic Sourcebook* (London, 1994), p182.

82   H Walter, 'Die Misere des "neuen Mittelstands" ', in A Kaes et al (eds), op cit, p189.
83   P Manstein, op cit, p70.
84   Ibid, p69.
85   R Grunberger, *A Social History of the Third Reich* (London, 1971), p198.
86   R Heberle, *From Democracy to Nazism: a Regional Case Study on Political Parties in Germany* (Baton Rouge, 1945), p97.
87   Ibid, p110.
88   R Hamilton, *Who Voted for Hitler?* (Princeton, 1982), p421.
89   C Fischer (ed), op cit, p243.
90   D Mühlberger, 'A Workers' Party or a "Party Without Workers"?', in C Fischer (ed), op cit, p53.
91   W Brustein, 'Blue Collar Nazism', in C Fischer (ed), op cit, pp150-151. See also W Brustein, *The Logic of Evil: the Social Origins of the Nazi Party, 1925-1933* (Yale, 1996).
92   W S Allen (ed), op cit, p76.
93   For a comprehensive survey of these see P Manstein, op cit.
94   M Kater, *The Nazi Party* (Cambridge, Massachusetts, 1983), pp241, 252.
95   E J Feuchtwanger, *From Weimar to Hitler* (London, 1984), p332.
96   J W Falter, 'Die Wähler der NSDAP 1928-1933: Sozialstruktur und Parteipolitische Herkunft', in W Michalka (ed), *Die Nationalsozialistische Machtergreifung* (Paderborn, 1984), quoted in P Manstein, op cit, appendix 28a.
97   See, for example, M Kater, op cit, p255.
98   Ibid, p254.
99   See ibid, pp140-141.
100 D Mühlberger in C Fischer (ed), op cit, p60.
101 Ibid, p61.
102 Ibid, p65.
103 Ibid, p65.
104 E Fromm, *The Working Class in Weimar Germany* (Leamington Spa, 1984), p85.
105 Ibid, p111.
106 Ibid, p183.
107 Figures from M Kater, op cit, p263, and P Manstein, op cit, appendix 17.
108 M Kater, op cit, p156.
109 C Fischer, *Stormtroopers*, op cit, p4.
110 Figures for 1920 to 30 January 1933 ibid, p49.
111 Figures from M Kater, op cit, discussed in C Fischer, op cit, p16. See also J M H Kele, op cit, p183.
112 Quoted in C Fischer, *Stormtroopers*, op cit, p47.
113 J Noakes, 'Nazism and High Society', in M Burleigh (ed), *Confronting the Nazi Past* (London, 1996), p55.
114 C Fischer, *Stormtroopers*, op cit, p39.
115 See, for details, C Fischer, *Stormtroopers*, op cit, pp211-212.
116 For details see K D Bracher, 'The Third Reich and the Problem of "Social Revolution" ', in V Berghahn and M Kitchen, *Germany in the Age of Total War* (London, 1981), p205.
117 C Fischer (ed), *The Rise of National Socialism and the Working Class in Weimar Germany* (Oxford, 1996), p238.
118 M N Dobkowski and I Wallimann (eds), op cit, p138.
119 C Fischer (ed), *The Rise etc*, op cit, p157.

120 Quoted in J M H Kele, op cit, p185.
121 Quoted in J M H Kele, op cit, p185. See also I Kershaw, Hitler, 1889-1936. Hubris, op cit, pp347-350.
122 J M H Kele, op cit, p165.
123 Rote Fahne, 17 August 1932.
124 M N Dobkowski and I Wallimann (eds), op cit, p132.
125 V Kratzenberg, op cit, p99.
126 G Mai, 'National Socialist Factory Cell Organisation', in C Fischer (ed), The Rise etc, op cit, p122.
127 Arbeitertum, NSBO newspaper, quoted in V Kratzenberg, op cit, p103.
128 Quoted in C Fischer, The German Communists and the Rise of Nazism (Basingstoke, 1991), p163.
129 G Mai in C Fischer (ed), The Rise etc, op cit, p163.
130 Quoted in V Kratzenberg, op cit, p101.
131 Details in M Broszat, The Hitler State (London, 1981), p41.
132 M Frese, Betriebspolitik im 'Dritten Reich' (Paderborn, 1991), p52.
133 Quoted ibid, p53.
134 F L Carsten, The German Workers and the Nazis (Aldershot, 1995), p7.
135 See Mai in C Fischer (ed), The Rise etc, op cit, p121.
136 Sources: F Deppe and W Rossmann (eds), Weltwirtschafte, Faschismus, Gewerkschaften, 1929-33 (Cologne, 1981), p41; H Weber, Die Wandlung des Deutschen Kommunismus, (Frankfurt am Main, 1969), p366; H E Schumann, Nationalsozialisten und Gewerkschaftsbewegung (Hanover and Frankfurt am Main, 1958), p167.
137 W Müller, Lohnkampf, Massenkampf, Sowjetmacht, Ziel und Grenzen der RGO (Cologne, 1988), p363.
138 F L Carsten, op cit, p8.
139 Mai, in C Fischer, The Rise etc, p122.
140 M Schneider, Unternehmer und Demokratie. Die Freien Gewerkschaften in der Unternehmerischen Ideologie der Jahre 1918 bis 1933 (Bonn, 1975), p193.
141 M Frese, op cit, p53.
142 Ibid, p456.

Chapter 5

1 C Harman, The Lost Revolution: Germany 1918-23 (London, 1984), p306.
2 R Hamilton, Who Voted for Hitler? (Princeton, 1982), pp440-441.
3 J Danos and M Gibelin, June '36: Class Struggle and the Popular Front in France (London, 1986), p381.
4 Ibid, p34.
5 Ibid, p34.
6 Ibid, p40.
7 Ibid, p145.
8 F Morrow, Revolution and Counter-revolution in Spain (New York, 1974), p45.
9 R Fraser, 'The Popular Experience of War and Revolution', in P Preston (ed), Revolution and War in Spain, 1931-39 (London, 1984), p226.
10 Ibid, p227.
11 Quoted in A Bauerkämpfer, Die 'Radikale Rechte' in Grossbritannien (Göttingen, 1991), p189.
12 P Piratin, Our Flag Stays Red (London, 1978), pp20, 23-24.

13 For example, Hamilton notes that in Norway, despite similarities with the economic crisis in Germany, Quisling's National Socialists took only 2 percent of the vote while the Labour Party actually grew. He ascribes this to the greater activism and efforts by the Norwegian Labour Party to provide an alternative to fascism: 'The lesson it would seem, is that many so-called petty bourgeois votes could as easily turn to socialism as others did to Nazism. The key factor determining the outcome in this two country comparison was the organisational one, the ability of a party to generate a plausible programme and to mobilise cadres to sell it.' R F Hamilton, *Who Voted for Hitler?* (Princeton, 1982), pp440-441.

14 C Fischer (ed), *The Rise of National Socialism and the Working Classes in Weimar Germany* (Oxford, 1996), p194.

15 Ibid, p194.

16 Ibid, p196.

17 Ibid, p198.

18 Ibid, p201.

19 For Hilferding see L Trotsky, *The Struggle Against Fascism in Germany* (Harmondsworth, 1975), p119. See also I Kershaw, *Hitler, 1889-1936. Hubris,* op cit, p424.

20 D Geary, 'Employers, Workers and the Collapse of Weimar', in I Kershaw (ed), *Why did Weimar Democracy Fail?* (London, 1990), pp113-114.

21 *Rote Fahne*, 3, 5, 6, 7 January 1932.

22 *Rote Fahne*, 16 October 1932.

23 R-M Huber-Koller, *Gewerkschaften und Arbeitlose* (Pfaffenweiler, 1992), p82.

24 Ibid, p82.

25 Report of Leipart, quoted ibid, p82.

26 S Pollard, 'German Trade Union Policy, 1929-1933', in J von Kruedener (ed), *Economic Crisis and Political Collapse* (New York, 1990), pp22-23.

27 Geary in I Kershaw (ed), *Why did Weimar Democracy Fail?*, op cit, p110.

28 H Weber, *Die Wandlung des Deutschen Kommunismus* (Frankfurt am Main, 1969), pp364-365.

29 E Rosenhaft, *Beating the Fascists?* (Cambridge, 1983), p211.

30 *Berliner Tageblatt*, 23 January 1933.

31 R Koshar, *Social Life, Local Politics and Nazism, Marburg 1880-1935* (Chapel Hill, N Carolina 1986), pp206-207.

32 W S Allen (ed), *The Infancy of Nazism: The Memoirs of ex-Gauleiter Albert Krebs, 1923-1933* (New York, 1976), pp106-107.

33 A Hitler, *Mein Kampf* (London, 1969), p454.

34 L Trotsky, op cit, pp92-93.

35 Ibid, p94.

36 Ibid, p233.

37 Ibid, pp29-30.

38 F Neumann, *Behemoth. The Structure and Practice of National Socialism* (New York, 1944), pp335-336.

39 Quoted in T Abel, *Why Hitler Came into Power* (Harvard, 1966), p36.

40 Szejnmann, in C Fischer (ed), *The Rise etc*, op cit, p210.

41 E Rosenhaft, 'Working Class Life and Working Class Politics', in V Berghahn and M Kitchen, *Germany in the Age of Total War* (London, 1981), p227. See also O Flechtheim, *Die KPD in der Weimarer Republik* (Frankfurt am Main), p253.

42   Speech of SPD Reichstag president Breitscheid on 16 December 1931 in
     W Ruge and W Schumann (eds), *Dokumente zur Deutschen Geschichte, 1924-1945* (Frankfurt am Main, 1977), p48.
43   D Abraham, *The Collapse of the Weimar Republic* (New York and Princeton, 1986), p324.
44   H A Winkler, 'Choosing the Lesser Evil: The German Social Democrats and the Fall of the Weimar Republic', in *Journal of Contemporary History*, vol 25 (1990), p209.
45   21 July 1932, in E Frölich (ed), *Die Tagebücher von Joseph Goebbels*, vol 1 (Munich, 1987), p208.
46   *Vorwärts*, 20 July 1932.
47   *Vorwärts*, 21 July 1932.
48   *Vorwärts*, 1 August 1932.
49   Quoted in D Harsch, *German Social Democracy and the Rise of Nazism* (North Carolina, 1993), p171.
50   Ibid, p175.
51   For details of the KPD's reaction see T Cliff, *Trotsky*, vol 4, *The Darker the Night the Brighter the Star* (London, 1993), p112.
52   D Harsch, op cit, p179.
53   *Vorwärts*, 5 September 1930.
54   *Vorwärts*, 7 September 1930.
55   Quoted in K M Mallmann, *Kommunisten in der Weimarer Republik* (Darmstadt, 1996), p265.
56   Quoted ibid, p274.
57   Ibid, p275.
58   *Vorwärts*, 22 January 1933.
59   L Trotsky, op cit, p61.
60   For a full description of this process see H A Weber, *Die Wandlung etc*, op cit.
61   O Flechtheim, op cit, p256.
62   Quoted ibid, p257.
63   Quoted in H Weber, *Hauptfiend Sozialdemokratie: Strategie und Taktik der KPD 1929-1933* (Düsseldorf, 1982), p18.
64   *Rote Fahne*, 16 September 1930.
65   Details in T Cliff, op cit, p114.
66   W Florin, 'The Approaching Prussian Election in the Context of our Struggle Against the Fraudulent Social Fascist Manoeuvre of "the Lesser Evil"', *Die Internationale*, January 1932, pp64-65.
67   Quoted in O Flechtheim, op cit, p266.
68   Quoted in E Anderson, *Hammer or Anvil* (London, 1945), p144.
69   L Trotsky, op cit, p89.
70   Ibid, p109.
71   *Rote Fahne*, 29 November 1931.
72   E Thälmann, *Reden und Aufsätze zur Geschichte der Deutschen Arbeiterbewegung*, vol 2 (Berlin, 1956), p484.
73   Local KPD paper, quoted in H Weber, *Hauptfiend etc*, op cit, p47.
74   H A Winkler, op cit, p220.
75   E D Weitz, *Creating German Communism, 1890-1990* (Princeton, 1997), p170.
76   Ibid, p162. See also Geary, in I Kershaw (ed), *Why did Weimar Democracy Fail?*, op cit, p112.
77   Ibid, p115.

78   K M Mallmann, op cit, p268.
79   Ibid, p269.
80   M Scharrer (ed), *Die Spaltung der Deutschen Arbeiterbewegung* (Stuttgart, 1985), p146; A Merson, *Communist Resistance in Nazi Germany* (London, 1985), p20.
81   O Flechtheim, op cit, p316.
82   A survey of the KPD in the late 1920s showed that it was marginally more blue collar and unskilled than the SPD. In terms of skill 49 percent of the KPD was composed of artisans and skilled workers; 28 percent were unskilled [F Borkenau, *World Communism* (Ann Arbor, 1971), p364]. The proportion of workers in 1928 was 63 percent while the SPD's stood at 60 percent. (KPD figures in F Borkenau, op cit, p364). By 1930 this had dropped to 32 percent due to unemployment. The SPD figure is for 1930 and is given in D Harsch, op cit, p28.
83   B Fowkes, *Communism in Germany under the Weimar Republic* (London, 1984), p175. Flechtheim makes the same point in O Flechtheim, op cit, pp312-321.
84   T Cliff, op cit, pp146-147.
85   H Weber, *Hauptfiend etc*, op cit, p64.
86   Quoted ibid, p24.
87   Ibid, p26.
88   E Thälmann, op cit, p484.
89   L Trotsky, *The First Five Years of the Communist International*, vol 2 (London, 1974), pp93-94.
90   H Weber, *Hauptfiend etc*, op cit, p28.
91   O Flechtheim, op cit, p271.
92   H Weber, *Hauptfiend etc*, p31.
93   *Rote Fahne*, 29 August 1930.
94   *Rote Fahne*, 28 November 1931.
95   *Rote Fahne*, 20 May 1932.
96   *Rote Fahne*, 1 November 1931.
97   Quoted in C Fischer, *The German Communists etc*, op cit, p179.
98   *Rote Fahne*, 30 April 1932.
99   *Rote Fahne*, 1 November 1932.
100   *Rote Fahne*, 24 July 1931.
101   Quoted in H Weber, *Hauptfiend etc*, op cit, pp41-42.
102   L Trotsky, *The Struggle etc*, op cit, p125.
103   O Flechtheim, op cit, p278.
104   F Kunstler quoted in K M Mallmann, op cit, p269.
105   Quoted ibid, p373.
106   Quoted in H Weber, *Hauptfiend etc*, op cit, p49.
107   Quoted ibid, p51.
108   Quoted ibid, p54.
109   *Rote Fahne*, 1 July 1932.
110   *Rote Fahne*, 20 July 1932.
111   Quoted in N Poulantzas, *Fascism and Dictatorship* (London, 1974), pp183-184.
112   *Rote Fahne*, 11 August 1932.
113   H Weber, *Hauptfiend etc*, op cit, p59.
114   *Der Streik der Berliner Verkehrs-Arbeiter*, published by the KPD (no place of publication, 1932), p6.
115   Ibid, p7.
116   Ibid, p7.

117 Ibid, p22.
118 Quoted in V Kratzenberg, *Arbeiter auf dem Weg zu Hitler?* (Frankfurt am Main, 1989), p107.
119 E Frölich (ed), op cit, 8 November 1932, p274.
120 O Flechtheim, op cit, p347.
121 C Fischer, *The German Communists etc*, op cit, p187.
122 *Rote Fahne*, 12, 13, 14, 19 and 21 December 1930.
123 O Flechtheim, op cit, p273.
124 L Trotsky, *The Struggle etc*, op cit, p216.
125 Fritz Schulte, RGO leader, quoted in H Weber, *Hauptfiend etc*, op cit, p57.
126 Ibid, p57.
127 Quoted in K M Mallmann, op cit, p263.
128 Details in M Frese, *Betriebspolitik im 'Dritten Reich'* (Paderborn, 1991), p193; and W Müller, *Lohnkampf, Massenkampf, Sowjetmacht, Ziel und Grenzen der RGO* (Cologne, 1988), p171.
129 K M Mallmann, op cit, p325. The figure is set at six in M Scharrer (ed), *Die Spaltung der Deutscher Arbeiterbewegung* (Stuttgart, 1985), p146.
130 Details in O Flechtheim, op cit, p73 .
131 K M Mallmann, op cit, p155; and B Fowkes, op cit, p189.
132 Berlin Communist youth quoted in K M Mallmann, op cit, p376.
133 *Rote Fahne*, 29 January 1932.
134 *Rote Fahne*, 15 July 1932.
135 Quoted in L Trotsky, *The Struggle etc*, op cit, p236.
136 *Rote Fahne*, 17 December 1931. See also *Rote Fahne*, 26 March 1931, for similar comments.
137 T Cliff, op cit, p155.
138 T Cliff, op cit, p155.
139 See C Rosenberg, 'Labour and the Fight Against Fascism', in *International Socialism*, summer 1988.
140 L Trotsky, *The Struggle etc*, op cit, p340.
141 T Mason, *Social Policy in the Third Reich* (Oxford, 1993), p73.
142 L Trotsky, *The Struggle etc*, op cit, p416.
143 H Schulze (ed), *Anpassung oder Widerstand? Aus den Akten des Parteivorstandes der Deutschen Sozialdemokratie* (Bonn-Bad Godesberg, 1975), pp131-135.
144 Ibid, pp145-147.
145 H Niemann, 'Die Haltung der SPD zur Faschistischen Machtergreifung 1933', in *Beitrag zur Geschichte* (1983), p42.
146 H Grebing, *History etc*, op cit, p135.
147 For example, on 1 February the SPD newspaper, *Vorwärts*, called for a demonstration (*Vorwärts*, 1 February 1933). On 2 February this demonstration was reported as banned as was the 4 February edition of *Vorwärts* itself.
148 D Harsch, op cit, p229.
149 E Frölich (ed), op cit, 1 February 1933, p362.
150 Ibid, 11 February 1933, p372.
151 W S Allen, *The Nazi Seizure of Power* (London, 1989), p191.
152 D Harsch, op cit, p224.
153 F L Carsten, *The German Workers etc*, op cit, p14.
154 K M Mallmann, op cit, p276.
155 D Harsch, op cit, p229.
156 *Vorwärts*, 7 February 1933.

157 Quoted in H Grebing, *History etc*, op cit, p135.

158 Ibid, p148.

159 D Harsch, op cit, p231; H Grebing, *History etc*, op cit, p135.

160 Quoted in D Harsch, op cit, p236.

161 SPD Reichstag statement on its voting for Hitler's 'peace resolution' in B Hebel-Kuntze (ed), *SPD und Faschismus. Zur Politischen und Organisatorischen Entwicklung der SPD, 1932-1935* (Frankfurt am Main, 1977), p227.

162 D Harsch, op cit, pp236-237.

163 *Die Illegale Tagung des Zentralkomitees der KPD am 7 Februar 1933 in Ziegenhals bei Baring* (Berlin, 1981), p31.

164 Ibid, p30.

165 Ibid, p40.

166 J Degras, *The Communist International, 1919-1943*, vol 3 1929-1943 (London, 1971), p249.

167 *Rote Fahne* 3, 4 February 1933; and A Merson, op cit, p27.

168 'Da Ist Nirgends Nichts Gewesen Ausser Hier', in *Rote Mossingen* (Berlin, 1982).

169 *Rote Fahne*, 4 February 1933.

170 Piatnitsky quoted in J Degras, op cit, p120.

171 *Die Illegale Tagung etc*, op cit, p29.

172 Ibid, p23.

173 Ibid, p34.

174 Ibid, p28.

175 Goering on 3 March 1933, quoted in A Bullock, *Hitler: A Study in Tyranny* (New York, 1962), p264.

176 Quoted in K P Fischer, *Nazi Germany. A New History* (London, 1995), p271.

177 L Trotsky, *The Struggle etc*, op cit, p348.

178 J A Moses, *Trade Unionism in Germany from Bismarck to Hitler*, vol 2 (London, 1982), p512.

179 ADGB executive committee meeting of 31 January 1933. *Quellen zur Geschichte der Deutschen Gewerkschaften im 20. Jahrhundert*, vol 4 (Cologne, 1988), p831.

180 H Deutschland and H Polzin, 'Der Zerschlagung der Freien Gewerkschaften am 2 Mai 1933', in *Beitrag zur Geschichte* (1983), p525.

181 G Beier (ed), 'Zur Entstehung des Führerkreises der Vereinigten Gewerkschaften, April 1933', in *Archiv für Sozialgeschichte*, vol 15 (1975), pp385-386.

182 ADGB statement of 9 April 1933 in H E Schumann, *Nationalsozialismus und Gewerkschaftsbewegung* (Hanover and Frankfurt am Main, 1958), p166.

183 H Deutschland and H Polzin, op cit, p525.

184 W Pahl in *Gewerkschaftszeitung* (Berlin), 29 April 1933.

185 ADGB statement on May Day in *Metallarbeiter-Zeitung*, 22 April 1933, in J Gross (ed), *Vorwärts und Nicht Vergessen!* (Gaggenau, 1988), p462.

186 *Rastatter Tageblatt*, 2 May 1933, in J Gross (ed), op cit, p462.

Chapter 6

1 D Schoenbaum, *Hitler's Social Revolution* (New York, 1966).

2 R Zitelmann, *Hitler: Selbstverständnis eines Revolutionärs* (Hamburg, 1987).

3 R Zitelmann in R Smelser and R Zitelmann, *The Nazi Elite* (Basingstoke, 1993), p116.

4 Hitler to Reichstag, 30 January 1937, in N H Baynes (ed), *The Speeches of Adolf Hitler* (Oxford, 1942), pp214-215.

5   M Hauner, 'A German Racial Revolution?', in *Journal of Contemporary History*, vol 19 (1984). Kershaw agrees with this description. See I Kershaw, *Hitler, 1889-1936. Hubris* (London, 1998), p436.

6   M Roseman, 'National Socialism and Modernisation', in R Bessel (ed), *Fascist Italy and Nazi Germany* (Cambridge, 1996), p202.

7   T Saunders, 'Nazism and Social Revolution', in G Martel (ed), *Modern Germany Reconsidered* (London, 1992), p164.

8   Quoted in G Remmling, 'The Destruction of the Workers' Mass Movements in Germany', in M N Dobkowski and I Wallimann (eds), *Radical Perspectives on the Rise of Fascism* (New York, 1989), p221.

9   Cited in H Soell, 'Von der Machterschleichung zur Machtergreifung', in C Gradmann and O von Mengersen (eds), *Das Ende der Weimarer Republik und die Nationalsozialistische Machtergreifung* (Frankfurt am Main, 1996), p27.

10   Quoted in N H Baynes (ed), op cit, p667.

11   Ibid, p639.

12   *Völkische Beobachter* (Munich edition), 21 March 1933.

13   Quoted in C Gradmann and O von Mengersen (eds), op cit, p33.

14   L E Jones, ' "The Greatest Stupidity of my Life": Alfred Hugenberg and the Formation of the Hitler Cabinet, January 1933', in *Journal of Contemporary History*, vol 27 (1992).

15   A Bullock, *Hitler: A Study in Tyranny* (New York, 1962), p257.

16   K D Bracher, *The German Dictatorship* (Harmondsworth, 1970), p253.

17   A J P Taylor, *The Course of German History* (London, 1993), p247.

18   R Kühnl, *Der Deutsche Faschismus in Quellen und Dokumenten* (Cologne, 1975), p196.

19   R Eatwell, *Fascism. A History* (London, 1995), p110.

20   Details in A Bullock, op cit, pp269-270.

21   M Broszat, *Der Staat Hitlers* (Munich, 1976), p82.

22   M Broszat, *The Hitler State* (London, 1981), p101.

23   Details in G Remmling, ' The Destruction etc', op cit, p224.

24   Quoted in M Broszat, *The Hitler State*, op cit, p123.

25   Quoted ibid, p125.

26   Details of the law in A Bullock, op cit, p275.

27   Details in G Remmling, ' The Destruction etc', op cit, pp222-223.

28   See the law of 31 March 1933 in H Hürten (ed), *Deutsche Geschichte in Quellen und Darstellung*, pp166-168. See also pp174-175.

29   Quoted in K D Bracher, op cit, p265.

30   Ibid, p264.

31   W S Allen, *The Nazi Seizure of Power* (London, 1989), p184.

32   Ibid, p188.

33   Ibid, p189.

34   Ibid, p199.

35   Ibid, p200.

36   Ibid, p208.

37   Ibid, p216.

38   Ibid, p221.

39   Ibid, p222.

40   Ibid, p231. See also I Kershaw, *Hitler, 1889-1936. Hubris*, op cit, pp478-479.

41   Heinrich Galm quoted in D Peukert, *Inside Nazi Germany* (Harmondsworth, 1989), p105.

42   W S Allen, *The Nazi Seizure of Power*, op cit, p232.

43   Ibid, pp296-297.

44   J Noakes and G Pridham, *Nazism 1919-1945* (Exeter, 1964), p266.

45   R Grunberger, *A Social History of the Third Reich* (Hemel Hempstead, 1984), p173.

46   N Frei, *National Socialist Rule in Germany* (Oxford, 1993), p55.

47   Quoted in A Bullock, op cit, p281.

48   N Frei, op cit, p49.

49   Quoted in G Mai, 'National Socialist Factory Cell Organisation', in C Fischer (ed), *The Rise of National Socialism and the Working Classes in Weimar Germany* (Oxford, 1996), p129.

50   Ley at fifth annual meeting of the DAF, September 1937, quoted in T Mason, *Social Policy in the Third Reich* (Oxford, 1993), p83.

51   Ibid, p91.

52   D Guerin, *Fascism and Big Business* (New York, 1973), p142.

53   D Schoenbaum, *Hitler's Social Revolution* (New York, 1966), p81.

54   T Mason, *Social Policy etc*, op cit, p100.

55   Ibid, p333.

56   Quoted ibid, p335.

57   N H Baynes (ed), op cit, pp328-329.

58   Ibid, p314.

59   Quoted in D Guerin, op cit, p142.

60   Quoted in K P Fischer, *Nazi Germany. A New History* (London, 1986), pp285-286.

61   Quoted in C Fischer, *Stormtroopers* (London, 1983), p218.

62   Letter of 1 January 1934, in N H Baynes (ed), op cit, p289.

63   According to the White Book published in Paris. See A Bullock, op cit, p305. Later estimates suggest figures in the low 80s. Bracher gives 150-200 as the figure. K P Fischer, op cit (p292) and H Höhne, *Mordsache Röhm* (Hamburg, 1984), pp319-321, set this at 85.

64   Quoted in K P Fischer, op cit, p293.

Chapter 7

1   K D Bracher, *The German Dictatorship* (Harmondsworth, 1970), p307.

2   A Bullock, *Hitler: A Study in Tyranny* (New York, 1962), pp419-420.

3   T Mason, *Nazism, Fascism and the Working Class* (Cambridge, 1995), p54.

4   See 'The Primacy of Politics', ibid, pp53-76.

5   *The Writings of Leon Trotsky, 1933-34* (New York, 1972), p104.

6   *The Writings of Leon Trotsky, 1934-35* (New York, 1971), p53.

7   *The Writings of Leon Trotsky, 1939-40* (New York, 1969), p410.

8   Hitler to Düsseldorf Industry Club in 1932, quoted in A Kaes et al (eds), *The Weimar Republik Sourcebook* (London, 1994), p140.

9   K Marx, *Capital*, vol 1 (Moscow, 1954), p712.

10   N I Bukharin, *Imperialism and World Economy* (London, 1987), p119.

11   Ibid, pp119-120.

12   Ibid, pp124-125.

13   A Tasca, 'Allgemeine Bedingungen der Entstehung und des Aufstieges des Faschismus', in O Bauer, H Marcuse, A Rosenberg et al, *Faschismus und Kapitalismus* (Frankfurt am Main, 1967), p181.

14   J Kuczynski, *Das Grosse Geschäft* (Berlin, 1967), p119.

15   K P Fischer, *Nazi Germany. A New History* (London, 1995), p374.

16   Quoted in G Mai, 'National Socialist Factory Cell Organisation', in C Fischer (ed),
      The Rise of National Socialism and the Working Classes in Weimar Germany (Oxford,
      1996), p131.
17   R Smelser, *Robert Ley. Hitler's Labor Leader* (Oxford, 1988), p302.
18   Ibid, pp305-306.
19   D Schoenbaum, *Hitler's Social Revolution* (New York, 1966), p75.
20   Ibid, p78.
21   Ibid, p79.
22   Hitler's press secretary, Otto Dietrich, quoted in R Smelser and R Zitelmann,
      The Nazi Elite (Basingstoke, 1993), p122.
23   R A Brady, *The Spirit and Structure of German Fascism* (London, 1937), p118.
24   Quoted ibid, p127.
25   Quoted in T Mason, *Social Policy in the Third Reich* (Oxford, 1993), p80.
26   Quoted in R A Brady, op cit, p129.
27   Ibid, p130.
28   Law quoted in T Mason, *Nazism etc*, op cit, p80.
29   Ibid, p81.
30   T Mason, *Social Policy etc*, op cit, p156.
31   Agreement of November 1933 quoted ibid, p102.
32   Ibid, p106.
33   Quoted ibid, p102.
34   DAF regulation of 24 October 1924, quoted in U Hörster-Philipps, *Grosskapital
      und Faschismus, 1918-1945* (Cologne, 1981), p218.
35   See T Mason, 'The Primacy of Politics', in T Mason, *Nazism etc*, op cit, pp53-76.
36   Details in T Mason, 'Labour in the Third Reich', in *Past and Present* 33, April
      1966, p125.
37   D Schoenbaum, op cit, p90.
38   A Schweitzer, *Big Business in the Third Reich* (Indiana, 1977), p368.
39   Ley in the autumn of 1933 quoted in T Mason, *Social Policy etc*, op cit, p97.
40   M Frese, *Betriebspolitik im 'Dritten Reich'* (Paderborn, 1991), pp452-453.
41   K Marx, *Capital*, vol 1 (Moscow, 1954), p386.
42   H Braverman, *Labor and Monopoly Capital* (New York, 1974), p110.
43   R Hachtmann, *Industriearbeit im 'Dritten Reich'* (Göttingen, 1989), p303.
44   K Dunkmann at the meeting to establish the German Institute for Technical
      Education and Training, 24 May 1925, in W Ruge and W Schumann (eds),
      Dokumente zur Deutschen Geschichte, 1924-1945 (Frankfurt am Main, 1977),
      1924-29, p39.
45   Quoted in R A Brady, op cit, p156.
46   Quoted in R Grunberger, *A Social History of the Third Reich* (London, 1971), p46.
47   H Braverman, op cit, p271.
48   T Mason, *Social Policy etc*, op cit, p159.
49   *Rote Fahne* 3, 1936.
50   N Frei, *National Socialist Rule in Germany* (Oxford, 1993), p82.
51   T Mason, *Social Policy etc*, op cit, p161.
52   H Braverman, op cit, p278.
53   T Mason, 'Labour in the Third Reich', op cit, p118.
54   Quoted in T Mason, *Nazism etc*, op cit, p80.
55   D Farnham and J Pimlott, *Understanding Industrial Relations* (Eastbourne, 1986),
      p64.
56   Ibid, p64.

57   R Smelser, op cit, p307.
58   Ibid, p307.
59   K H Roth, 'Revisionist Tendencies in Historical Research into German
      Fascism', in *International Review of Social History*, vol 30, December 1994, p439.
60   D Bankier, *The German People and the Final Solution* (Oxford, 1996), p18.
61   Quoted in K Heiden, *A History of National Socialism* (London, 1935), p276.
62   N Frei, op cit, p72.
63   T Mason, *Social Policy etc*, op cit, p113; D Petzina, *Die Deutsche Wirtschaft in der
      Zwischenkriegszeit* (Wiesbaden, 1977), p112.
64   T Mason, *Social Policy etc*, op cit, p111.
65   D Schoenbaum, op cit, p79.
66   T Mason, *Social Policy etc*, op cit, p118.
67   D Petzina, op cit, p113.
68   Quoted in L Herbst, 'Die Nationalsozialistische Wirtschaftspolitik im
      Internationalen Vergleich', in W Benz, H Buchheim, H Mommsen (eds), *Das
      Nationalsozialismus. Studien zur Ideologie und Herrschaft* (Frankfurt am Main,
      1993), p157. See also I Kershaw, *Hitler, 1889-1936. Hubris* (London, 1998),
      pp441-446.
69   For details see D Petzina, op cit, p113.
70   A Barkai, *Nazi Economics* (Oxford, 1990), p158.
71   L Herbst, 'Die Nationalsozialistische etc', op cit, p157.
72   T Mason, *Social Policy etc*, op cit, p123.
73   L Herbst, 'Die Nationalsozialistische etc', op cit, p157.
74   Ibid, p158.
75   G Bry, *Wages in Germany, 1871-1945* (Princeton, 1960), p264.
76   R Hachtmann, *Industriearbeit im 'Dritten Reich'* (Göttingen, 1989), p51.
77   Ibid, p228.
78   Source: D Petzina, op cit, p122.
79   N Frei, op cit, pp79-80.
80   R Grunberger, *A Social History of the Third Reich* (London, 1971), pp247-248.
81   R Hachtmann, op cit, p286.
82   G Bry, op cit, p313.
83   Quoted in D Guerin, *Fascism and Big Business* (New York, 1973), p285.
84   A Speer, *Inside the Third Reich* (London, 1995), p230.
85   Ibid, p300. For a full treatment of this question see T Mason, 'The Legacy of
      1918 for National Socialism', in T Mason, *Social Policy etc*, op cit, pp19-40.
86   N Poulantzas, *Fascism and Dictatorship* (London, 1974), p256.
87   M Broszat, *Der Staat Hitlers* (Munich, 1976), p208.
88   Quoted ibid, p212.
89   Ibid, p214.
90   Discussion on 2 August 1933, in W Ruge and W Schumann (eds), op cit, 1933-35,
      p56.
91   M Broszat, op cit, p215.
92   Ibid, p217.
93   Ibid, p217.
94   Preamble to the May 1933 law, quoted in N Poulantzas, op cit, p287.
95   D Peukert, *Inside Nazi Germany* (Harmondsworth, 1989), p88; and A Barkai, op
      cit, p230.
96   N Frei, op cit, p77.
97   A Bullock, op cit, p259.

98   N Frei, op cit, p55.
99   A Schweitzer, *Big Business in the Third Reich* (Indiana, 1977), p398. See also figures given in R Kühnl, *Der Deutsche Faschismus in Quellen und Dokumenten* (Cologne, 1975), p264.
100   J Taylor and W Shaw, *A Dictionary of the Third Reich* (London, 1987), pp291-297.
101   M Broszat, op cit, p218.
102   R Grunberger, op cit, p228.
103   M Broszat, op cit, p219.
104   Quoted in G C Boehnert, 'The Third Reich and the Problem of "Social Revolution" ', in V Berghahn and M Kitchen, *Germany in the Age of Total War* (London, 1981), p203.
105   Schröder to the Military Tribunal at Nuremberg, quoted in R Kühnl, op cit, p477.
106   Details in W Ruge and W Schumann (eds), op cit, 1936-39, p21.
107   N Frei, op cit, p76.
108   U Hörster-Philipps, *Im Schatten des Grossen Geldes* (Cologne, 1985), pp55-56.
109   J Borkin, *The Crime and Punishment of IG Farben* (London, 1970), pp58, 72.
110   M Kettle, in 'GM and Ford Face New Accusations', in the *Guardian*, 1 December 1998.
111   The *Berliner Handelsgesellschaft*, details in *Rote Fahne* 5, 1938.
112   R Grunberger, op cit, p231.
113   D Guerin, op cit, p281.
114   Quoted in A Schweitzer, op cit, p258.
115   M Broszat, op cit, p223.
116   C Bettelheim, *L'Économie Allemande Sous le Nazisme*, vol 1 (Paris, 1971), p77.
117   R Beckenbach, *Der Staat im Faschismus* (Berlin, 1974), p83.
118   Ibid, p122.
119   K Hildebrand, *The Third Reich* (Hemel Hempstead, 1984), p41.
120   Details in J Hiden, *Germany and Europe 1919-1939* (London, 1977), p173.
121   L Herbst, op cit, p159.
122   Ibid, pp160-163.
123   Ibid, p164.
124   G C Allen, *A Short Economic History of Modern Japan* (London, 1964), p136.
125   Figures in U Hörster-Philipps, op cit, p210.
126   C Harman, *Explaining the Crisis* (London, 1984), pp67-68.
127   R Beckenbach, op cit, p91.
128   T Mason, *Nazism etc*, op cit, p113.
129   8-11 August 1941. *Hitler's Secret Conversations* (New York, 1976), p20.
130   K Hildebrand, op cit, p41. Schweitzer makes the same point.
131   *Frankfurter Zeitung*, quoted in D Guerin, op cit, p247.
132   D E Kaiser, 'Hitler and the Coming of the War', in G Martel (ed), *Modern Germany Reconsidered* (London, 1992), p181.
133   D Guerin, op cit, p155.
134   Quoted in P Heider, 'Der Totale Krieg—seine Vorbereitung durch Reichswehr und Wehrmacht', in L Nestler et al (eds), *Der Weg der Deutschen Eliten in dem Zweiten Weltkrieg* (Berlin, 1990), p43.
135   Ibid, p43.
136   J Taylor and W Shaw, *A Dictionary of the Third Reich* (London, 1987), p54.
137   Quoted in P Heider, op cit, p58. See also F L Carsten, *Reichswehr and Politics, 1918-1933* (Oxford, 1966), p311.

138 Quoted in P Heider, op cit, p75.

139 Documents of 16 and 19 July 1938, quoted in H Hürten (ed), *Deutsche Geschichte in Quellen und Darstellung*, p305.

140 Quoted in P Heider, op cit, p77.

141 R Grunberger, op cit, p180.

142 P Heider, op cit, p77.

143 L Trotsky, *The Struggle Against Fascism in Germany* (Harmondsworth, 1975), p413.

Chapter 8

1 H R Trevor-Roper, 'A J P Taylor, Hitler and the War', in E M Robertson (ed), *The Origins of the Second World War* (London, 1971), p90.

2 M Domarus, quoted in J Joll, 'The Conquest of the Past', in E M Robertson, op cit, p78.

3 A J P Taylor, *The Origins of the Second World War* (Harmondsworth, 1965), pp135-136.

4 E H Carr, *International Relations Between the Two World Wars, 1939-1939* (Basingstoke, 1990), pp262-263.

5 J Noakes and G Pridham, *Nazism 1919-1945* (Exeter, 1964), p633. Reported remarks of Hitler, Berlin, 20 June 1941.

6 *Hitler's Secret Conversations* (New York, 1976), 19-20 August 1941, p23.

7 G Fleming, *Hitler and the Final Solution* (London, 1985), p14.

8 12 October 1939, in J Goebbels, *Diaries, 1939-1941* (London, 1982), p18.

9 Quoted in J Hiden, *Germany and Europe 1919-1939* (London, 1977), p79.

10 24 May 1941, J Goebbels, op cit, p380.

11 Quoted in K P Fischer, *Nazi Germany. A New History* (London, 1995), p469.

12 Quoted in A Bullock, *Hitler: A Study in Tyrrany* (New York, 1962), p660.

13 J Noakes and G Pridham, op cit, p607.

14 Hitler on 17 September 1944 quoted in W Maser (ed), *Hitler's Letters and Notes* (New York, 1976), p151.

15 Meeting between Halifax and Hitler on 19 November 1937, in W Ruge and W Schumann (eds), *Dokumente zur Deutschen Geschichte* (Frankfurt am Main), 1936-39, pp62-63. For the attitude of the Lord Rothermere's *Daily Mail* see I Kershaw, *Hitler, 1889-1936. Hubris* (London, 1998), pp336-337.

16 For a full description of this process see E H Carr, op cit.

17 Record of a conference of 5 November 1937 drawn up by Colonel von Hossbach in *Documents on German Foreign Policy, 1918-1945*, series D, vol I (London, 1949), p29.

18 M Geyer, 'The Nazi Pursuit of War', in R Bessel (ed), *Fascist Italy and Nazi Germany* (Cambridge, 1996), pp141-142.

19 Quoted in J Hiden, *Germany and Europe 1919-1939* (London, 1977), p105.

20 T Mason, 'Internal Crisis and War of Aggression, 1938-1939', in T Mason, *Nazism, Fascism and the Working Class* (Cambridge, 1995), p116. Mason's arguments are backed up by H-E Volkmann, 'Die NS-Wirtschaft in Vorbereitung des Krieges', in *Ursachen und Voraussetzungen der Deutschen Kriegspolitik* (Stuttgart, 1979).

21 R J Overy, 'Germany, Domestic Crisis and War in 1939', in *Past and Present*, August 1987, p158.

22 T Mason, 'Internal Crisis', in T Mason, *Nazism etc*, op cit, pp116-117.

23 U Herbert, 'The Real Mystery', in M Burleigh (ed), *Confronting the Nazi Past*
    (London, 1996), p30; and T Mason, *Nazism etc*, op cit, pp201-202.
24 Quoted in U Hörster-Philipps, *Grosskapital und Faschismus, 1918-1945*
    (Cologne, 1981), p217.
25 Speech of 17 December 1936, quoted in K Hildebrand, *The Third Reich* (Hemel
    Hempstead, 1984), p43.
26 H Röchling, iron and steel industrialist, on 17 August 1936, in W Ruge and
    W Schumann (eds), op cit, 1936-1939, p29; and M Kettle, in the *Guardian*,
    1 December 1998.
27 R Hilberg, *The Destruction of the European Jews* (New York, 1985), p246n.
28 R Grunberger, *A Social History of the Third Reich* (London, 1971), pp232-233.
29 *The Brown Book*, published by the DDR (no place of publication, no date),
    pp29-30.
30 J Borkin, *The Crime and Punishment of IG Farben* (London, 1970), p97.
31 J Goebbels, *Diaries 1939-1941* (London 1982), 5 November 1940, p165.
32 Kaiser, in G Martel (ed), *Modern Germany Reconsidered* (London, 1992), p189.
33 W Maser, op cit, p283.
34 Adapted from J Hiden, *Germany and Europe 1919-1939* (London, 1977), p171.
35 G Meier, *Forever in the Shadow of Hitler?* (New Jersey, 1993), p178.
36 R Hilberg, *The Destruction of the European Jews* (New York, 1985), p863.
37 This is the argument of his book *Hitler's War*. For a discussion of German
    Holocaust deniers see S Berger, *The Search for Normality: National Identity and
    Historical Consciousness* (Oxford, 1997). For the US see D E Lipstadt, *Denying
    the Holocaust* (New York, 1993). Other Holocaust deniers include
    F Leuchter, P Rassinier and R Faurisson.
38 22 February 1942, in *Hitler's Secret Conversations*, op cit, pp269-270.
39 J von Lang and C Sibyll (eds), *Eichmann Interrogated* (London, 1983), p81.
40 R Hilberg, op cit, p983.
41 J von Lang and C Sibyll (eds), op cit, p110.
42 M Gilbert, *The Holocaust* (London, 1987), p824.
43 A furious dispute in German academic circles (the *Historikerstreit* or Clash of
    Historians) recently brought this to the surface. Referring to the war years, one
    writer praised as 'responsibly ethical' those Nazis who carried out the Holocaust
    because 'everything depended on building up at least a weak veil of defences on
    the eastern Prussian border in order to avoid the worst...' Nolte, the best known
    historian of this school, argues that Auschwitz was the result of a 'reaction to
    the acts of annihilation that took place during the Russian Revolution'. It was 'a
    distorted copy and not a first act or an original' [E Nolte, 'Between Historical
    Legend and Revisionism?', in *Forever in the Shadow of Hitler?* (New Jersey, 1993),
    p14]. The counter-revolutionary element in Nazi thinking had nothing to do
    with Russian 'acts of annihilation'. Hitler's fanatical ideology was a reaction to
    the stopping of war that was begun in Russia and completed by the German
    Revolution, and it was directed against fellow countrymen who strove for a
    genuine socialist society.
44 K Hildebrand, *The Third Reich* (Hemel Hempstead, 1984), p150, discussing the
    views of S Haffner. His own views are similar. See p48, for example.
45 L Dawidowicz, *The War Against the Jews, 1933-1945* (Harmondsworth, 1977), p27.
46 J M Glass, *Life Unworthy of Life* (New York, 1998), pxiii.
47 D Goldhagen, *Hitler's Willing Executioners* (London, 1997), p9.
48 M Gilbert, op cit, p36.

49   P Burrin, *Hitler and the Jews: the Genesis of the Holocaust* (London, 1994), p42.
      Gilbert gives the figure of 36.

50   D Bankier, *The German People and the Final Solution* (Oxford, 1996), p69. See
      also I Kershaw, *Hitler, 1889-1936. Hubris*, op cit, pp476-477.

51   For examples see H Krausnick and M Broszat, *Anatomy of the SS State* (London,
      1970), p45; or D Bankier, op cit, pp82-83.

52   For details see J Noakes and G Pridham, *Documents on Nazism, 1919-1945*, op
      cit, pp463-465.

53   Quoted in R Hilberg, op cit, p38.

54   D Bankier, op cit, p80.

55   K A Schleunes, *The Twisted Road to Auschwitz* (London, 1975), p261.

56   J Noakes and G Pridham, op cit, pp473-475.

57   See I Kershaw, 'Working towards the Führer: Reflections on the Nature of the
      Hitler Dictatorship', in I Kershaw and M Lewin, *Stalinism and Nazism:
      Dictatorships in Comparison* (Cambridge, 1997), p100.

58   R Hilberg, op cit, pp39-40.

59   Quoted in J Noakes and G Pridham, op cit, p477.

60   Ibid, p473.

61   D Bankier, op cit, p86.

62   *Rote Fahne* 5, 1938.

63   For a discussion of how much was known in German society about the Holocaust
      see R Breitman, 'Secrecy and the Final Solution', in R L Millan (ed), *New
      Perspectives on the Holocaust* (New York, 1996), and L D Stokes, 'The German
      People and the Destruction of the European Jews', in M R Marrus (ed), *Public
      Opinion and Relations to the Jews in Nazi Europe*, vol 1 (Westport, 1989), pp61-85.

64   H Krausnick and M Broszat, op cit, p47.

65   Ibid, p56.

66   Ibid, p203.

67   M Burleigh and W Wippermann, *The Racial State* (Cambridge, 1991), p86.

68   H Krausnick and M Broszat, op cit, pp62-63.

69   R Hilberg, op cit, pp96-97.

70   U Hörster-Philipps, *Im Schatten des Grossen Geldes* (Cologne, 1985), pp52-53.

71   Quoted in P Burrin, *Hitler and the Jews: the Genesis of the Holocaust* (London,
   • 1994), p52.

72   Quoted in H Krausnick and M Broszat, op cit, p63.

73   J Goebbels, *Diaries 1939-1941*, op cit, 5 December 1939, p60.

74   P Burrin, op cit, p86.

75   Notes by Admiral Raeder after a meeting with Hitler on 20 June 1940 quoted in
      P Burrin, op cit, p77.

76   J von Lang and C Sibyll (eds), op cit, p65.

77   Even here the level of approval for the Nazis' anti-Semitic policies may have
      been limited. The Muller-Claudius study, in M Housden, *Resistance and
      Conformity in the Third Reich* (London, 1997), pp147-148, the only survey of
      NSDAP members' opinions on this issue, produced the following interesting
      results. When Jewish policy was discussed the reaction of members who joined
      before 1933 was as follows (percentages):

	1938	1942
indignation	63	26
non-committal/indifferent	32	69
approval	5	5

For discussion of the findings see I Kershaw, 'German Popular Opinion and the Jewish Question. Some Further Reflections', in M R Marrus (ed), op cit, pp198-199.

78   M Burleigh and W Wippermann, *The Racial State* (Cambridge, 1991), p34.

79   P Weindling, *Health, Race and German Policies between National Unification and Nazism* (Cambridge, 1989), p445.

80   See G Bock, *Zwangssterilisation im Nationalsozialismus* (Opladen, 1986).

81   R Grunberger, op cit, pp288-289.

82   Frick's estimate. See G Bock, 'Antinatalism in National Socialist Racism', in D F Crew (ed), *Nazism and German Society, 1933-1945* (London, 1994), p114.

83   G Bock, *Zwangssterilisation*, op cit, p238; and G Bock, 'Antinatalism etc', in D F Crew (ed), op cit, pp112, 114.

84   Ibid, pp117, 122.

85   Ibid, p118.

86   G Aly, P Chroust and C Pross, *Cleansing the Fatherland* (Baltimore, 1994), pp48-49.

87   M Burleigh, 'Saving Money, Spending Lives: Psychiatry, Society and the "Euthanasia" Programme', in M Burleigh (ed), *Confronting the Nazi Past*, op cit, p108.

88   Projected law drafted by Dr E Mezger quoted ibid, p178.

89   P Burrin, op cit, p66.

90   V Brack, senior official in Hitler's chancellery, quoted in G Aly, 'The Planning Intelligentsia and the "Final Solution" ', in M Burleigh (ed), op cit, p143.

91   Quoted in N Frei, op cit, p120.

92   H Friedlander, 'Euthanasia and the Final Solution', in D Cesarini (ed), *The Final Solution* (London, 1994), pp53-54.

93   P Burrin, op cit, p92.

94   H Friedlander in D Cesarini (ed), op cit, pp58-59.

95   P Burrin, op cit, p67.

96   Quoted in H Krausnick and M Broszat, op cit, p194.

97   Heydrich, quoted ibid, p200.

98   J Noakes and G Pridham, op cit, pp485-486.

99   24 February, 30 September, 8 November. He also deliberately falsified the date of the 'prophecy' as being 1 September 1939. E Jäckel, *Hitlers Weltanschauung, Entwurf einer Herrschaft* (Tübingen, 1969), pp81-82.

100   J Noakes and G Pridham, op cit, p611.

101   15 March 1940, quoted in R Ainzstein, *Jewish Resistance in Nazi-Occupied Eastern Europe* (London, 1974), p216.

102   See J Förster, 'The Relation between Operation Barbarossa as an Ideological War of Extermination and the Final Solution', in D Cesarini (ed), op cit, p87, and P Burrin, op cit, p68.

103   Heydrich's estimate quoted in H Krausnick and M Broszat, op cit, p73.

104   Quoted in *The Brown Book*, op cit, p234.

105   M Gilbert, op cit, p154.

106   Quoted in E Jäckel, op cit, p77.

107   Quoted in H Krausnick and M Broszat, op cit, p61.

108   Quoted ibid, p62.

109   General Halder, Chief of General Staff, quoted in J Noakes and G Pridham, op cit, pp619-620.

110   Quoted in H Krausnick and M Broszat, op cit, p80.

111   Quoted in M Gilbert, op cit, p195.

112 Quoted in O Bartov, 'Savage War', in M Burleigh (ed), op cit, p129.
113 Quoted in M Gilbert, op cit, p615.
114 M Gilbert, op cit, p175.
115 C Streit in D Cesarini (ed), op cit, p109.
116 See P Burrin and C Streit, 'Wehrmacht, Einsatzgruppen, Soviet POWs and Anti-Bolshevism in the Emergence of the Final Solution', in D Cesarini (ed), op cit, pp103-136. Gilbert puts 'day one of the Final Solution' as 7 December 1941, M Gilbert, op cit, p240. See also C Browning, 'The Euphoria of Victory', in D Cesarini (ed), pp137-147.
117 Hitler's directive on Barbarossa from December 1940, in J Noakes and G Pridham, op cit, p593.
118 R Ainzstein, Jewish Resistance in Nazi-Occupied Eastern Europe (London, 1974), p243.
119 P Burrin, op cit, p120.
120 Ibid, p112.
121 Ibid, p113.
122 R Hilberg, op cit, p863.
123 See N G Finkelstein and R B Birn, A Nation on Trial (New York, 1998); and C Browning, Ordinary Men: Reserve Police Battalion 101 and the Final Solution in Poland (New York, 1992).
124 M Burleigh (ed), op cit, pp306-307.
125 C Browning, op cit, p189. See also C Browning, 'One Day in Josefow', in D F Crew (ed), op cit, p314.
126 R Hilberg, op cit, pp56-62.
127 The Writings of Leon Trotsky, 1939-40 (New York, 1969), pp193-194.
128 R Hilberg, op cit, p411.
129 Quoted in U Herbert, Hitler's Foreign Workers (Cambridge, 1997), p226.
130 Quoted by Frank, ruler of the General Gouvernement area of Poland, on 25 March 1941 in W Ruge and W Schumann (eds), op cit, 1939-42, p59.
131 R Höss, Commandant of Auschwitz (London, 1959), p132.
132 Quoted in U Herbert, 'Labor as Spoils of Conquest, 1933-1935', in D F Crew (ed), op cit, p255.
133 Ibid.
134 Hitler's Secret Conversations, op cit, 17 September 1941, p32.
135 See discussion document of 1 June 1940 in W Ruge and W Schumann (eds), op cit, 1939-42, pp39-42.
136 Such as IG Farben, the Association of Berlin Merchants and the School of Economy. See R E Herzstein, When Nazi Dreams Come True (London, 1982), pp103-125.
137 G Aly, 'The Planning Intelligentsia and the "Final Solution"', in M Burleigh (ed), Confronting the Nazi Past (London, 1996), pp145, 147.
138 G Aly and S Heim, Vordenker der Vernichtung (Frankfurt am Main, 1993), p392.
139 U Herbert, op cit, p139.
140 Plan of 3 August 1940, in W Ruge and W Schumann (eds), op cit, 1939-42, pp52-53.
141 A Barkai, From Boycott to Annihilation (London, 1990), p240.
142 D Peukert, op cit, pp126-127; U Herbert, 'Labor as Spoils of Conquest, 1933-1935', in D F Crew (ed), op cit, p233.
143 U Herbert, Hitler's Foreign Workers, op cit, p99.
144 Ibid, p69.

145 P Weindling, *Health, Race and German Policies between National Unification and Nazism* (Cambridge, 1989), p556.
146 D Peukert, op cit, p127.
147 U Herbert, *Hitler's Foreign Workers*, op cit, p225.
148 R Höss, op cit, p121.
149 D Peukert, op cit, p128.
150 W Sofsky, *The Order of Terror: The Concentration Camp* (New Jersey, 1997), p180.
151 Ibid, p182.
152 Ibid, p182.
153 Details in H-G Stümke, 'From the "People's Consciousness of Right and Wrong" to "the Healthy Instincts of the Nation": the Persecution of Homosexuals in Nazi Germany', in M Burleigh (ed), op cit, p164.
154 D Goldhagen, op cit, p317. Hilberg rightly emphasises that the direct costs of the killing operation to the state outweighed direct profits. See R Hilberg, op cit, pp1005-1007.
155 A Barkai, *Nazi Economics* (Oxford, 1990), p238.
156 U Herbert, *Hitler's Foreign Workers*, op cit, p157.
157 G Aly and S Heim, op cit, p318.
158 Ibid, p327.
159 Quoted in U Herbert, 'Labor etc', op cit, p251.
160 K-J Siegfried, 'Racial Discrimination at Work: Forced Labour in the Volkswagen Factory, 1939-1945', in M Burleigh (ed), op cit, p42.
161 Quoted in U Herbert, 'Labor etc', op cit, pp265-266.
162 R Ainzstein, op cit, p234.
163 H Krausnick and M Broszat, op cit, p229.
164 R Hilberg, op cit, p929.
165 J Borkin, op cit, p113
166 R Hilberg, op cit, p888.
167 W Sofsky, op cit, p262.
168 Ibid, pp259, 264.
169 Ibid, p277.
170 R Hildebrand, op cit, p92.
171 K Marx, 'Communist Manifesto', in *The Revolutions of 1848* (Harmondsworth, 1973), pp70, 72, 74.

Chapter 9

1 Hitler quoted in A Speer, *Inside the Third Reich* (London 1995), p588.
2 Statistics in R Kühnl, *Der Deutsche Faschismus in Quellen und Dokumenten* (Cologne, 1975), p477.
3 P Hoffman, *German Resistance to Hitler* (Cambridge, Massachusetts, 1988), p51.
4 T Mason, *Social Policy in the Third Reich* (Oxford, 1993), pp331-332.
5 This distinction is suggested by T Mason, 'The Workers' Opposition in Nazi Germany', *History Workshop Journal* 11 (1981), pp120-137.
6 H Krausnick and M Broszat, *Anatomy of the SS State* (London, 1970), p154.
7 Details in A Merson, *Communist Resistance in Nazi Germany* (London, 1985), p61.
8 Quoted in N Frei, *National Socialist Rule in Germany* (Oxford, 1993), p103.
9 Ibid, p103.
10 *Berichte der Sozialdemokratischen Partei Deutschlands (SOPADE) 1934-1940* (henceforth SOPADE) (Frankfurt am Main, 1986), May 1937, p684.

11   This figure include those who were victims of Stalin's purges. E D Weitz,
      Creating German Communism, 1890-1990 (Princeton, 1997), p280.
12   Quoted ibid, p289.
13   E Anderson, *Hammer or Anvil* (London, 1945), pp166-167.
14   *SOPADE*, June 1937, p780.
15   Ibid, p724.
16   Ibid, p792.
17   Ibid, p795.
18   Ibid, p798.
19   Ibid, p821.
20   Siegfried in M Burleigh (ed), *Confronting the Nazi Past* (London, 1996), p40.
21   *SOPADE*, July 1937, p956.
22   C Koonz, *Mothers in the Fatherland* (London, 1987), p313.
23   *SOPADE*, July 1937, p961.
24   Stümke in M Burleigh (ed), op cit, p161.
25   H Krausnick and M Broszat, op cit, p210.
26   Details in A Merson, op cit, p261.
27   K-M Mallmann and G Paul, 'Omniscient, Omnipotent, Omnipresent? Gestapo,
      Society and Resistance', in D F Crew (ed), *Nazism and German Society, 1933-45*
      (London, 1994), pp181-182.
28   Quoted in E D Weitz, op cit, p291.
29   Quoted ibid, p291.
30   A Kenkmann, 'Navajos, Kittelbach- und Edelweisspiraten. Jugendliche
      Dissidenten im "Dritten Reich" ', in W Breyvogel (ed), *Piraten, Swings und
      Junge Garde* (Bonn, 1991), p151.
31   *SOPADE*, September 1937, p1249.
32   R Gellately, 'The Political Policing of Nazi Germany', in F R Nicosia and L D
      Stokes (eds), *Germans Against Nazism* (Oxford, 1990), p18.
33   For a discussion of this issue see K-M Mallmann and G Paul, op cit, pp166-
      196.
34   Study by R Mann quoted in R Gellately, *The Gestapo and German Society*
      (Oxford, 1990), p135.
35   R Grunberger, *A Social History of the Third Reich* (London, 1971), p145.
36   R Gellately, op cit, p146.
37   K-M Mallmann and G Paul, op cit, p176. In 1939 only 3,000 out of its 20,000
      employees had SS rank.
38   M Burleigh (ed), op cit, p274.
39   Figures based on social status of fathers of SD (Security Service—a section of
      the Gestapo) in G C Browder, *Hitler's Enforcers: The Gestapo and the SS Security
      Service in the Nazi Revolution* (New York, 1996), p273.
40   Evidence from Hüttenberger's study of the Munich Special Court cited in
      R Gellately, op cit, p144.
41   K von Klemperer, *German Resistance against Hitler* (Oxford, 1992), p3.
42   There are only two significant exceptions to this. One was Fritz Thyssen, an
      early supporter of Nazism who later objected to its rejection of corporatism. For
      a discussion of this point see A Barkai, *Nazi Economics* (Oxford, 1990),
      pp120-121. The other was Robert Bosch, the Stuttgart industrialist who
      financed Gördeler's trips abroad.
43   K von Klemperer, op cit, p169-170.
44   Ibid, pp169-170.

45 C Gördeler's secret memorandum of 26 March 1943 to general officers in the event of a coup, in H Royce, E Zimmermann and H-A Jacobsen, *Germans against Hitler* (Bonn, 1960), p70.

46 Quoted in H Royce, E Zimmermann and H-A Jacobsen, op cit, p31.

47 K von Klemperer, op cit, p145n.

48 Ibid, p24.

49 E Gerstenmaier, 'The Kreisau Circle', in H Royce et al, op cit, p33.

50 Wheeler-Bennett quoted in K von Klemperer, op cit, p376.

51 Ibid, p155.

52 Note by Ludwig Beck for the report to the commander-in-chief of the army, Brauchitsch, on 16 July 1938, in H Royce et al, op cit, p21.

53 Weizsäcker quoted in K von Klemperer, op cit, p219.

54 P Steinbach, 'The Conservative Resistance', in D Clay Large (ed), *Contending with Hitler* (Cambridge, 1994), p96. For a further discussion of this see also C Dipper, 'The German Resistance and the Jews', in M R Marrus (ed), *Public Opinion and Relations to the Jews in Nazi Europe*, vol 1 (Westport, 1989), pp204-246.

55 Goering's contacts were with Birger Dahlerus. See K von Klemperer, op cit, p162.

56 Ibid, p395.

57 Denunciation of the totalitarian claim of the state from the pulpit of the Provisional church leadership, 23 August 1936, in H Royce et al, op cit, p25.

58 Quoted in J Bentley, *Martin Niemoeller* (Oxford, 1984), p147.

59 R P Eriksen, 'Resistance in the German Protestant Church', in F R Nicosia and L D Stokes (eds), op cit, p130.

60 Quoted in G Lewy, *The Catholic Church and Nazi Germany* (London, 1968), p104.

61 Encyclical of Pope Pius XI of 3 March 1937, in H Royce et al, op cit, p22.

62 Quoted in M Burleigh and W Wippermann, *The Racial State* (Cambridge, 1991), pp152-153.

63 Summary of the Catholic church's argument in D Dietrich, 'Catholic Resistance to Racist Eugenics', in F R Nicosia and L D Stokes (eds), op cit, p141.

64 Ibid, p152.

65 J F Morley, *Vatican Diplomacy and the Jews during the Holocaust* (New York, 1980), pp126-127.

66 F L Carsten, *The German Workers and the Nazis* (Aldershot, 1995), p114.

67 Y Suhl (ed), *They Fought Back. The Story of Jewish Resistance in Nazi Europe* (London, 1968), p13.

68 E Rosenhaft, 'The Uses of Remembrance', in F R Nicosia and L D Stokes (eds), op cit, p374; and B Mark, 'The Herbert Baum Group', in Y Suhl (ed), op cit.

69 R Ainzstein, *Jewish Resistance in Nazi-Occupied Eastern Europe* (London, 1974), p255.

70 Ibid, p262.

71 Ibid, p288.

72 See ibid, pp463-681.

73 M Gilbert, *The Holocaust* (London, 1987), p557.

74 General Jerzy Kirchmayer, quoted in R Ainzstein, op cit, p671.

75 R Ainzstein, op cit, p737. Gilbert gives different figures: M Gilbert, op cit, p597.

76 Ibid, pp618-619.

77 Message of 24 June 1943, quoted in H Langbein, *Against all Hope* (London, 1994), p59.

78   U Herbert, 'Labor as Spoils of Conquest, 1933-1935', in D F Crew (ed), op cit, p263.

79   Ibid, p264; and U Herbert, *Hitler's Foreign Workers* (Cambridge, 1997), pp345-358.

80   Quoted in M von Hellfeld, *Edelweisspiraten in Köln* (Cologne, 1981), p15.

81   Quoted ibid, p15.

82   G Rempel, *Hitler's Children* (North Carolina, 1989), p90.

83   D Peukert, 'Youth in the Third Reich', in R Bessel (ed), *Life in the Third Reich* (Oxford, 1987), p39.

84   G Rempel, op cit, p92.

85   C Moll, 'Acts of Resistance: The White Rose in the Light of New Archival Evidence', in M Geyer and J W Boyer (eds), *Resistance against the Third Reich* (Chicago, 1994), pp173-200; and *Die Weisse Rose und das Erbe des Deutschen Widerstandes* (Munich, 1993).

86   D Peukert, in R Bessel (ed), op cit, p32.

87   Oberhausen HJ denunciation of 11 June 1941 quoted in D Peukert, *Die Edelweisspiraten* (Cologne, 1980), p85.

88   D Peukert, *Inside Nazi Germany*, op cit, p165.

89   G Rempel, op cit, p91.

90   D Peukert, in R Bessel (ed), op cit, pp34-35.

91   Details in M Burleigh (ed), op cit, p224.

92   M von Hellfeld, op cit, p9.

93   Ibid, p52.

94   Ibid, p56.

95   Ibid, p9.

96   Ibid, p59.

97   L Trotsky, *The Struggle Against Fascism in Germany* (Harmondsworth, 1975), p420.

98   J Noakes and G Pridham, *Documents on Nazism, 1919-1945* (London, 1974), p607.

99   Quoted in U Herbert, *Hitler's Foreign Workers*, op cit, p149.

100   Ibid, p173.

101   Minutes of inter-departmental conference on 10 November 1939, in J Noakes and G Pridham, op cit, p638.

102   Ley's proclamation of 19 November 1939 quoted in J Noakes and G Pridham, op cit, p639.

103   Figures calculated from J Noakes and G Pridham, op cit, p646.

104   A Speer, op cit, p300.

105   Figures calculated from J Noakes and G Pridham, op cit, p646.

106   *SOPADE*, November 1937, p1523.

107   Quoted in F L Carsten, op cit, p123.

108   Quoted in J Noakes and G Pridham, *Nazism 1919-1945* (Exeter, 1964), p581; and *SOPADE*, July 1938, p697.

109   *Rote Fahne* 8, 1938.

110   Quoted in I Kershaw, *Popular Opinion and Political Dissent in the Third Reich* (Oxford, 1983), pp24-29.

111   C Browning, 'One Day in Josefow', in D F Crew (ed), op cit, p304.

112   For a discussion of this see O Bartov, 'German Workers, German Soldiers', in *German History* (1990), pp46-65; and O Bartov in M Burleigh (ed), op cit, p133. See also the dubious argumentation of A Lüdtke, 'The Appeal of Exterminating "Others": German Workers and the Limits of Resistance', in M Geyer and J W Boyer (eds), *Resistance Against the Third Reich* (Chicago, 1994), pp53-74.

113   D Peukert, *Inside Nazi Germany*, op cit, p51.

114 A Merson, op cit, p109. There were also plebiscites with similarly pro-Nazi results in 1936 and 1938.

115 I Kershaw, *The Hitler Myth* (Oxford, 1987), p82.

116 *The Writings of Leon Trotsky, 1938-1939* (New York, 1974), p19.

117 M Frese, *Betriebspolitik im 'Dritten Reich'* (Paderborn, 1991), p54.

118 G Gross, *Der Gewerkschaftliche Widerstandskampf der Deutschen Arbeiterklasse Während der Faschistischen Vertrauensräte Wahlen, 1934* (Berlin, 1962), p52.

119 Ibid, p55.

120 Ibid, p57.

121 Ibid, p58.

122 Ibid, p59.

123 *SOPADE*, June 1937.

124 L Trotsky, *The Struggle etc*, op cit, p406.

125 I Kershaw quoting S Haffner, *The Meaning of Hitler* (London, 1979), p34, in I Kershaw, *The Hitler Myth*, op cit, p1.

126 I Kershaw, 'Hitler and the Germans', in R Bessel (ed), op cit, p50.

127 Ibid, p54.

128 *SOPADE*, October 1936, p1249.

129 Reports of Dortmund Gestapo, July 1935, and Kassel, 1934, quoted in F L Carsten, op cit, p38.

130 A Speer, op cit, pp240-241.

131 U Herbert, '"The Real Mystery in Germany". The German Working Class During the Nazi Dictatorship', in M Burleigh (ed), op cit, p31.

132 M Pikarski and E Warning, 'Über den Antifaschistischen Widerstandskampf der KPD', in *Beitrag zur Geschichte* (1983), p85.

133 Situation report for October 1935 from Munster in Westphalia, quoted in A Merson, op cit, p139.

134 M Pikarski and E Warning, op cit (situation report for July to September 1935), p405.

135 F L Carsten, op cit, p59.

136 M Pikarski and E Warning, op cit, p539.

137 Ibid, p705.

138 Ibid, p81.

139 Ibid. Report of October to December 1935, p409.

140 M R D Foot quoted in K von Klemperer, op cit, p4.

141 Quoted in D Peukert, *Ruhrarbeiter Gegen den Faschismus* (Frankfurt am Main, 1976), p156.

142 *Rote Fahne*, October 1935.

143 KPD Central Committee statement, 'Against the Shame of the Jewish Pogrom', from mid-November 1938, quoted in R Kühnl, op cit, p422.

144 Quoted in B Hebel-Kuntze (ed), *SPD und Faschismus, zur Politischen und Organisatorischen Entwicklung der SPD, 1932-1935* Frankfurt am Main, 1977), pp231, 234.

145 *Rote Fahne*, June 1933.

146 *Rote Fahne*, November 1933.

147 F L Carsten, op cit, p70.

148 *Rote Fahne*, mid-July 1933.

149 *Rote Fahne*, August 1934.

150 *Rote Fahne*, first half of November 1935.

151 *Rote Fahne* 7, May 1933.

152 *Rote Fahne* 2 , 1937.
153 Ibid.
154 *Rote Fahne* 3, 1937.
155 *Rote Fahne* 4, 1936.
156 F L Carsten, op cit, p124.
157 Quoted in D Ziegs, 'Die Leipziger SPD im Kampf um die Republik', in
      H Grebing, H Mommsen and K Rudolph (eds), *Demokratie und Emanzipation
      Zwischen Saale und Elbe* (Essen, 1993), p327.
158 For details see T Meyer et al (eds), *Lern- und Arbeitsbuch der Deutschen
      Arbeiterbewegung*, vol 2 (Bonn, 1984), p672.
159 Quoted in I Kershaw, *Popular Opinion etc*, op cit, p74.
160 *SOPADE*, 4 September 1937.
161 F L Carsten, op cit, p62.
162 M Schneider, *A Brief History of the German Trade Unions* (Bonn, 1991), p218.
163 M Pikarski and E Warning, op cit (situation reports for July to September and
      October to December 1935), pp400, 407.
164 P Steinbach and J Tuchel (eds), *Widerstand Gegen die Nationalsozialisten* (Berlin,
      1994), p136.
165 Ibid, p133.
166 Ibid, p142.
167 Ibid, p137.
168 Ibid, p193.
169 Ibid, p140.
170 For a discussion of the specific role of women see C Wickert, 'Frauen im
      Hintergrund—das Beispiel von Kommunistinnen und Bibelforscherinnen', in
      H Grebing and C Wickert (eds), *Das 'Andere Deutschland' im Widerstand Gegen
      den Nationalsozialismus* (Essen, 1994), pp200-225.
171 An analysis of 100 disputes was published in 1937 in *Rote Fahne* 1. The
      following is the full breakdown: 26 against wage cuts, 21 for wage rises, 14
      against speed ups, 12 against compulsory overtime, 10 against compulsory
      donations to Nazi causes, 5 against higher prices of basic goods, 5 over health
      and safety issues, 4 against higher contributions to DAF and KdF, and 3 for
      democratic rights and against the presence of spies. Of these, 61 were apparently
      successful, 13 partially successful, 22 were defeated and four continued.
172 T Mason, 'Workers Opposition in Nazi Germany', op cit, p121.
173 M Pikarski and E Warning, op cit (situation report for July to September 1935),
      p400.
174 M Pikarski and E Warning, op cit (monthly report on left movement for August
      1936), p554.
175 M Pikarski and E Warning, op cit (situation report for 1 October to
      31 December 1935), p407.
176 *SOPADE*, December 1937, p1678.
177 *SOPADE*, August 1937, p1295.
178 F L Carsten, op cit, p130.
179 *SOPADE*, June 1937, p781.
180 *SOPADE*, June 1937, p784.
181 U Herbert, ' "The Real Mystery in Germany" etc', in M Burleigh (ed), op cit,
      p29; F L Carsten, op cit, p101; and T Mason, 'Workers' Opposition etc', op cit,
      p124. Figures for strike action vary with the Gestapo recording 356 strikes
      between 1936 and 1938.

182 *SOPADE*, December 1937.
183 Herbert cites numerous examples in his study of German reactions to foreign workers in U Herbert, *Hitler's Foreign Workers*, op cit.
184 *SOPADE*, December 1937, p1669.
185 J Goebbels, *Diaries, 1939-1941* (London, 1982), 4 April 1945, p317.
186 T Mason, *Social Policy etc*, op cit, p359.
187 Quoted in H Hürten (ed), *Deutsche Geschichte in Quellen und Darstellung*, pp383-384.
188 Hildebrand gives estimates ranging from 245,000 to 35,000 in K Hildebrand, *The Third Reich* (Hemel Hempstead, 1984), p81.
189 J Noakes and G Pridham, op cit, p667.
190 Quoted in D Bankier, *The German People and the Final Solution* (Oxford, 1996), p148.
191 I Kershaw, *Popular Opinion etc*, op cit, p109.
192 L Niethammer, U Borsdorf and P Brandt (eds), *Arbeiterinitiative 1945* (Wuppertal, 1976), p392.
193 Ibid, pp237-242.
194 *SOPADE*, December 1937, p1669.
195 L Niethammer et al (eds), op cit, p286
196 Ibid, p324.
197 Ibid, p298.
198 Ibid, p400.
199 Ibid, p403.
200 Ibid, p405.
201 Ibid, p533
202 Ibid, p282.
203 Ibid, p291.
204 For example, ibid, p288.
205 For example, ibid, p290.
206 For example, ibid, pp475, 512.
207 Retranslated from L Niethammer et al (eds), op cit, pp701-702.
208 Summary of report by the Joint Intelligence Comittee on 'Anti-Fascism Type Movements in Germany', 30 June 1945, in L Niethammer et al (eds), op cit, p702.

Bibliography
of works cited in text

Primary sources
Newspapers and contemporary journals

Berliner Tageblatt
Deutsche Allgemeine Zeitung
Deutsche Tageszeitung
Deutsche Zeitung
Frankfurter Zeitung
Gewerkschaftszeitung
Die Internationale
Rote Fahne
Vorwärts
Völkische Beobachter

Collections of documents

Berichte der Sozialdemokratischen Partei Deutschlands (SOPADE) 1934-1940 (Frankfurt am Main, 1986).

J Degras, *The Communist International, 1919-1943*, vol 3 1929-1943, (London, 1971).

Documents on German Foreign Policy, 1918-1945, series D, vol I (London, 1949).

H Hürten (ed), *Deutsche Geschichte in Quellen und Darstellung*.

A Kaes, M Jay and E Dimendberg (eds), *The Weimar Republik Sourcebook* (London, 1994).

R Kühnl, *Der Deutsche Faschismus in Quellen und Dokumenten* (Cologne, 1975).

J Noakes and G Pridham, *Documents on Nazism, 1919-1945* (London, 1974).

J Noakes and G Pridham, *Nazism 1919-1945* (Exeter, 1964).

M Pikarski and E Warning, 'Über den Antifaschistischen Widerstandskampf der KPD', in *Beitrag zur Geschichte*, 1983.

Quellen zur Geschichte der Deutschen Gewerkschaften im 20 Jahrhundert, vol 4 (Cologne, 1988).

J C G Röhl, *From Bismarck to Hitler* (London, 1970).

W Ruge and W Schumann (eds), *Dokumente zur Deutschen Geschichte, 1924-1945* (Frankfurt am Main, 1977).

H Schulze (ed), *Anpassung oder Widerstand? Aus den Akten des Parteivorstandes der Deutschen Sozialdemokratie* (Bonn-Bad Godesberg, 1975).

Other primary sources

N H Baynes (ed), *The Speeches of Adolf Hitler* (Oxford, 1942).

Der DMV in Zahlen (Berlin, 1932).

E Frölich (ed), *Die Tagebücher von Joseph Goebbels*, vol 1 (Munich, 1987).

J Goebbels, *Diaries, 1939-41* (London, 1982).

Hitler's Secret Conversations (New York, 1976).

A Hitler, *Mein Kampf* (London, 1969).

A Hitler, *Zweites Buch* (Stuttgart, 1961).

Die Illegale Tagung des Zentralkomitees der KPD am 7 Februar 1933 in Ziegenhals bei Baring (Berlin, 1981).

W Maser (ed), *Hitler's Letters and Notes* (New York, 1976).

Alfred Rosenberg, *Selected Writings* (London, 1970).

A Speer, *Inside the Third Reich* (London, 1995).

Statistisches Jahrbuch für das Deutsche Reich (Berlin, 1934).

Der Streik der Berliner Verkehrs-Arbeiter, published by the KPD, 1932.

E Thälmann, *Reden und Aufsätze zur Geschichte der Deutschen Arbeiterbewegung*, vol 2 (Berlin, 1956).

Secondary sources
Journals

Archiv für Sozialgeschichte
Beitrag zur Geschichte
German History
History Workshop Journal
International Review of Social History
International Socialism
Journal of Contemporary History
Past and Present

Articles

G Aly, 'The Planning Intelligentsia and the "Final Solution" ', in M Burleigh (ed), *Confronting the Nazi Past* (London, 1996).

P Baldwin, 'Social Interpretations of Nazism: Review of a Tradition', in *Journal of Contemporary History*, 1990, vol 25.

O Bartov, 'German Workers, German Soldiers', in *German History*, 1990.

O Bartov, 'Savage War', in M Burleigh (ed), *Confronting the Nazi Past* (London, 1996).

G Beier (ed), 'Zur Entstehung des Führerkreises der Vereinigten Gewerkschaften, April 1933', in *Archiv für Sozialgeschichte*, vol 15, 1975.

R Bessel, 'Violence as Propaganda: The Role of the Storm Troopers in the Rise of National Socialism', in T Childers (ed), *The Mobilisation of Nazi Support 1918-1933* (Beckenham, 1986).

R Bessel, 'Why did the Weimar Republic Collapse?', in I Kershaw (ed), *Why did Weimar Democracy Fail?* (London, 1990).

G Bock, 'Antinatalism in National Socialist Racism', in D F Crew (ed), *Nazism and German Society, 1933-1945* (London, 1994).

G C Boehnert, 'The Third Reich and the Problem of "Social Revolution" ', in V Berghahn and M Kitchen (eds), *Germany in the Age of Total War* (London, 1981).

K D Bracher, 'Democracy and the Power Vacuum: the Problem of the Party State during the Disintegration of the Weimar Republic', in V Berghahn and M Kitchen (eds), *Germany in the Age of Total War* (London, 1981).

K D Bracher, 'The Third Reich and the Problem of "Social Revolution" ', in V Berghahn and M Kitchen (ed), *Germany in the Age of Total War* (London, 1981).

R Breitman, The 'Final Solution', in G Martel (ed), *Modern Germany Reconsidered* (London, 1992).

R Breitman, 'Secrecy and the Final Solution', in R L Millan (ed), *New Perspectives on the Holocaust* (New York, 1996).

C Browning, 'The Euphoria of Victory', in D Cesarini (ed), *The Final Solution* (London, 1994).

C Browning, 'One Day in Josefow', in D F Crew (ed), *Nazism and German Society, 1933-1945* (London, 1994).

W Brustein, 'Blue Collar Nazism', in C Fischer (ed), *The Rise of National Socialism and the Working Classes in Weimar Germany* (Oxford, 1996).

M Burleigh, 'Saving Money, Spending Lives: Psychiatry, Society and the "Euthanasia" Programme', in M Burleigh (ed), *Confronting the Nazi Past* (London, 1996).

J Caplan, 'The Rise of National Socialism 1919-1933', in G Martel (ed), *Modern Germany Reconsidered* (London, 1992).

H Deutschland and H Polzin, 'Der Zerschlagung der Freien Gewerkschaften am 2 Mai 1933', in *Beitrag zur Geschichte*, 1983.

D Dietrich, 'Catholic Resistance to Racist Eugenics', in F R Nicosia and L D Stokes (eds), *Germans against Nazism* (Oxford, 1990).

C Dipper, 'The German Resistance and the Jews', in M R Marrus (ed), *Public Opinion and Relations to the Jews in Nazi Europe*, vol 1 (Westport, 1989).

G Eley, 'Bismarckian Germany', in G Martel (ed), *Modern Germany Reconsidered* (London, 1992).

R P Eriksen, 'Resistance in the German Protestant Church', in F R Nicosia and L D Stokes (eds), *Germans against Nazism* (Oxford, 1990).

J W Falter, 'The First German Volkspartei: the Social Foundations of the NSDAP', in K Rohe (ed), *Elections, Parties and Political Traditions* (Oxford, 1990).

J W Falter, 'Unemployment and the Radicalisation of the German Electorate, 1928-1933', in P D Stachura (ed), *Unemployment and the Great Depression in Weimar Germany* (London, 1986).

J W Falter, 'Die Wähler der NSDAP 1928-1933: Sozialstruktur und Parteipolitische Herkunft', in W Michalka (ed), *Die Nationalsozialistische Machtergreifung* (Paderborn, 1984).

G Feldman, 'The Weimar Republic: A Problem of Modernisation?' in *Archiv Für Sozialgeschichte*, vol XXVI, 1986.

W Florin, 'The Approaching Prussian Election in the Context of our Struggle against the Fraudulent Social Fascist Manoeuvre of "the Lesser Evil" ', *Die Internationale*, January 1932.

J Förster, 'The Relation between Operation Barbarossa as an Ideological War of Extermination and the Final Solution', in D Cesarini (ed), *The Final Solution* (London, 1994).

R Fraser, 'The Popular Experience of War and Revolution', in P Preston (ed), *Revolution and War in Spain, 1931-39* (London, 1984).

S Friedlander, 'Euthanasia and the Final Solution', in D Cesarini (ed), *The Final Solution* (London, 1994).

D Geary, 'Employers, Workers and the Collapse of Weimar', in I Kershaw (ed), *Why did Weimar Democracy Fail?* (London, 1990).

D Geary, 'The Industrial Elite and the Nazis in the Weimar Republic', in P D Stachura (ed), *The Nazi Machtergreifung* (London, 1983).

R Gellately, 'The Political Policing of Nazi Germany', in F R Nicosia and L D Stokes (eds), *Germans against Nazism* (Oxford, 1990).

H Geyer, 'Munich in Turmoil: Social Protest and the Revolutionary
Movement 1918-19' in C Wrigley (ed), *Challenges of Labour:
Central and Western Europe, 1917-1920* (London, 1993).

M Geyer, 'The Nazi Pursuit of War', in R Bessel (ed), *Fascist Italy
and Nazi Germany* (Cambridge, 1996).

M Geyer, 'Professionals and Junkers', in R Bessel and
E J Feuchtwanger (eds), *Social Change and Political Development in
Weimar Germany* (London, 1981).

M Hauner, 'A German Racial Revolution?' in *Journal of
Contemporary History*, vol 19, 1984.

P Heider, 'Der Totale Krieg—seine Vorbereitung durch Reichswehr
und Wehrmacht', in L Nestler et al (eds), *Der Weg der Deutschen
Eliten in dem Zweiten Weltkrieg* (Berlin, 1990).

U Herbert, 'Labor as Spoils of Conquest, 1933-1935', in D F
Crew (ed), *Nazism and German Society, 1933-1945* (London,
1994).

U Herbert, ' "The Real Mystery in Germany". The German
Working Class during the Nazi Dictatorship', in M Burleigh (ed),
Confronting the Nazi Past (London, 1996).

L Herbst, 'Die Nationalsozialistische Wirtschaftspolitik im
Internationalen Vergleich', in W Benz, H Buchheim,
H Mommsen (eds), *Das Nationalsozialismus. Studien zur
Ideologie und Herrschaft* (Frankfurt am Main, 1993).

J Jacobs, 'Marxism and Anti-Semitism: Kautsky', in *International
Review of Social History*, vol 30, 1985.

J Joll, 'The Conquest of the Past', in E M Robertson (ed),
The Origins of the Second World War (London, 1971).

L E Jones, ' "The Greatest Stupidity of my life". Alfred Hugenberg
and the Formation of the Hitler Cabinet, January 1933', in *Journal
of Contemporary History*, vol 27 (1992).

D E Kaiser, 'Hitler and the Coming of the War', in G Martel (ed),
Modern Germany Reconsidered (London, 1992).

A Kenkmann, 'Navajos, Kittelbach- und Edelweisspiraten.
Jugendliche Dissidenten im "Dritten Reich" ', in W Breyvogel
(ed), *Piraten, Swings und Junge Garde* (Bonn, 1991).

I Kershaw, 'German Popular Opinion and the Jewish Question.
Some Further Reflections', in M R Marrus (ed), *Public Opinion and
Relations to the Jews in Nazi Europe*, vol 1 (Westport, 1989).

I Kershaw, 'Ideology, Propaganda, and the Nazi Party', in
P D Stachura (ed), *The Nazi Machtergreifung* (London, 1983).

J Kocka, 'German History before Hitler: the Debate about the German
Sonderweg', in *Journal of Contemporary History*, vol 23 (1988).

A Lüdtke, 'The Appeal of Exterminating "Others": German Workers and the Limits of Resistance', in M Geyer and J W Boyer (eds), *Resistance Against the Third Reich* (Chicago, 1994).

G Mai, 'National Socialist Factory Cell Organisation', in C Fischer (ed), *The Rise of National Socialism and the Working Classes in Weimar Germany* (Oxford, 1996).

K-M Mallmann and G Paul, 'Omniscient, Omnipotent, Omnipresent? Gestapo, Society and Resistance', in D F Crew (ed), *Nazism and German Society, 1933-1945* (London, 1994).

B Mark, 'The Herbert Baum Group', in Y Suhl (ed), *They Fought Back. The Story of Jewish Resistance in Nazi Europe* (London, 1968).

K Marx, 'Communist Manifesto', in *The Revolutions of 1848* (Harmondsworth, 1973).

K Marx, 'The 18th Brumaire of Louis Bonaparte', in K Marx, *Surveys from Exile* (Harmondsworth, 1973).

T Mason, 'Labour in the Third Reich', in *Past and Present 33*, April 1966.

T Mason, 'The Workers' Opposition in Nazi Germany', *History Workshop Journal* 11, 1981.

C Moll, 'Acts of Resistance: The White Rose in the Light of New Archival Evidence', in M Geyer and J W Boyer (eds), *Resistance against the Third Reich* (Chicago, 1994).

D. Mühlberger, 'A Workers' Party or a "Party Without Workers"?' in C Fischer (ed), *The Rise of National Socialism and the Working Classes in Weimar Germany* (Oxford, 1996).

H Niemann, 'Die Haltung der SPD zur Faschistischen Machtergreifung 1933', in *Beitrag zur Geschichte*, 1983.

E Nolte, 'Between Historical Legend and Revisionism?' in G Meier, *Forever in the Shadow of Hitler?* (New Jersey, 1993).

R J Overy, 'Germany, Domestic Crisis and War in 1939', in *Past and Present*, August 1987.

D Petzina, 'Problems in the Social and Economic Development of the Weimar Republic', in M N Dobkowski and I Wallimann (eds), *Towards the Holocaust, The Social and Economic Collapse of the Weimar Republic* (Westport, 1983).

D Petzina, 'Was there a Crisis before the Crisis?' in J von Kruedener (ed), *Economic Crisis and Political Collapse* (New York, 1990).

D Peukert, 'Youth in the Third Reich', in R Bessel (ed), *Life in the Third Reich* (Oxford, 1987).

S Pollard, 'German Trade Union Policy, 1929-1933', in J von Kruedener (ed), *Economic Crisis and Political Collapse* (New York, 1990).

G Remmling, 'The Destruction of the Workers' Mass Movements in Germany', in N Dobkowski and I Wallimann (eds), *Radical Perspectives on the Rise of Fascism* (New York, 1989).

G Ritter, 'The Historical Foundations of the Rise of National Socialism', in *The Third Reich* (New York, 1955).

C Rosenberg, 'Labour and the Fight against Fascism', in *International Socialism*, Summer 1988.

E Rosenhaft, 'The Uses of Remembrance', in F R Nicosia and L D Stokes (eds), *Germans against Nazism* (Oxford, 1990).

E Rosenhaft, 'Working Class Life and Working Class Politics', in V Berghahn and M Kitchen (eds), *Germany in the Age of Total War* (London, 1981).

K H Roth, 'Revisionist Tendencies in Historical Research into German Fascism', in *International Review of Social History*, vol 30, December 1994.

T Saunders, 'Nazism and Social Revolution', in G Martel (ed), *Modern Germany Reconsidered* (London, 1992).

H Soell, 'Von der Machterschleichung zur Machtergreifung', in C Gradmann and O von Mengersen (eds), *Das Ende der Weimarer Republik und die Nationalsozialistische Machtergreifung* (Heidelberg, 1994).

C Sparks, 'Fascism and the Working Class: the German Experience', in *International Socialism*, Autumn 1978.

P Steinbach, 'The Conservative Resistance', in D Clay Large (ed), *Contending with Hitler* (Cambridge, 1994).

G Steinmetz, 'The Myth of an Autonomous State', in G Eley (ed), *Society, Culture and the State in Germany, 1870-1930* (Ann Arbor, 1996).

K-J Siegfried, 'Racial Discrimination at Work: Forced Labour in the Volkswagen Factory, 1939-1945', in M Burleigh (ed), *Confronting the Nazi Past* (London, 1996).

L D Stokes, 'The German People and the Destruction of the European Jews', in M R Marrus (ed), *Public Opinion and Relations to the Jews in Nazi Europe*, vol 1 (Westport, 1989).

C Streit, 'Wehrmacht, Einsatzgruppen, Soviet POWs and Anti-Bolshevism in the Emergence of the Final Solution', in D Cesarini (ed), *The Final Solution* (London, 1994).

H-G Stümke, 'From the "People's Consciousness of Right and Wrong" to "the Healthy Instincts of the Nation": the Persecution of Homosexuals in Nazi Germany', in M Burleigh (ed), *Confronting the Nazi Past* (London, 1996).

A Tasca, 'Allgemeine Bedingungen der Entstehung und des Aufstieges des Faschismus', in O Bauer, H Marcuse, A Rosenberg et al, *Faschismus und Kapitalismus* (Frankfurt am Main, 1967).

A Thalheimer, 'Über den Faschismus', in O Bauer, H Marcuse, A Rosenberg et al, *Faschismus und Kapitalismus* (Frankfurt am Main, 1967).

H R Trevor-Roper, 'A J P Taylor, Hitler and the War', in E M Robertson (ed), *The Origins of the Second World War* (London, 1971).

E Vermeil, 'The Origin, Nature and Development of German Nationalist Ideology in the 19th and 20th Centuries', in *The Third Reich* (New York, 1955).

H-E Volkmann, 'Die NS-Wirtschaft in Vorbereitung des Krieges', in *Ursachen und Voraussetzungen der Deutschen Kriegspolitik* (Stuttgart, 1979).

C Wickert, 'Frauen im Hintergrund—das Beispiel von Kommunistinnen und Bibelforscherinnen', in H Grebing and C Wickert (eds), *Das 'Andere Deutschland' im Widerstand gegen den Nationalsozialismus* (Essen, 1994).

H A Winkler, 'Choosing the Lesser Evil: The German Social Democrats and the Fall of the Weimar Republic', in *Journal of Contemporary History*, vol 25 (1990).

D Ziegs, 'Die Leipziger SPD im Kampf um die Republik', in H Grebing, H Mommsen and K Rudolph (eds), *Demokratie und Emanzipation zwischen Saale und Elbe* (Essen, 1993).

Books

T Abel, *Why Hitler Came into Power* (Harvard, 1966).

D Abraham, *The Collapse of the Weimar Republic* (New York and Princeton, 1986).

R Ainzstein, *Jewish Resistance in Nazi-Occupied Eastern Europe* (London, 1974).

G C Allen, *A Short Economic History of Modern Japan* (London, 1964).

W S Allen (ed), *The Infancy of Nazism: The Memoirs of Ex-Gauleiter Albert-Krebs, 1923-1933* (New York, 1976).

W S Allen, *The Nazi Seizure of Power* (London, 1989).

G Aly and S Heim, *Vordenker der Vernichtung* (Frankfurt am Main, 1993).

G Aly, P Chroust and C Pross, *Cleansing the Fatherland* (Baltimore, 1994).

E Anderson, *Hammer or Anvil* (London, 1945).

D Bankier, *The German People and the Final Solution* (Oxford, 1996).

A Barkai, *Nazi Economics* (Oxford, 1990).

A Barkai, *From Boycott to Annihilation* (London, 1990).

O Bauer, H Marcuse, A Rosenberg et al, *Faschismus und Kapitalismus* (Frankfurt am Main, 1967).

A Bauerkämpfer, *Die 'Radikale Rechte' in Grossbritannien* (Göttingen, 1991).

R Beckenbach, *Der Staat im Faschismus: Ökonomie und Politik im Deutschen Reich, 1920-45* (Frankfurt am Main, 1964)

J Bentley, *Martin Niemoeller* (Oxford, 1984).

W Benz, H Buchheim, H Mommsen (eds), *Das Nationalsozialismus. Studien zur Ideologie und Herrschaft* (Frankfurt am Main, 1993).

S Berger, *The Search for Normality: National Identity and Historical Consciousness* (Oxford, 1997).

R Bessel (ed), *Fascist Italy and Nazi Germany* (Cambridge, 1996).

R Bessel and E J Feuchtwanger (eds), *Social Change and Political Development in Weimar Germany* (London, 1981).

C Bettelheim, *L'Économie Allemande sous le Nazisme*, vol 1 (Paris, 1971).

D Blackbourn, *Fontana History of Germany. The Long 19th Century* (London, 1997).

G Bock, *Zwangssterilisation im Nationalsozialismus* (Opladen, 1986).

H Böhme, *Deutschlands Weg zur Grossmacht* (Cologne, 1966).

H Böhme, *An Introduction to the Social and Economic History of Germany* (Oxford, 1978).

F Borkenau, *World Communism* (Ann Arbor, 1971).

J Borkin, *The Crime and Punishment of IG Farben* (London, 1970).

K D Bracher, *Die Auflösung der Weimarer Republik* (Villingen, 1955).

K D Bracher, *The German Dictatorship* (Harmondsworth, 1970).

R A Brady, *The Spirit and Structure of German Fascism* (London, 1937).

H-J Braun, *The German Economy in the 20th Century* (London, 1990).

H Braverman, *Labor and Monopoly Capital* (New York, 1974).

W Breyvogel (ed), *Piraten, Swings und Junge Garde* (Bonn, 1991).

M Broszat, *Hitler and the Collapse of Weimar Germany* (Leamington Spa, 1987).

M Broszat, *The Hitler State* (London, 1981).

M Broszat, *Der Staat Hitlers* (Munich, 1976).

G C Browder, *Hitler's Enforcers: The Gestapo and the SS Security Service in the Nazi Revolution* (New York, 1996).

The Brown Book, published by the DDR.

C Browning, *Ordinary Men: Reserve Police Battalion 101 and the Final Solution in Poland* (New York, 1992).

W Brustein, *The Logic of Evil: the Social Origins of the Nazi Party, 1925-1933* (Yale, 1996).

G Bry, *Wages in Germany, 1871-1945* (Princeton, 1960).

N I Bukharin, *Imperialism and World Economy* (London, 1987).

A Bullock, *Hitler: A Study in Tyranny* (New York, 1962).

M Burleigh (ed), *Confronting the Nazi Past* (London, 1996).

M Burleigh and W Wippermann (eds), *The Racial State* (Cambridge, 1991).

P Burrin, *Hitler and the Jews: the Genesis of the Holocaust* (London, 1994).

E H Carr, *International Relations Between the Two World Wars, 1939-1939* (Basingstoke, 1990).

F L Carsten, *Essays in German History* (London, 1985).

F L Carsten, *The German Workers and the Nazis* (Aldershot, 1995).

F L Carsten, *Reichswehr und Politik* (Cologne, 1964).

F L Carsten, *Reichswehr and Politics, 1918-1933* (Oxford, 1966).

D Cesarini (ed), *The Final Solution* (London, 1994).

T Childers (ed), *The Mobilisation of Nazi support 1918-1933* (Beckenham, 1986).

T Childers, *The Nazi Voter* (Chapel Hill and London, 1983).

T Cliff, *Trotsky*, vol 4, *The Darker the Night the Brighter the Star* (London 1993).

D F Crew (ed), *Nazism and German Society, 1933-1945* (London, 1994).

'Da ist Nirgends Nichts Gewesen Ausser Hier', *Rote Mossingen* (Berlin, 1982).

J Danos and M Gibelin, *June '36: Class Struggle and the Popular Front in France* (London, 1986).

L Dawidowicz, *The War against the Jews, 1933-1945* (Harmondsworth, 1977).

M N Dobkowski and I Wallimann (eds), *Radical Perspectives on the Rise of Fascism* (New York, 1989).

M N Dobkowski and I Wallimann (eds), *Towards the Holocaust, The Social and Economic Collapse of the Weimar Republic* (Westport, 1983).

F Deppe and W Rossmann (eds), *Weltwirtschaftskrise, Faschismus, Gewerkschaften, 1929-1933* (Cologne, 1981).

A Dorpalen, *Hindenburg and the Weimar Republic* (Princeton, 1964).

J B Drabkin, *Die Novemberrevolution 1918 in Deutschland* (Berlin, 1968).

R Eatwell, *Fascism. A History* (London, 1995).

F Engels, *The Peasant War in Germany* (Moscow, 1969).

R J Evans, *Rereading German History, 1880-1996* (London, 1997).

J W Falter, T Lindenberger and S Schumann (eds), *Wahlen und Abstimmungen in der Weimarer Republik* (Munich, 1986).

D Farnham and J Pimlott, *Understanding Industrial Relations* (Eastbourne, 1986).

G A Feldman, *Army, Industry and Labor in Germany 1914-18* (Princeton, 1966).

N G Finkelstein and R B Birn, *A Nation on Trial* (New York, 1998).

C Fischer, *The German Communists and the Rise of Nazism* (Basingstoke, 1991).

C Fischer (ed), *The Rise of National Socialism and the Working Classes in Weimar Germany* (Oxford, 1996).

C Fischer, *Stormtroopers* (London, 1983).

F Fischer, *From Kaiserreich to Third Reich* (London, 1986).

F Fischer, *Hitler war kein Betriebsunfall* (Munich, 1992).

F Fischer, *War of Illusions* (London, 1975).

K P Fischer, *Nazi Germany. A New History* (London, 1995).

O Flechtheim, *Die KPD in der Weimarer Republik* (Frankfurt am Main, 1976).

G Fleming, *Hitler and the Final Solution* (London, 1985).

N Frei, *National Socialist Rule in Germany* (Oxford, 1993).

M Frese, *Betriebspolitik im 'Dritten Reich'* (Paderborn, 1991).

E Fromm, *The Working Class in Weimar Germany* (Leamington Spa, 1984).

E J Feuchtwanger, *From Weimar to Hitler* (London, 1984).

M Gilbert, *The Holocaust* (London, 1987).

J M Glass, *Life Unworthy of Life* (New York, 1998).

D Gluckstein, *The Western Soviets: Workers' Councils Versus Parliament 1915-20* (London, 1984).

D Goldhagen, *Hitler's Willing Executioners* (London, 1997).

N Goodrick-Clarke, *The Occult Origins of Nazism* (London, 1992).

H J Gordon, *The Reichswehr and the German Republic* (London, 1957).

C Gradmann and O von Mengerson, *Das Ende der Weimarer Republik und die Nationalsozialistische Machtergriefung* (Frankfurt am Main, 1996).

H Grebing, H Mommsen and K Rudolph (eds), *Demokratie und Emanzipation zwischen Saale und Elbe* (Essen, 1993).

H Grebing, *History of the German Labour Movement* (Leamington Spa, 1985).

H Grebing and C Wickert (eds), *Das 'Andere Deutschland' im Widerstand gegen den Nationalsozialismus* (Essen, 1994).

D Groh, *Überlegung zum Verhältnis von Intensivierung der Arbeit und Arbeitskämpfen im Organisierten Kapitalismus in Deutschland* (Heidelberg, 1976).

G Gross, *Der Gewerkschaftliche Widerstandskampf der Deutschen Arbeiterklasse während der Faschistischen Vertrauensräte Wahlen, 1934* (Berlin, 1962).

J Gross (ed), *Vorwärts und Nicht Vergessen!* (Gaggenau, 1988).

R Grunberger, *A Social History of the Third Reich* (London, 1971).

D Guerin, *Fascism and Big Business* (New York, 1973).

W Guttmann and P Meehan, *The Great Inflation* (Farnborough, 1975).

R Hachtmann, *Industriearbeit im 'Dritten Reich'* (Göttingen, 1989).

S Haffner, *The Meaning of Hitler* (London, 1979).

G W F Hallgarten, *Hitler, Reichswehr und Industrie* (Frankfurt am Main, 1986).

R Hamilton, *Who Voted for Hitler?* (Princeton, 1982).

E W Hansen, *Reichswehr und Industrie* (Boppard am Rhein, 1978).

C Harman, *Explaining the Crisis* (London, 1984).

C Harman, *The Lost Revolution: Germany 1918-23* (London, 1982).

D Harsch, *German Social Democracy and the Rise of Nazism* (North Carolina, 1993).

B Hebel-Kuntze (ed), *SPD und Faschismus. Zur Politischen und Organisatorischen Entwicklung der SPD, 1932-1935* (Frankfurt am Main, 1977).

R Heberle, *From Democracy to Nazism: a Regional Case Study on Political Parties in Germany* (Baton Rouge, 1945).

K Heiden, *A History of National Socialism* (London, 1935).

M von Hellfeld, *Edelweisspiraten in Köln* (Cologne, 1981).

U Herbert, *Hitler's Foreign Workers* (Cambridge, 1997).

R E Herzstein, *When Nazi Dreams Come True* (London, 1982).

J Hiden, *Germany and Europe 1919-1939* (London, 1977).

R Hilberg, *The Destruction of the European Jews* (New York, 1985).

R Hilferding, *Finance Capital* (London, 1981).

K Hildebrand, *The Third Reich* (Hemel Hempstead, 1984).

A Hillgruber, *Germany and the Two World Wars* (Cambridge, Massachusetts, 1981).

E Hobsbawm, *Age of Extremes* (London, 1995).

H Höhne, *Mordsache Röhm* (Hamburg, 1984).

U Hörster-Philipps, *Grosskapital und Faschismus, 1918-1945* (Cologne, 1981).

U Hörster-Philipps, *Im Schatten des Grossen Geldes* (Cologne, 1985).

R Höss, *Commandant of Auschwitz* (London, 1959).

P Hoffman, *German Resistance to Hitler* (Cambridge, Massachusetts, 1988).

M Housden, *Resistance and Conformity in the Third Reich* (London, 1997).

R-M Huber-Koller, *Gewerkschaften und Arbeitslose* (Pfaffenweiler, 1992).

E Jäckel, *Hitlers Weltanschauung, Entwurf einer Herrschaft* (Tübingen, 1969).

H James, *The German Slump* (Oxford, 1986).

M Kater, *The Nazi Party* (Cambridge, Massachusetts, 1983).

J M H Kele, *Nazis and Workers* (Chapel Hill, 1972).

W Kendall, *The Labour Movement in Europe* (London, 1975).

I Kershaw, *Hitler, 1889-1936. Hubris* (London, 1998).

I Kershaw, *The Hitler Myth* (Oxford, 1987).

I Kershaw, *Popular Opinion and Political Dissent in the Third Reich* (Oxford, 1983).

I Kershaw (ed), *Why did Weimar Democracy Fail?* (London, 1990).

I Kershaw and M Lewin, *Stalinism and Nazism: Dictatorships in Comparison* (Cambridge, 1997).

K von Klemperer, *German Resistance against Hitler* (Oxford, 1992).

C Koonz, *Mothers in the Fatherland* (London, 1987).

R Koshar, *Social Life, Local Politics and Nazism, Marburg 1880-1935* (Chapel Hill, North Carolina, 1986).

K Koszyk, *Deutsche Presse, 1914-1945*, vol 3 (Berlin, 1972).

V Kratzenberg, *Arbeiter auf dem Weg zu Hitler?* (Frankfurt am Main, 1989).

H Krausnick and M Broszat, *Anatomy of the SS State* (London, 1970).

J von Kruedener (ed), *Economic Crisis and Political Collapse* (New York, 1990).

J Kuczynski, *Das Grosse Geschäft* (Berlin, 1967).

D Landes, *The Unbound Prometheus* (Cambridge, 1969).

J von Lang and C Sibyll (eds), *Eichmann Interrogated* (London, 1983).

H Langbein, *Against all Hope* (London, 1994).

V I Lenin, *Collected Works*.

V I Lenin, *On Britain* (London, 1959).

A Leon, *The Jewish Question* (New York, 1970).

G Lewy, *The Catholic Church and Nazi Germany* (London, 1968).

D E Lipstadt, *Denying the Holocaust* (New York, 1993).

E Lucas, *Zwei Formen von Radikalismus in der Deutschen Arbeiterbewegung* (Frankfurt am Main, 1976).

R Luxemburg, *The National Question* (New York, 1976).

R Luxemburg, *Rosa Luxemburg Speaks* (New York, 1970).

C S Maier, *Recasting Bourgeois Europe* (Princeton, 1975).

K-M Mallmann, *Kommunisten in der Weimarer Republik* (Darmstadt, 1996).

P Manstein, *Die Mitglieder und Wähler der NSDAP* (Frankfurt am Main, 1989).

T Mason, *Nazism, Fascism and the Working Class* (Cambridge, 1995).

T Mason, *Social Policy in the Third Reich* (Oxford, 1993).

K Marx, *Capital*, vol 1 (Moscow, 1954).

K Marx and F Engels, *Collected Works*.

K Marx and F Engels, *The German Ideology* (London, 1970).

K Marx, *Introduction to Contribution to a Critique of Political Economy* (Moscow, 1981).

G Meier, *Forever in the Shadow of Hitler?* (New Jersey, 1993).

A Merson, *Communist Resistance in Nazi Germany* (London, 1985).

T Meyer et al (eds), *Lern-und Arbeitsbuch der Deutschen Arbeiterbewegung*, vol 2 (Bonn, 1984).

B Miller Lane and L J Rupp, *Nazi Ideology before 1933* (Manchester, 1978)

J F Morley, *Vatican Diplomacy and the Jews during the Holocaust* (New York, 1980).

F Morrow, *Revolution and Counter-revolution in Spain* (New York, 1974).

J A Moses, *Trade Unionism in Germany from Bismarck to Hitler*, vol 2 (London, 1982).

D Mühlberger, *Hitler's Followers: Studies in the Sociology of the Nazi Movement* (London, 1991).

W Müller, *Lohnkampf, Massenkampf, Sowjetmacht, Ziel und Grenzen der RGO* (Cologne, 1988).

R Neebe, *Grossindustrie, Staat und NSDAP, 1930-33* (Göttingen, 1981).

F Neumann, *Behemoth. The Structure and Practice of National Socialism* (New York, 1944).

L Niethammer, U Borsdorf and P Brandt (eds), *Arbeiterinitiative 1945* (Wuppertal, 1976).

F R Nicosia and L D Stokes (eds), *Germans against Nazism* (Oxford, 1990).

R Opitz, *Faschismus und Neofaschismus*, vol 1 (Frankfurt am Main, 1984).

G Paul, *Aufstand der Bilder* (Bonn, 1990).

D Petzina, *Die Deutsche Wirtschaft in der Zwischenkriegszeit* (Wiesbaden, 1977).

D Peukert, *Die Edelweisspiraten* (Cologne, 1980).

D Peukert, *The Weimar Republic* (Harmondsworth, 1991).

D Peukert, *Inside Nazi Germany* (Harmondsworth, 1989).

D Peukert, *Ruhrarbeiter gegen den Faschismus* (Frankfurt am Main, 1976).

E H Phelps Brown, *A Century of Pay* (London, 1968).

P Piratin, *Our Flag Stays Red* (London, 1978).

N Poulantzas, *Fascism and Dictatorship* (London, 1974).

G Pridham, *Hitler's Rise to Power* (London, 1973).

E M Robertson (ed), *The Origins of the Second World War* (London, 1971).

G Rempel, *Hitler's Children* (North Carolina, 1989).

G A Ritter and S Miller (eds), *Die Deutsche Revolution 1918-19*.

K Rohe (ed), *Elections, Parties and Political Traditions* (Oxford, 1990).

Arthur Rosenberg, *A History of the German Republic* (London, 1936).

E Rosenhaft, *Beating the Fascists?* (Cambridge, 1983).

H Royce, E Zimmermann and H-A Jacobsen, *Germans against Hitler* (Bonn, 1960).

M Ruck, *Gewerkschaften-Staat-Unternehmer* (Cologne, 1990).

M Scharrer (ed), *Die Spaltung der Deutschen Arbeiterbewegung* (Stuttgart, 1985).

K A Schleunes, *The Twisted Road to Auschwitz* (London, 1975).

M Schneider, *A Brief History of the German Trade Unions* (Bonn, 1991).

M Schneider, *Unternehmer und Demokratie. Die Freien Gewerkschaften in der Unternehmerischen Ideologie der Jahre 1918 bis 1933* (Bonn, 1975).

D Schoenbaum, *Hitler's Social Revolution* (New York, 1966).

H E Schumann, *Nationalsozialisten und Gewerkschaftsbewegung* (Hanover and Frankfurt am Main, 1958).

A Schweitzer, *Big Business in the Third Reich* (Indiana, 1977).

R Smelser and R Zitelmann, *The Nazi Elite* (Basingstoke, 1993).

R Smelser, *Robert Ley. Hitler's Labor Leader* (Oxford, 1988).

W Sofsky, *The Order of Terror: the Concentration Camp* (New Jersey, 1997).

A Sohn-Rethel, *The Economy and Class Structure of German Fascism* (London, 1978).

H Speier, *German White Collar Workers and the Rise of Hitler* (Yale, 1986).

P D Stachura (ed), *The Nazi Machtergreifung* (London, 1983).

P D Stachura (ed), *Unemployment and the Great Depression in Weimar Germany* (London, 1986).

P Stearns, *Lives of Labour* (London, 1975).

P Steinbach, J Tuchel (eds), *Widerstand gegen den Nationalsozialisten* (Berlin, 1994).

J M Steiner, *Power Politics and Social Change in National Socialist Germany* (The Hague, 1976).

J P Stern, *Hitler: The Führer and the People* (no place of publication, 1975).

O Strasser, *Hitler et Moi* (Paris, 1940).

Y Suhl (ed), *They Fought Back. The Story of Jewish Resistance in Nazi Europe* (London, 1968).

A J P Taylor, *The Course of German History* (London, 1993).

A J P Taylor, *The Origins of the Second World War* (Harmondsworth, 1965).

J Taylor and W Shaw, *A Dictionary of the Third Reich* (London, 1987).

The Third Reich (London, 1955).

D Thomas and M McAndrew, *Russia, Soviet Union, 1917-1945* (New South Wales, 1995).

F Thyssen, *I Paid Hitler* (London, 1941).

H Trevor-Roper, *Introduction to Goebbels' Diaries, The Last Days* (London, 1978).

L Trotsky, *The First Five Years of the Communist International*, vol 2 (London, 1974).

L Trotsky, *The Struggle against Fascism in Germany* (Harmondsworth, 1975)

The Writings of Leon Trotsky, 1933-40 (New York).

H A Turner, *German Big Business and the Rise of Hitler* (Oxford, 1987).

H Weber, *Hauptfiend Sozialdemokratie: Strategie und Taktik der KPD 1929-1933* (Düsseldorf, 1982).

H Weber, *Die Wandlung des Deutschen Kommunismus* (Frankfurt am Main, 1969).

H U Wehler, *Deutsche Gesellschaftsgeschichte*, vol 3 (Munich, 1995).

P Weindling, *Health, Race and German Policies between National Unification and Nazism* (Cambridge, 1989).

Die Weisse Rose und das Erbe des Deutschen Widerstandes (Munich, 1993).

E D Weitz, *Creating German Communism, 1890-1990* (Princeton, 1997).

H A Winkler, *Mittelstand, Demokratie und Nationalsozialismus* (Cologne, 1972).

C Wrigley (ed), *Challenges of Labour: Central and Western Europe, 1917-1920* (London, 1993).

R Zitelmann, *Hitler: Selbstverständnis eines Revolutionärs* (Hamburg, 1987).

Index

© Penny Gower

About the author

Donny Gluckstein's previous books include *The Paris Commune: A Revolution in Democracy*, *The Tragedy of Bukharin*, and *The Western Soviets: Workers' Councils Versus Parliament 1915–1920*. He is the coauthor with Tony Cliff of *The Labour Party: A Marxist History* and *Marxism and Trade Union Struggle: The General Strike of 1926*. Gluckstein is a lecturer in history in Edinburgh and is a member of the Socialist Workers Party (UK).